ANNUAL EDITIONS

Educational Psychology

08/09

Twenty-Third Edition

EDITORS

Kathleen M. Cauley
Virginia Commonwealth University

Kathleen M. Cauley received her PhD in Educational Studies/Human Development from the University of Delaware in 1985. Her current research interests are student transitions to a new school, and the influence of assessment practices on motivation.

Gina M. Pannozzo
Virginia Commonwealth University

Gina M. Pannozzo received her PhD in Educational Psychology from the University of Buffalo in 2005. Her current research examines the relationships among student engagement patterns in school and dropping out.

Boston Burr Ridge, IL Dubuque, IA New York San Francisco St. Louis
Bangkok Bogotá Caracas Kuala Lumpur Lisbon London Madrid Mexico City
Milan Montreal New Delhi Santiago Seoul Singapore Sydney Taipei Toronto

ANNUAL EDITIONS: EDUCATIONAL PSYCHOLOGY, TWENTY-THIRD EDITION

Published by McGraw-Hill, a business unit of The McGraw-Hill Companies, Inc., 1221 Avenue of the Americas, New York, NY 10020.

Annual Editions is published by the **Contemporary Learning Series** group within the McGraw-Hill Higher Education division.

1 2 3 4 5 6 7 8 9 0 QPD/QPD 0 9 8

ISBN 978–0–07–339769–6
MHID 0–07–339769–5
ISSN 1731–1141

Managing Editor: *Larry Loeppke*
Senior Managing Editor: *Faye Schilling*
Developmental Editor: *Dave Welsh*
Editorial Assistant: *Nancy Meissner*
Production Service Assistant: *Rita Hingtgen*
Permissions Coordinator: *Lenny Behnke*
Senior Marketing Manager: *Julie Keck*
Marketing Communications Specialist: *Mary Klein*
Marketing Coordinator: *Alice Link*
Project Manager: *Sandy Wille*
Design Specialist: *Tara McDermott*
Senior Administrative Assistant: *DeAnna Dausener*
Senior Production Supervisor: *Laura Fuller*
Cover Graphics: *Kristine Jubeck*

Compositor: Laserwords Private Limited
Cover Images: Stockbyte/Getty Images and Richard Lewisohn/Getty Images

Library in Congress Cataloging-in-Publication Data
Main entry under title: Annual Editions: Educational Psychology, 23/e
1. Educational Psychology—Periodicals by Kathleen M. Cauley, Gina M. Pannozzo, *comp.* II. Title: Educational Psychology
658'.05

www.mhhe.com

Editors/Advisory Board

Members of the Advisory Board are instrumental in the final selection of articles for each edition of ANNUAL EDITIONS. Their review of articles for content, level, currentness, and appropriateness provides critical direction to the editor and staff. We think that you will find their careful consideration well reflected in this volume.

Preface

In publishing ANNUAL EDITIONS we recognize the enormous role played by the magazines, newspapers, and journals of the public press in providing current, first-rate educational information in a broad spectrum of interest areas. Many of these articles are appropriate for students, researchers, and professionals seeking accurate, current material to help bridge the gap between principles and theories and the real world. These articles, however, become more useful for study when those of lasting value are carefully collected, organized, indexed, and reproduced in a low-cost format, which provides easy and permanent access when the material is needed. That is the role played by ANNUAL EDITIONS.

Educational psychology is an interdisciplinary subject that includes human development, learning, intelligence, motivation, assessment, instructional strategies, and classroom management. The articles in this volume give special attention to the application of this knowledge to teaching.

Annual Editions: Educational Psychology 08/09 is divided into six units, and an overview precedes each unit, which explains how the unit articles are related to the broader issues within educational psychology.

The first unit, Perspectives on Teaching, presents issues that are central to the teaching role. The articles' authors provide perspectives on being an effective teacher and the issues facing teachers in the twenty-first century.

The second unit, entitled Development, is concerned with child and adolescent development. It covers the biological, cognitive, social, and emotional processes of development. The essays in this unit examine the issues of parenting, moral development, the social forces affecting children and adolescents, as well as the personal and social skills needed to cope with school learning and developmental tasks.

The third unit, considers the many individual differences among learners and how to meet those needs. It focuses on inclusive teaching, serving students who are gifted, gender issues, and multicultural education. Diverse students require an individualized approach to education. The articles in this unit review the characteristics of these children and suggest programs and strategies to meet their needs.

In the fourth unit, Learning and Instruction, articles about theories of learning and instructional strategies are presented. The selections on learning and cognition provide a broad view of different aspects of learning covering areas such as constructivist learning, critical thinking, differentiation, and cooperative learning. Although they cover a broad variety of topics, the common thread is that learning is an active process and involves construction of meaning. In the instructional strategies section of the unit the articles provide a range of strategies for improving student learning from a framework to foster deep understanding to project based learning.

The topic of motivation is perhaps one of the most important aspects of school learning. Effective teachers need to motivate their students both to learn and to behave responsibly. How to manage children and what forms of discipline to use are issues that concern parents as well as teachers and administrators. The articles in the fifth unit, Motivation and Classroom Management, present a variety of perspectives on motivating students and discuss approaches to managing student behavior.

The articles in the sixth unit review assessment approaches that can be used to diagnose learning and improve instruction. The focus is on how standards and high stakes assessments influence students, involving students in the assessment process, formative assessment, and grading. Throughout, assessment is integrated with instruction to enhance student learning.

A feature that has been added to this edition are selected World Wide Web sites, which can be used to further explore the articles' topics. These sites are cross-referenced by number in the topic guide.

This twenty-third *Annual Editions: Educational Psychology* has been revised in order to present articles that are current and useful. Your responses to the selection and organization of materials are appreciated. Please complete and return the postage-paid article rating form on the last page of the book.

Kathleen M. Cauley
Editor

Gina M. Pannozzo
Editor

Contents

UNIT 1
Perspectives on Teaching

UNIT 2
Development

The concepts in bold italics are developed in the article. For further expansion, please refer to the Topic Guide.

UNIT 3
Individual Differences Among Leaders

The concepts in bold italics are developed in the article. For further expansion, please refer to the Topic Guide.

UNIT 4
Learning and Instruction

The concepts in bold italics are developed in the article. For further expansion, please refer to the Topic Guide.

UNIT 5
Motivation and Classroom Management

The concepts in bold italics are developed in the article. For further expansion, please refer to the Topic Guide.

The concepts in bold italics are developed in the article. For further expansion, please refer to the Topic Guide.

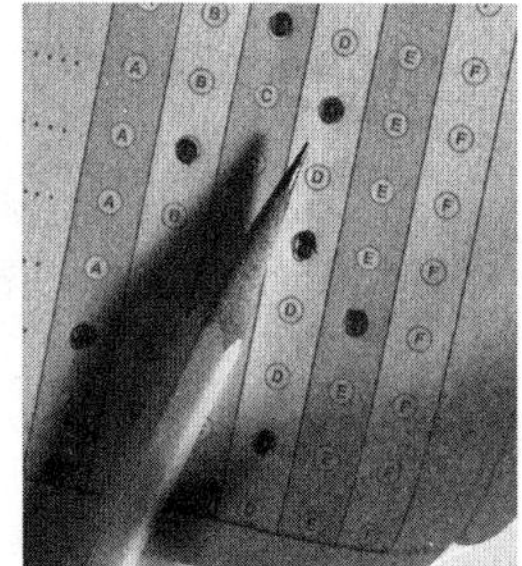

UNIT 6
Assessment

The concepts in bold italics are developed in the article. For further expansion, please refer to the Topic Guide.

Correlation Guide

The Annual Editions series provides students with convenient, inexpensive access to current, carefully selected articles from the public press. **Annual Editions: Educational Psychology, 23/e** is an easy-to-use reader that presents articles on important topics such as teaching perspectives, development, learning, individual differences, motivation, and many more. For more information on Annual Editions and other McGraw-Hill Contemporary Learning Series titles visit www.mhcls.com.

This convenient guide matches the units in **Annual Editions: Educational Psychology, 23/e** with the corresponding chapters in one of our best-selling McGraw-Hill Educational Psychology textbooks by Santrock.

Annual Editions: Educational Psychology, 23/e	Educational Psychology, 3/e by Santrock
Unit 1: Perspectives on Teaching	**Chapter 1:** Educational Psychology: A Tool for Effective Teaching
Unit 2: Development	**Chapter 2:** Cognitive and Language Development **Chapter 3:** Social Contexts and Socioemotional Development
Unit 3: Individual Differences Among Leaders	**Chapter 3:** Social Contexts and Socioemotional Development **Chapter 4:** Individual Variations **Chapter 5:** Sociocultural Diversity
Unit 4: Learning and Instructions	**Chapter 6:** Learners Who Are Exceptional **Chapter 7:** Behavioral and Social Cognitive Approaches **Chapter 11:** Learning and Cognition in the Content Areas **Chapter 12:** Planning, Instruction, and Technology **Chapter 13:** Motivation, Teaching, and Learning
Unit 5: Motivation and Classroom Management	**Chapter 14:** Managing the Classroom
Unit 6: Assessment	**Chapter 15:** Standardized Tests and Teaching **Chapter 16:** Classroom Assessment

Topic Guide

This topic guide suggests how the selections in this book relate to the subjects covered in your course. You may want to use the topics listed on these pages to search the Web more easily.

On the following pages a number of Web sites have been gathered specifically for this book. They are arranged to reflect the units of this *Annual Edition*. You can link to these sites by going to the student online support site at *http://www.mhcls.com/online/*.

ALL THE ARTICLES THAT RELATE TO EACH TOPIC ARE LISTED BELOW THE BOLD-FACED TERM.

Internet References

The following Internet sites have been carefully researched and selected to support the articles found in this reader. The easiest way to access these selected sites is to go to our student online support site at *http://www.mhcls.com/online/*.

AE: Educational Psychology, 08/09

The following sites were available at the time of publication. Visit our Web site—we update our student online support site regularly to reflect any changes.

General Sources

American Psychological Association

http://www.apa.org/topics/homepage.html

By exploring the APA's "PsycNET," you will be able to find links to an abundance of articles and other resources that are useful in the field of educational psychology.

Educational Resources Information Center

http://www.eric.ed.gov

This invaluable site provides links to all ERIC sites: clearinghouses, support components, and publishers of ERIC materials. Search the ERIC database for what is new.

National Education Association

http://www.nea.org

Something—and often quite a lot—about virtually every education-related topic can be accessed at or through this site of the 2.3-million-strong National Education Association.

National Parent Information Network/ERIC

http://npin.org

This is a clearinghouse of information on elementary and early childhood education as well as urban education. Browse through its links for information for parents.

U.S. Department of Education

http://www.ed.gov/pubs/TeachersGuide/

Government goals, projects, and grants are listed here, plus many links to teacher services and resources.

UNIT 1: Perspectives on Teaching

The Center for Innovation in Education

http://www.center.edu

The Center for Innovation in Education, self-described as a "not-for-profit, non-partisan research organization," focuses on K–12 education reform strategies. Click on its links about school privatization.

Classroom Connect

http://www.classroom.net

This is a major Web site for K–12 teachers and students, with links to schools, teachers, and resources online. It includes discussion of the use of technology in the classroom.

Education World

http://www.education-world.com

Education World provides a database of literally thousands of sites that can be searched by grade level, plus education news, lesson plans, and professional-development resources.

Goals 2000: A Progress Report

http://www.ed.gov/pubs/goals/progrpt/index.html

Open this site to survey a progress report by the U.S. Department of Education on the Goals 2000 reform initiative. It provides a sense of the goals that educators are reaching for as they look toward the future.

Teacher Talk Forum

http://education.indiana.edu/cas/tt/tthmpg.html

Visit this site for access to a variety of articles discussing life in the classroom. Clicking on the various links will lead you to electronic lesson plans, covering a variety of topic areas, from Indiana University's Center for Adolescent Studies.

UNIT 2: Development

Association for Moral Education

http://www.amenetwork.org/

AME is dedicated to fostering communication, cooperation, training, curriculum development, and research that link moral theory with educational practices. From here it is possible to connect to several sites on moral development.

Center for Adolescent and Families Studies

http://www.indiana.edu/~cafs

This site provides information on research practices of instruction. Also included is a link to other resources.

Child Welfare League of America

http://www.cwla.org

The CWLA is the United States' oldest and largest organization devoted entirely to the well-being of vulnerable children and their families. This site provides links to information about issues related to morality and values in education.

The National Association for Child Development

http://www.nacd.org/

This international organization is dedicated to helping children and adults reach their full potential. Its home page presents links to various programs, research, and resources into such topics as ADD/ADHD.

National Association of School Psychologists (NASP)

http://www.nasponline.org/

The NASP offers advice to teachers about how to help children cope with the many issues they face in today's world. The site includes tips for school personnel as well as parents.

Scholastic News Zone

http://www.scholasticnews.com

At this site, Scholastic Classroom magazines provide up-to-date information to children, teachers, and parents online to help explain timely issues.

Unit 3: Exceptional and Culturally Diverse Children

The Council for Exceptional Children

http://www.cec.sped.org/index.html

This page will give you access to information on identifying and teaching gifted children, attention-deficit disorders, and other topics in gifted education.

Global SchoolNet Foundation

http://www.gsn.org

Access this site for multicultural education information. The site includes news for teachers, students, and parents, as well as chat rooms, links to educational resources, programs, and contests and competitions.

International Project: Multicultural Pavilion

http://curry.edschool.virginia.edu/curry/centers/multicultural/papers.html

Here is a forum, sponsored by the Curry School of Education at the University of Virginia, for sharing stories and resources and for learning from the stories and resources of others. These articles on the Internet cover every possible racial, gender, and multicultural issue that could arise in the field of multicultural education.

Let 100 Flowers Bloom/Kristen Nicholson-Nelson

http://teacher.scholastic.com/professional/assessment/100flowers.htm

Open this page for Kristen Nicholson-Nelson's discussion of ways in which teachers can help to nurture children's multiple intelligences. She provides a useful bibliography and resources.

National Association for Multicultural Education

http://www.nameorg.org

NAME is a major organization in the field of multicultural education. The Web site provides conference information and resources including lesson plans, advice for handling touchy issues, and grant information.

National Attention Deficit Disorder Association

http://www.add.org

This site, some of which is under construction, will lead you to information about ADD/ADHD. It has links to self-help and support groups, outlines behaviors and diagnostics, answers FAQs, and suggests books and other resources.

National MultiCultural Institute (NMCI)

http://www.nmci.org

NMCI is one of the major organizations in the field of diversity training. At this Web site, NMCI offers conference data, resource materials, diversity training and consulting service information, and links to other related sites.

Tolerance.org

http://www.tolerance.org

This site promotes and supports anti-bias activism in every venue of life. The site contains resources, a collection of print materials, and downloadable public service announcements.

UNIT 4: Learning and Instruction

The Critical Thinking Community

http://criticalthinking.org

This site promotes educational reform through fair-minded critical thinking. The site also provides information and resources on critical thinking.

Education Week on the Web

http://www.edweek.org

At this page you can open archives, read special reports, keep up on current events, and access a variety of articles in educational psychology. A great deal of this material is helpful in learning and instruction.

Online Internet Institute

http://www.oii.org

A collaborative project among Internet-using educators, proponents of systemic reform, content-area experts, and teachers who desire professional growth, this site provides a learning environment for integrating the Internet into educators' individual teaching styles.

Teachers Helping Teachers

http://www.pacificnet.net/~mandel/

This site provides basic teaching tips, new teaching-methodology ideas, and forums for teachers to share their experiences. It features educational resources on the Web, with new ones added each week.

The Teachers' Network

http://www.teachers.net/

Bulletin boards, classroom projects, online forums, and Web mentors are featured on this site, as well as the book *Teachers' Guide to Cyberspace* and an online, 4-week course on how to use the Internet.

UNIT 5: Motivation and Classroom Management

I Love Teaching

http://www.iloveteaching.com

This site is a resource for new and veteran teachers as well as preservice teachers and student teachers. Information is broken out into various links such as "Encouraging Words," and "Classroom Management."

The Jigsaw Classroom

http://jigsaw.org

The jigsaw classroom is a cooperate learning technique that reduces racial conflict among school children, promotes better learning, improves student motivation, and increases enjoyment of the learning experience. The site includes history, implementation tips, and more.

North Central Educational Regional Laboratory

http://www.ncrel.org/sdrs/

This site provides research, policy, and best practices on issues critical to educators engaged in school improvement. A number of critical issues are covered.

Teaching Helping Teachers

http://www.pacificnet.net/~mandel/

This site is a resource tool for all teachers. It includes links to "Classroom Management," "Special Education," and more.

UNIT 6: Assessment

Awesome Library for Teachers

http://www.neat-schoolhouse.org/teacher.html

Open this page for links and access to teacher information on everything from assessments to child development topics.

FairTest

http://fairtest.org

This site is the homepage for the National Center for Fair and Open Testing. The main objective of this group is to end the misuses and flaws of standardized testing and to ensure that evaluation of students, teachers, and schools is fair, open, valid, and educationally beneficial.

Kathy Schrocks's Guide for Educators: Assessment

http://school.discovery.com/schrockguide/assess.html

Sponsored by Discovery School.com, this webpage has a comprehensive compilation of sites about classroom assessment and rubics.

Phi Delta Kappa International

http://www.pdkintl.org

This important organization publishes articles about all facets of education. You can check out the online archive of the journal, *Phi Delta Kappan,* which has resources such as articles having to do with assessment.

Washington (State) Center for the Improvement of Student Learning

http://www.k12.wa.us/

This Washington State site is designed to provide access to information about the state's new academic standards, assessments, and accountability system. Many resources and Web links are included.

We highly recommend that you review our Web site for expanded information and our other product lines. We are continually updating and adding links to our Web site in order to offer you the most usable and useful information that will support and expand the value of your Annual Editions. You can reach us at: *http://www.mhcls.com/annualeditions/.*

UNIT 1

Perspectives on Teaching

Unit Selections

1. **A Learner's Bill of Rights,** Charles H. Rathbone
2. **Letters to a Young Teacher,** Jonathan Kozol
3. **Memories from the 'Other,'** Thomas David Knestrict
4. **The Skill Set,** Lawrence Hardy
5. **A National Tragedy: Helping Children Cope,** *National Association of School Psychologists*

Key Points to Consider

- What questions would you like to see educational psychologists study?
- Describe several characteristics of effective teachers. How is effective teaching viewed differently by different constituents?
- As we move into the twenty-first century, what new expectations should be placed on teachers and schools? What expectations will fade?

Student Web Site

www.mhcls.com/online

Internet References

Further information regarding these Web sites may be found in this book's preface or online.

The Center for Innovation in Education
http://www.center.edu

Classroom Connect
http://www.classroom.net

Education World
http://www.education-world.com

Goals 2000: A Progress Report
http://www.ed.gov/pubs/goals/progrpt/index.html

Teacher Talk Forum
http://education.indiana.edu/cas/tt/tthmpg.html

Banana Stock/Picture Quest

The teaching-learning process in school is enormously complex. Many factors influence pupil learning—such as family background, developmental level, prior knowledge, motivation, and, of course, effective teachers. Educational psychology investigates these factors to better understand and explain student learning. We begin our exploration of the teaching-learning process by considering the characteristics of effective teaching.

In the first article, the author describes the rights of the learner that all educators ought to endorse. In the next article, a new teacher receives advice from an experienced educator. The third article dramatically shows how important it is for teachers to believe that each student can learn. The fourth article discusses the skill set that graduates will need to compete in a global society.

Finally, the fifth article discusses the range of reactions that children and adolescents have experienced in response to tragedies such as the terrorism attacks of September 11, 2001 or the recent hurricanes, and suggests ways that educators can help them to cope and continue their schooling.

Educational psychology is a resource for teachers that emphasizes disciplined inquiry, a systematic and objective analysis of information, and a scientific attitude toward decision making. The field provides information for decisions that are based on quantitative and qualitative studies of learning and teaching rather than on intuition, tradition, authority, or subjective feelings. It is our hope that this aspect of educational psychology is communicated throughout these readings, and that, as a student, you will adopt the analytic, probing attitude that is part of the discipline.

While educational psychologists have helped to establish a knowledge base about teaching and learning, the unpredictable, spontaneous, evolving nature of teaching suggests that the best they will ever do is to provide concepts and skills that teachers can adapt for use in their classrooms. The issues raised in these articles about effective teaching, and the issues facing teachers in the twenty-first century, help us understand the teaching role and its demands. As you read articles in other chapters, consider the demands they place on the teaching role as well.

A Learner's Bill of Rights

In looking back at the progressive education movement, Mr. Rathbone identifies the rights of the learner that all educators should embrace and protect.

CHARLES H. RATHBONE

Celebrating its 35th year, the Fayerweather Street School of Cambridge, Massachusetts, is one of the few extant schools associated with the "open education" movement of the late Sixties.[1] Not only has the school flourished, but it has managed to stick to its original progressive principles. Fayerweather recently hosted a panel discussion on progressive education, which prompted me to write this article. Listening to the panelists discuss progressive education—its politics, its commitment to social responsibility, its emphasis on the individual learner as the maker of meaning—I found myself formulating a bill of rights, intellectual rights, that I imagine my progressive colleagues, past and present, might endorse.

The Right to Choose

The progressive teacher acknowledges each student's right to make important decisions about what is learned, how it is learned, when, and with whom. As a British head (principal) once put it, "The basis for learning should be that the child wants to know, not that somebody else knows or that somebody says he ought to know."[2] Relevance, in other words, is to be determined by the learner herself. The pseudo-progressive teacher, while he may offer "choice time," presents only options chosen by himself and only at limited times. At worst, this teacher uses choice as a reward and withholds it as punishment.

The Right to Follow Through

An active learner often skips past conventional age- and grade-level expectations, ignoring the traditional boundaries of the disciplines and oblivious to the notion of social appropriateness. This means a progressive teacher cannot be skittish when the student shows an interest in sex, politics, religion, or rap. The entire world is available for exploration, with nothing predetermined, nothing censored, and certainly no one saying, "You mustn't learn that now because it is going to be taught later at some higher grade."

The Right to Take Action

Activity-based, developmentally appropriate learning by doing, using manipulatives, means noise, mess, and much active, often unplanned collaboration. This requires a flexible teacher prepared to share in decision making. Progressive teachers recognize that the right to take meaningful action is a logical corollary of the right to choose.

The Right to Remain Engaged

Full engagement of the mind is a desired educational objective. To interrupt a learner's focused attention risks teaching the student not to trust her own preferences, her own intellectual rhythms, her own mind. Though the teacher and school invariably have a program, a schedule, and a curriculum, the progressive teacher seeks also to honor the learner's interests, style, and tempo.

The Right to Wallow

As David Hawkins eloquently explains in "Messing About in Science," some wallowing is worthwhile—perhaps even necessary—prior to that moment when the learner can articulate a question or define a pursuable problem.[3] When students are simply *given* all the problems, they never learn how to formulate one—a crippling intellectual restriction.

The Right to Err

Answer-driven teaching and testing are anathema to those who want to foster genuine, personal learning. So long as one's self-esteem isn't on the line, error is a wonderful teacher. Moreover, as Hawkins points out in "I-Thou-It," inanimate materials provide immediate, objective, and emotionally safe feedback.[4] Progressives try to talk with students about their work without jumping to judgment. They seek to protect students against the debilitating effects of unsolicited criticism, and most would agree with British educator John Coe that all praise, to some degree, is condescending.

The Right to Concentrate

So long as a student continues to learn new things, the progressive teacher trusts that this learning is likely to be worthwhile and does not worry that the student will somehow grow lopsided. Specialization often leads to deep understanding and powerful intellectual commitment. Progressives seem less anxious about curriculum "coverage," as they know that the clever teacher will find a way of merging the school's agenda with the child's. Moreover, they operate from an intrinsic optimism that the growing mind knows what it needs.

The Right to Take Learning Personally

To the teacher who says it doesn't matter what the student writes about as long as she produces six sentences before the bell rings, the progressive teacher would respond, "What the student chooses to write is the *only* thing that matters!" Writing, inquiring mathematically, drawing, dancing, or thinking scientifically are all extensions of the self. For, as Sylvia Ashton-Warner and Elwyn Richardson remind us, it is those words nearest and dearest to the child's heart that she needs to learn, not an alphabetized list provided by a publisher.[5] The personal urge toward understanding is often linked to a drive to act upon newly acquired knowledge. A young child will simply want to share; an older student may wish to change the world. Either way, learning is both personal and social.

The Right of Collaboration

So much of learning takes place within the communal group, especially in the younger years. Schools that provide opportunities for collaborative projects, for mixed-age grouping, and for cooperative performance capitalize on the social aspect of how children learn. Unfortunately, such approaches are susceptible to corruption: performance can promote competition and create a "star" culture; mixed grouping can place an enormous burden upon teachers who mistakenly think they must then teach two or three classes in one room.

The Right to Respect

The unresolved problem and the unfinished thought are a very real part of learning, and they deserve the considered attention of a teacher who cares about the student's thought process as much as the end product. When there *is* a work product, it is seen as an extension of the student's thinking and therefore deserving of similar respect. Thoughtful, aesthetically pleasing displays of children's work honor that work and encourage everyone around to take it seriously. Teachers committed to progressive principles become students of their students, respectful researchers of how children think and what excites their imagination. The teachers then provision the environment accordingly.

The Right of Centrality

"At the heart of the educational process lies the child," begins the *Plowden Report*.[6] When the learner's interests, needs, and intellectual style drive the educational enterprise, then scheduling, curriculum, teacher behavior, school architecture, and even budget decisions all fall, if not always into place, at least into perspective. John Dewey knew how important this was when he wrote:

> The change which is coming into our education is the shifting of the center of gravity. It is a change, a revolution, not unlike that introduced by Copernicus when the astronomical center shifted from the earth to the sun. In this case the child becomes the sun about which the appliances of education revolve; he is the center about which they are organized.[7]

These rights of the learner, like their constitutional analogs, are forever balanced in the real world against the greater good of the group. Naturally, there is a tension: just as free spee ded theater, so the necessities of teachers to coordinate scheduling with specialists, of schools to maintain enrollments and not appear too wacko, and of publishers to sell their wares to nonprogressive schools all weigh against the undiluted implementation of these and other rights. Each time a compromise is made, however, I would want it to be publicly acknowledged and personally painful. I want teachers to flinch at each violation of a learner's rights. And I want the rest of us—like some shrill, educational ACLU—to point our fingers and demand that, if a right be restricted, it be with the least limiting restriction possible.

References

1. See Charles H. Rathbone and Lydia A. H. Smith, "Open Education," in James W. Guthrie, ed., *The Encyclopedia of Education,* 2nd ed. (New York: Macmillan Reference, 2003); and Lydia A. H. Smith, "'Open Education' Revisited: Promise and Problems in American Educational Reform (1967–1976)," *Teachers College Record,* vol. 99, 1997, pp. 371–415.
2. Roy Illsley, head, Battling Brook Primary School, Leicestershire, in Charles H. Rathbone, "Examining the Open Education Classroom," *School Review,* vol. 80, 1972, p. 535.
3. David Hawkins, "Messing About in Science," in *The Informed Vision: Essays on Learning and Human Nature* (New York: Agathon Press, 1974), pp. 63–75.
4. Hawkins, "I-Thou-It," in idem, pp. 48–62.
5. Sylvia Ashton-Warner, *Teacher* (New York: Bantam Books, 1963); and Elwyn S. Richardson, *In the Early World* (Wellington: New Zealand Council of Educational Research; New York: Pantheon, 1969).
6. Central Advisory Council for Education (England), *Children and Their Primary Schools* (known as the *Plowden Report*), vol. 1 (London: Her Majesty's Stationery Office, 1966).
7. John Dewey, *The School and Society*, 2nd ed. (Chicago: University of Chicago Press, 1915), p. 34.

Charles H. Rathbone, a former teacher and administrator, currently works with student teachers at Wheaton College, Norton, Mass. (e-mail: ceorathbone@comcast.net).

Letters to a Young Teacher

JONATHAN KOZOL

In the following passages, adapted from Mr. Kozol's newest book, the author and a beginning first-grade teacher share their reflections on the life of a teacher, the kids they have come to know, and how to put the fun back into learning.

Dear Francesca,
I was very happy that you wrote to me and I apologize for taking two weeks to reply. I was visiting schools in others cities in the first part of the month and I didn't have a chance to read your letter carefully until tonight.

The answer to your question is that I would love to come and visit in your classroom and I'm glad that you invited me. I'd also like to reassure you that you didn't need to worry that I'd think your letter was presumptuous. I like to hear from teachers and, as you have probably suspected, I feel very close to quite a few of them, especially the ones who work with little children in the elementary grades, because those are the grades I used to teach. I think that teaching is a beautiful profession and that teachers of young children do one of the best things that there is to do in life: bring joy and beauty, mystery and mischievous delight into the hearts of little people in their years of greatest curiosity.

Sometimes when I'm visiting a school, a teacher whom I may have met once when she was in college, or with whom I may have corresponded briefly, or a teacher whom I've never met but who's read one of my books and feels as if she knows me, sees me standing in the corridor and comes right up and tells me, "Come and visit in my classroom!" Sometimes she doesn't give me any choice. She simply grabs me by the arm and brings me to the classroom. Then, when I get there, typically she puts me on the spot and asks if I would like to teach a lesson or ask questions of her children.

I love it when teachers let me do this, but I almost always do it wrong at first, because it's been a long time since I was a teacher, and I often ask the kind of question that gets everybody jumping from their seats and speaking out at the same time. Six-year-olds, when they become excited, as you put it in your letter, have "only a theoretical connection with their chairs." They do the most remarkable gymnastics to be sure you see them. A little girl sitting right in front of me will wave her fingers in my face, climbing halfway out of her chair, as if she's going to poke me in the eyes if I won't call on her, and making the most heartrending sounds—"Oooh! Oooh! Oooh! Oooh!"—in case I still don't notice that she's there. Then, when I finally call on her, more often than not she forgets the question that I asked, looks up at me in sweet bewilderment, and asks me, "What?" It turns out she didn't have a thing to say. She just wanted me to recognize that she was there.

The best teachers believe that every child who has been entrusted to their care comes into their classroom with inherent value to begin with.

The teacher usually has to bail me out. She folds her arms and gives the class one of those looks that certain teachers do so well, and suddenly decorum is restored.

It's a humbling experience, but I think that it's a good one too, for someone who writes books on education to come back into the classroom and stand up there as the teacher does day after day and be reminded in this way of what it's like to do the real work of a teacher. I sometimes think that every education writer, every would-be education expert, and every politician who pontificates, as many do so condescendingly, about the "failings" of the teachers in the front lines of our nation's public schools ought to be obliged to come into a classroom once a year and teach the class, not just for an hour with the TV cameras watching but for an entire day, and find out what it's like. It might at least impart some moderation to the disrespectful tone with which so many politicians speak of teachers.

In my writings through the course of nearly 40 years, I have always tried to bring the mighty and ferocious educational debates that dominate the pages of the press and academic publications, in which the voices of our teachers are too seldom heard, back from the distant kingdom of intimidation and abstraction—lists of "mandates," "sanctions," "incentives," "performance standards," and the rest—into the smaller, more specific world of colored crayons, chalk erasers, pencil sharpeners, and tiny quarrels, sometimes tears and sometimes uncontrollably contagious jubilation of which daily life for a real teacher and her students is, in fact, composed.

I'm often disappointed, when I visit some of the allegedly sophisticated schools of education, to recognize how very little of the magic and the incandescent chemistry that forms between a truly gifted teacher and her children is conveyed to those who are about to come into our classrooms. Many of these schools of education have been taken over, to a troubling degree, by people who have little knowledge of the classroom but are the technicians of a dry and mechanistic, often business-driven version of "proficiency and productivity." State accountability requirements, correlated closely with the needs and wishes of the corporate community, increasingly control the ethos and the aims of education that are offered to the students at some of these schools.

But teachers, and especially the teachers of young children, are not servants of the global corporations or drill sergeants for the state and should never be compelled to view themselves that way. I think they have a higher destiny than that. The best of teachers are not merely the technicians of proficiency; they are also ministers of innocence, practitioners of tender expectations. They stalwartly refuse to see their pupils as so many future economic units for a corporate society, little pint-sized deficits or assets for America's economy, into whom they are expected to pump "added value," as the pundits of the education policy arena now declaim. Teachers like these believe that every child who has been entrusted to their care comes into their classroom with *inherent* value to begin with.

Many of the productivity and numbers specialists who have rigidified and codified school policy in recent years do not seem to recognize much preexisting value in the young mentalities of children and, in particular, in children of the poor. Few of these people seem to be acquainted closely with the lives of children and, to be as blunt as possible about this, many would be dreadful teachers because, in my own experience at least, they tend to be rather grim-natured people who do not have lovable or interesting personalities and, frankly, would not be much fun for kids to be with.

A bullying tone often creeps into their way of speaking. A cocksure overconfidence, what Erik Erikson described as "a destructive conscientiousness," is not unfamiliar either. The longer they remain within their institutes of policy or their positions in the government, the less they seem to have a vivid memory of children's minuscule realities, their squirmy bodies and their vulnerable temperaments, their broken pencil points, their upturned faces when the teacher comes and leans down by their desk to see why they are crying.

I suspect that you and I will come back to this matter many times. For now I simply want to say I'm very, very glad you're teaching here in Boston, because that means that I can visit sometimes in your class without needing to make plans long in advance. Thank you for saying it's okay if I stop by one day without much prior warning, which makes things a whole lot easier for me. As you know, you're teaching in the neighborhood where I began to teach, so I definitely will not need to ask you for directions!

I promise to visit as soon as I can. Meanwhile, I hope the next few weeks are not too intimidating for you. You said you like your principal and that she's been kind to you. That's one big victory to start with. I'm sure there will be many more during the weeks ahead. In spite of the butterflies you said are making "many, many loop-the-loops" within your stomach almost every morning as you head for school, try hard to enjoy this first month with your children if you can.

It will someday be a precious memory.

Jonathan

Winning the Heart of Captain Black

Dear Francesca,

I've been wrestling with your question about children who come into school with a defiant attitude that seems to challenge every effort that we make to teach them and who seem to mock our very presence in the classroom, as if they've decided in advance that we are people they won't like and who probably should not be trusted.

I meet many children like this sitting in the classrooms of the public schools I visit in the poorest sections of Los Angeles, Chicago, and New York. These are usually the hardest kids to teach and pose the greatest challenges to teachers. And this is especially the case with teachers who are just beginning their careers and whose initial insecurity may function as an invitation to such children to confront them and to break down their self-confidence right from the start. Some of these children are so outright rude, sarcastic, and denunciatory to the teacher—and so loaded with hostility to other children—that they singlehandedly can bring almost all serious instruction to a halt.

Many young teachers, as compassionate and patient as they try to be, tend to react to kids like these by making what is basically a surgical decision: "I cannot do a good job for the other children in the room if I permit this boy to take up so much of my time and ruin things for everybody else." So, even though it goes against their principles, they tend to isolate that child in whatever way they can and try to lock him out of their attention for extended periods of time.

I noticed, when I visited your class the first time, that there was a child like this in your room who gave you so much trouble that you had to put him at a table in the corner where he could not constantly distract the other children from their work. I knew that you felt bad about this because you reluctantly conceded that you thought he was a fascinating child. You said, "I kind of love him for his style, his defiance, but he has no common sense and absolutely no politeness."

His tall and loose-limbed body had a gangly and slightly comical appearance, which I thought that he exploited like a stage comedian when he was walking through the room. You said, "He acts as if he's made of Silly Putty. He never just sits down like other children do. He makes it a theatrical performance just to get back to his chair." You also told me that the first week of the year, before you put him at the table in the corner, he vaulted over the back of his chair one afternoon and kicked someone behind him in the face.

On the morning I was there, he didn't strike me as malicious to the other children. He had his head down on his table, pressed against his folded arms, and simply seemed to have decided to ignore you and the other students altogether. When I went and stood there near him in his corner and said "Hi" to him, he looked me over briefly and then blew me off without a word. He didn't even bother to lift up his head. He just sized me up from where he was and closed his eyes again.

One of the other kids, however, told me, "He is mean!" And there was one week, as I recall—it might have been the week after I visited—when you said you had to ask your principal to keep him in her office for the first part of each day because he kept on getting up and wandering around the room and looking over children's desks and doing irritating things like grabbing their erasers or their pencils.

The only time I saw him acting somewhat less resistant was when he was on the reading rug one day while you were reading from that lovely book about "the grouchy ladybug," one of the many books by Eric Carle I noticed in your room. He obviously liked the story and paid good attention for a while, although even then he kept on pushing other kids who were taking up the space he seemed to think he needed for himself so he could stretch out on his belly and lean on his elbows and look up at you as you were pointing to the pictures.

As soon as the story was over, however, he reverted to his customary manner and, by a circuitous route which I thought was clearly meant to be annoying to you and the other children, he made his way back to his table, where he thoroughly turned you off as if he had a TV clicker and decided that your program wasn't good enough to watch.

The next time I was there, I saw that you had moved him to a desk beside the blackboard where you had a better chance to keep an eye on him and where you could try to bring him in from time to time to join some of the class activities, a few of which, like moving around those red and blue and yellow bars of different lengths, he seemed to find intriguing. You told me that he finally confessed to you that he had gotten bored from doing almost nothing all day long and gave you to understand that he was now prepared to let you make his life more interesting, if you had the skill to do it, for the hours when he had to be in class.

In November, when I visited again, he didn't look so hostile anymore but still would interrupt the other kids while they were working on their journals or were doing independent reading, and he still kept getting into quarrels about pencils, colored crayons, or whatever other objects he could grab from other children's desks and then insist they were his own. When he did this, I was impressed to see you use your sternest-looking frown—you got quite good at that—to get him to stay relatively quiet and polite at least for periods of time.

You told me that his name was Dobie but that he insisted upon being known as "Captain Black." And I recall that, on an impulse just before Thanksgiving, you made a visit to his home and brought him a box of brownies you had baked for him. You said that you were shocked to find he didn't have a bedroom but was sleeping on a small bed in the same room as his sister and his mom. But you also told me you were heartened by the way that he reacted to your visit. His tendency to mock a friendly gesture and distrust its meaning seemed to have dissolved somewhat by then. You said that you were startled when he told his mother you were "a nice lady," "the best teacher in my school." How could he possibly say that to his mother when he gave you so much trouble all day long? And he gave you at least what you said was "a ho-hum hug" when it was time to leave.

In academic terms, the first sign of a breakthrough I could sense was when he started filling up his spiral pad with bits of narrative that opened up some of those angry memories and fears he'd been reluctant to reveal to you before. You said that you began to use these sentences to introduce him to the very grown-up task of looking at his own words and rewriting them so that the vowels, some of which you said that he already knew but stubbornly ignored, began to go where they belonged. After you had told him that old saying about "silent e," which, when it follows a consonant, makes the vowel that comes just before the consonant into a "long O" or "long A" or "E" or "I" or "U"—I think you said it makes that vowel "brave enough to say its name"—you told me he kept "jumping" you by telling you this rule, as if you'd never heard of it, each time that it applied.

It was only eight weeks earlier that you had thought of recommending him for a "referral," which would probably have led to his assessment as a boy who was "developmentally delayed" or "psychologically impaired" or something worse—one of those many labels that so often end up as the self-fulfilling prophecies that stigmatize a child not just for one year but for the course of his career in public school.

I try to bend over backwards not to start extracting overly big meanings from small spurts of progress. In doing so, we tend to dwarf and overstate the first few modest steps that previously resistant children suddenly begin to take once the dam that held them back is broken and at least a little stream of curiosity and stirrings of their intellectual vitality begin to flow. Nonetheless, if there's a lesson to be learned from his experience with you, and yours with him—because relationships like these have always struck me as a kind of complicated and mysterious duet between a teacher and a very vulnerable child—it may be simply this: None of us should make the error of assuming that a child who is hostile to us at the start, or who retreats into a sullenness and silence or sarcastic disregard for everything that's going on around him in the room, does not have the will to learn and plenty of interesting stuff to teach us too, if we are willing to invest the time and the inventiveness to penetrate his seemingly implacable belief that grown-ups do not mean him well and that, if he trusts us, we will probably betray or disappoint him.

I do not mean, Francesca, in saying what I did about assigning "labels" to a student, that children who have serious psychological problems, or other kinds of problems such as speech pathology or difficulty in the processing of words they hear, cannot benefit tremendously from being given extra help by speech or language specialists, for instance, or by school psychologists. Clinical needs, when they're real, require clinical solutions. And special education teachers, like the one who taught a number of severely damaged children in the room right next to mine in Boston and who helped me so much at the start of my career, are priceless assets in a school in almost any neighborhood at all.

At the same time, I think that teachers need to be as patient as they can, and rely on every bit of ingenuity that they command, before they assign these kids to categories out of which, as they move from grade to grade, they sometimes never can escape."It becomes a trap," you said. "It's so much easier for children to go in than to get out." In Dobie's case I think that time has proven that you made the right decision.

When Dobie finally started writing longer, more coherent entries in his spiral pad, and when the floodgates opened up enough so he could vent more of the anguish he had hidden up until that time, you told me you were startled once again to find out how much turbulence and social violence he had already undergone. Turning that pent-up anguish into satisfaction at the progress he was making in his literacy skills may not have saved him from the other sorrows and endangerments he's likely to encounter in the years ahead. Even if the progress he is making now should be sustained during his next four years in elementary school, there are the ever-present risks that he will face when he moves on into the less protective world of middle school.

Still, victories are victories. And I recall that when he wrote that powerful piece of narrative for you about the Sunday afternoons on which he visited his father, who was in a prison out in western Massachusetts (I think you said that he's still there) several hours from his home, you said it made you cry. You told me that you put it on your bedroom wall.

It seems that Dobie has accepted you at last and sees you as a special friend. The letter you showed me that he gave you just before the holidays will, I bet, soon earn a place up on your wall as well. "Dear Lady Mamalade," he wrote—you told me he had asked you what you liked for breakfast and you said that you loved orange marmalade and butter on your toast—"I think yur wunder full, plus also cheezy, plus also good and wunder full. Love, Captin Black." I liked especially what he squeezed in down at the bottom of the page: "PS. And you beter tell me Thank You for this leter be kuz I workt hard on it!"

You said he told you that this was your Christmas present—"the only one" you'd get from him, he added. It's hard to imagine any other present that was likely to have made you happier. If I were Dobie's teacher, I'd be every bit as proud as you were to receive a letter like that from a child who was so determined to dislike you when he walked into your classroom in September.

You told me once you knew that you were fortumate to have a class of only 20 children and one in which there weren't a bunch of other kids who started out distrusting you the way that Dobie did. I know a teacher in New York who had three boys like Dobie in her class last year and several girls with very hostile attitudes as well. And these were older children—I think they were third-graders—and it was a big class, nearly 30 students, so she couldn't give each of these kids the time and the attention that she knew they needed and deserved. She told me that she often cried at night out of frustration.

This is why I think that class size is so terribly important. In a class of 20 children or, as I saw not long ago in one of the elementary schools not far from Boston, only 16 children in one room, kids who come into the class with an edgy attitude but a lot of pent-up energy, as Dobie did, are far more likely to be given personal attention than are children in the badly overcrowded classes that I visit in so many other inner-city schools. The likable humor that emerged at last in Dobie's personality and the powerful feelings that he finally got down on paper get "locked in" for kids like these. When they're not disrupting class, they sit and brood and look as if they feel encaged. It's like seeing spirit trapped in stone.

Langston Hughes wrote something strong and memorable about the often-gifted litte rebels who, because of their rebellious ways, are written off too rapidly and ultimately penalized severely by society:

> Nobody loves a genius child.
> "Kill him—and let his soul run wild!"

Well, all these little rebels who begin by flaunting their distrust and adversarial abilities in front of teachers in the first months of the school year are not "genius children." But many of these children do have gifts to bring us if we grant ourselves—and if our schools allow us—time enough to listen to them carefully and also time to forge the subtle bond that will permit them to reveal themselves.

I think that Dobie has been blessed to have you as his teacher, but blessings in the very special world of elementary school have always had a lovely reciprocity. I can tell from the elation and the tenderness for Dobie that were so apparent when you phoned me here last night that you feel you have been blessed by knowing him as well. He dared to open up his heart to you. You made that possible.

Jonathan

Wiggly and Wobbly and Out!

Dear Francesca,

I promised I would think about the question that you asked me in the playground of your school the other day after the children were dismissed and most of them had already gone home. Shaniqua and another child were still waiting for their mothers and were studying some kind of very big and ugly-looking bug they had discovered crawling on a spot of grass that had appeared as the snow was melting.

While you were watching them, you asked me whether anyone I know who's setting education policy these days ever speaks about the sense of fun that children have, or ought to have, in public school or the excitement that they feel when they examine interesting creatures such as beetle bugs and ladybugs and other oddities of nature that they come upon—or even merely whether they are happy children and enjoy the hours that they spend with us in school.

The truth is that in all the documents I read that come from Washington, or from the various state capitals, or from the multitude of government-supported institutes where goals are set and benchmarks for performance of our students are spelled out in what is usually painstaking detail, I never come upon words such as "delight" or "joy" or "curiosity"—or, for that matter, "kindness," "empathy," or "compassion for another child." Nothing, in short, that would probably come first for almost any teacher working with young children.

There is no "happiness index" for the children in our public schools, and certainly not for children in the inner-city schools, where happiness is probably the last thing on the minds of overburdened state officials. Perhaps there ought to be. The school boards measure almost every other aspect of the lives our children lead in school but never ask if they look forward to the days they spend with us.

Fortunately, there are many teachers who, no matter what pressures the states and federal government impose, refuse to banish these considerations and, by their nature, could not do so even if they tried. I told you once of a young teacher whom I met some years ago in the South Bronx whose name was April Gamble, a perfect name, I thought, for someone in the springtime of her life who was starting out on her career in the third grade. Her students had sent me one of those fat envelopes of friendly letters children sometimes send to writers, asking if I'd visit them someday when I was in their neighborhood. One of the children wrote, "My name is Pedro. I am 7 years old. Would you come and visit us for 6 hours so we could tell you everything about our life?" He signed his letter, "From my heart to my eyes, Pedro."

"Wonderment" is a word you seldom find in any of those documents that tabulate the items of essential knowledge children are supposed to learn.

I couldn't resist those invitations, so one day I called the principal and went to meet the class. Pedro happened to be sick that day, so I didn't get to meet him. But I got to know some of the other children in the classroom pretty well and later kept in touch with them.

At one point during the morning, the discussion I was having with the children got a little out of hand—you've noted that this happens to me now and then—and the teacher realized that I wasn't sure how I should handle things. She seemed to know exactly what to do.

She rose to her feet and put one hand, with fingers curled up slightly, just beneath her mouth, and curled her other hand in the same way but held it out about twelve inches to the right. I watched with fascination as the class subsided from the chaos I'd created and the children stood and did the same thing Mrs. Gamble did. All these children with one hand before their mouth, one to the side, and with their eyes directed to the teacher. What was this about?

Then the teacher started humming softly. Then she briefly trilled a melody in her soprano voice, and some of the children started trilling their own voices too. And suddenly I understood: It was an orchestra, and they were the flute section! In their hands were the imaginary flutes. Their little fingers played the notes, and when the teacher bent her head as if she were so deeply stirred by the enchanted music she was hearing that she had to tilt her body in response, the children bent their bodies too.

The principal, who was standing in the doorway, seemed to be as fascinated by the sight of this as I was. I could see that she admired Mrs. Gamble as a teacher but was obviously taken also by the sweetness of her manner—the precision of her fingers on the keys! And then the teacher danced a bit from foot to foot before the children, and I thought of Papageno and Tamino and the lovely tune Tamino plays in Mozart's *Magic Flute,* and the children danced from foot to foot as well. And then the music ended and the teacher put away her flute with an efficient and conclusive motion of her hands, and all the children did the same and we began our class discussion once again.

What I remembered later wasn't only an effective trick for bringing third-grade children who had grown a trifle wild back into a calm and quiet state of mind. It was also the impromptu dance the teacher did, only a step or two, but just enough to fill the moment with gratuitous amusement so that, even in regaining grownup governance over those joyful little protons and electrons that I'd inadvertently set into motion, she also showed herself to be a woman who was not too overly "mature" or too "professional" to show the happiness she felt at making magic music for the children with a magic, and imaginary, flute.

When Mrs. Gamble trilled her voice and ran her fingers through the air, she didn't simply play the flute. She also played the playfulness within herself and seemed to play the spirits of the children too. She later told me that one-third of all the children in her class and in the school suffered from asthma, which was common in the South Bronx as a consequence of New York City's policy of placing toxic installations like waste burners in the neighborhood. You wouldn't have guessed it on that morning. For a minute there, we might have been a thousand miles from the city in a magic forest where the evening air smells fresh and green and not one of the spirits of the woods has any trouble breathing.

I've watched other teachers use their own inventive ways to spice the school day for their children with brief words and moments that are like their evanescent tributes to the need for impulse and for beauty in the classroom. This doesn't mean that they ignore the necessary skills they need to teach but that they feel the confidence to interweave the teaching of those skills into a context of aesthetic merriment that satisfies and does not enervate the children's sense of curiosity and joy.

I remember a first-grade class in Minnesota where the bookshelves and the color-coded reading bins were filled with hundreds of children's books and stories, organized according to the levels of ability they would require for a child to understand them. Books on bears and worms and caterpillars had positions of particular distinction in the sun-filled corner room in which the class took place. *The Very Hungry Caterpillar* and some of the other works of Eric Carle were favorites of the children, and for a memorable period of time they had their own real caterpillar in the room, a "woolly bear caterpillar," as these 6-year-old researchers ascertained with some assistance from their teacher.

On the day the teacher brought him into school, all other class activities came to a halt for a good period of time. He was a beautiful creature, with rich brown and orange hair that looked like fur, and in the weeks that followed, children often slipped out of their chairs to pet him softly with their fingers or simply to study him with wonderment.

The day he disappeared into the gray cocoon that he was spinning was, of course, momentous for the children too. And when he at length emerged as a very splendid tiger moth and the teacher opened the window and he flew away one April afternoon, celebratory rites were held for him but were followed by a study of life cycles among caterpillars and additional small members of his species.

I used the word "wonderment" in speaking of the feelings that the presence of this caterpillar had awakened in the children. That's another word you seldom find in any of those documents that tabulate the items of essential knowledge children are supposed to learn in order to assume their place someday, as we are told, in the national economy and help to "sharpen our competitive edge" in "the global marketplace." (I actually saw a "mission statement" with those words posted in an inner-city elementary school not long ago. Why on Earth should kids in elementary school be asked to care about their future role within the global marketplace? Why should teachers foist this mercenary nonsense on them in the first place?)

I loved the reflections that you sent me on the role of whim and wonderment within the classroom. "If at the end of the day," you said, "I find Arturo standing at the window instead of reading at his seat," and if you notice that he's "wide-eyed" and "entranced" by looking at a squirrel in a tree, you said you would not call to him "to sit down and pick up his book." In fact, you said, "I might even join him there" in order to remember what it feels like to be young enough to take so much amazement in a squirrel. "I won't be responsible," you wrote, "for hurrying my children out of that age when many things are interesting and so much is new."

Even in the presentation of mandated lessons, I've noticed that you try hard to adapt them with a sense of playfulness to the concerns that have immediate connections with your children's lives. The last time I visited your class, I saw a time line posted on the wall above the reading rug. I know that time lines are a commonplace device that first-grade teachers use to introduce their students to a recognition of progressions from one day or month or season to the next. But this was no commonplace variety of time line. I would call it "a time line with a sense of humor."

In fact, as I remember this, it wasn't even called a time line. It was called a "Tooth Line," as the sign you'd written just above it read. Very convincing-looking teeth, which I think you said that you had cut out of a piece of cardboard, had been placed in litle slots along the left side of a sheet of something that resembled fiberboard. All the children in the class could find their own teeth somewhere in one of those slots: I saw "Shaniqua's Tooth," "Arturo's Tooth," "Dobie's Tooth," et cetera.

At the top of the chart you had created four "tooth-status" columns. The first column was for teeth that hadn't yet come loose. The second column was for "Wiggly Teeth," the third for "Wobbly Teeth." The fourth column was for teeth that had come "Out!" (I liked the exclamation point you put there because it's a big event for children when they finally lose a tooth, whether or not they get rewarded every time with a quarter or a dollar underneath their pillow.)

As children reported on the status of a tooth, their cardboard tooth would be advanced across the chart to "Wiggly Teeth," then "Wobbly Teeth," then "Out!" The thing about this time line that I think had caught the fancy of the children was not only that it had been built upon a series of events that obviously matter very much to 6-year-olds but also that it clearly had been done with a degree of frolicsome intent. "Wiggly" and "wobbly" are fun to say. They're slightly silly-sounding words. I wouldn't be surprised if that's one reason why you picked them.

The teaching of sequences, progressions, and categories is, I know, a very important part of early education. But, as you demonstrated in this instance, there's no reason why these concepts must be taught in shopworn terms that are external to the students' lives. Immediacy, and a sense of fun in the immediate, can infiltrate the teaching of these concepts too.

The march of little teeth across that chart was, in itself, inherently amusing. When I asked one of the children which one was her tooth, she went right up and pointed to it. "This one is my tooth," she said, then stuck her fingers in her mouth to show me which one of her teeth it was. On the chart it said that it was "wiggly," but after she had moved it around awhile with her forefinger and thumb, she took the cardboard tooth out of its slot and slipped it into "wobbly." I know that you like to have the children do these things collectively when everyone is seated on the rug. I guess I should have told her to hold off and do it the next morning, but she did it out of impulse.

Francesca, I know this letter, like some others I've been writing to you recently, is proving to be more rambling than I intended it to be. But if there's a common theme in all of this, it has to do with the upholding of a sense of artistry and imaginative creativity on the part of teachers at a time when both are under serious assault. A couple of years ago, a high official in the U.S. Department of Education said that the objective of the White House was "to change the face of reading instruction across the United States from an art to a science," a statement that could not have brought much comfort to those teachers who believe that books have more to do with artistry than metrics and that teaching children how to read them calls for somewhat different skills than teaching physics or geometry.

But this longing to turn art into science, as it turned out, didn't stop with reading methodologies. In many schools, it now extends to almost every aspect of the school day and the lives that children lead within it. Artistry and furry caterpillars do not stand much of a chance against these cold winds blowing down from Washington. All the more reason, then, for teachers to resist these policies and to use their ingenuity in every way they can to undermine the consequences of this pseudoscientific push for uniformity.

In a class in North Carolina that I visited last year, the teacher had tacked up a pleasantly defiant poster on one of the classroom walls. "How to Be an Artist" was the heading. "Stay loose, learn to watch snails, plant impossible gardens, . . . make friends with freedom and uncertainty, look forward to dreams. . . . "

The teacher didn't slight the basic skills. Her low-income students did okay on their exams. But when I asked about the reading method she was using, whether every aspect of her reading lessons was prescribed for her or whether she was free to innovate in any ways at all, she shook her head like someone who was shaking off an irritant—a flea or a mosquito.

"I like to mix it up!" she said and tossed her long hair gleefully, then pivoted around to keep an eye on one of the rambunctious boys sitting in the back part of the room.

I like the way you "mix it up" as well. I hope that many other teachers coming into urban schools will feel the wish to do the same. Down with concerns about "the global marketplace"! Up with "Wiggly" and "Wobbly" and "Out!" Childhood does not exist to serve the national economy. In a healthy nation, it should be the other way around. We have a major battle now ahead of us, not just about the tone and style of a child's education but about the purposes it should espouse and whether we, as teachers, need to go down on our knees before a brittle business-driven ethos that is not our own. We need the teachers who are coming to our classrooms making up their minds, before they even get here, which side they are on.

Jonathan

Goodbye for Now

Dear Francesca,

This will be my final letter to you for a while. You'll be traveling with your sister for a good part of the summer, and I'm going to be traveling for several weeks as well.

Before I say goodbye for now, I hope that you will understand if I want to take this opportunity to say a few brief words about a recently departed friend who's given me more affirmation of my own ideas about the sensibilities and education of our children than any other grown-up I have known since I was a young teacher.

I suspect you know that I am thinking of Fred Rogers, since I've told you how important he became to me as a steadfast presence in my life during the 10 years prior to his death and how hard it is to fully recognize, even to this day, that he is really gone.

I met Mr. Rogers late in 1992 when I was in Pittsburgh to be interviewed at the public television station where "Mr. Rogers' Neighborhood" was taped. At the end of my interview, as the studio technicians were untangling the wire and the microphone they had attached to me, I heard a voice behind me calling me by my first name as if we already knew each other. There, only a couple feet away, looking exactly as he did on television except that his hair was turning gray, was Mr. Rogers.

He brought me into his studio and, at my request, showed me the closet where he put away his jacket at the start of every show, and then the setup for "The Neighborhood of Make-Believe," and, naturally, the trolley train. And he introduced me to the man who played the role of Mr. McFeely on the show, all of which impressed me every bit as much as I imagine it might have impressed a 4- or 5-year-old.

Then we sat down on his sofa for the first of many conversations we would have in years to come. He questioned me about my book *Savage Inequalities,* which I had published earlier that year, and he was so courteous and patient when I gave him rambling or awkward answers (I was at first a little nervous to be chatting suddenly with somebody whose mannerisms and whose face were so familiar to me) that I soon felt utterly at ease and no longer had that sense of something "just a bit unreal" that I usually feel in talking to a person who, to me, belongs within the borders of a TV screen.

From that point on, we spoke on the phone or corresponded with each other every month or so. We also managed to arrange things so that we could meet from time to time, once in Washington, the second time in New York City, where he asked if he could go with me to the South Bronx to meet the kids I wrote about. On that occasion, he asked me first if I thought his presence in the neighborhood might be "intimidating" to the children, a thought that never would have come into my mind. I teased him a little and replied, "I bet they can handle it!" So he said, "Okay! Then let's go to the Bronx!" When he asked me how I went there from Manhattan, I told him that the quickest way was by the Number 6 train to Brook Avenue. The idea of going on the subway seemed to please him very much.

The ride on the train, the visit to an elementary school where several of my favorite teachers taught, the hours spent with children in the kindergarten classes, the visit we made later to a nearby afterschool, where a little boy named Mario descended on him instantly (and wrapped his arms around his head and gave him a big kiss right in the middle of his forehead, then looked him in the eyes and told him, "Welcome to *my* neighborhood!")—all of this became imprinted on my memory as one of the most joyful days I ever spent in the South Bronx.

He later sent me photographs he took that day, assembled in an album with handwritten annotations next to pictures that held special meaning for him. Next to a picture of Mario, who was holding a stuffed animal beneath his arm, he wrote, "This one is my favorite." In subsequent months and years he kept on asking about Mario.

In retrospect, though, I think it was the teachers we had visited who were most affected by the time he spent with them. He squeezed himself into the kindergarten chairs so that he was at eye level with the children who surrounded him. He questioned them about their lives or objects on their desks or in the room that were of interest to them, and he listened to their answers with his usual respectfulness and did not try to hurry them. He met with teachers in the older grades as well and asked them many questions about children in their classes. One thing that he didn't ask them about was the test scores of their pupils.

That visit took place in 1996. He made another visit with me to the neighborhood in autumn of 2000. As the momentum for intensive testing of young children and for scripted and didactic methods of instruction rapidly intensified during that period, he told me he had grown increasingly disturbed. The quiet way in which he spoke of his disconsolate reactions to this rising tide of what he viewed as an unnatural severity to children at a vulnerable moment in their lives reinforced my own beliefs more powerfully than any of the words or writings of the more specifically credentialed and established critics of these policies.

He also used to ask about my private life and would then return to something I had mentioned, maybe even six months after I had told it to him. For reasons that I didn't understand until a little later on, he grew especially attached to my dog, Sweetie Pie.

After Fred had seen a photograph of Sweetie Pie, he began to ask about her all the time and soon began to send her letters, usually for no particular occasion, but always on her birthdays. He would also call her on the phone at times and ask to speak to her, and, when I put her floppy ear beside the phone, he'd talk to her, and she would sometimes give a good woof in reply.

He must have kept a careful calendar of birthdays of his friends because he never missed one of her birthdays and, if we were not at home, he always sang her "Happy Birthday" on my answering machine. He later told me she reminded him of his first dog, "whom," he said, "I loved beyond all measure. . . . I got her for taking terrible-tasting medicine when I was 3. She lived until I was 21. You can imagine how I loved her."

A few years after that, when Sweetie Pie grew ill with a malignant tumor on her nose that pressed against her optic nerve and threatened to invade the bone around her brain, he asked me for repeated updates on the chemotherapy she had to undergo. At one point that fall, her right eye had to be removed, and I hesitated for almost a month to tell Fred of her worsening condition. He wrote me a long and worried letter in which he said, "I hope your silence about Sweetie Pie doesn't mean the worst." It was, by then, the middle of December. He didn't mention in his letter that he too had recently been diagnosed with a malignancy. That letter about Sweetie Pie was the final message I received from him. Seven weeks later I read in the *Boston Globe* that he had died.

Francesca, I've spoken of the emphasis Mr. Rogers used to place on leaving open space and open time for children to express themselves and, when they do, the need for us to listen to them carefully. Now he's gone, and we are in an age of stern intentionality in which the possibilities for leaving open space and open times in which our children can reveal their secrets and unveil their souls have been diminished greatly in too many of our schools. The sacredness he saw in children has now been supplanted by more chastening concerns as to their future economic value, their "utility" and "productivity," words and ideas, as you can imagine, that he did not like at all.

Fred had studied theology as a young man, as I think I may have told you, and had been ordained in the Presbyterian denomination with "a ministry to children." But he also identified with children in a manner more intrinsic to his personality than that which is perhaps suggested by a word like "ministry." He wrote a song in the last year of his life, one he never had a chance to finish, that he called "The Child Who's in Me Still, and Sometimes Not So Still!" I love that title. It reminds me of the look of sheer exhilaration on his face when we were riding to the South Bronx on the subway. He seemed as excited as a young boy might have been by all the lights and noises and the people coming through the train to sell CDs and flashlight batteries and those many other items that are sold, illegally perhaps, for bargain prices to the passengers.

That song inevitably makes me think, as well, of all those easily exhilarated and impulsive first-year teachers that I meet and many older teachers too who have never wholly given up the child in themselves and might not be nearly as good teachers if they ever did. I look to those teachers to hold to their hearts the legacy that Mr. Rogers left us. It's a fragile legacy because, although he was immersed in Eriksonian ideals and had studied with Erikson scholars and, of course, knew Erikson himself, nothing about his way of listening to children or *being* with young children is considered "research-based" or "scientific," which are the code words of acceptability these days, as you know all too well.

Mr. Rogers' legacy is viewed as "soft" and "too impressionistic" in an age when very hard and measurable outcomes have been stringently demanded by the overseers of public education, whose certitude about the practices that they enforce seems nearly absolute. I pray that teachers of all ages will reject the cheap rewards of overstated absolutes and honor instead the self-effacing virtues of the kindest man and wisest friend of children we may have the opportunity to know for many years

Jonathan

JONATHAN KOZOL is the National Book Award-winning author of *Death at an Early Age, Savage Inequalities, Amazing Grace,* and, most recently, *The Shame of the Nation* (Crown, 2005). This article is adapted from his newest book, *Letters to a Young Teacher,* published by Crown Publishers, a division of Random House.

Memories from the 'Other'

Lessons in Connecting with Students

Thanks to the good work of some significant teachers, Mr. Knestrict learned an important lesson: all children deserve to feel lovable and capable.

THOMAS DAVID KNESTRICT

I hated school. I struggled with it from the moment I started kindergarten. Before that, I had been so happy as a young child. I can remember when I was 4 years old, coloring with my mom at home. I can still hear her telling me how smart I was and how much she loved me. I remember quite vividly entering Hayes Elementary School in September of 1964 and walking into the large kindergarten room. I came into the room excited about school and eager to learn. I had perfect attendance the first semester of that year and received a certificate for my achievement.

But as the year progressed, things changed. My memories of that year have faded somewhat over time, but there are certain recurrent themes that stay with me today. The first is that I very clearly was different from most of the other children. I had trouble sitting on the floor "Indian style." I needed to get up and move. The next theme I clearly recall is that I wasn't as smart as the other boys and girls. Learning to read was difficult; learning to write was even harder. In fact, anything that required me to focus for an extended period of time or to use fine motor skills was lost on me. The final general recollection I have is discovering that I was a "problem" in class. I remember being sent to the "cloak room" several times that year for "not playing nice" or "disrupting the class."

Mrs. L. came over to me and took the paper fire truck I had just completed. She peeled the wheels off of the fire truck and told me that she knew I could do better. I had tried to cut out round wheels but was unable to create anything better than octagon shapes. Obviously this was not good enough.

In first grade I was placed in a class with an almost entirely new group of children. The only student I already knew was a boy named Tommy. We had been in kindergarten together, he came to first grade with me, and he was with me until my senior year of high school. But the rest of the students we had been with the previous year were placed in the two other classrooms. The children I met in first grade were to be my classmates for the next five years. Students were tracked back then, and I was in the "slow class." This was the term that Mr. P., our principal, used on more than one occasion. It was true. All of us had trouble reading, witting, and behaving. I can't imagine what the teacher must have been thinking when she received her class list in August. This might explain why many of the teachers we had did not return the following year.

Class was so boring. The print made no sense to me. So I found ways to entertain myself, especially during reading. I can remember looking for Tommy during reading group. I knew if I could catch his eye, I could make him laugh. I was always searching for a way to escape the monotony. When I got his attention I turned both of my eyelids inside out and stared at

him. Pretty soon every boy in the reading group was doing the same thing. Mrs. S. became very angry and made all of us stay in for recess.

The overwhelming message I received every day was that I was different, not as good, and defective. I had different books. I completed different assignments. I was not asked to join in any of the extra activities my fellow students in the other classes participated in. There were only a few kids in our class each year who excelled. The next year they would be moved to one of the other classrooms. Their spot was always taken by a new kid—usually a kid like me or a new student who couldn't speak English. The funny thing is that after a new kid learned to speak English, he usually excelled and left our class. My grades were horrible. The school used to trust me to bring my report card home for my parents to sign. But it never found its way home. Every year my mom would have to call about the whereabouts of my report card.

I dreaded oral reading groups. My handwriting was illegible, and the teachers always claimed that I was very smart but lazy. By third grade I had discovered some "truths" about myself. The first truth was that I was stupid. This was reinforced daily by teacher comments and by the eventual absence of teacher concern—a kind of teaching boycott put into effect because of my perceived bad attitude. Second, I was different from the "cool" kids in the other classes. I was viewed by my peers and my teachers as different, and because of this I had a very limited group of people around me from whom to draw friends. Last, I did possess a significant talent. I was one funny guy. I could make people laugh. Turning my eyelids inside out was just one trick. I had a million of them. But it worked only within the context of school. Outside of the classroom, the group were even more rigidly defined, and I had no capital.

The middle grades of elementary school were very tough. These years were marked by a tremendous lack of accomplishment. I never read a book. I never completed a book report. I rarely passed a test. I never completed any homework. But I continued to be passed to the next grade with little or no assistance for my increasing academic deficits.

In fourth grade I had Ms. S. for a teacher. She was determined to whip me into shape. I remember turning in some kind of written assignment to her and having her hand it back to me to be recopied. It was far too messy, and there were too many misspelled words. I recopied it, and she handed it back to me again. I handed it in a third time, and again she handed it back to me. I was not allowed to go to recess or gym that day. I stayed after school until 4:00. I started to cry, and she told me that if I continued to cry I would have to stay in the next day as well. I stayed inside for three consecutive days. She finally gave up. I did, too.

In fifth grade I had Mr. H. for math. It was in this class that I really learned my place in school. The pain and humiliation I and my fellow students suffered in this class were remarkable. By fifth grade you should be learning fractions, long division, pre-algebra, equations, probability. We were still on two-digit times two-digit multiplication. One day, Mr. H. caught me clowning around in class. As punishment he had me get up in front of the class to complete the following problem:

$$23 \times 13$$

Mr. H. knew that I could complete this problem only to the point of putting the place-holding zeros down. I got lost and could not go any further. As I froze and tried to climb inside of the chalkboard, Mr. H. said these words: "Mr. Knestrict, I could teach and teach and teach, and you still would not get this. I give up." What I heard was, "You're stupid, Mr. Knestrict. You can't do math, Mr. Knestrict. You are not a capable student, Mr. Knestrict." This is a moment I would relive many times in my academic career. His is a voice I still hear today. I hear it when I bounce a check. I heard it when I took my first statistics course in college. I hear it when I am at the grocery store figuring my bill or when I am figuring the tip at a restaurant. Like so many kids with learning differences, I had these words burned into my heart, into my brain. At that moment Mr. H. verbalized 10 years of my internal dialogue. When he voiced this condemnation, it made it so for me, for my peers, and for him. At that moment I was defined.

Beth was a smart girl. She attended the same elementary school I did but was always in the "smart class." In junior high, members of my class were mixed in with the "smart kids" for art, music, and industrial arts. I sat next to Beth in music. We had to do a report together about a famous musician. We picked John Denver. We began reading some books on him, and Beth started taking notes on index cards. I asked her what she was doing, and she showed me how she would read a fact about John Denver that she thought was interesting and write it down on the card. "A different card for every fact. Then when it's time to write, we can just copy down what we wrote on the cards." I was stunned. I could do this. It took a 12-year-old girl to show me that I could complete a meaningful academic task.

In junior high, things changed a bit for me. I was still tracked with the same kids. However, several elementary schools merged, and all the "dumb kids" from each school were grouped together. At least there were some new faces. And there were the "mixed-ability" groups for some subjects. Beth was the first "smart girl" I had ever made friends with. She helped me get my first A in any class . . . ever! Our paper on John Denver was a thing of beauty. During the writing process, Beth told me that it was okay that I had trouble writing. "I'll carry us, Tom." And she did. But she also taught me that I could do a few things myself. During the research part of the assignment, she could not find some basic biographical data on Mr. Denver. I had all of his albums at home, and on one of them there was a John Denver biography. I brought this in and wrote out five fact cards to contribute to the effort. Beth was so pleased. I felt like Einstein.

I remember sitting in Mrs. A.'s English class. We were diagramming sentences. I could not figure out the appropriate lines to draw for the various parts of speech. So I invented my own. I brought my paper up to Mrs. A., and she looked at it and told me to sit down and reread the assignment because I had done it completely wrong. She handed the paper back to me and continued to work at her desk. She did not know I could barely read the book we were using.

I had to go to other classes in junior high. I had to take Spanish in sixth grade. I never could figure out how a kid who couldn't master English was supposed to learn Spanish. I failed. In fact, I took Spanish I three years in a row. I think it still stands as a record at Harding Junior High School. Math was still a mystery. Physical education, an enjoyable class for me in elementary school, became a daily nightmare in junior high. Taking your clothes off in front of others? Taking showers? All of the "smart" boys and all of the "dumb" boys were in gym together. In one respect, the playing field was leveled in gym class. Luckily, intelligence had little to do with the tasks in Mr. S.'s gym class. It was all about testosterone. Who could withstand pain, tumble, run, jump, and wrestle? I was a good athlete, and I went into this class feeling good.

But that wouldn't last. Mr. S. had a rule. If you did not remember to bring your uniform, you had to wear the "community clothes": a pair of very dirty shorts that smelled funny and had brown stains in the seat and a smelly tank-style top with the words "Lakewood" on the front. It was a well known fact that the girls wore the shirts that said "Lakewood" and the boys wore the shirts that said "Rangers." Because I sometimes forgot my uniform, I was now clearly a girl. I missed a record number of days during my sixth-grade year. Thirty-four to be exact.

There was a spelling bee in sixth grade. The entire sixth grade participated. I can remember standing in line, on stage, in front of all of the seventh-and eighth-graders, waiting for my word. The first round was usually seen as a practice round, and the students were given a simple word to spell in order to get comfortable. It came to me. My word was "Lakewood." Simple enough, my hometown. "L...a...k...w...o...o...d, Lakewood." Silence. "Incorrect." The auditorium erupted. I laughed and joked, but I was dying inside. I then had to sit down in the front row for the next 30 minutes until another speller made a mistake and left the competition.

In high school I attempted to take Spanish again. I failed again. But my Spanish teacher, Ms. D., referred me to the school counselor, telling me, "Thomas, you must first learn the English language before learning Spanish." She referred me for academic testing. The year was 1975, and P.L. 94-142 had just been passed. I sometimes think I was the first child identified after its ratification. I was given a tutor and had to attend certain classes in the resource room for extra help. I made sure nobody saw me go into that room. It would be social suicide. Although, given my social status, I had very little to lose.

I was told that I was learning disabled and that I had to go to special education classes. The school psychologist told me this as if it were cause for celebration. "Hooray, we finally know what is wrong with Tom." But I wasn't ready to celebrate the fact that there was yet another thing that made me different.

Sometime during my sophomore year, a counselor met with me and talked to me about vocational school. "Tom," she said, "it's clear you are not on the college track here at LHS. So I would like you to start thinking about vocational school or even the military." I was devastated. My entire family had attended Bowling Green State University. I was going to go, too. But now, it looked like I would barely get out of high school. I finished that year in special education. I was 16, low on the social ladder, attending school on the special education track. I'd been told I couldn't attend the "regular" (read "normal") high school the next year, and I could barely read and write. I became very depressed. I started to cut class and feign illness to avoid going to school. There were days I came to school just for homeroom, so I could be counted as present, and then I would leave for home. I did this easily 50% of the time and never got caught. Still, I passed to the 11th grade. Remarkable!

In my junior year, I was required to take the ACT exam. I posted a total score of 7. I have been told that you could guess and score higher than this. I didn't guess.

At the end of my senior year, I had a grade-point average of 1.7. I read at about the fourth-grade level, still had not mastered my multiplication facts, had never read a book, had developed a consistent pattern of starting and then quitting new activities, thought of myself as stupid, could not write a coherent paragraph, had few friends, and in June was handed a diploma and graduated with my class from high school. It still ranks as the most inexplicable moment of my life. I kept thinking that my fellow classmates would attack if they knew that I was getting the same piece of paper they were that stated that I, too, had completed all the requisite coursework to graduate. No, I had not!

I woke up after graduation and wondered what had just happened. School was over—they let me graduate? Huh?

Somewhere between my graduation and the following school year, I had an epiphany. During that summer I worked at a gas station and a pizza place. I was very aware of how the people I was working with had been working these jobs for most of their adult lives and didn't seem real happy. I went home that night and talked to my father, and he convinced me to try taking a class at Cuyahoga Community College, also known as Tri C. I signed up for a series of high school-level reading and writing classes affectionately known as the 0900 courses. There were adults in these classes older than I was, and somehow that fact made me feel better about myself.

I signed up for all the high school-level courses I could that year, and in my first writing course I had a professor who saved my life. He taught me how to write and how to love to read. We read *Death of a Salesman* and books by Hemingway and Poe, and then we talked and wrote about the books. It would take me forever to finish a book, and sometimes it would be a combination of reading the book, watching the movie, and using the Cliff notes that got me through the assignments, but I loved every minute of it. It was the most amazing thing I had ever experienced. I was learning about metaphor and simile, seeing how the literature gave me insight into my life, writing reflections on my feelings about these books. It was wonderful. It was life changing. I learned more in that one year at Tri C than I had learned in the previous 12 years of school.

What was different was that I was seen as capable. The professors knew I could do it and expected me to do it. Also, they wanted me to enjoy the process and worry about the products later. One professor I had during this time stated, "Process over product. If you learn the process of reading and writing, the products will follow." But most important, they knew me and I knew them. We had a relationship. They cared about me. I had never, in 12 years of school, had that before.

As I was leaving my last writing and reading class at Tri C, the professor looked at me and said, "Make sure you read the comments I wrote on your last paper." When I got to my car, I pulled the paper out and read, "Thomas, this paper was one of the most insightful and inspired papers I have ever received from a student. I am so pleased with your progress this year. Grade for the quarter: A." I cried.

Later that year I ended up being accepted "conditionally" to Kent State University. During that year I met a man who ran a camp for children with learning disabilities and behavior problems. He was at Kent to hire counselors for the summer. I started talking to him a bit about my school experience. He hired me on the spot. I worked that summer leading hikes, camping, doing crafts, and canoeing with children who were experiencing some of the same things I had gone through in school. I found I had a real talent for working with children. From that point on, I knew I would teach.

That summer, the director of the camp, Jerry Dunlap, taught me something that has become a fundamental part of my teaching philosophy: he told me that all children deserve to feel lovable and capable. He then asked me if I felt lovable and capable. And for the first time in my life, I could say yes. I had spent most of my school years believing that I was not lovable and not capable. The system had beaten me up. But thanks to the good work of some significant teachers in my life, I was on the mend, with a focus on teaching and helping kids.

During my first year of teaching in the classroom, I had a student named Dante. He was 7 years old, could not read or write, and spoke only sparingly. As I introduced myself to Dante and his parents on the first day of school, I laughed at the joke God had played on me. Dante was me, and I was quite possibly the only person able to help him. We had a wonderful year, filled with lots of loving and learning. In June I asked Dante if he felt lovable and capable. He looked at me and smiled and said, "I know you love me, Mr. Knestrict, but what does 'capable' mean?"

Postscript

As I reflect on my life in school, I am struck by the times teachers failed to connect with me on any real human level. I am a professor of education now, and I am still struck by the lack of emphasis on this human connection in education. We spend so much of our time as teachers worrying about the standards, giving tests, and focusing entirely on content that the child as a person seems to disappear. One of the fundamental theories we teach undergraduates in our education programs is Abraham Maslow's hierarchy of needs. We know that human connection is crucial to child development, but our schools fail to manifest this knowledge in practice. Classes get bigger and bigger, and test scores matter more and more. Our cultural obsession with measurement and testing often serves to sort students, not help them. These values define students very early in life. Once defined, individuals begin to see themselves that way, and the perception becomes a self-fulfilling prophecy. In fact, when a child is identified with a special need and placed on an Individualized Education Plan, he or she will actually have that label for a minimum of three years—and, as research suggests, much longer emotionally.[2]

I can tell you firsthand that I still hold internalized notions of myself as a child. I still have trouble seeing myself as smart, lovable, and capable. I believe that this difficulty is a result of the damage caused by my experience in schools and in particular our education system's notion of how to help children with different needs. I am not advocating de-emphasizing content. However, it is not unreasonable to assume that we can teach a solid curriculum and at the same time treat students with dignity and care.

Notes

1. Joan Wink and Dawn Wink, *Teaching Passionately: What's Love Got to Do with It?* (Boston: Pearson/Allyn and Bacon, 2004).
2. John R. Weisz et al., "Cognitive Development, Helpless Behavior, and Labeling Effects in the Lives of the Mentally Retarded," *Applied Developmental Psychology,* vol. 24, 1985, pp. 672–83.

Thomas David Knestrict is an assistant professor of education at Xavier University, Cincinnati. He taught in the public schools for 15 years.

The Skill Set

What do graduates need to be successful in the 21st century?

LAWRENCE HARDY

The reports, studies, and initiatives keep coming—dire assessments of the weak skills of U.S. high school graduates and the increasing competition they face in a burgeoning global economy. We have *The Urgency Gap, America's Perfect Storm, Tough Choices or Tough Times,* and most frightening of all, *Be Very Afraid.*

All right, we made up that last one. There is no report called *Be Very Afraid.* But since 1983's *A Nation at Risk* and its provocative, if rather absurd, charge that the mediocre U.S. public schools—if foisted on us by a foreign power—would constitute an act *of war,* we have operated at somewhere between code yellow and orange with respect to our ongoing crisis in the public schools.

But is the world truly different now, in the 21st century? And have U.S. students kept up? The flurry of reports makes a good case that it is, and they haven't. Consider:

- "Employing demographic projections combined with current skills distributions, we estimate that by 2030 the average levels of literacy and numeracy in the working-age population will have decreased by about 5 percent . . . Over this same period, nearly half the projected job growth will be concentrated in occupations associated with higher education and skill levels."—*America's Perfect Storm: Three Forces Changing Our Nation's Future,* a February report of the Educational Testing Service (ETS).
- "Thirty years ago, the United States could lay claim to having 30 percent of the world's population of college students. Today that proportion has fallen to 14 percent and is continuing to fall."—*Tough Choices or Tough Times,* the 2007 report of the New Commission on the Skills of the American Workforce.

The decrease in literacy and numeracy predicted by ETS will be driven by increasing numbers of low-skilled Hispanic immigrants and their children. But the graduation rate among current students also is disturbingly low, having dropped to about 70 percent after peaking at 77 percent in 1969. Numerous groups—including the National Governors Association, which issued a report called *The Silent Epidemic*—say the dropout rate threatens the nation's economic security.

The Emergence of Globalization

But what about our high school graduates? Several reports say they're not doing well enough either. For example, an ACT report on the Class of 2006 found that just 42 percent of those taking the test had sufficient algebra preparation for college-level math, and only 62 could do college-level English. The proportion meeting ACT benchmarks in all four core subjects (English, Algebra, Biology, and Social Sciences) was just 21 percent.

Not surprisingly, many of these students fare poorly in college. According to Thomas Toch and Kevin Carey of Education Sector, only half of the 75 percent of high school graduates who go on to college earn degrees.

On the other hand, the United States continues to produce a substantial number of well-prepared high school graduates who can compete on a world-class level. And indeed, as accomplished members of the "Echo Boom" generation will tell you, the competition to get into the best colleges is fiercer than ever.

For example, a student from a competitive high school in Northern Virginia may have earned an A-minus average to go with her five Advanced Placement courses—and still have little chance of making the cut at the prestigious University of Virginia. Meanwhile, Lehigh University in Pennsylvania—a solid institution that may lack the cachet of Virginia or the Ivy League—has seen applications increase 50 percent over seven years to more than 10 times the 1,150 available spaces in the freshmen class, according to the *New York Times.*

So clearly, a large number of students are performing extremely well, but an even greater number are not. And while that might have been fine 50 years ago, when non-college-bound students could find well-paying jobs in manufacturing, it is no longer the case today.

The reason, of course, is globalization. The emergence of foreign markets accelerated the decline of U.S. manufacturing over the past half-century, and today it is challenging even college-educated Americans with competition from a growing class of highly skilled workers. "Today, Indian engineers make $7,500 a year against $45,000 for an American engineer with the same qualifications," says *Tough Choices or Tough Times.*

Former senator and labor secretary William E. Brock III, a member of the commission that wrote the report, puts it in more gut-check terms: "Everybody's coming after us—we've got to keep that in mind," he says. "They want what we got. And they're willing to educate and train their workers to compete with us and—they think—win."

Regaining a Competitive Edge

What, then, do today's graduates need to compete? It will take more than mere parity, *Tough Choices* asserts: "If we succeed in matching the very high levels of mastery of mathematics and science of these Indian engineers—an enormous challenge for this country—why would the world's employers pay us more than they have to pay the Indians to do their work? They would be willing to do that only if we could offer something that the Chinese and Indians, and others, cannot."

The Partnership for 21st Century Skills, whose members include education-related firms such as Apple, Microsoft, and McGraw-Hill Education, has devised a six-point plan for "a unified, collective vision for 21st century learning." It includes core subjects; 21st century content, such as global awareness and civic literacy; learning and thinking skills like creativity, communication, and contextual learning; ICT (information and community technology) literacy; life skills, such as leadership, ethics, and social responsibility; and assessments that can measure things like thinking skills and life skills.

How does No Child Left Behind fit into this new conception of creative thinking and assessment? Critics, such as Princeton economist Alan S. Blinder, say it doesn't.

"I would emphasize—and have emphasized in congressional testimony and many other places—that No Child Left Behind is pushing the United States in exactly the wrong direction—toward rote memorization," Blinder says. "Now how in the world are American students going to out memorize a memory chip? That's a losers' game. We need to teach students how to think, not how to memorize."

Others, like Partnership President Ken Kay, see no contradiction between NCLB and the kind of new learning and assessment his group espouses. He says NCLB has helped to identify low-performing schools even if its content-heavy assessments must evolve into something broader.

"What would happen if we had a set of metrics that measures problem-solving, global awareness, and self-directed learning?" Kay asks. "We don't need to view NCLB and 21st century skills as at odds with each other. It's healthier to see them as the future of NCLB, seeing our work as the metrics to aspire to."

What most observers agree on is that the United States is in the midst of a wrenching economic and societal shift that will change the way people work and live their lives. As the example of the Indian engineers illustrates, outsourcing will not be confined to low-level manufacturing jobs but will reach well into the educated sector as well.

Indeed, Blinder says, it will be felt throughout the wage spectrum among occupations that are "portable"—everything from computer programming to contract law. Brain surgeons will stay put, as will housekeepers and taxi drivers. "Architects could be endangered," he writes, "but builders aren't."

The nation has weathered bigger changes before. Most notable was the shift of labor off the farm and into manufacturing during the 19th and early 20th centuries, Blinder says. "On a less dramatic level, something like a third of all Americans worked in factories around the year 1960 or 1967. . . . Now it's down to 10 (percent)."

"So I do think we're going to weather it," he concludes. "But the question is, do we do it in a more painful, slow, agonizing way, or do we do it in a less painful, faster way? And that's where these policy changes, such as in the education system, come in."

Lawrence Hardy (lhardy@nsba.org) is a senior editor of *American School Board Journal.*

A National Tragedy: Helping Children Cope

Tips for Parents and Teachers

Whenever a national tragedy occurs, such as terrorist attacks or natural disasters, children, like many people, may be confused or frightened. Most likely they will look to adults for information and guidance on how to react. Parents and school personnel can help children cope first and foremost by establishing a sense of safety and security. As more information becomes available, adults can continue to help children work through their emotions and perhaps even use the process as learning experience.

All Adults Should:

1. **Model calm and control**. Children take their emotional cues from the significant adults in their lives. Avoid appearing anxious or frightened.
2. **Reassure children that they are safe** and (if true) so are the other important adults in their lives. Depending on the situation, point out factors that help insure their immediate safety and that of their community.
3. **Remind them that trustworthy people are in charge**. Explain that the government emergency workers, police, firefighters, doctors, and the military are helping people who are hurt and are working to ensure that no further tragedies occur.
4. **Let children know that it is okay to feel upset**. Explain that all feelings are okay when a tragedy like this occurs. Let children talk about their feelings and help put them into perspective. Even anger is okay, but children may need help and patience from adults to assist them in expressing these feelings appropriately.
5. **Observe children's emotional state**. Depending on their age, children may not express their concerns verbally. Changes in behavior, appetite, and sleep patterns can also indicate a child's level of grief, anxiety or discomfort. Children will express their emotions differently. There is no right or wrong way to feel or express grief.
6. **Look for children at greater risk**. Children who have had a past traumatic experience or personal loss, suffer from depression or other mental illness, or with special needs may be at greater risk for severe reactions than others. Be particularly observant for those who may be at risk of suicide. Seek the help of mental health professional if you are at all concerned.
7. **Tell children the truth**. Don't try to pretend the event has not occurred or that it is not serious. Children are smart. They will be more worried if they think you are too afraid to tell them what is happening.
8. **Stick to the facts**. Don't embellish or speculate about what has happened and what might happen. Don't dwell on the scale or scope of the tragedy, particularly with young children.
9. **Keep your explanations developmentally appropriate**. ***Early elementary school*** children need brief, simple information that should be balanced with reassurances that the daily structures of their lives will not change. ***Upper elementary and early middle school*** children will be more vocal in asking questions about whether they truly are safe and what is being done at their school. They may need assistance separating reality from fantasy. ***Upper middle school and high school*** students will have strong and varying opinions about the causes of violence in schools and society. They will share concrete suggestions about how to make school safer and how to prevent tragedies in society. They will be more committed to doing something to help the victims and affected community. ***For all children, encourage them to verbalize their thoughts and feelings. Be a good listener!***
10. **Monitor Your Own Stress Level.** Don't ignore your own feelings of anxiety, grief, and anger. Talking to friends, family members, religious leaders, and mental health counselors can help. It is okay to let your children know that you are sad, but that you believe things will get better. You will be better able to support your children if you can express your own emotions in a productive manner. Get appropriate sleep, nutrition, and exercise.

What Parents Can Do

1. **Focus on your children over the next week following the tragedy**. Tell them you love them and everything will be okay. Try to help them understand what has happened, keeping in mind their developmental level.
2. **Make time to talk with your children**. Remember if you do not talk to your children about this incident someone else will. Take some time and determine what you wish to say.

3. **Stay close to your children.** Your physical presence will reassure them and give you the opportunity to monitor their reaction. Many children will want actual physical contact. Give plenty of hugs. Let them sit close to you, and make sure to take extra time at bedtime to cuddle and to reassure them that they are loved and safe.
4. **Limit your child's television viewing of these events.** If they must watch, watch with them for a brief time; then turn the set off. Don't sit mesmerized re-watching the same events over and over again.
5. **Maintain a "normal" routine.** To the extent possible stick to your family's normal routine for dinner, homework, chores, bedtime, etc., ***but don't be inflexible***. Children may have a hard time concentrating on schoolwork or falling asleep at night.
6. **Spend extra time reading or playing quiet games with your children before bed.** These activities are calming, foster a sense of closeness and security, and reinforce a sense of normalcy. Spend more time tucking them in. Let them sleep with a light on if they ask for it.
7. **Safeguard your children's physical health.** Stress can take a physical toll on children as well as adults. Make sure your children get appropriate sleep, exercise, and nutrition.
8. **Consider praying or thinking hopeful thoughts for the victims and their families.** It may be a good time to take your children to your house of worship, write a poem, or draw a picture to help your child express their feelings and feel that they are somehow supporting the victims and their families.
9. **Find out what resources your school has in place to help children cope.** Most schools are likely to be open and often are a good place for children to regain a sense of normalcy. Being with their friends and teachers can help. Schools should also have a plan for making counseling available to children and adults who need it.

What Schools Can Do

1. **Assure children that they are safe** and that schools are well prepared to take care of all children at all times.
2. **Maintain structure and stability within the schools.** It would be best, however, not to have tests or major projects within the next few days.
3. **Have a plan for the first few days back at school.** Include school psychologists, counselors, and crisis team members in planning the school's response.
4. **Provide teachers and parents with information** about what to say and do for children in school and at home.
5. **Have teachers provide information directly to their students**, not during the public address announcements.
6. **Have school psychologists and counselors available** to talk to student and staff who may need or want extra support.
7. **Be aware of students who may have recently experienced a personal tragedy** or a have personal connection to victims or their families. Even a child who has been to visit the Pentagon or the World Trade Center may feel a personal loss. Provide these students extra support and leniency if necessary.
8. **Know what community resources are available** for children who may need extra counseling. School psychologists can be very helpful in directing families to the right community resources.
9. **Allow time for age appropriate classroom discussion and activities.** Do not expect teachers to provide all of the answers. They should ask questions and guide the discussion, but not dominate it. Other activities can include art and writing projects, play acting, and physical games.
10. **Be careful not to stereotype people or countries that might be home to the terrorists.** Children can easily generalize negative statements and develop prejudice. Talk about tolerance and justice versus vengeance. ***Stop any bullying or teasing of students immediately***.
11. **Refer children who exhibit extreme anxiety, fear or anger to mental health counselors** in the school. Inform their parents.
12. **Provide an outlet for students' desire to help.** Consider making get well cards or sending letters to the families and survivors of the tragedy, or writing thank you letters to doctors, nurses, and other health care professionals as well as emergency rescue workers, firefighters and police.
13. **Monitor or restrict viewing scenes** of this horrendous event as well as the aftermath.

For information on helping children and youth with this crisis, contact NASP at (301) 657-0270 or visit NASP's website at www.nasponline.org.

UNIT 2

Development

Unit Selections

6. **Mind and Body,** Kathleen Vail
7. **Understanding Families,** Linda Garris Christian
8. **The Curriculum Superhighway,** Thomas Armstrong
9. **The Role of the Generations in Identity Formation,** Doug Hamman and C. Bret Hendricks
10. **Risk Taking in Adolescence,** Laurence Steinberg

Key Points to Consider

- How can physical activity be built into the regular classroom day?
- How do families differ, and how could teachers interact differently with each?
- How can schools and teachers provide an environment that is conducive to adolescent development?

Student Web Site

www.mhcls.com/online

Internet References

Further information regarding these Web sites may be found in this book's preface or online.

Association for Moral Education
http://www.amenetwork.org/

Center for Adolescent and Families Studies
http://www.indiana.edu/~cafs

Child Welfare League of America
http://www.cwla.org

The National Association for Child Development
http://www.nacd.org

National Association of School Psychologists (NASP)
http://www.nasponline.org/

Scholastic News Zone
http://www.scholasticnews.com

Creatas

The study of human development provides us with knowledge of how children and adolescents mature and learn within the family, community, and school environments. Educational psychology focuses on description and explanation of the developmental processes that make it possible for children to become intelligent and socially competent adults. Psychologists and educators are presently studying the idea that biology as well as the environment influence cognitive, personal, social, and emotional development and involve predictable patterns of behavior.

The perceptions and thoughts that young children have about the world are often quite different when compared to adolescents and adults. That is, children may think about moral and social issues in a unique way. Children need to acquire cognitive, moral, and social skills in order to interact effectively with parents, teachers, and peers. Human development encompasses all of the above skills and reflects the child's intelligent adaptation to the environment.

Today the physical, cognitive, moral, social, and emotional development of children takes place in a rapidly changing society. As the article on "Mind and Body" suggests, maintaining a focus on student health helps children cope with the pressures of academics and daily life. The article "Understanding Families: Applying Family Systems Theory to Early Childhood Practice," explains how different families cope, how those differences might manifest themselves in the classroom, and how teachers might best work with students and their families.

Adolescence brings with it the ability to think abstractly and hypothetically and to see the world from many perspectives. Adolescents strive to achieve a sense of identity by questioning their beliefs and tentatively committing to self-chosen goals. Their ideas about the kinds of adults they want to become and the ideals they want to believe in sometimes lead to conflicts with parents and teachers. Adolescents are also sensitive about espoused adult values versus adult behavior. The articles in this section address identity formation, risk-taking, and how the implicit "social curriculum" of middle schools can affect social development.

Mind and Body

New Research Ties Physical Activity and Fitness to Academic Success

KATHLEEN VAIL

When Garrett Lydic's students scale the climbing wall in their physical education classes, they are doing more than exercising their bodies—they are giving their brains a workout, as well. In Ellen Smith's PE class, students play a revamped version of the familiar sharks and minnows game that includes a science lesson.

Lydic, a PE teacher at North Laurel Elementary School in Laurel, Del., ordered a magnetized climbing wall so he could place numbers, letters, and other symbols on it. "Kids can climb and spell or solve math problems at the same time," says Lydic, who is the current Delaware State Teacher of the Year. "They are solving 20 to 30 problems as they climb across the wall. It occupies their minds while they are getting strong."

In Smith's reinvented game, students are asteroids instead of sharks. To win, other students must get through the asteroid belt and name the planets in the solar system. "Students will tell you their favorite class is PE because they think they are playing, but we are teaching through the playing," says Smith, who teaches at Gove Elementary School, a bilingual magnet school in Palm Beach County, Fla.

Academics and physical education used to exist in two separate universes, and never the twain did meet. In fact, some educators continue to see them as competing factions, one fighting for the mind, the other for the body. These days, however, the demarcation between mind and body, between academic education and physical education, is wavering. PE teachers such as Lydic and Smith are adding academic elements to their lessons, and regular classroom teachers are using physical exercises and activities to help boost students' concentration and focus.

Some of this change has been spurred by mounting research suggesting physical activity and fitness may actually help students do better in the classroom. Concern over childhood obesity also is fueling interest in the mind-body connection. But while child obesity rates continue to soar, more and more schools are cutting back on or eliminating physical education classes—especially at the elementary level—to make more time for academic instruction. By taking away recess and other opportunities for physical activity in response to the requirements of the No Child Left Behind Act, schools could be depriving their students of an element of what they need to do well in the classroom.

"There absolutely is an association with grades and fitness levels. As schools had more kids in higher fitness levels, they had higher grades—math in particular," says Alicia Moag-Stahlberg, the executive director of Action For Healthy Kids. Founded by Surgeon General David Satcher to help address the growing childhood obesity problem in the United States, Action For Healthy Kids released a report in 2004 looking at the research on the academics-fitness link.

Brains vs. Brawn

It turns out the old stereotypes of the dumb jock and the smart nerd don't exactly hold true. Probably the best known of the recent research on the academics-fitness link is a 2004 study by the California Department of Education, which found that students who do better on achievement tests are also more physically fit than their peers who don't score as well.

The study looked at students' FitnessGram scores and compared them with reading and math scores on the Stanford Achievement Test. (The FitnessGram is a nationally recognized test that measures aerobic capacity, body composition, muscle strength, endurance, and flexibility.) The students were in fifth, seventh, and ninth grades in California public schools.

According to the study's author, Jim Grissom, "results indicate a consistent positive relationship between overall fitness and academic achievement. That is, as overall fitness scores improved, mean achievement scores also improved. This relationship appeared to be stronger for females than males and stronger for higher socioeconomic status than lower SES students."

So should we be sending our children to the spinning class to raise their test scores? Not so fast. The study contained a large caveat: "Results should be interpreted with caution. It cannot be inferred from these data that physical fitness causes academic achievement to improve. It is more likely that physical and mental processes influence each other in ways that are still being understood."

With this said, the study continues: "However, if there is evidence that physical education has a direct positive effect on important educational domains such as reading and mathematics, it could be argued that physical education is not extracurricular. Rather, it is a vital component in students' academic success."

No one yet knows what it is about being physically fit that makes students do better on tests and get better grades. It could be that some superachieving students also seek to shine in athletics. It could be that physically fit students are healthier, and we know that healthier students do better in school. (Ample research shows how health and nutrition influence achievement.) Students who get regular physical education and exercise are better able to concentrate in the classroom. Exercise can help reduce asthma symptoms, a major cause for student absenteeism, especially in low-income areas. Regular exercise can alleviate stress, anxiety, and depression—problems that can affect school performance—and can even boost self-esteem.

Exercise and fitness might actually affect brain function. Studies on elderly adults show that exercise can help them maintain cognitive functioning; the same could apply to children. Researchers are busy trying to find out more. One of those researchers is University of Illinois professor of kinesiology Darla Castelli. She and colleague Charles Hillman have been studying fitness and cognitive functioning in preadolescents. "We found a strong association between math and aerobic fitness," says Castelli.

They looked at children ages 8, 9, and 10, comparing their fitness scores with how well they performed on five to seven different cognitive tasks. They also compared the fitness scores with the students' math and reading scores on the Illinois Standards Achievement Test. In addition to the correlation between aerobic fitness and math, the researchers found that the higher the students' Body Mass Index, the lower their scores. (A measurement of the relative percentages of fat and muscle mass in the human body, the BMI is an indicator of obesity.)

"It's common sense," says Castelli. "We think that children who are healthier are more ready to learn. If you have a higher BMI, you're not as prepared to learn."

Castelli urges caution in how the research, still in its nascent stages, is interpreted: "We can't say that if you jog a couple more laps, you'll do better with math. We need to investigate more." But since the association does exist, she says, schools that are eliminating or curtailing physical education programs should rethink the idea. "Maybe we should keep physical activity and promote play after the school day," she says. "Don't eliminate them, because we have these associations."

Some in the health and physical education fields are leery of making a case for more PE and recess on the basis of a possible link to improved academic performance. Schools should consider the health benefits of physical activity, even if exercise does or does not affect test scores, says Dr. Howard Taras, a San Diego pediatrician who works with school districts in southern California. After all, he says, schools do many other things purely for health reasons, such as provide immunizations.

The health benefits of physical activity—including having children carry those habits of exercise to adulthood—are pretty obvious, says Tom Templin, head of the Department of Health and Kinesiology at Purdue University and the president of the National Association for Sport and Physical Education. "I wouldn't put all my eggs in that basket. I would put my eggs in the physical benefits. The evidence is really solid there," he says. "What we are seeing is that physical education plays a critical role in moving kids toward a healthy and active lifestyle."

Other Mind-Body Links

Taras, a member of the American Academy of Pediatrics Task Force on Obesity, published a paper in the *Journal of School Health* in October [2005] examining the research on the association of obesity and academics. Taras says there is strong evidence that physical activity helps students concentrate and focus, at least in the short term.

Mike Wendt, superintendent of Wilson Central School District in Wilson, N.Y., explored this idea with researchers at the University of Buffalo, with interesting results. Their study looked at children with ADHD who went through a six-week exercise course. "We saw a dramatic behavior change at the end of six weeks," Wendt says. After that study, the district applied for and won a federal Physical Education Program (PEP) grant for $250,000 to build fitness centers at its schools. The district used the centers for, among other things, exercise labs for at-risk students. The key, says Wendt, is getting the heart rate up to 135 to 175 beats a minutes for 20 minutes a day, five days a week. "If endorphins are released at this point, then the kids will settle down," he says.

Indoor exercise is especially important in an area like upstate New York, Wendt says, where it gets too cold in the winter for outdoor activities. In fact, he says, the schools usually see a spike in misbehavior during the months when children are stuck indoors most days.

Certain types of exercises can enhance focus and relieve stress. "You might have the best lesson on the planet, but if [the students] are stressed out, it will bounce off them," says Florida's Ellen Smith. "If they are uptight and their brain, mind, and body are not ready to learn, it will be a wasted effort."

Smith uses a program called Brain Gym in her classes. Classroom teachers noticed their students doing the exercises before tests and asked Smith about the techniques so they could use them, too. "It's a routine that helps calm [students] down," she says.

The exercises in Brain Gym, which was developed by educators Paul and Gail Dennison, are meant to be done slowly. Carla Hannaford, author of *Smart Moves: Why Learning Is Not All in Your Head*, says it's important to have cross-lateral movements, such as the left hand crossing the body to touch the right leg. Tai chi is another form of exercise that includes such movements. The advantage of twisting and crossing arms or legs is that these movements encourage the brain's right and left hemispheres to work together, enabling the organization of brain functions.

"When you start doing this, you see a massive difference in children," says Hannaford. "They aren't acting out. They focus. It takes them out of the survival part of the brain and moves them into where they can think and learn. It makes life a lot easier, even for adults."

Learning through physical activity, whether it's in PE or in the regular classroom, helps many students who have trouble concentrating, sitting still, and paying attention. PE teacher Garrett Lydic found that integrating academics into PE allowed active or kinesthetic learners to excel. "The kids love it," he says. "It adds another element of challenge and gives them a way to learn in an active way. At-risk students learn especially well that way. It lets them learn in a way that they are best suited for."

The Motivation Factor

Along with PE, athletics are also being cut back in some schools, particularly in urban areas. And that could spell trouble for academics, because sports can be a great motivator. In many cases, students come to school and study just so they can participate in sports. They keep their grades up so they can maintain their spot on the team.

Jack Kemp spent 13 years as a pro football quarterback before going to Congress, serving as the U.S. secretary of Housing and Urban Development and as a vice presidential candidate in 1996. He says he was told as a student there would be no football if he didn't get better grades—and that in itself was enough for him to buckle down. But he believes sports have other benefits as well. "You can't succeed in sports without discipline in mind and body," Kemp says. "That discipline spills over, to study and get prepared for college."

Kemp serves as chairman of USA Football, a nonprofit organization founded by the NFL and the NFL Players Association, which is giving the National Association of State Boards of Education a $400,000 grant to study the link between athletics and academics in high school.

In urban schools especially, says NASBE Executive Director Brenda Welburn, coaches serve as powerful mentors to students. Often, coaches are the only adult student athletes connect with. Players spend three to four hours a day with their coach, who reminds them that they have to practice and keep up their grades to keep their spot on the team. "Anecdotal evidence suggests that students who are active in athletics and cocurricular activities perform better academically and are less inclined to use drugs and engage in other risky behaviors," says Welburn. However, she points out, "sound policy is not made on the basis of anecdotal evidence."

While we wait for more research on the connection between fitness and academics, some educators and health officials are calling for schools to be more aware of student health issues—including ensuring that physical education and activity are available to students despite growing testing pressures.

Pat Cooper, superintendent in McComb, Miss., started a districtwide wellness program several years ago. He acknowledges that the wellness focus has brought grades up, but he says that the boost is almost beside the point. "[Students] are healthier if they are taking part in physical activity every day," Cooper says. "They are coming to school, and they are coming to school with a better attitude." PE and recess give students a chance to let their guard down and have fun—and that, in turn, motivates them to like school. "PE teachers can be friends and mentors to our kids," he says. "They can do things that the regular teachers can't do. These are folks with special relationships with kids."

Focusing on student health can only help kids, including their ability to perform academically. "It's critical that school boards understand that the best thing they could do for the kids' grade point averages and test scores is to ensure kids are healthy," says Paul Rosengard, the executive director of SPARK, a physical education program developed by researchers at San Diego State University. "One core way to ensure healthy kids is make sure they have a good physical education program by a qualified phys ed teacher," he adds. "We have a ton of data supporting that fact."

Kathleen Vail (kvail@nsba.org) is a senior editor of *American School Board Journal.*

Understanding Families

Applying Family Systems Theory to Early Childhood Practice

LINDA GARRIS CHRISTIAN

Working with families is one of the most important aspects of being an early childhood professional, yet it is an area in which many educators have received little preparation (Nieto 2004). We spend hours learning about child development, developmentally appropriate practices, health and safety, playgrounds, and play. At times it seems that we focus on children as if they appear from nowhere, land in our classrooms, and merely disappear at the end of the day. We may ignore the settings in which they spend their time away from us, believing they are not very important. In fact the home environment greatly influences what goes on in school. Much has been written on parent involvement (Ginott 1965; Henderson & Berla 1981; Epstein et al. 1997), and the literature includes a growing number of references to family involvement (Birckmayer et al. 2005; Crosser 2005; Diss & Buckley 2005). However, a limited amount of research (Bredekamp & Copple 1997; Couchenour & Chrisman 2004) directly addresses understanding of family systems as a key component of early Childhood Education.

To serve children well, we must work with their families. To be effective in this work, we must first understand families who are diverse in ways such as culture, sexual orientation, economic status, work, religious beliefs, and composition. Single-parent families, families of divorce, blended families, extended families, homeless families, migrant families, and gay and lesbian families represent some of the diversity in families that we work with as early childhood professionals. Yet no matter how different families appear to outside observers, all have certain characteristics in common. Families just show them in different ways. Examining these characteristics helps educators engage families in ways that foster optimal child development.

Family Systems Theory

Family systems theory comes from the work of individuals like Ackerman (1959), Jackson (1965), Minuchin (1974), and Bowen (1978). While this theory is typically used in family counseling and therapy, much can be learned from examining it in the context of early childhood settings. Family systems theory has been used in trying to understand problems of students in school settings (Sawatzky, Eckert, & Ryan 1993; Widerman & Widerman 1995; Kraus 1998; Van Velsor & Cox 2000). The need for understanding family systems theory in early childhood settings has been underscored by professional organizations in their guidelines for preparing early childhood and elementary professionals (NAEYC, CEC/DEC, & NBPTS 1996; ACEI 1997a,b).

Family systems theory can explain why members of a family behave the way they do in a given situation.

A primary concept in family systems theory is that the family includes interconnected members, and each member influences the others in predictable and recurring ways (Van Velsor & Cox 2000). From our families we learn skills that enable us to function in larger and more formal settings, such as school and the workplace. Family experiences also shape our expectations of how the larger world will interact with us (Kern & Peluso 1999; Nieto 2004).

Family systems theory focuses on family behavior rather than individual behavior. The theory considers communication and interaction patterns, separateness and connectedness, loyalty and independence, and adaptation to stress in the context of the whole as opposed to the individual in isolation. Family systems theory can explain why members of a family behave the way they do in a given situation (Fingerman & Bermann 2000). It is critical to use these explanations to better serve children and families rather than for the purpose of blaming or trying to "fix" families.

While there are many aspects of the theory that could be applied in early childhood settings, I will limit this discussion to a few basics that I have found useful in my work with

Boundaries

Eight-year-old Miguel knows about the call to his house today. His after-school program director, Mr. Chin, told him that unless his spelling improved, he would be ineligible to compete at the city spelling meet. When the flyer on after-school classes came out in August, Miguel said he wanted to try pottery or chess. His mother insisted on his participation in the spelling bee and the challenging preparation for it. As he studied, Miguel felt a sense of pride in carrying on a family tradition. His mother, uncle, and older cousin had all won competitions when they were his age. However, Miguel has been frustrated by the rigor of the activities and the lack of time for other interests. By the time he gets home, a family meeting has already been planned to determine how best to help him to prepare. Miguel is nervous but knows his family will have good suggestions.

When Miguel's best friend, Mark, asked his mom which after-school class to take, she responded, "Whatever you want." Last year he tried and enjoyed swimming but got discouraged when his parents did not attend his meets. He signed up for the spelling bee this year, but only so he could be with Miguel. He isn't doing much better than Miguel, but when Mr. Chin calls Mark's family, their response is quite different from that of Miguel's family. Mark's dad takes the call and mentions it at dinner: "Mr. Chin called. It seems you're not doing so well with the spelling thing. Is there anything we can do to help?" Mark says, "No, I'm just tired of school stuff by the end of the day. Next time I'm going to try a sport or maybe chess." Mark's mom replies, "Sounds like a good plan, but what about Miguel?" Mark shrugs, "I did the spelling with him to keep him company. Maybe next time he'll do something with me."

families and children. There are six characteristics of the family as a system that are especially relevant for early childhood professionals: boundaries, roles, rules, hierarchy, climate, and equilibrium. Each of these characteristics lies on a continuum. For example, while all families have rules, some have many and others have few; some adhere strictly to rules and others are inconsistent. While few families fall on the extreme end of a continuum, they do tend to be more to one side.

Boundaries relate to limits, togetherness, and separateness—what or who is "in" or "out of" the family (Walsh & Giblin 1988). Some families are open to new people, information, and ideas. Family members tend to be independent and able to make decisions on their own. They value separateness and autonomy over a sense of belonging. Each person's identity is encouraged and respected. These families are sometimes described as *disengaged.* In other families boundaries tend to be more closed and restrictive; the families emphasize togetherness, belonging, emotional connectedness, and at times, conformity. They may control rather than monitor their children's friends and activities. Discipline is one way a family can enforce the boundaries within the family (Kern & Peluso 1999). Behaviors are seen as a reflection on the family, not just the individual. These families are sometimes referred to as *enmeshed.* An individual's identity is very much tied to the family when he or she is part of an enmeshed family.

Boundaries relate to limits, togetherness, and separateness—what or who is "in" or "out of" the family.

Early childhood professionals should remain open when thinking about these two types of families. One is not positive and the other negative; the types are just different from each other. Families may show signs and degrees of each type; this may vary at any given point, depending on factors such as age of the children, economic circumstances, and the family's stage of development (for example, first-time parents versus a family with several children). Other factors, including the families in which the parents grew up, the social and political climate of the times, the culture and values of the family, and health or mental issues in the family, also influence the degree of enmeshment or disengagement. Over time families may change from one style to another. For example, during times of stress and crisis a family that had operated in a disengaged manner may move toward a more closed system.

Miguel's family is closer to the enmeshed end of the continuum while Mark's family tends to be more disengaged. Mark may sometimes wish his parents would become more involved with his activities, while Miguel may secretly wish his family would occasionally keep their opinions to themselves! The family's involvement in his preparation for the competition indicates their enmeshment.

In a conversation with Mark's parents about next term's activities, you may learn that while Mark's mother thinks sports would help his lagging physical development, his father fears self-esteem issues could arise if Mark struggles because of this lag. However, both feel that it is Mark's decision and they will support it. Mark's family's disengagement works to foster his independence and develop his identity, while Miguel's identity is closely related to that of his family.

As an educator, you would foster both Miguel's and Mark's sense of identity while respecting their families: share what you know about each boy's real strengths with them and their families. Help each child and his family to see the characteristics that make him unique and wonderful. Work with Miguel to identify family rituals, traditions, and values in which he believes. Help him find ways to appreciate and honor his family's support. As Mark's teacher you may plan activities that allow his family to see Mark's uniqueness or activities that lend themselves to family involvement. Help Mark to see the ways in which his family does support his development.

Ideas for Working with Families—Boundaries

1. **Recognize different parenting styles and family boundaries.** Educators often perceive the family who comes to meetings and responds with active and enthusiastic involvement and participation (helps with learning or discipline issues, provides materials for a special project, serves as a volunteer) as more caring and as a "good family." The family who responds politely to requests but leaves day-to-day decisions and work on school matters to the child and teacher (allows child to experience consequences due to lack of preparation for a quiz or forgetting their share item for the day) is seen as less caring and uninvolved. Build on family strengths and avoid labeling and allowing personal bias to influence your interactions with families.
2. **Avoid stereotypes.** Just because a student is of a certain culture does not automatically mean that student's family is of a given religion, does not have legal status, has a certain discipline style, or has a specific socioeconomic status (Kagan & Garcia 1991). It is critical for teachers to become familiar with the cultural background of individual students.
3. **Recognize that for some families *everything* is a family affair.** Be sure to have enough chairs, snacks, and materials to accommodate extended families at events and conferences. For some families, an invitation to family night includes aunts, uncles, cousins, friends who serve as family, and even neighbors (Trawick-Smith 2005).
4. **Balance children's activities and curriculum to incorporate both individual and group identity.** Whether their families are disengaged or enmeshed, children need opportunities to experience who they are individually and as a part of a group.
5. **Respect families' need for control.** When introducing new ideas, materials, or experiences to children, involve families as well. Also recognize that some family members did not have positive experiences with education as they were growing up. While they may display anger, hostility, or mistrust, and these may be directed at you, the source may be events from the past. It will take time and persistence to build a relationship with these families. Teachers need to demonstrate that families can depend on and trust them to help in the education of their children.

Roles

"Lela, go and join the others on the playground. I'll finish the rest of cleanup for you. You've been a big help today," says Kathy as she hugs the four-year-old. Lela hesitates at the door and asks, "Are you sure?" Kathy smiles reassuringly. "Yes, now go play!"

Once on the playground, Lela pushes Sadie, one of the younger children, on the swing. When Sadie tires of swinging and goes off to play in the sand, Lela helps the teacher carry toys from the storage shed to set up an activity. Later, Lela mediates a dispute over tricycles between two classmates. A visiting teacher taking anecdotal notes that day writes, "Lela's play was limited to 'helping' for outdoor playtime and much of the rest of the day. How can we encourage her to expand her play activities to include other roles?"

In all families, individual members have roles (Walsh & Giblin 1988; Tarnowski-Goodell, Hanson, & May 1999; Fingerman & Bermann 2000). There is usually a peacemaker, a clown, a rescuer, and a victim, although there can be many other roles as well. Each role has certain behavioral expectations. For example, if someone is the responsible one within the family, this person has a tendency to fix problems and take care of others, and others depend on him. The victim in the family is the person who gets blamed for everything. This person often acts out in ways that are sure to bring responses of anger, threats, and punishment.

Family roles can be carried over to work, school, and social settings. A child who has spent four years practicing every day to be the peacemaker will bring those skills to the classroom. While each role can have positive behavior, there can also be negative consequences. For example, if the responsible person in the family always solves the problems, others do not have opportunities to develop problem-solving skills.

Lela has a clear idea of her role in her family: she is a helper. Helping is a wonderful attribute and not one that teachers want to disappear. Having Lela teach others how to help is a way to build on her strength. To facilitate her whole-child development, teachers could set up a situation that does not lend itself to her helping anyone and encourage her play in that area. They could also refuse some of her offers to help, but with careful wording. For example, "You were such a great help yesterday, you deserve a day off today! But you can choose someone to do this job today."

Lela's teachers will need patience, consistency, and creative ideas to help her learn new roles. Look for her other strengths and channel her energies in that direction. For example, Lela has strong fine motor skills; she could be paired with a child who is creative to design and construct new signs for the play areas. It is also important to find ways

Rules

Jason teaches a toddlers' class. Soon after parents Sam and Imelda met at a party, they began sharing rides and helping each other out on weekends. The relationship blossomed into something more than two single parents sharing the trials and tribulations of their two-year-olds. The two families have recently joined together as one.

As the assistant director, Jason needs to find out which families need child care over an upcoming holiday. When he broaches the subject with Sam and Imelda, he detects a stony silence. Finally Sam says, "I thought it would be nice for our first holiday to go away together with the children. My uncle has offered the use of his house in the mountains." Imelda chimes in quickly, "But I've always spent the holidays with my family here in town. It's just expected that everybody will be there. If someone doesn't, they hear about it for years."

Jason remembers a huge fight with his wife the first year after they became parents. It was about when to open Christmas presents. He understands Sam and Imelda's dilemma, but he isn't sure how to support them as a new family.

to share positive information with Lela's family that allow them to foster opportunities for new roles at home.

Ideas for Working with Families—Roles

1. **Give children ample opportunity for role play, in both structured and unstructured situations.** Children need to experience new roles as well as work through their current roles. Recognize the importance of children's cultural backgrounds in the roles they adopt (Noel 2000; Garcia 2002).
2. **Observe children carefully.** Many "problems" that educators identify are very role bound. A child who seems to be a magnet for disruptive events may be the child who gets blamed for everything at home. Set up situations for that child to see herself in different roles. For example, engage the child in working with you to negotiate a dispute between two other children or allow the child to lead an activity.
3. **Help families recognize their children's many and varied strengths.** A note home might read, "Sally taught Ki how to put on his shoes today! She was a very good teacher" or "I appreciate Ricky's sense of humor. He always makes us smile!"

Family roles can be carried over to work, school, and social settings.

Rules are sets of standards, laws, or traditions that tell us how to live in relation to each other. Our patterns and rules for interaction have long-term and far-reaching effects. For example, if we believe in the predictability of life, we tend to plan ahead. If we believe what happens is out of our control, we may deal with circumstances as they arise rather than trying to prevent or avoid problems (Fingerman & Bermann 2000).

Rules may be spoken or unspoken. If we have been informed about a rule, we can discuss, problem solve, and make choices. If we are unaware of a rule, we may behave in ways that are not consistent with that rule. We usually find out about an unspoken rule by breaking it and then experiencing the consequences. Rules are often embedded in a cultural context; therefore, they can contribute to the feeling of cultural discontinuity that some children experience at school. When home and school cultures conflict, misunderstandings and even hostility can occur for children, families, and teachers (Delpit 1995; Noel 2000). Sam and Imelda are experiencing problems with procedural kinds of rules. Jason needs to support this family in a positive way without crossing professional and personal boundaries. There may be resources to which he can direct them.

Jason must be very careful in how he responds; he is not a counselor. Is this a simple issue, or is it one in which the family may need outside help? Jason can share his experience—that he and his wife found it helpful to talk to their priest, and that the center resource director has a list of local counselors that other families have used in the past. On a practical level he can acknowledge the importance of bringing both familiar rituals to the new family as well as new experiences that will bond the members together. He can encourage Sam and Imelda to keep talking and listening to each other so that they can determine what is important to each of them.

Ideas for Working with Families—Rules

1. **Make distinctions between home rules and school rules.** When children challenge you on a specific school rule, it may be because it differs from home rules. Proceed carefully; it is critical to respect the home environment. For example, you may allow children to serve themselves at mealtimes, although at home their plates are prepared by adults.
2. **Watch for unspoken rules,** especially those related to gender, power, and how we treat each other; discuss them with care. While you may want girls and boys to enjoy cooking experiences, recognize that in some traditional families this may create a conflict. Discuss the skills, rationale, and benefits for children and families. You may uncover alternate activities that meet the goals of all.
3. **Ask for families' input and assistance when conflict arises over rules.** Explain the reasons behind school rules and, equally important, listen to the

Hierarchy

Nancy, a preschool teacher, notices that the Hudson family has been rather short with her and almost cold since the last family meeting. Up until now they had been supportive and friendly. Puzzled, she schedules an appointment with Kate, the center director. Kate thoughtfully listens to Nancy's dilemma, and together they re-create the events of the last meeting with families.

After much thought, they focus on one activity. Several teachers had presented three curriculum designs on which they wanted family input. A couple of parents had given ideas, but then the communication stopped. In an effort to get things going again, Nancy had said, "Mrs. Hudson, you and Mr. Hudson have been active volunteers and observers of our curriculum for several months now. What do you think?" While Mr. Hudson offered several ideas, Mrs. Hudson averted her eyes and did not respond. Thinking back, Kate and Nancy remember Mr. Hudson looked rather startled and almost angry. But what was the source of this animosity?

family. They can share information that may help resolve a problem or address changes that may need to be made in school rules. They may also be willing to modify home rules or talk with their child about the differences between home and school.

Hierarchy helps answer the question "Who's the boss?" This characteristic is related to decision making, control, and power in the family. In some families, the hierarchy is a parental one. The parents share family responsibilities. One may defer to the other based on a specific situation or individual strength, but there is a definite balance and trading back and forth of power and control. Early childhood professionals may also observe family hierarchies based on gender and age and influenced by culture, religion, or economic status. At times there may be a clear and strong message but other times it may be difficult to discern. You may observe at the center's family picnic that the males are seated, served, and encouraged to eat first. In other families, the elder grandmother may be the decision maker, and everyone may look to her for leadership and guidance. The role of extended family in understanding hierarchy may be very important in some families (Morton 2000).

Rules are often embedded in a cultural context; therefore, they can contribute to the feeling of cultural discontinuity that some children experience at school.

Early childhood professionals need to understand hierarchy because of the diversity of families with whom we work. Each time the family composition changes, there is a shift in where family members are in the hierarchy. For example, one family consists of a child, a younger sibling, a mother, and a grandmother at the beginning of the year. After a midyear marriage, the family home has the child, the sibling, the mother, the grandmother, the new father figure, and two new older stepsiblings. The hierarchy has changed. In families with large extended kin networks, hierarchy can be confusing to outsiders.

Each time the family composition changes, there is a shift in where family members are in the hierarchy.

The Hudson family may feel that Nancy and her colleagues did not respect the hierarchy in their family. There are two issues for Nancy and her colleagues: prevention and repair. In terms of prevention, they could add some items to the information sheets distributed at the beginning of the year and returned by each family that respectfully ask about how the family would like to be approached in certain situations. Sample items might read:

Decisions about children in our family are usually made by ________.

How and with whom would you like information about your child shared?

We want to respect your family in our work with you and your child at this center. Please share any information that you feel will help us in these efforts.

Most important, Nancy and her colleagues should make conscious efforts to observe families and their children in center activities, social gatherings at the center, and in home visits to notice cues the family gives as to the hierarchy. They can become "family watchers" in addition to being "child watchers." For example, does a mother always defer to the grandmother on questions that the teacher asks?

Climate is about the emotional and physical environments a child grows up in.

To repair the relationship with the Hudsons, Nancy and her colleagues will need to be sincere, diligent, and focused on respect and what is best for the child and family. If conferences with the family don't illicit a response that allows Nancy to address the change in their behavior, she may choose to directly state her concern that she has offended them in some way. She may ask for their help in understanding so that she will not repeat her mistake and stress how much she values and respects the family as part of her classroom. She may

Climate

Climate is about the emotional and physical environments a child grows up in. Some families compensate for hurtful or inadequate parts of the environment, such as living in a dangerous neighborhood, as best as they can (Nieto 2004). Other families have the best that money can buy, but the emotional quality of the home environment is not optimal for the children. The culture, economic status, or educational level of the family does not cause the emotional quality of the environment to be positive or negative. Emotional quality is related to beliefs about children and families. To determine the climate of a family system, consider the answers to the following questions: What would it feel like to be a child in this family? Would I feel safe, secure, loved, encouraged, and supported? Or would I feel scared, fearful, angry, hated, and unhappy?

communicate to them how vital they are to the success of the program and especially to their children. She may also ask if they have a need that she has failed to address.

Ideas for Working with Families—Hierarchy

1. **Engage in careful and keen observation.** "Family watching" is essential. Who signs the permission forms? Who returns the phone call? How does the child role-play his family members in dramatic play? Does a youngster assume that a male teacher is the boss of the female teachers? While answers to these questions are not always indicative of hierarchy, they may offer clues.
2. **Note the signs that a family's hierarchy is in the process of changing.** Be aware that children can respond by testing hierarchy in the classroom. A child who often leads at school may appear lost or unsure of herself as a new stepbrother takes her place "in charge" of younger siblings. Help her to reclaim her confidence through activities that allow her to experience success.
3. **Watch out for hierarchies emerging in the classroom and on the playground.** While hierarchy can lead to a sense of order and security, it can also lead to a pecking order and in the worst cases, bullying. Avoid activities that reinforce the same hierarchy over time. Vary activities so that different children's strengths are showcased.

Equilibrium

It is critical for early childhood professionals to understand the balance or sense of equilibrium within a family. Changes or inconsistency in a family can create confusion or resentment in its members, including children (Kern & Peluso 1999). Consistency in families can be difficult to maintain, but it is essential to children's development of a sense of security and trust. Rituals and customs often keep a family together during times of change and stress (Fingerman & Bermann 2000). All families, even ones with ongoing difficulties, have a sort of balance that tells members what to expect. When there is change, positive or negative, it impacts the balance of the family. That is one reason change is so difficult to maintain.

For example, in a family where sweets, fried foods, and lots of bread are meal staples, a family member with a heart condition is told to change to a healthier diet. While other family members may wish to be supportive, it can be difficult. They may resent that their eating habits must change too, because preparing two meals is usually not feasible.

Ideas for Working with Families—Climate

1. **Provide opportunities for families to discuss their beliefs about children,** what they want for their children, and how they support their children's development. Staff can facilitate at the events. These discussions help teachers learn how they can best support families as the families support their children (Delpit 1995; Garcia 2001). An additional benefit is that families often value information and advice from their peers more than through a lecture on good parenting.
2. **Create a classroom climate of safety, positive feedback and guidelines, and healthy sensory experiences.** Even if home environments do not offer these (or especially!), children need to feel school is a wonderful place to be.

Ideas for Working with Families—Equilibrium

1. **Consider inviting a trained family professional to facilitate discussion** when a big change or issue is impacting a number of families (for example, a bond issue will impact the public schools the children

attend). Families need to have safe places to vent, discuss, and talk about their changing worlds.

Consistency in families can be difficult to maintain, but it is critical to children's development of a sense of security and trust.

2. **Provide as much consistency as possible** when you are aware of changes within a family (a new baby or sick grandparent). This is usually not a good time to change the routine, rearrange the classroom, or introduce new staff. Recognize that in some cases, the teacher, the environment, and the school routine are the most stable forces in the child's life.
3. **Encourage families to plan ways to increase stability and security.** For example, parents may have to meet the needs of their young children while also caring for an older relative in failing health. Nevertheless, they can set aside time for a bedtime routine that involves reading a story and talking about the day's events.

Conclusion

The suggestions in this article are not absolutes nor meant to be perfect. Each family is unique, as is each teacher. Some educators are comfortable with direct interactions, while others of us need to begin discussions with an activity that demonstrates our connections to and caring for families before tackling these kinds of conversations. While establishing relationships with families before problems arise is essential, it doesn't always happen. We need nonconfrontational ways to broach sensitive topics.

The keys to win-win resolutions are awareness, willingness, sincerity, and respect. Making an effort to understand families will open up opportunities for you to better serve children and their families.

References

ACEI (Association for Childhood Education International). 1997a. Preparation of early childhood teachers. *Childhood Education* 73 (3): 164–65.

ACEI (Association for Childhood Education International). 1997b. Preparation of elementary teachers. *Childhood Education* 73 (3): 166–67.

Ackerman, N. 1959. Theory of family dynamics. *Psychoanalysis and the Psychoanalytic Review* 46 (4): 33–50.

Birckmayer, J., J. Cohen, I. Jensen, & D. Variano. 2005. Supporting grandparents who raise grandchildren. *Young Children* 60 (3): 100–04.

Bowen, M. 1978. *Family therapy in clinical practice.* New York: Jason Aronson.

Bredekamp, S., & C. Copple, eds. 1997. *Developmentally appropriate practice in early childhood programs.* Rev. ed. Washington, DC: NAEYC.

Couchenour, D., & K. Chrisman. 2004. *Families, schools, and communities: Together for young children.* Canada: Delmar Learning.

Crosser, S. 2005. *What do we know about early Childhood Education? Research based practice.* Clifton Park, NY: Thomson Delmar Learning.

Delpit, L. 1995. *Other people's children: Cultural conflict in the classroom.* New York: The New Press.

Diss, R., & P. Buckley. 2005. *Developing family and community involvement skills through case studies and field experiences.* Upper Saddle River, NJ: Pearson.

Epstein, J., L. Coates, K.C. Salinas, M.G. Saunders, & B.S. Simon. 1997. *School, family, and community partnerships: Your handbook for action.* Thousand Oaks, CA: Corwin.

Fingerman, K., & E. Bermann. 2000. Applications of family systems theory to the study of adulthood. *International Journal of Aging and Human Development* 51 (1): 5–29.

Garcia, E. 2001. *Hispanic education in the United States: Raices y Alas.* Lanham, MD: Rowman and Littlefield.

Garcia, E. 2002. *Student cultural diversity: Understanding and meeting the challenge.* Boston, MA: Houghton Mifflin.

Ginott, H. 1965. *Between parent and child: New solutions to old problems.* New York: Macmillian.

Henderson, A.T., & N. Berla. 1981. *The evidence grows: Parent involvement improves student achievement.* Columbia, MD: National Committee for Citizens in Education.

Jackson, D.D. 1965. Family rules: Marital quid pro quo. *Archives of General Psychiatry* 12: 589–94.

Kagan, S., & E. Garcia. 1991. Educating culturally and linguistically diverse preschoolers: Moving the agenda. Urbana, IL: ERIC Clearinghouse on Elementary and Early Childhood Education, University of Illinois.

Kern, R., & P. Peluso. 1999. Using individual psychology concepts to compare family systems processes and organizational behavior. *Family Journal* 7 (3): 236–45.

Kraus, I. 1998. A fresh look at school counseling: A family systems approach. *Professional School Counseling* 1 (4): 12–17.

Morton, D. 2000. Beyond parent education: The impact of extended family dynamics in deaf education. *American Annals of the Deaf* 145 (4): 359–66.

Minuchin, S. 1974. *Families and family therapy.* Cambridge, MA: Harvard University Press.

NAEYC, CEC/DEC (Council for Exceptional Children, Division of Early Childhood), & NBPTS (National Board for Professional Teaching Standards). 1996. *Guidelines for preparation of early childhood professionals.* Washington, DC: NAEYC.

Nieto, S. 2004. *Affirming diversity: The sociopolitical context of multicultural education.* Boston: Pearson.

Noel, J. 2000. *Developing multicultural educators.* New York: Longman.

Sawatzky, D.D., C. Eckert, B.R. Ryan. 1993. The use of family systems approach by school counselors. *Canadian Journal of Counseling* 27: 113–12.

Tarnowiski-Goodell, T., H. Hanson, & S. May. 1999. Nurse-family interactions in adult critical care: A Bowen family systems perspective. *Journal of Family Nursing* 5 (1): 72–92.

Trawick-Smith, J. 2005. *Early childhood development: A multicultural perspective*. Upper Saddle River, NJ: Pearson.

Van Velsor, P., & D. Cox. 2000. Use of the collaborative drawing technique in school counseling practicum: An illustration of family systems. *Counselor Education and Supervision* 40 (2): 141–53.

Walsh, W., & N. Giblin. 1988. *Family counseling in school settings*. Springfield, IL: Charles C. Thomas.

Widerman, J. L., & E. Widerman. 1995. Family systems-oriented school counseling. *The School Counselor* 43: 66–73.

Linda Garris Christian, PhD, is a professor of education at Adams State College in Alamosa, Colorado, working primarily with preservice teachers. Linda is also involved in local Even Start, Head Start, and other nonprofit early childhood centers.

You can also view this article online in Beyond the Journal: www.journal.naeyc.org/btj.

The Curriculum Superhighway

In the race to get kids to the finish line, let's not bypass their developmental needs.

THOMAS ARMSTRONG

A superhighway is being built across today's education landscape. It has been under construction for some time. Initially, this project focused on connecting kindergarten to the elementary grades. Gradually, it has broadened its vision until now it extends from preschool to graduate school.[1] All the byways, narrow routes, and winding paths that have traditionally filled the journey from early childhood to early adulthood are now being "aligned" so that the curriculum (a Latin word meaning "a lap around a racetrack") can move along at breakneck speed.

So far, this project has received the approbation of most educators and policymakers. Such a colossal undertaking, however, extracts a great cost.

An Environmental Impact Report

Educators today are almost entirely engaged in *academic achievement discourse* (Armstrong, 2006). The topics of this discourse—test scores, benchmarks, data, accountability, and adequate yearly progress—are the bulldozers, backhoes, cement mixers, and asphalt pavers that are constructing the curriculum superhighway. A more appropriate focus of educators' dialogue would be *human development discourse,* which recognizes that human beings travel through different stages of life, each with its own requirements for optimal growth.

The curriculum superhighway is carving an asphalt swath through several distinct areas of the human development countryside, threatening to damage or destroy their delicate ecosystems. Let's consider some of the eco-disasters likely to ensue from this multi-billion-dollar road project.

Human beings travel through different stages of life, each with its own requirements for optimal growth.

Early Childhood

In early childhood, the developmental bottom line is *play.* When I say play, I'm not talking about playing checkers or soccer; I'm referring to open-ended play in a rich, multimodal environment, with supportive facilitators and a minimum of adult interference. Between the ages of 2 and 6, children's brains go through an incredible process of development. Metabolism is twice that of an adult, and brain connections are formed or discarded in response to the kinds of stimulation the child does or doesn't receive.

At this time of life, it makes the most sense to encourage open-ended engagement with the world in an environment like that of Habibi's Hutch, a preschool in Austin, Texas, that calls itself a "natural childlife preserve." Children spend most of their day playing on swing sets, in sand piles, in playhouses, and with art materials and toys. They perform their own plays and participate in a cooking class (Osborne, 2007). The preschool's Web site (http://habibishutch.com/philosophy.html) explains, "Our kids leave the Hutch with so much more than their ABCs and 123s. They all leave with a sense of themselves and a wonder and drive to know more about themselves and their surroundings."

This approach to early childhood education is a good example of a developmentally appropriate program. Unfortunately, the curriculum superhighway is delivering academic goods and materials as well as formal teaching lessons from the higher grades down to the preschool level—a trend that could ultimately destroy this precious ecology.

Middle Childhood

In middle childhood, the developmental bottom line is *learning how the world works.* Naturally, children of all ages are constantly learning about the world. But from age 7 to 10, this need becomes especially important. Kids are becoming a more significant part of the broader society, and they want to understand the rules of this more complex world. Their brains have matured to the point where they can begin to learn the formal rules of reading, writing, and math; but they also need to satisfy their insatiable curiosity by learning how governments work, how butterflies grow, how their community developed, and countless other things.

The "children's museum" model of learning, recommended by Howard Gardner (1994) among others, is a good example of how we can preserve this developmental ecology. "In a children's museum," Gardner explains, "kids have an opportunity to work with very interesting kinds of things, at their own pace, in their own way, using the kinds of intelligence which they're strong in." In a unit developed by the Minnesota Children's Museum, for example, 1st grade students spend six weeks studying insects using the museum's Insect Discovery Kit and then take a trip to the museum's anthill exhibit (Association of Children's Museums, 2003).

"In all the world there is no other child exactly like you. In the millions of years that have passed, there has never been another child exactly like you. You may become a Shakespeare, a Michelangelo, a Beethoven. You have the capacity for anything. Yes, you are a marvel."

—Pablo Casals

Because schools today are spending more and more class time preparing students for academic tests that are part of the superhighway scheme (a project aptly called "No Child Left Behind"), students have fewer opportunities to engage in a rich exploration of our incredible world. As a result, this ecosystem could eventually decay and disappear.

Early Adolescence

The developmental needs of early adolescence consist primarily of *social, emotional, and metacognitive growth.* Surges of testosterone at puberty swell the amygdala, especially in boys, generating strong emotions (Giedd et al., 1996). For girls, estrogen levels appear to affect serotonin levels, leading to high rates of depression (Born, Shea, & Steiner, 2002). The curriculum needs to reflect young adolescents' greater sensitivity to emotional and social issues. For example, at Benjamin Franklin Middle School in Ridgewood, New Jersey, students read about the Warsaw ghetto and then discuss how they can combat injustices that they see in their own lives (Curtis, 2001).

Just before puberty, children's brains experience a surge in the growth of gray matter in the frontal, parietal, and temporal lobes, which may be related to what Piaget called *formal operational thinking*—the ability to "think about thinking." This new capacity represents an incredible resource, enabling young teens to begin to reflect at a more abstract level—not only to gain perspective on their own emotional responses, but also to engage intellectually with such universal issues as justice and individual rights.

Unfortunately, the project managers of the curriculum superhighway appear to regard this newly acquired metacognitive capacity as merely an opportunity to teach algebra and reading comprehension. The components of the superhighway's infrastructure—tougher requirements, more homework, and harder tests—leave teachers little chance to engage students' emotions, social needs, and metacognitive thinking in any substantial way. The resulting deterioration in this ecosystem may lead to environmental hazards such as gangs, violence, and mental disorders.

Late Adolescence

In late adolescence, the developmental bottom line is *preparing to live independently in the real world.* At this age, neural pathways in the brain are becoming increasingly sheathed, or myelinated, so that nerve impulses travel more quickly—especially in the frontal lobes, which control planning and decision making (National Institute of Mental Health, 2001). At this age, young people in many states are legally empowered to set up their own individual retirement accounts, drive a car, marry, vote, and engage in other adult responsibilities. But in a typical high school classroom, these same adolescents have to raise their hand for permission to go to the bathroom.

At this stage of life, kids need less classroom time and more time out in the real world, in apprenticeships, internships, job shadowing, career-based work experiences, and other situations in which they can experience themselves as incipient adults. The traffic on the curriculum superhighway, however, is especially intense at this point. High school students are deluged with pressures to pass high-stakes tests, meet strict graduation requirements, and take advanced courses that will prepare them for four-year academic colleges. Many of them aren't even allowed to dip their toes into the currents of the real world, because to take this time would mean falling behind their peers in an increasingly competitive society The curriculum superhighway's attack on this ecosystem may erode students' ability to think for themselves, reflect on their futures, and make responsible choices that mirror their own proclivities and interests.

Restoring a Human Development Curriculum

Schools need to approach curriculum in a way that is environmentally sensitive to the ecologies of different developmental stages of life. Let's start with literacy. In early childhood, literacy needs to take place in the context of play. According to developmental psychologist David Elkind (2001), children aren't even cognitively ready to learn formal reading and math skills until they reach Piaget's operational stage of cognitive development around age 6 or 7. In early childhood, literacy should be just another part of the child's rich multisensory environment. A playhouse area, for example, should include books and magazines along with dolls and furniture. If a child wants to play at being mommy reading a story to baby, that's up to her (experts call this process *emergent literacy*).

At the elementary school level, we can appropriately teach formal reading and writing skills, because the symbol systems of literacy are an important component of how the world works. Literacy will develop best, however, not with boring worksheets and sterile reading programs, but with reading and writing experiences that give students a chance to learn about all aspects of the world, from science to history to social relationships. In such programs, students may read historical narratives, guidebooks on science topics, and other reading materials (such as reference sources, Internet text, or high-quality fiction) that whet their curiosity to find out more about the world. Likewise, they may take field notes on nature hikes, write letters to people of influence, and create reports based on what they've discovered about their community's history.

In middle school, literacy needs to take place in the context of a young teen's social, emotional, and metacognitive growth. Journal writing, therefore, is developmentally more important than book report writing. Reading material should include emotional themes that speak to the adolescent's inner turmoil. Teachers should assign collaborative and cooperative reading and writing assignments to honor the social needs of early adolescence. They need to teach students how to use metacognitive strategies to monitor their own reading and writing habits.

Finally, in high school, literacy needs to serve the interests of the student becoming an independent person in the real world. Here, college preparation reading lists are appropriate for some students. But all students should learn more practical literacy skills, including how to write a résumé, how to skim for essential information on the Internet, and how to develop a lifelong interest in reading as a hobby.

Math and science instruction should also evolve as children move through each developmental ecosystem. In early childhood, math and science are an integral part of daily play activities as kids build with blocks, examine insects, and dangle from the jungle gym. In elementary school, kids are developmentally ready to learn the formal systems of mathematics and the use of science to answer questions about the world, from why the sky is blue to how a car works.

In middle school, math and science become vehicles for exploring the biology of life, the ultimate nature of the cosmos, the consequences of a nuclear war, and other emotionally laden and thought-provoking topics. Students need to work on high-interest, group-oriented math and science projects (for example, preserving a bird habitat or monitoring junk food habits) and communicate their findings to others through the Internet, science fairs, and other means.

At the high school level, students need to study for preparatory exams in math and science to help them apply for college or technical schools. They also need to learn the practical math and technical skills necessary for living independently (for example, financial planning and using computer software) and develop the science and math literacy necessary to vote intelligently on such issues as taxation, global warming, and the costs of war.

Schools need to approach curriculum in a way that is environmentally sensitive to the ecologies of different developmental stages of life.

A human development curriculum also extends beyond literacy, math, and science to other subjects, including the arts, physical education, social skills training, and imaginative, moral, and spiritual development. In far too many schools, these subjects have been crushed beneath the heavy weight of the concrete (benchmarks), asphalt (standardized tests), and steel (adequate yearly progress) that make up the bulk of the curriculum superhighway.

As educators, we need to rescue these important components of person-building from the rubble of the superhighway construction site and preserve the delicate ecologies that make up our students' stages of human growth and development. By dismantling the curriculum superhighway, we can ensure that our students will not stress out in traffic jams, keel over from road fatigue, or be maimed or killed in collisions along the way. By focusing on the whole child, we can prepare our students to meet the challenges of the real world in the years to come.

Note

1. See, for example, the 2004 publication of the California Alliance of PreK–18 Partnerships, *Raising Student Achievement Through Effective Education Partnerships: Policy and Practice* (available at www.ced.csulb.edu/California-alliance/documents/AllianceReport-printversion.pdf).

References

Armstrong, T. (2006). *The best schools: How human development research should inform educational practice.* Alexandria, VA: ASCD.

Association of Children's Museums. (2003, May 2). *Whether with public schools, childcare providers, or transit authorities, children's museums partner creatively with their communities* [Online news release]. Available: www.childrensmuseums.org/press_releases/5_2_03.htm

Born, L., Shea, A., & Steiner, M. (2002). The roots of depression in adolescent girls: Is menarche the key? *Current Psychiatry Reports, 4,* 449–460.

Curtis, D. (2001, Spring). We're here to raise kids. *Edutopia,* 8–9. Available: www.edutopia.org/EdutopiaPDF/Spring01.pdf

Elkind, D. (2001). Much too early. *Education Next, 1*(2), 9–15.

Gardner, H. (1994). *Reinventing our schools: A conversation with Howard Gardner.* [Videotape]. Bloomington, IN: AIT & Phi Delta Kappa.

Giedd, J. N., Vaituzis, A. C., Hamburger, S. D., Lange, N., Rajapakse, J. C., Kaysen, D., et al. (1996). Quantitative MRI of the temporal lobe, amygdala, and hippocampus in normal human development: Ages 4–18 years. *Journal of Comparative Neurology, 366*(2), 223–230.

National Institute of Mental Health. (2001). *Teenage brain: A work in progress* (NIH Publication No. 01-4929). Washington, DC: Department of Health and Human Services. Available: www.nimh.nih.gov/Publicat/teenbrain.cfm

Osborne, C. (2007, January 22). South Austin preschool doesn't make children learn their ABCs, *Austin American-Statesman.* Available: www.statesman.com/news/content/news/stories/local/01/22/22preschool.html

Thomas Armstrong (Thomas@thomasarmstrong.com; www.thomasarmstrong.com) is a speaker with more than 30 years of teaching experience from the primary through the doctoral level. He is the author of 13 books, including *The Best Schools: How Human Development Research Should Inform Educational Practice* (ASCD, 2006).

The Role of the Generations in Identity Formation

Erikson Speaks to Teachers of Adolescents

DOUG HAMMAN AND C. BRET HENDRICKS

There is no shortage of important research findings describing how educators may improve the academic and social achievement of adolescents (Ames and Archer 1988; Anderman 2002; Goodenow 1993; Committee on Increasing High School Student Engagement and Motivation to Learn 2003; Turner et al. 2003). Despite the soundness of this research and the earnest application of its recommendations, teachers of early and middle adolescents may still feel themselves in last place when it comes to their position in adolescents' pantheon of influence and admiration. Add to this differences in race, ethnicity, or socioeconomic status, and teachers can truly find themselves marginalized as they attempt to hold sway over the academic efforts and career goals of their developing students.

This article is concerned with the importance of adults in the lives of adolescents. It provides a description of Erikson's (1968) theory that, almost forty years earlier, detailed the process of identity formation during adolescence and the prominent role played by adults. Erikson's work points to ways of thinking about the teacher-pupil relationship that, along with more recent research findings, may help teachers exert a positive influence on adolescents' future, especially those at greatest risk of failure or dropping out of school.

Erikson's Theory of Psychosocial Development

Erikson's theory is unique among developmental theories in that he attempted to describe the process of development over the course of the lifespan. He described this process as one that requires individuals to accomplish specific psychosocial tasks during eight developmental periods. Across the lifespan, these tasks may generally be described as an attempt, on the part of each individual, to figure out how he or she relates to the world.

Adolescents' Psychosocial Task

Adolescents, according to Erikson, are trying to figure out how they relate to the world. Their specific developmental task involves identifying, evaluating, and selecting values and roles for their adult life. Given such a serious and potentially tumultuous undertaking, it is normal for adolescents' behavior during this period to appear unsettled and even rebellious because they are actively exploring possibilities for self-definition, which may require questioning or rejecting previously held beliefs.

Erikson was clear that establishing identity during adolescence is no easy task. He believed that for an identity to be truly viable, it must confer both a sense of uniqueness and, simultaneously, provide a sense of unity or sameness. In order to achieve a sense of uniqueness, adolescents must define themselves as distinct from parents and peers, not merely as extensions of them. Even though adolescents will incorporate many aspects of their identities from parents, peers, and culture, their identities must allow them to have a self that is capable of making choices that diverge from those made by parents and peers. Adolescents must view themselves as autonomous agents.

A viable identity must also help the adolescent to feel some sense of unity or sameness. The adolescent's identity must maintain continuity among the past, present, and future. To do this, the identity must be plausible, in the adolescent's mind, based on his or her experiences in the past in order to be one that can realistically forecast the future. With this type of identity, an adolescent will not only know who she is in the present and how she arrived at her present state, but also who she will be in the future. Any identity that does not have such continuity will be viewed as false or fabricated.

Example and Analysis

The case of Robert, a sixth-grader in a large suburban middle school, provides some illustration. In the elementary school Robert attended the year before, he had been an average student who was best known for his interest in soccer and baseball.

After the first few weeks of the new school year, Robert arrived at school sporting cowboy boots and a black western hat. Although this apparel was not unusual for the school, it was out of the ordinary for Robert, who previously wore mostly sports attire. His dress was very similar, however, to that of a new group of friends with whom Robert has recently become affiliated. His choice of attire might be all the more surprising to his teachers and his peers if they knew that Robert's mother is an accountant and his father is a medical technician; and neither has family roots in farming or ranching.

Robert is definitely grappling with questions about values and roles, and has made some preliminary decisions about his attire and friends. Robert's new identity may also confer some partial sense of uniqueness in that he is distinct from his parents, but he may eventually view his new attire (along with his identity) as false because it provides no integrative benefits for him due to its inconsistency with his past or future experiences. In the parlance of current adolescents, Robert would likely feel that he is a "poser." The psychological moratorium for adolescents is a time when important decisions about future life roles are being tried on, evaluated, and shaped in an attempt to figure out where one fits in. It is a process that takes place over time, and in any circumstance or setting where identity is called into question (Nakkula 2003).

The Role of Generations in Adolescents' Identity Formation

"The function of the identity search is to discover the standards for adulthood and to select from those standards what is truly important" (Erikson 1968, 37). Erikson believed that adults hold an especially privileged position during the time when adolescents are exploring and evaluating standards for their future. He explicitly described the role of the older generation as the bearers of societal standards.

By virtue of their age and position, the older generation provides adolescents with (*a*) information about what is important for a "successful" life, and (*b*) a metric by which adolescents may evaluate themselves. Adolescents use information about adult roles and expectations to learn about societal standards, and then define themselves in terms of—and perhaps in opposition to—the adult roles they find in their lives. Adolescents also use this information to evaluate their current and future capabilities to fulfill adult roles and to make decisions about their future.

Although these interactions between adolescent and adult may sound one-sided, Erikson argued that in their role as bearers, confirmers, and bestowers of standards, adults are also under scrutiny. "[I]n youth the tables of childhood dependence begin slowly to turn: no longer is it merely for the old to teach the young the meaning of life. It is the young who, by their responses and actions, tell the old whether life as represented to them has some vital promise, and it is the young who carry in them the power to confirm those who confirm them, to renew and regenerate, to disavow what is rotten, to reform and rebel" (258). For adolescents, the choice to "buy into" standards is a natural part of their identity formation. For adults, adolescents' response to them is likewise a natural part of the stage of adult life Erikson described as dealing with the issue of generativity versus stagnation. There is a reciprocal relationship, according to Erikson, between the youth and the adult. This reciprocal relationship between adolescent and adult is especially important within the context of school (Sadowski 2003).

Unique Role of Teachers in Adolescents' Development

By most accounts, teachers play a particularly prominent role in adolescents' lives. For example, teachers affect students' achievement, their involvement in school, and their motivation for learning (see Anderman 2002; Wentzel 2002). Teachers also play an important role in the intergenerational exchange between adults and adolescents. Erikson described two specific ways teachers help students make progress toward a true, viable, authentic, and healthy identity.

Become a Sanctioner of Capabilities

One of the most important tasks for a teacher in this intergenerational exchange is to become a "sanctioner" (Erikson 1968, 87) of adolescents' capabilities. For a teacher, sanctioning adolescents' capabilities involves more than simply encouraging students' efforts (Ames and Archer 1988). Instead, it involves identifying, and perhaps even searching out and uncovering, what adolescents do well. Teachers who act as sanctioners of adolescents' capabilities give students information about roles for which they might be well suited as adults. These may include roles that are both personal and academic, such as student, friend, artist, or physician. By sanctioning capabilities in adolescents, teachers communicate to them that their talents and potential have been noticed, and are valuable in an adult world. In terms of the generational roles, teachers are communicating to adolescents that their capabilities compare favorably with adult roles and standards that they may adopt when they become older.

Usually, it is very easy to find aspects to value in students who are high achieving. Identifying positive capabilities in low-achieving, disengaged students, however, is often much more of a challenge (Phelan, Davidson, and Yu 1998). In cases where students are disengaged or even rebellious, Erikson believed that teachers should avoid making judgments about adolescents that are ultimately defining, because an ultimately defining judgment goes right to the core of an adolescent who is seeking identity. Negative judgments of this type from the adult world, from a teacher, give adolescents information that they have not differentiated themselves as unique individuals in any way that is valued by the adult world, and that what they have chosen as a possible identity does not really count. Erikson suggested that identifying and valuing some capability might be an effective starting point for addressing the obstacles preventing students from engaging in academic tasks.

A positive evaluation from a teacher about one's capabilities has many desirable effects. Erikson believed that acknowledging students' capabilities helps students sustain initiative and assists them in differentiating more accurately among possible adult roles they might choose for themselves. Negative evaluations from teachers, on the other hand, have the undesirable potential of destroying academic initiative and alienating adolescents from adults who could be sources of accurate information about future capabilities.

Although Erikson wrote that the teacher should be supportive, he also stated that the role of the teacher should not establish a perception in students that she or he is all-permissive. Instead, the teacher should be supportive in directing students to find new ways of directly achieving what the students truly want and need. It is imperative that teachers model natural consequences for adolescents. If adolescents perceive that they can bypass systems and still achieve gain, they do not learn appropriate role tasks.

Most teachers are probably aware that they are not the only adult in their students' lives. Adolescents may have a wide variety of adults with whom to compare themselves and ultimately learn about their capabilities as soon-to-be-adults. The challenge for teachers is to be one of those voices adolescents hear when they listen to messages that are personally defining. Erikson suggested one way of ensuring that this will happen is to create an environment that is responsive to adolescents' identity needs.

Create an Environment Safe for Identity Growth

Educational and adolescent development literatures are full of studies and good advice about creating positive school and classroom climates (Goodenow 1993; James 1986; Marzano, Marzano, and Pickering 2003; Turner et al. 2003), and about teacher actions intended to maximize students' engagement and achievement in school (Phelan et al. 1998; Wentzel 2002). Underlying all of these successful interventions, Erikson might argue, are teacher actions that, on some level, communicate to adolescents about identity by creating an environment that permits adolescents to explore identity issues.

Creating an environment that is safe for identity growth is critical, according to Erikson, because, "[t]he dominant issue of this stage is the assurance that the active, the selective ego is in charge and enabled to be in charge by a social structure which grants a given age group the place it needs—and in which it is needed" (246). The creation of an identity-safe environment provides the social setting adolescents need to continue creating their own identities, and an identity-safe environment communicates that the identity task is vitally important. Educators may create identity-safe environments in two ways. The first is a matter of attitude or approach to teaching adolescents that is highly consistent with a philosophy of providing educational opportunities and settings that are developmentally responsive to adolescent learners (see National Middle School Association 2003). The second is related to the core of the teacher's role—providing effective instruction.

First, teachers should create a classroom environment that is supportive of adolescents as they grapple with identity issues of fidelity, choice, and trust. Many adolescents ages twelve to fifteen are in the initial stages of identity formation and are "trying on" new identities. Erikson stated that it is especially important for adults to tolerate public displays, fluctuations, growth, experimentation, and peer cliques because it is through this type of activity and experimentation that adolescents learn future adult roles. Teachers are called on to see the broader significance of adolescents' actions that for some may appear obnoxious, irresponsible, or disengaged. Above all, the environment of the classroom should convey a sense of tolerance and acceptance with the caveat that teachers should accept the person, while not always accepting the adolescents' behavior.

Second, beyond creating an environment of personal acceptance, teachers should also create an environment that offers and expands adolescents' views of what they can become and the roles they may adopt as their own. This action is one a teacher achieves primarily through instruction—creating opportunities for students to take on roles as historians, scientists, and authors rather than simply learning facts about the subject matter. Creating classroom environments where students may become active learners is important from a practical standpoint, because it may enhance students' learning, but it is also important from a psychosocial standpoint, because it may enable adolescents to explore possible roles and to learn about their capabilities. This task takes on added significance in a time when students are contemplating adult careers. The classroom where instruction is teacher-centered and -directed, on the other hand, provides the adolescent with little opportunity for active learning about subject matter or identity. Classrooms that are supportive of adolescents' identity development are likely to be those that communicate a value for effort and learning (Anderman 2002) while at the same time are tolerant of adolescents' role explorations and provide opportunities that enable adolescents to learn about their capabilities in light of adult standards.

Conclusion

Erikson suggested that teachers should find ways of sanctioning the capabilities of students by paying close attention to their activities and identifying and communicating with them about some valued area in which they demonstrate competence. Opportunities for this type of interaction to occur increases as the time teachers spend with their students increases, and the goals for interaction varies among academic, service, and recreation purposes (see Billig 2004; James 1986). Erikson also suggested that teachers should create an environment where students can explore dimensions of their identities. This identity "safe zone" involves having tolerance for adolescents' displays as well as having a commitment to effective instruction that fosters real engagement with content. Such engagement helps adolescents realize their capability for intellectual pursuits and confers a sense of mastery over tasks that are valued by adults. These two activities provide the means to meet adolescents' developmental needs while at the same time improve their academic achievement. These suggestions seem especially important as possible ways teachers might actively engage students who are at risk of dropping out of school.

Some education critics may find it distracting to consider the psychological dimension of teaching adolescents, especially at a time when accountability seems to be foremost on the minds of educators and policymakers. There is considerable evidence, however, that pursuit of both academic and personal goals in the school setting may be associated with positive outcomes for adolescent learners in the middle and secondary school (Committee on Increasing High School Student Engagement and Motivation to Learn 2003). Erikson's advice concerning teachers' generational role in adolescents' psychosocial development is, in no way, meant to detract from or minimize concerns about student achievement. Rather, we acknowledge these concerns, but offer that adolescents see themselves as much more than a score on a state-level assessment, and so should their teachers. Doing so allows teachers to take on their generational role and make a positive and lasting contribution to adolescents' identity development.

References

Ames, C., and J. Archer. 1988. Achievement goals in the classroom: Students' learning strategies and motivation processes. *Journal of Educational Psychology*, no. 80:260–70.

Anderman, E. M. 2002. School effects on psychological outcomes during adolescence. *Journal of Educational Psychology*, no. 94:795–809.

Billig, S. H. 2004. *Impacts of service-learning on youth, schools and communities: Research on K–12 school-based service-learning, 1990–1999*. Denver, CO: Education Commission of the States. http://www.ecs.org/ecsmain.asp?page=/html/IssuesK12.asp.

Committee on Increasing High School Student Engagement and Motivation to Learn. 2003. *Engaging schools: Fostering high school students' motivation to learn*. Washington, DC: National Academies Press.

Erikson, E. H. 1968. *Identity: Youth in crisis*. New York: W. W. Norton.

Goodenow, C. 1993. The psychological sense of school membership among adolescents: Scale development and educational correlates. *Psychology in the Schools*, no. 30:79–90.

James, M. 1986. *Adviser-advisee programs: Why, what and how*. Columbus, OH: National Middle School Association.

Marzano, R. J., J. S. Marzano, and D. J. Pickering. 2003. *Classroom management that works: Research-based strategies for every teacher*. Alexandria, VA: Association for Supervision and Curriculum Development.

Nakkula, M. 2003. Identity and possibility: Adolescent development and the potential of schools. In *Adolescents at school: Perspectives on youth, identity and education*, ed. M. Sadowski, 7–18. Cambridge, MA: Harvard Education Press.

National Middle School Association. 2003. *This we believe: Successful schools for young adolescents*. Columbus, OH: National Middle School Association.

Phelan, P., A. Davidson, and H. C. Yu. 1998. *Adolescents' worlds: Negotiating family, peers and school*. New York: Teachers College Press.

Sadowski, M. 2003. *Adolescents at school: Perspectives on youth, identity and education*. Cambridge, MA: Harvard Education Press.

Turner, J. C., D. K. Myer, C. Midgley, and H. Patrick. 2003. Teacher discourse and sixth-graders' reported affect and achievement behaviors in two high-mastery/high-performance mathematics classrooms. *Elementary School Journal* 103 (4): 357–82.

Wentzel, K. R. 2002. Are effective teachers like good parents? Teaching styles and student adjustment in early adolescence. *Child Development* 73 (1): 287–301.

Doug Hamman is an assistant professor of teacher education and **C. Bret Hendricks** is an assistant professor of counselor education in the College of Education at Texas Tech University, in Lubbock.

From *The Clearing House*, November/December 2005, pp. 72–75. Reprinted by permission of the Helen Dwight Reid Educational Foundation. Published by Heldref Publications, 1319 Eighteenth St., NW, Washington, DC 20036-1802.

Risk Taking in Adolescence

New Perspectives from Brain and Behavioral Science

Trying to understand why adolescents and young adults take more risks than younger or older individuals do has challenged psychologists for decades. Adolescents' inclination to engage in risky behavior does not appear to be due to irrationality, delusions of invulnerability, or ignorance. This paper presents a perspective on adolescent risk taking grounded in developmental neuroscience. According to this view, the temporal gap between puberty, which impels adolescents toward thrill seeking, and the slow maturation of the cognitive-control system, which regulates these impulses, makes adolescence a time of heightened vulnerability for risky behavior. This view of adolescent risk taking helps to explain why educational interventions designed to change adolescents' knowledge, beliefs, or attitudes have been largely ineffective, and suggests that changing the contexts in which risky behavior occurs may be more successful than changing the way adolescents think about risk.

LAURENCE STEINBERG

Adolescents and college-age individuals take more risks than children or adults do, as indicated by statistics on automobile crashes, binge drinking, contraceptive use, and crime; but trying to understand why risk taking is more common during adolescence than during other periods of development has challenged psychologists for decades (Steinberg, 2004). Numerous theories to account for adolescents' greater involvement in risky behavior have been advanced, but few have withstood empirical scrutiny (but see Reyna & Farley, 2006, for a discussion of some promising approaches).

False Leads in Risk-Taking Research

Systematic research does not support the stereotype of adolescents as irrational individuals who believe they are invulnerable and who are unaware, inattentive to, or unconcerned about the potential harms of risky behavior. In fact, the logical-reasoning abilities of 15-year-olds are comparable to those of adults, adolescents are no worse than adults at perceiving risk or estimating their vulnerability to it (Reyna & Farley, 2006), and increasing the salience of the risks associated with making a potentially dangerous decision has comparable effects on adolescents and adults (Millstein & Halpern-Felsher, 2002). Most studies find few age differences in individuals' evaluations of the risks inherent in a wide range of dangerous behaviors, in judgments about the seriousness of the consequences that might result from risky behavior, or in the ways that the relative costs and benefits of risky activities are evaluated (Beyth-Marom, Austin, Fischoff, Palmgren, & Jacobs-Quadrel, 1993).

Because adolescents and adults reason about risk in similar ways, many researchers have posited that age differences in actual risk taking are due to differences in the information that adolescents and adults use when making decisions. Attempts to reduce adolescent risk taking through interventions designed to alter knowledge, attitudes, or beliefs have proven remarkably disappointing, however (Steinberg, 2004). Efforts to provide adolescents with information about the risks of substance use, reckless driving, and unprotected sex typically result in improvements in young people's thinking about these phenomena but seldom change their actual behavior. Generally speaking, reductions in adolescents' health-compromising behavior are more strongly linked to changes in the contexts in which those risks are taken (e.g., increases in the price of cigarettes, enforcement of graduated licensing programs, more vigorously implemented policies to interdict drugs, or condom distribution programs) than to changes in what adolescents know or believe.

The failure to account for age differences in risk taking through studies of reasoning and knowledge stymied researchers for some time. Health educators, however, have been undaunted, and they have continued to design and offer interventions of unproven effectiveness, such as Drug Abuse Resistance Education (DARE), driver's education, or abstinence-only sex education.

A New Perspective on Risk Taking

In recent years, owing to advances in the developmental neuroscience of adolescence and the recognition that the conventional decision-making framework may not be the best way to think about adolescent risk taking, a new perspective on the subject has emerged (Steinberg, 2004). This new view begins from the premise that risk taking in the real world is the product of both logical reasoning and psychosocial factors. However, unlike logical-reasoning abilities, which appear to be more or less fully developed by age 15, psychosocial capacities that improve decision making and moderate risk taking—such as impulse control, emotion regulation, delay of gratification, and resistance to peer influence—continue to mature well into young adulthood (Steinberg, 2004; see Figure 1). Accordingly, psychosocial immaturity in these respects during adolescence may undermine what otherwise might be competent decision making. The conclusion drawn by many researchers, that adolescents are as competent decision makers as adults are, may hold true only under conditions where the influence of psychosocial factors is minimized.

Evidence from Developmental Neuroscience

Advances in developmental neuroscience provide support for this new way of thinking about adolescent decision making. It appears that heightened risk taking in adolescence is the product of the interaction between two brain networks. The first is a socioemotional network that is especially sensitive to social and emotional stimuli, that is particularly important for reward processing, and that is remodeled in early adolescence by the hormonal changes of puberty. It is localized in limbic and paralimbic areas of the brain, an interior region that includes the amygdala, ventral striatum, orbitofrontal cortex, medial prefrontal cortex, and superior temporal sulcus. The second network is a cognitive-control network that subserves executive functions such as planning, thinking ahead, and self-regulation, and that matures gradually over the course of adolescence and young adulthood largely independently of puberty (Steinberg, 2004). The cognitive-control network mainly consists of outer regions of the brain, including the lateral prefrontal and parietal cortices and those parts of the anterior cingulate cortex to which they are connected.

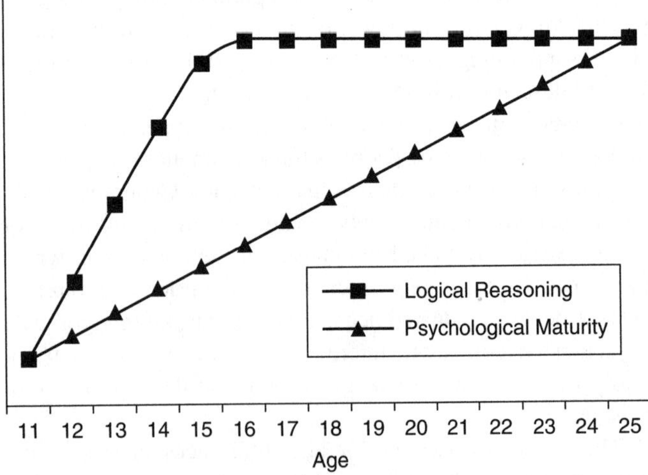

Figure 1 Hypothetical graph of development of logical reasoning abilities versus psychosocial maturation. Although logical reasoning abilities reach adult levels by age 16, psychosocial capacities, such as impulse control, future orientation, or resistance to peer influence, continue to develop into young adulthood.

In many respects, risk taking is the product of a competition between the socioemotional and cognitive-control networks (Drevets & Raichle, 1998), and adolescence is a period in which the former abruptly becomes more assertive (i.e., at puberty) while the latter gains strength only gradually, over a longer period of time. The socioemotional network is not in a state of constantly high activation during adolescence, though. Indeed, when the socioemotional network is not highly activated (for example, when individuals are not emotionally excited or are alone), the cognitive-control network is strong enough to impose regulatory control over impulsive and risky behavior, even in early adolescence. In the presence of peers or under conditions of emotional arousal, however, the socioemotional network becomes sufficiently activated to diminish the regulatory effectiveness of the cognitive-control network. Over the course of adolescence, the cognitive-control network matures, so that by adulthood, even under conditions of heightened arousal in the socioemotional network, inclinations toward risk taking can be modulated.

It is important to note that mechanisms underlying the processing of emotional information, social information, and reward are closely interconnected. Among adolescents, the regions that are activated during exposure to social and emotional stimuli overlap considerably with regions also shown to be sensitive to variations in reward magnitude (cf. Galvan, et al., 2005; Nelson, Leibenluft, McClure, & Pine, 2005). This finding may be relevant to understanding why so much adolescent risk taking—like drinking, reckless driving, or delinquency—occurs in groups (Steinberg, 2004). Risk taking may be heightened in adolescence because teenagers spend so much time with their peers, and the mere presence of peers makes the rewarding aspects of risky situations more salient by activating the same circuitry that is activated by exposure to nonsocial rewards when individuals are alone.

The competitive interaction between the socioemotional and cognitive-control networks has been implicated in a wide range of decision-making contexts, including drug use, social-decision processing, moral judgments, and the valuation of alternative rewards/costs (e.g., Chambers, Taylor, & Potenza, 2003). In all of these contexts, risk taking is associated with relatively greater activation of the socioemotional network. For example, individuals' preference for smaller immediate rewards over larger delayed rewards is associated with relatively increased activation of the ventral striatum, orbitofrontal cortex, and medial prefrontal cortex—all regions linked to the socioemotional network—presumably because immediate rewards are especially emotionally arousing (consider the difference between how you might feel if a crisp $100 bill were held in front of you versus being told that you will receive $150 in 2 months). In contrast, regions implicated in cognitive control are engaged equivalently across decision conditions (McClure, Laibson, Loewenstein, & Cohen, 2004). Similarly, studies show that increased activity in regions of the socioemotional network is associated with the selection of comparatively risky (but potentially highly rewarding) choices over more conservative ones (Ernst et al., 2005).

Evidence from Behavioral Science

Three lines of behavioral evidence are consistent with this account. First, studies of susceptibility to antisocial peer influence show that vulnerability to peer pressure increases between preadolescence and mid-adolescence, peaks in mid-adolescence—presumably when the imbalance between the sensitivity to socioemotional arousal (which has increased at puberty) and capacity for cognitive control (which is still immature) is greatest—and gradually declines thereafter (Steinberg, 2004). Second, as noted earlier, studies of decision making generally show no age differences in risk processing between older adolescents and adults when decision making is assessed under conditions likely associated with relatively lower activation of brain systems responsible for emotion, reward, and social processing (e.g., the presentation of hypothetical decision-making dilemmas to individuals tested alone under conditions of low emotional arousal; Millstein, & Halpern-Felsher, 2002). Third, the presence of peers increases risk taking substantially among teenagers, moderately among college-age individuals, and not at all among adults, consistent with the notion that the development of the cognitive-control network is gradual and extends beyond the teen years. In one of our lab's studies, for instance, the presence of peers more than doubled the number of risks teenagers took in a video driving game and increased risk taking by 50% among college undergraduates but had no effect at all among adults (Gardner & Steinberg, 2005; see Figure 2). In adolescence, then, not only is more merrier—it is also riskier.

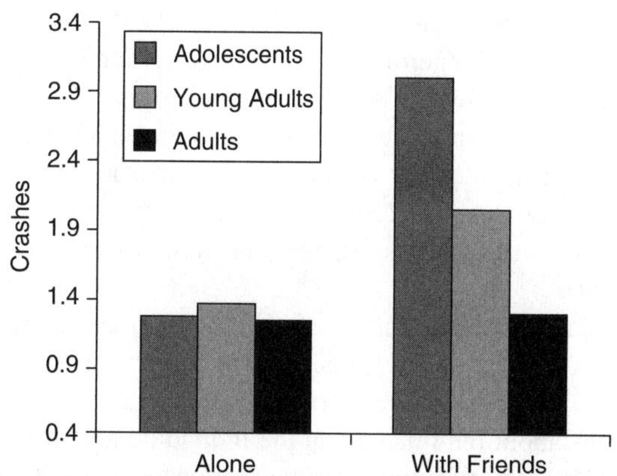

Figure 2 Risk taking of adolescents, young adults, and adults during a video driving game, when playing alone and when playing with friends. Adapted from Gardner & Steinberg (2004).

What Changes During Adolescence?

Studies of rodents indicate an especially significant increase in reward salience (i.e., how much attention individuals pay to the magnitude of potential rewards) around the time of puberty (Spear, 2000), consistent with human studies showing that increases in sensation seeking occur relatively early in adolescence and are correlated with pubertal maturation but not chronological age (Steinberg, 2004). Given behavioral findings indicating relatively greater reward salience among adolescents than adults in decision-making tasks, there is reason to speculate that, when presented with risky situations that have both potential rewards and potential costs, adolescents may be more sensitive than adults to variation in rewards but comparably sensitive (or perhaps even less sensitive) to variation in costs (Ernst et al., 2005).

It thus appears that the brain system that regulates the processing of rewards, social information, and emotions is becoming more sensitive and more easily aroused around the time of puberty. What about its sibling, the cognitive-control system? Regions making up the cognitive-control network, especially prefrontal regions, continue to exhibit gradual changes in structure and function during adolescence and early adulthood (Casey, Tottenham, Liston, & Durston, 2005). Much publicity has been given to the finding that synaptic pruning (the selective elimination of seldom-used synapses) and myelination (the development of the fatty sheaths that "insulate" neuronal circuitry)—both of which increase the efficiency of information processing—continue to occur in the prefrontal cortex well into the early 20s. But frontal regions also become more integrated with other brain regions during adolescence and early adulthood, leading to gradual improvements in many aspects of cognitive control such as response inhibition; this integration may be an even more important change than changes within the frontal region itself. Imaging studies using tasks in which individuals are asked to inhibit a "prepotent" response—like trying to look away from, rather than toward, a point of light—have shown that adolescents tend to recruit the cognitive-control network less broadly than do adults, perhaps overtaxing the capacity of the more limited number of regions they activate (Luna et al., 2001).

In essence, one of the reasons the cognitive-control system of adults is more effective than that of adolescents is that adults' brains distribute its regulatory responsibilities across a wider network of linked components. This lack of cross-talk across brain regions in adolescence results not only in individuals acting on gut feelings without fully thinking (the stereotypic portrayal of teenagers) but also in thinking too much when gut feelings ought to be attended to (which teenagers also do from time to time). In one recent study, when asked whether some obviously dangerous activities (e.g., setting one's hair on fire) were "good ideas," adolescents took significantly longer than adults to respond to the questions and activated a less narrowly distributed set of cognitive-control regions (Baird, Fugelsang, & Bennett, 2005). This was not the case when the queried activities were not dangerous ones, however (e.g., eating salad).

The fact that maturation of the socioemotional network appears to be driven by puberty, whereas the maturation of the cognitive-control network does not, raises interesting questions about the impact—at the individual and at the societal levels—of early pubertal maturation on risk-taking. We know that there is wide variability among individuals in the timing of puberty, due to both genetic and environmental factors. We also know that there has been a significant drop in the age of pubertal maturation over the past 200 years. To the extent that the temporal disjunction between the maturation of the socioemotional system and that of the cognitive-control system contributes to adolescent risk taking, we would expect to see higher rates of risk taking among early maturers and a drop over time in the age of initial experimentation with risky behaviors such as sexual intercourse or drug use. There is evidence for both of these patterns (Collins & Steinberg, 2006; Johnson & Gerstein, 1998).

Implications for Prevention

What does this mean for the prevention of unhealthy risk taking in adolescence? Given extant research suggesting that it is not the way adolescents think or what they don't know or understand that is the problem, a more profitable strategy than attempting to change how adolescents view risky activities might be to focus on limiting opportunities for immature judgment to have harmful consequences. More than 90% of all American high-school students have had sex, drug, and driver education in their schools, yet large proportions of them still have unsafe sex, binge drink, smoke cigarettes, and drive recklessly (often more than one of these at the same time; Steinberg, 2004). Strategies such as raising the price of cigarettes, more vigilantly enforcing laws governing the sale of alcohol, expanding adolescents' access to mental-health and contraceptive services, and raising the driving age would likely be more effective in limiting adolescent smoking, substance abuse, pregnancy, and automobile fatalities than strategies aimed at making adolescents wiser, less impulsive, or less shortsighted. Some things just take time to develop, and, like it or not, mature judgment is probably one of them.

The research reviewed here suggests that heightened risk taking during adolescence is likely to be normative, biologically driven, and, to some extent, inevitable. There is probably very little that can or ought to be done to either attenuate or delay the shift in reward sensitivity that takes place at puberty. It may be possible to accelerate the maturation of self-regulatory competence, but no research has examined whether this is possible. In light of studies showing familial influences on psychosocial maturity in adolescence, understanding how contextual factors influence the development of self-regulation and knowing the neural underpinnings of these processes should be a high priority for those interested in the well-being of young people.

References

Baird, A., Fugelsang, J., & Bennett, C. (2005, April). *"What were you thinking?": An fMRI study of adolescent decision making.* Poster presented at the annual meeting of the Cognitive Neuroscience Society, New York.

Beyth-Marom, R., Austin, L., Fischoff, B., Palmgren, C., & Jacobs-Quadrel, M. (1993). Perceived consequences of risky behaviors: Adults and adolescents. *Developmental Psychology, 29,* 549–563.

Casey, B.J., Tottenham, N., Liston, C., & Durston, S. (2005). Imaging the developing brain: What have we learned about cognitive development? *Trends in Cognitive Science, 9,* 104–110.

Chambers, R.A., Taylor, J.R., & Potenza, M.N. (2003). Developmental neurocircuitry of motivation in adolescence: A critical period of addiction vulnerability. *American Journal of Psychiatry, 160,* 1041–1052.

Collins, W.A., & Steinberg, L. (2006). Adolescent development in interpersonal context. In W. Damon & R. Lerner (Series Eds.) & N. Eisenberg (Vol. Ed.), *Handbook of Child Psychology: Social, emotional, and personality development* (Vol. 3, pp. 1003–1067). New York: Wiley.

Drevets, W.C., & Raichle, M.E. (1998). Reciprocal suppression of regional cerebral blood flow during emotional versus higher cognitive processes: Implications for interactions between emotion and cognition. *Cognition and Emotion, 12,* 353–385.

Ernst, M., Jazbec, S., McClure, E.B., Monk, C.S., Blair, R.J.R., Leibenluft, E., & Pine, D.S. (2005). Amygdala and nucleus accumbens activation in response to receipt and omission of gains in adults and adolescents. *Neuroimage, 25,* 1279–1291.

Galvan, A., Hare, T., Davidson, M., Spicer, J., Glover, G., & Casey, B.J. (2005). The role of ventral frontostriatal circuitry in reward-based learning in humans. *Journal of Neuroscience, 25,* 8650–8656.

Gardner, M., & Steinberg, L. (2005). Peer influence on risk-taking, risk preference, and risky decision-making in adolescence and adulthood: An experimental study. *Developmental Psychology, 41,* 625–635.

Johnson, R., & Gerstein, D. (1998). Initiation of use of alcohol, cigarettes, marijuana, cocaine, and other substances in US birth cohorts since 1919. *American Journal of Public Health, 88,* 27–33.

Luna, B., Thulborn, K.R., Munoz, D.P., Merriam, E.P., Garver, K.E., Minshew, N.J., et al. (2001). Maturation of widely distributed brain function subserves cognitive development. *Neuroimage, 13,* 786–793.

McClure, S.M., Laibson, D.I., Loewenstein, G., & Cohen, J.D. (2004). Separate neural systems value immediate and delayed monetary rewards. *Science, 306,* 503–507.

Millstein, S.G., & Halpern-Felsher, B.L. (2002). Perceptions of risk and vulnerability. *Journal of Adolescent Health, 31S,* 10–27.

Nelson, E., Leibenluft, E., McClure, E., & Pine, D. (2005). The social re-orientation of adolescence: A neuroscience perspective on the process and its relation to psychopathology. *Psychological Medicine, 35,* 163–174.

Reyna, V., & Farley, F. (2006). Risk and rationality in adolescent decision-making: Implications for theory, practice, and public policy. *Psychological Science in the Public Interest, 7,* 1–44.

Spear, P. (2000). The adolescent brain and age-related behavioral manifestations. *Neuroscience and Biobehavioral Reviews, 24,* 417–463.

Steinberg, L. (2004). Risk-taking in adolescence: What changes, and why? *Annals of the New York Academy of Sciences, 1021,* 51–58.

Acknowledgments—Thanks to Nora Newcombe for comments on an earlier draft and to Jason Chein for his expertise in developmental neuroscience.

Address correspondence to Laurence Steinberg, Department of Psychology, Temple University, Philadelphia, PA 19122; lds@temple.edu.

UNIT 3

Individual Differences Among Leaders

Unit Selections

Key Points to Consider

- What are some of the issues and concerns of including children with exceptionalities in regular classrooms?
- Who are the gifted and talented? How can knowledge of their characteristics and learning needs help to provide them with an appropriate education?
- How will understanding the needs of culturally diverse and language minority students help them achieve success in school?
- What instructional strategies are more successful with boys as opposed to girls, and why?

Student Web Site

www.mhcls.com/online

Internet References

Further information regarding these Web sites may be found in this book's preface or online.

The Council for Exceptional Children
http://www.cec.sped.org/index.html

Global SchoolNet Foundation
http://www.gsn.org

International Project: Multicultural Pavilion
http://curry.edschool.virginia.edu/curry/centers/multicultural/papers.html

Let 100 Flowers Bloom/Kristen Nicholson-Nelson
http://teacher.scholastic.com/professional/assessment/100flowers.htm

National Association for Multicultural Education
http://www.nameorg.org

National Attention Deficit Disorder Association
http://www.add.org

National MultiCultural Institute (NMCI)
http://www.nmci.org

Tolerance.org
http://www.tolerance.org

The Equal Educational Opportunity Act for All Handicapped Children (Public Law 94-142) gives children with disabilities the right to an education in the least-restrictive environment, due process, and an individualized educational program that is specifically designed to meet their needs. Professionals and parents of children with special needs are responsible for developing and implementing an appropriate educational program for each child. The application of these ideas to classrooms across the nation at first caused great concern among educators and parents. Classroom teachers whose training did not prepare them for working with children who have special needs expressed negative attitudes about mainstreaming. Special resource teachers also expressed concern that mainstreaming would mitigate the effectiveness of special programs for the disabled and would force cuts in services. Parents feared that their children would not receive the special services they required because of governmental red tape and delays in proper diagnosis and placement.

In 1991, P.L. 94-142 was amended as the Individuals with Disabilities Education Act (IDEA) and the term "inclusion" was introduced. Inclusion tries to assure that children with disabilities will be fully integrated within the classroom. Many of the above concerns have been studied by psychologists and educators, and their findings have often influenced policy. For example, research has indicated that inclusion is more effective when regular classroom teachers and special resource teachers collaborate and work cooperatively.

The articles concerning students with exceptional learning needs confront some of these issues. The first article by Michael Giangreco discusses curricular modifications that can be used to meet the needs of students with special needs in an inclusive classroom. Jody Sherman, Carmen Rasmussen, and Lola Baydala help us understand the positive qualities of students with ADHD, and instructional strategies that support those strengths. The article by Heidi Silver-Pacuilla and Steve Fleischman addresses issues of universal design, and how technologies can benefit all struggling learners.

Other exceptional children are the gifted and talented. These children are rapid learners who can absorb, organize, and apply concepts more effectively than the average child. They often have IQs of 140 or more and are convergent thinkers (i.e., they give the correct answer to teacher or test questions). Convergent thinkers are usually models of good behavior and academic performance, and they respond to instruction easily; teachers generally value such children and often nominate them for gifted programs. There are other children, however, who do not score well on standardized tests of intelligence because their thinking is more divergent (i.e., they can imagine more than one answer to teacher or test questions). These gifted divergent thinkers may not respond to traditional instruction. They may become bored, respond to questions in unique and disturbing ways, and appear uncooperative and disruptive. Many teachers do not understand these unconventional thinkers and fail to identify them as gifted. In fact, such children are sometimes labeled as emotionally disturbed or mentally retarded because of the negative impressions they make on their teachers. Because of the differences between these types of students, a great deal of controversy surrounds programs for the gifted. Such programs should enhance the self-esteem of all gifted and talented children, motivate and challenge them, and help them realize their creative potential. The two articles in the subsection on gifted children consider the characteristics of giftedness, and they explain how to identify gifted students and provide them with an appropriate education.

Banana Stock/PunchStock

The third subsection of this unit concerns student diversity. Just as labeling may adversely affect the disabled child, it may also affect the child who comes from a minority ethnic background where the language and values are quite different from those of the mainstream culture. The term "disadvantaged" is often used to describe these children, but it is negative, stereotypical, and apt to result in a self-fulfilling prophecy whereby teachers perceive such children as incapable of learning. Teachers should provide academically and culturally diverse children with experiences that they might have missed in the restricted environment of their homes and neighborhoods. The articles in this section suggest ways to create culturally compatible classrooms. The first article challenges us to identify the tacit assumptions and practices that unwittingly maintain the deficit view of urban students in particular. The second article specifies ways to meet the needs of culturally diverse learners.

The fourth subsection concerns gender differences in the classroom. Gender refers to the traits and behaviors often associated with either boys or girls. In the 1980's issues were raised about whether girls were receiving an appropriate education in school. Much has been done since to raise their achievement in mathematics and science, for example, and to address bias in the curriculum. More recently questions have been raised about the compatibility of boys and school. The articles in this section address some of these issues. The first article revisits bias in the curriculum, and addresses the progress that has been made in the area of literacy. The last two articles consider instructional techniques that accommodate the needs of boys and girls in the classroom.

Extending Inclusive Opportunities

MICHAEL F. GIANGRECO

Ms. Santos,[1] a 5th grade teacher, had successfully included students with learning disabilities or physical limitations in her classroom for years. Even in years when none of her students had been identified as having disabilities, her students' abilities and needs had varied, sometimes substantially. She regularly taught students whose native languages were not English and students who displayed challenging behaviors or fragile emotional health. The range of her students' reading abilities typically spanned several years.

Ms. Santos had confidently made *instructional* accommodations for all her students, for example, by modifying materials and giving individualized cues—but she had rarely needed to modify her curriculum. Students with and without disabilities in her class worked on the same topics, although sometimes at differing levels and paces. But when a boy who worked far below 5th grade level was assigned to her class, Ms. Santos faced a question that looms large for teachers trying to make inclusion work: How can we achieve true curricular inclusion for students who function substantially below grade level?

Facing a New Challenge

Last school year, Ms. Santos welcomed Chris into her 5th grade class. A boy new to the school, Chris had a good sense of humor, liked many kinds of music, and had a history of making friends and liking school. Unfortunately, in the eyes of most people, these qualities were overshadowed by the severity of his intellectual, behavioral, sensory, and physical disabilities. Because Chris came to her class functioning at a kindergarten or pre-kindergarten level in all academic areas, Ms. Santos had trouble conceiving of how he could learn well in a 5th grade class, and she worried about what Chris's parents and her colleagues would expect. By suggesting how a teacher might handle this kind of situation, I hope to assist teachers and other professionals who are attempting to successfully include students with significant disabilities within mainstream classrooms.

Extending Student Participation

The Individuals with Disabilities Education Improvement Act of 2004 presumes that the first placement option a school system must consider for each student with a disability, regardless of disability category or severity, is the regular classroom. Students with disabilities are entitled to supplemental supports that enable them to meaningfully pursue individually determined learning outcomes—including those from the general education curriculum. The question to be asked is not whether a student is able to pursue the same learning outcomes as his or her age-level peers, but whether that student's needs can be appropriately addressed in the general education setting.

The participation of students with disabilities within general education classes can be broadly characterized along two dimensions: each student's *program* (such as the goals of the student's individualized education program) and each student's *supports*. Supports are anything that the school provides to help the student pursue education goals—for example materials, adaptations, or a classroom aide (Giangreco, 2006).

Within a school day, or even within a single activity, an individual student will sometimes require modifications to the general education program and at other times be able to work within the standard program. Likewise, the number of supports teachers will need to provide for students will fluctuate greatly. In some scenarios, a student with a disability can do the same academic work his or her classmates are doing. These kinds of opportunities help teachers and students interact in a natural way, show classmates that students with learning needs don't always need special help, and allow students to avoid unnecessary supports.

Setting the Stage for Curricular Modifications

Chris was fortunate that he was assigned a teacher who already had good practices in place for including students with IEPs. Ms. Santos created opportunities for many types of instructional interactions through a busy classroom schedule of inquiry-based activities. Her ability to teach students with disabilities grew out of her belief that the core of teaching and learning was the same, regardless of whether a student had a disability label.

Although Ms. Santos was not sure how to meet the challenge of including Chris in her classroom, she asked important questions to clarify her own role as a team member, understand the curricular expectations for Chris, and get a vision for how to teach a class with a wider mix of abilities than she had encountered before. As part of that vision, she drew on the power of relationships, both in drawing Chris into her plans for students and in building a collaborative team of special educators, parents, and others. In her classroom community, she expected students to help one another learn and be responsible for helping the classroom run smoothly. As much as possible, she also planned for Chris to have an active voice in telling his teachers which supports helped him and which did not.

For Chris to be a viable social member of the classroom, he would have to participate in the academic work, not just be physically present or socially accepted. Ms. Santos knew how frustrating and embarrassing it can be for students when curriculum content is over their heads, and she also knew the hazards of underestimating students. She sought ways to adjust the curriculum to an appropriate level of difficulty for Chris, while leaving opportunities for him to surprise her with his capabilities.

When Curriculum Modifications Are Essential

In many inclusion scenarios, such as the one Ms. Santos faced, modifications to the general education program will be essential. Sometimes the student will need individualized content but will not require specialized supports to work with that content. For example, the teacher might assign a student five new vocabulary words instead of 10, or assign that learner single-digit computation instead of decimals.

In some situations, the classroom teacher will need to both modify the general education program and provide individualized supports. Although students with more severe disabilities may often need both program and support accommodation to succeed in a mainstream class, teachers may not need to alter both the curriculum and the types of support available for all classroom work a student with a disability undertakes. Even a student with significant disabilities, like Chris, rarely needs both an individualized education program and individualized supports all the time.

Multilevel Curriculum and Curriculum Overlapping

Multilevel curriculum and *curriculum overlapping* are two approaches to adapting curriculum that facilitate participation of students with significant disabilities. In the multilevel curriculum approach, students with disabilities and their peers participate in a shared activity. Each student has individually appropriate learning outcomes that are within the same curriculum area but that may be at grade level or below (or above) grade level (Campbell, Campbell, Collicott, Perner, & Stone, 1988; Peterson & Hittie, 2003). Students of different ability levels may be working on the same or different subject matter within the same academic area. In curriculum overlapping, students with disabilities and nondisabled peers participate together in an activity, but they pursue learning outcomes from different curriculum areas, including such broadly defined curriculum areas as social skills.

Multilevel Curriculum in Action

Let's go back to Ms. Santos's challenge of including Chris as an academic member of her class and see how she used multilevel curriculum. In class work for a social studies unit, Chris and his classmates studied the Revolutionary War. But Ms. Santos adapted Chris's level of learning outcomes to suit him: His goals were to become familiar with historical people, places, and events, whereas his classmates' goals were to demonstrate knowledge of political and economic factors that led to the war.

To reinforce students' learning, Ms. Santos created a Revolutionary War board game that drew on both the class's grade-appropriate learning goals and Chris's lower-level goals to advance in the game. The game board had colored spaces, and each color a student landed on corresponded to a stack of question cards related to the desired content, with blue cards for historical people, green cards for historical places, and so on. Ms. Santos and a special educator had set aside specially prepared cards for Chris with questions matched to his learning outcomes. The rest of the class drew cards matched to their goals.

Another player read aloud for Chris each question and the multiple-choice answers, which were given both verbally and with images. For example, the question, "What American Revolutionary War hero became the first president of the United States?" might be followed by the labeled images of George Washington and two other famous people. When Chris was learning new content, Ms. Santos made the distracter choices substantially different and included at least one absurd choice (such as George Washington, Abraham Lincoln, and LeBron James). As Chris became more proficient, she used distracter choices that were more difficult to spot. When Chris answered a question correctly, he rolled dice and moved forward. Although this activity focused on social studies, Chris also learned the social skill of taking turns and such math skills as counting.

Curriculum Overlapping in Action

Curriculum overlapping is a vital strategy for classrooms in which there are substantial differences between the learning outcomes most of the students are pursuing and the outcomes a student with a disability is pursuing.

For example, in a human biology unit, a group of four students might assemble a model of the human cardiovascular system. The primary goal of three students is to learn anatomical structures and their functions. The fourth student, who has significant disabilities, shares the activity, but has learning goals within the curriculum area of communications and social skills, such as learning to follow directions, taking turns, or making requests using a communication device.

One way to start planning for curriculum overlapping with a student who has significant disabilities is to make a simple matrix with the student's individually determined learning outcomes down the side and a list of regularly occurring classes or activities across the top. Team members can then identify where they should focus additional energy to ensure meaningful participation.

Ms. Santos and her team did this. They established cross-lesson routines through which Chris's individual learning outcomes could be embedded within many class activities. For example, Chris had a series of learning objectives involving communication and social skills, including matching to a sample; discriminating between different symbols and photos; following one- and two-step instructions; responding to questions; and describing events, objects, or emotions. Ms. Santos routinely embedded these skills in activities and lessons Chris participated in across different content areas as a form of curriculum overlapping.

While pursuing these learning outcomes, Chris might also work with the actual curricular content. For example, in a geography activity Chris might distinguish between maps of European countries, first discriminating between highly different pairs (a map of Italy paired with an image that is not a map); followed by slightly more similar pairs (a map of Greece and a map of China); followed by even more similar pairs (maps of France and Germany).

When first using multilevel curriculum and curriculum overlapping, teams often feel that they don't have enough for their student with a significant disability to do within the typical classroom activities. But as they persist in collaborative planning, seek input directly from the student, and involve classmates in problem solving, they find new opportunities for the student's meaningful participation and learning.

Although multilevel curriculum and curriculum overlapping are primarily ways to include students with disabilities, they also enable more meaningful participation for students functioning above grade level. Applying multilevel curriculum allows teachers to stretch their curriculum away from a "middle zone" in which all students share the same curricular content, level, and amount of work. The practices many people associate with differentiated instruction (Tomlinson, 2001) occur within the boundaries of this middle zone. Multilevel curriculum stretches the concept of differentiated instruction. With curriculum overlapping, the boundaries of curriculum planning expand even further to create effective learning situations for students working both far above and far below their peers.

In the interest of access to the general education curriculum, teachers and teams working with students with disabilities should first consider whether the student can pursue the same learning outcomes as classmates or whether multilevel curriculum and instruction will provide enough accommodation before using curriculum overlapping.

Making It Happen

Implementing either multilevel curriculum and instruction or curriculum overlapping requires time, collaboration, and creativity. But the reward is the authentic inclusion of students who function substantially below grade level. Approaching inclusive education this way contributes to a positive classroom culture, acknowledges differences, promotes acceptance, and provides opportunities for real-life problem solving.

Some claim that inclusion of students with certain disabilities is impossible because in many schools the curriculum is one-size-fits-all and differentiation is minimal or nonexistent. Although it is difficult to include a student with significant disabilities in such classes, this begs the question of whether one-size-fits-all classes are what we want for anyone. Instructional practices such as cooperative learning and differentiated instruction are often beneficial for general education students, too.

Students with disabilities bring educators a challenge to make our teaching practices more inclusive. Meeting the challenge invariably improves the way we teach the broader range of students who don't have disabilities.

Note

1. Ms. Santos is a composite of teachers I have observed who work with students with severe disabilities.

References

Campbell, C., Campbell, S., Collicott, J., Perner, D., & Stone, J. (1988). Individualized instruction. *Education New Brunswick,* 3, 17–20.

Giangreco, M. F. (2006). Foundational concepts and practices for educating students with severe disabilities. In M. E. Snell & F. Brown (Eds.), *Instruction of students with severe disabilities* (6th ed., pp. 1–27). Upper Saddle River, NJ: Pearson Education/Prentice-Hall.

Peterson, J. M., & Hittie, M. M. (2003). *Inclusive teaching: Creating effective schools for all learners.* Boston: Allyn and Bacon.

Tomlinson, C. A. (2001). *How to differentiate instruction in mixed-ability classrooms* (2nd ed.). Alexandria, VA: ASCD.

Thinking Positively

How some characteristics of ADHD can be adaptive and accepted in the classroom.

JODY SHERMAN, CARMEN RASMUSSEN, AND LOLA BAYDALA

Attention deficit/hyperactivity disorder (ADHD) has received much attention over the past several years in both the scientific literature and the popular press, yet confusion still exists with respect to the origin of the disorder, factors that trigger or aggravate it, the trajectory of symptoms, and treatment options, particularly for young children (Gimpel & Kuhn, 2000; Mash & Wolfe, 1999). Entering the term "ADHD" into a popular search engine revealed 624,000 hits on the Web, highlighting the diversity and overwhelming range of information available to those seeking to learn about this condition. Most, if not all, sources describe ADHD as a "disorder," and list the various deficits and difficulties that children with ADHD experience. Parents, teachers, health care professionals, and the children themselves can become discouraged as they learn about the negative aspects associated with a diagnosis of ADHD. This article reviews the challenges associated with ADHD, as well as more recent discussions that center around a positive view of this "disorder."

ADHD occurs in 3 to 5 percent of school-age children, making it the most common psychiatric disorder among children.

ADHD occurs in 3 to 5 percent of school-age children (MTA Cooperative Group, 1999), making it the most common psychiatric disorder among children (Sciutto, Terjesen, & Bender Frank, 2000). ADHD's characteristics can be broken down into specific subtypes that capture differences in children who display predominantly hyperactive and impulsive behaviors, inattentive behaviors, or a combination of both (American Psychiatric Association, 2000). Because some children will exhibit mainly inattentive behaviors and some children will exhibit mainly hyperactive behaviors, not all treatments work equally well with all children diagnosed with ADHD. Most children with ADHD will continue to experience symptoms into adulthood (Mercugliano, Power, & Blum, 1999), although the behaviors tend to change over the course of development. The disorder often manifests in difficulties in school, trouble creating and maintaining social relations, low self-esteem, and deficits in the area of executive functioning (Barkley, 1998). Executive functioning refers to goal-directed, future-oriented behaviors, including planning, organized searches, inhibition, working memory, set-shifting, strategy employment, and fluency (Welsh & Pennington, 1988; Welsh, Pennington, & Grossier, 1991). Barkley (1998) proposed a model of executive functions in children with ADHD that includes deficits in inhibition, working memory, and self-regulation, which relates to the deficits children with ADHD typically demonstrate on tasks requiring split attention and organization (Zentall, 1993).

After reviewing the literature related to academic deficits in children with ADHD, Zentall (1993) noted that children with ADHD selectively attend to stimuli that are salient and/or novel in some way, such as color or movement. This characteristic may compromise performance on tasks in which selective attention is required for stimuli that are subtle or neutral. Selective attention is required to learn most new tasks, whereas tasks that are practiced and have a fairly constant level of performance, such as reading, require sustained attention. Thus, attention problems can interfere with both the learning of new tasks and the rehearsal of tasks requiring sustained attention, such as reading and writing. Teaching children with ADHD to read and write may be optimized when modifications address the unique needs of children with the disorder. Rief (2000) suggested numerous strategies for helping these children read, including paraphrasing, limiting distractions, and scanning for chapter headings and outlines. Writing can be enhanced by using such graphic organizers as flow charts, providing models of written work, and aiding in self-editing. The author also noted that most children with ADHD will need additional help with studying and organizational skills. Rief further noted that most teaching strategies found to be useful for children with ADHD are actually ideal for the entire classroom.

Changing the Way We Think of ADHD

Despite the negative attitudes toward behavior consistent with a diagnosis of ADHD, not all of those characteristics should be thought of negatively. In fact, many researchers now view some ADHD behaviors as potentially adaptive in some situations and contexts (Hartmann, 1996, 2003; Jensen et al., 1997), and they believe that parents, teachers, and health care professionals may need to reconsider the way they view the disorder. The very name, which includes the word "disorder," does not reflect the variability among children diagnosed with ADHD, and may bias individuals against realizing the potential, strengths, and gifts that many children with ADHD have. Similarly, Hallowell and Ratey (1994), both psychiatrists who happen to have ADHD, state that the diagnosis can become a way of life, and they place a more optimistic spin on the topic than is found in typical medical discussions on ADHD.

Having ADHD can be viewed either as a disorder defined by deficits, or as an advantage defined by unique characteristics and strengths that, in the appropriate contexts, are adaptive and advantageous (Hartmann, 2003). Had he lived today, the famous composer Wolfgang Amadeus Mozart might have been diagnosed as having ADHD, as his behaviors contribute to his description as being: "impatient, impulsive, distractible, energetic, emotionally needy, creative, innovative, irreverent, and a maverick" (Hallowell & Ratey, 1994, p. 43). These behaviors worked together in a beneficial manner for the musical genius, and may be part of what makes ADHD "powerfully positive" (Hallowell & Ratey, 1994, p. 43). Although Hallowell and Ratey believe that ADHD is a serious condition that should be treated sensitively and appropriately when diagnosed, they also point out that many historical figures, including Albert Einstein, Edgar Allan Poe, Salvador Dali, and Henry Ford, displayed characteristics consistent with ADHD, and that every individual with or without ADHD carries within him or herself extraordinary potential. It is this process of identifying potential, capitalizing on unique strengths, and encouraging physical, academic, and social/emotional development that is especially important to apply with every child who is diagnosed with ADHD.

Some researchers and authors do not believe that ADHD is a negative diagnosis at all, but rather it is society's perception of the diagnosis that is negative. Hartmann referred to ADHD as a *trait* rather than a *disorder*, and outlined an argument in which ADHD characteristics are associated with a specific gene, which he called the "Edison gene" after the inventor who is believed to have had ADHD. The trait, Hartmann claimed, is associated with behaviors and skills that worked to the advantage of hunter-gatherer societies and has been passed down over the course of evolution. He described how many of the symptoms of ADHD, including short attention spans, poor planning skills, daydreaming, and impatience, can be viewed as adaptive characteristics. That is, these characteristics were perhaps vital to the survival of hunter-gatherer societies. For example, what might be considered "short attention span" and "poor planning" also could be described as continually monitoring the environment and being flexible, ready to change strategies and react instantly to new sights or sounds. These characteristics stand in contrast to what so-called "farmer" societies possess. Farmers exhibit such characteristics as patience, being purposefully organized, and focusing on tasks until completion. Although being alert to changes in surroundings and reacting quickly may be advantageous to hunters, farmers fare better when they plan ahead, are patient, and maintain focus until goal completion.

Unfortunately for children with hunter-like traits, modern North American cultures typically favor farmer characteristics over hunter traits, particularly in the classroom. Children are expected to sit at their desks quietly and keep their hands still as they listen to the teacher; they must work on projects or topics for prolonged periods of time; homework must be completed after school hours; and information is typically absorbed through reading, listening, or seeing as opposed to doing. Children with farmer characteristics often perform well under these "normal" conditions. Children with ADHD characteristics, on the other hand, often find it difficult to achieve academic goals and obey classroom rules. Learning about how ADHD can be a positive trait in the classroom, however, can affect how educators deal with students diagnosed with ADHD, and, in turn, can benefit such students' academic, social, and behavioral outcomes.

The manner in which ADHD is viewed can affect the strategies that teachers employ in the classroom. Alcock and Ryan (2000) state that ADHD could be thought of as a gift, despite its negative reputation. They suggest that teachers should attempt to identify the unique ADHD characteristics of each child, and tailor their instruction and teaching behaviors to emphasize the child's strengths and abilities. ADHD can give children an advantage in that they are "polyactive"—that is, they are able to work on numerous tasks—and that they are often excellent brainstormers (Alcock & Ryan, 2000, p. 9). The notion of being polyactive, however, may refer more to the tendency to pursue multiple activities, rather than the ability to coordinate and process numerous tasks simultaneously. That is, although children with ADHD may be able to carry out various tasks sequentially and with great energy and enthusiasm, their ability to pursue multiple tasks simultaneously typically is compromised. Often, children's attention to one task is diverted to new tasks or stimuli, resulting in fragmented attention rather than processing numerous task demands at one time. Alcock and Ryan recommend techniques for making use of students' excess energy, such as allowing these children to do classroom errands. Such errands can include walking notes from the teacher down to the school's administrative office, putting chairs up on desks at the end of the day, and helping the teacher put supplies away or hanging up visuals. They also suggest that teachers establish quiet zones, create times for one-on-one interactions, and listen to students' needs and solve problems together. Based on the research, teachers may consider valuing and exploiting students' natural energy by engaging them in numerous activities, both academic and otherwise. Yet, they also must realize that being polyactive may not equate to success and appropriate focus on all the tasks simultaneously.

Just as Hartmann (1996, 2003) and others (Jensen et al., 1997) believe that ADHD is actually an adaptive trait with a negative image, Hughes (1990) also cautions about the danger of labeling children with diagnoses that may carry prejudicial stereotypes. Hughes (1990) suggests that teachers go beyond the label of ADHD and identify the specific needs of their students. Too often, the label marks the child as somehow inadequate, rather than identifying a specific pattern of learning and behaving. Even pointing out that children with ADHD have attention difficulties may be simplistic, because attention has many facets, including the ability to be directed, switched, divided, sustained, or withheld. Hughes recommends that teachers determine the specific characteristics and difficulties of each child and states that, with appropriate programming, children with ADHD can succeed academically, and even achieve average levels of attentional performance when tasks are self-paced. With respect to classroom instruction, the author suggests that teachers call on the students frequently, use various cues and immediate feedback, be specific about lesson goals, and emphasize the importance of setting goals.

Schirduan (2001) found that children with ADHD are successful in situations in which their unique learning patterns and strengths were identified. Specifically, Schirduan examined 87 students (Grades 2–7) from Schools Using a Multiple Intelligences Theory (SUMIT). In these schools, the curricula were designed to reflect the various cognitive profiles of the students. The author pointed out that traditional schools use curricula that reflect the dominant culture, rather than addressing individual children's learning styles, intelligences, and interests. In considering Gardner's (1993) eight intelligences (musical, bodily kinesthetic, logical mathematical, spatial, linguistic, interpersonal, intrapersonal, and naturalist), Schirduan found that most schools focus on logical mathematical and linguistic domains at the expense of the other areas (see Table 1). This focus places students whose primary areas of intelligence lie in one or some of the other six domains at a disadvantage. Schirduan found that most of the children in the program had average self-concepts, as well as average achievement levels. Because academic underachievement is a valid concern for most children with ADHD (Barkley, 1998), the results from this study were encouraging. When taught in settings that implement a multiple intelligences approach, children with ADHD perform and feel better than children with ADHD in traditional school settings (Schirduan, 2001).

Working With ADHD in the Classroom

Children with ADHD often are polyactive, excellent brainstormers, eager to please, energetic, and creative. Teachers can use these gifts in the classroom by asking students to carry out special tasks (such as those mentioned above), and creating hands-on lessons and stimuli to keep students with ADHD engaged. Teachers can capitalize on children's creativity and natural desire for exploration by setting up mini-experiments and lessons presented in various media (such as through music, art, crafts, and dance). Teachers also can enhance and capitalize on students' gifts by recognizing each child's individual learning styles, and by using a multiple intelligences approach to teaching. To help children achieve their best academically, Alcock and Ryan (2000) suggest that educators teach demanding course work in the morning hours, keep the classroom setting structures, and use a variety of media in their instruction (such as chalkboards, overhead projectors, objects, charts, videos, etc.).

Altering perceptions and classroom practices to benefit the whole classroom is a larger goal related to reshaping our views of ADHD. Realizing that children with ADHD may have strengths that are hidden behind misleading terminology and restrictive requirements can help teachers and support staff to re-examine many of their approaches to education and behavior management. Cooper and O'Regan (2001) proposed that teachers arrange their classrooms to limit distraction and increase teacher availability to address attention and behavioral issues. Furthermore, the authors suggested that complex tasks and instructions be broken down into smaller, more manageable components. Students with ADHD may need additional support completing multiple tasks. The authors recommended that teachers should provide students with a written copy of the instructions that they can refer back to,

Table 1 Children's Strengths in Relation to Gardner's Intelligences

Intelligences:	Potential Strengths:
Linguistic	Child expresses him- or herself clearly through written or spoken language; can use language to achieve goals
Musical	Child has strong musical talents or inclinations; can appreciate musical patterns, rhythms, etc.
Logical-Mathematical	Child is good at reasoning logically, solving mathematical problems, and/or exploring issues scientifically
Spatial	Child is aware of the space, locations, and/or dimensions around him or her
Bodily-Kinesthetic	Child performs well at sports, is aware of his or her body in motion, and can use mental ability to coordinate physical movements
Interpersonal	Child has success at interacting with other people, having empathy for others' feelings, and interpreting others' motivations and desires
Intrapersonal	Child is good at interpreting his or her own feelings
Naturalist	Child knows a lot about nature; can retain facts about the environment, animals, etc.

or have students repeat instructions back to the teacher. Lerner, Lowenthal, and Lerner (1995) discussed how educators might help children with ADHD improve their organizational and listening skills, and how to sustain their attention (De La Paz, 2001; DuPaul & Stoner, 1994; Hughes, 1990). Lerner et al. (1995) state that students with ADHD often need an external structure to help them organize and prioritize assignments, including rewards for being prepared, as well as such tools as day-planners to list homework assignments and deadlines. To increase sustained attention, the authors suggest that teachers shorten task and instructions, and include interesting and novel stimuli.

Taking some measures, such as shortening instructions and re-arranging desk in the classroom, can help children diagnosed with ADHD reach their creative, academic, and behavioral goals. Perhaps more fundamentally, altering perceptions about the disorder, if it is in fact a disorder, is vital to unlocking the unique strengths and skills of children diagnosed with ADHD. For example, although children with ADHD often are accused of daydreaming, Hartmann (2003) suggests that teachers view such behavior as an indication that children are bored with mundane tasks and that all the students would benefit from a change. Another example is the common complaint by teachers that students with ADHD have difficulty converting ideas into words. If ADHD is in fact an adaptive trait, rather than a disorder, then teachers would do well to realize that many students are visual or concrete thinkers who can clearly visualize a goal or product, even when they do not have the words to describe it. Allowing children to represent their ideas, inventions, or emotions through other means can open up alternative means of communication and education. Many students in the classroom, whether or not they are diagnosed with ADHD, could have more success solving problems or summarizing stories by using paints, molding clay, dramatic skits, or music. In fact, Zentall (1993) proposed that teachers incorporate new activities and experiences into their lesson plans. The author found that children with ADHD behaved better while watching films and during games than when they were partaking in more mundane tasks. In addition, art provides many therapeutic benefits for children with ADHD by giving the children an opportunity to express themselves; in addition, art is associated with increased attention and decreased impulsive behavior (Safran, 2002; Smitheman-Brown & Church, 1996). When implementing curricula, teachers should select hands-on material whenever possible, use multiple modalities when presenting information, modify testing strategies in accordance to students' special needs, and introduce any new vocabulary prior to delivering lessons (Lerner et al., 1995).

To deny that students diagnosed with ADHD experience various degrees of difficulty in academic, social, and behavioral domains would be, at the very least, irresponsible. At worst, denying the challenges associated with ADHD might hinder students from receiving the attention and help they may need to achieve their potential. Although some ADHD characteristics may be adaptive and despite the fact that North American societies' overwhelming allegiance to a farmer-type behavioral system may be limiting, some genuine concerns must be addressed. In fact, some researchers vehemently oppose viewing ADHD as an adaptive trait at all cautioning that doing so might underestimate the specific needs and limitations associated with the disorder (Barkley, 2000; Goldstein & Barkley, 1998). For example, children with ADHD frequently disrupt classroom tasks and other classmates, are often defiant, and have problems with peers and difficulty making friends (DuPaul & Stoner, 1994). Furthermore, students diagnosed with ADHD may have difficulty with selective and sustained attention (Zentall, 1993). Many teachers and educators face challenges associated with teaching children with ADHD. These students often have behavioral problems, difficulties maintaining focus in the classroom, and challenges meeting academic and social goals. Unfortunately for students diagnosed with ADHD, many teachers and health care professionals view the disorder as just that, a disorder. Yet, maintaining a positive attitude about ADHD can allow parents and educators to move beyond the diagnosis and focus on children's strengths and unique learning styles to encourage optimal development.

Conclusion

The authors are not denying that children diagnosed with ADHD do in fact face many real challenges, nor are we necessarily supporting the notion that ADHD is an evolved, adaptive trait. Rather, we argue that thinking positively about ADHD and recognizing all children's unique strengths is important for helping children reach their social emotional, and academic potential.

References

Alcock, M. W., & Ryan, P. M. (2000). ADD, type, and learning. *Journal of Psychological Type, 52,* 5–10.

American Psychiatric Association. (2000). *Diagnostic and statistical manual of mental disorders* (4th ed., text revision). Washington, DC: Author.

Barkley, R. A. (1998). *Attention-deficit disorder: A handbook for diagnosis and treatment* (2nd ed.). New York: Guilford Press.

Barkley, R. A. (2000). More on evolution, hunting, and ADHD. *The ADHD Report, 8,* 1–7.

Cooper, P., & O'Regan, F. J. (2001). *Educating children with AD/HD: A teacher's manual.* London: RoutledgeFalmer.

De La Paz, S. (2001). Teaching writing to students with attention deficits disorders and specific language impairment. *Journal of Educational Research, 95,* 37–47.

DuPaul, G. J., & Stoner, G. (1994). *ADHD in the schools: Assessment and intervention strategies.* New York: Guilford Press.

Gardner, H. (1993). *Frames of mind: The theory of multiple intelligences.* New York: Basic Books.

Gimpel, G. A., & Kuhn, B. R. (2000). "Maternal report of attention deficit hyperactivity disorder symptoms in preschool children": Authors' response. *Child: Care, Health and Development, 26,* 178–179.

Goldstein, S., & Barkley, R. A. (1998). Commentary: ADHD, hunting and evolution: "Just so" stories. *The ADHD Report, 6,* 1–4.

Hallowell, E. M., & Ratey, J. J. (1994). *Driven to distraction: Recognizing and coping with attention deficit disorder from childhood through adulthood.* New York: Touchstone.

Hartmann, T. (1996). *Beyond ADD: Hunting for reasons in the past and present.* Grass Valley, CA: Publishers Group West.

Hartmann, T. (2003). *The Edison gene: ADHD and the gift of the hunter child.* Rochester, VT: Park Street Press.

Hughes, S. (1990). Appropriate programming for children with attention deficits. *Arizona Reading Journal, 19,* 21–22.

Jensen, P. S., Mrazek, D., Knapp, P., Steinberg, L., Pfeffer, C., Schowalter, J., & Shapiro, T. (1997). Evolution and revolution in child psychiatry: ADHD as a disorder of adaptation. *Journal of the American Academy of Child & Adolescent Psychiatry, 36,* 1672–1681.

Lerner, J. W., Lowenthal, B., & Lerner, S. R. (1995). *Attention deficit disorders: Assessment and teaching.* Pacific Grove, CA: Brooks/Cole Publishing.

Mash, E. J., & Wolfe, D. A. (1999). Attention-deficit/hyperactivity disorder. In E. J. Mash & D. A. Wolfe (Eds.), *Abnormal child psychology* (pp. 143–184). Belmont, CA: Books/Cole-Wadsworth Publishing.

Mercugliano, M., Power, T. J., & Blum, N. J. (1999). *The clinician's practical guide to attention-deficit/hyperactivity disorder.* Baltimore: Paul H. Brookes.

MTA Cooperative Group. (1999). A 14-month randomized clinical trial of treatment strategies for attention-deficit/hyperactivity disorder. *Archives of General Psychiatry, 56,* 1073–1086.

Rief, S. (2000). ADHD: Common academic difficulties and strategies that help. Attention!, *September/October,* 47–51.

Safran, D. S. (2002). *Art therapy and AD/HD: Diagnostic and therapeutic approaches.* London: Jessica Kingsley.

Schirduan, V. (2001, April). *Mindful curriculum leadership for students with attention deficit hyperactivity disorder (ADHD): Leading in elementary schools by using multiple intelligences theory (SUMIT).* Paper presented at the annual meeting of the American Educational Research Association, Seattle, WA.

Sciutto, M. J., Terjesen, M. D., & Bender Frank, A. S. (2000). Teachers' knowledge and misperceptions of attention-deficit/hyperactivity disorder. *Psychology in the Schools, 37,* 115–122.

Smitheman-Brown, V., & Church, R. P. (1996). Mandala drawing: Facilitating creative growth in children with ADD or ADHD. *Art Therapy, 13,* 252–260.

Welsh, M. C., & Pennington, B. F. (1988). Assessing frontal lobe function in children: Views from developmental psychology. *Developmental Neuropsydtology, 4,* 199–230.

Welsh, M. C., Pennington, B. F., & Grossier, D. B. (1991). A normative-developmental study of executive function: A window of prefrontal function in children. Developmental *Neuropsychology, 7,* 131–149.

Zentall, S. S. (1993). Research on the educational implications of attention deficit hyperactivity disorder. *Exceptional Children, 60,* 143–153.

Jody Sherman is graduate student, Department of Psychology, Carmen Rasmussen is Research Associate, PhD, Department of Pediatrics, and Lola Baydala is MD, MSc, FRCP, FAAP, Department of Pediatrics, University of Alberta, Edmonton, Alberta, Canada.

Authors' Note—This project was funded by the Charles Fried Memorial Fund through the Misericordia Hospital, Edmonton, Alberta, Canada.

Technology to Help Struggling Students

HEIDI SILVER-PACUILLA AND STEVE FLEISCHMAN

Many technology features that were originally developed to help people with specific sensory impairments are now widely in use. We have begun to take for granted the ability to zoom in on small print or to have written text speak to us. Closed captioning of video programs, originally developed to support viewers who are hard of hearing, also has mainstream uses, allowing us to "tune in" to a program across a noisy room by reading the captions.

Such accessibility features, particularly text-to-speech and speech recognition, are increasingly available in educational technologies as well. Although schools commonly use them to support students with sensory impairments and learning disabilities, these features can help a broad range of students. Research is beginning to show the benefits of giving all students access to these capabilities.

What We Know

Research in psychology has shown the power of simultaneous, multiple modes of input to gain and hold a person's attention and to improve memory. Lewandowski and Montali (1996) conducted a study that compared the learning of poor readers and skilled readers who were both taught through a text-to-speech application with simultaneous on-screen highlighting of the spoken word. This study showed that experiencing the text bimodally (visually and aurally) enabled poor readers to perform as well as skilled readers in word recognition and retention. Research by Allinder, Dunse, Brunken, and Obermiller-Krolikowski (2001) and Meyer and Felton (1999) confirms that highlighting text as it is spoken can help learners pay attention and remember more.

Text-to-speech also relieves the burden of decoding for struggling readers, allowing them to focus on comprehension (Wise, Ring, & Olson, 2000) and improving their endurance in completing reading assignments (Hecker, Burns, Elkind, Elkind, & Katz, 2002). Research has also shown that students with learning disabilities identify and correct more errors in their compositions when they use text-to-speech for proofreading (Higgins & Raskind, 1995).

The inverse of text-to-speech is speech recognition, in which the technology takes spoken words and translates them into type. Speech recognition provides access to computers not only for users who have physical disabilities, but also for those who have constraints related to fatigue, poor handwriting, spatial organization, or spelling. Speech recognition also provides immediate constructive feedback, as users see their own words transformed into written text with correct formatting and grammar (Silver-Pacuilla, in press).

Technology features can support learning by building literacy and language skills and independence.

Early research conducted with previous versions of the technology, which had considerable problems with accuracy, indicated that the strategic use of speech recognition improved users' literacy skills (Higgins & Raskind, 2000). The researchers attributed these benefits to the heightened, strategic engagement with print and language that users experience while dictating and correcting errors.

A third technology application that has received research attention is computer-based graphic organizers. These tools facilitate brainstorming, concept mapping, and outlining in much the same way that teacher-led instruction does, but with the advantages of providing word processing and text-to-speech support and the ability to rearrange elements or switch between outline and map view. In one study (Sturm & Rankin-Erickson, 2002), middle school students with and without disabilities were taught concept-mapping strategies and then were asked to write descriptive essays using either no map, a hand-drawn map, or a computer-drawn map. Students who constructed concept maps during the prewriting stage—either by hand or with the computer—produced significantly more sophisticated and complete essays. Students who used computer-based mapping also reported a more positive attitude toward the writing process.

What You Can Do

Educators should not hesitate to integrate technology features into instruction for students who struggle with academic tasks. These approaches can support learning by building literacy and language skills and independence.

- *Text-to-speech.* You can use text-to-speech to increase the amount of reading that struggling readers do. For early readers and young English language learners, use digital storybooks as a fun and interactive way to engage with books. Encourage older readers to use text-to-speech to access motivating, content-specific texts on the Internet. For students who struggle to read classic literature, consider downloading the texts as e-books that students can read with text-to-speech. Much e-book software includes annotation, highlighting, and linked dictionary tools to facilitate studying. To help with writing, have students proofread their compositions as the software reads them aloud. You can install free, downloadable text-to-speech programs or find this feature bundled in many operating systems and stand-alone applications.
- *Speech recognition.* Use speech recognition technology to help struggling writers and spellers get their ideas on paper. The immediacy of the dictation process reinforces the vocabulary and use of writing conventions and punctuation. Special programs can help struggling math students dictate and organize mathematical expressions. If you haven't tried speech recognition software lately, you'll find vastly improved capabilities, reduced training requirements, and better microphones available at very reasonable costs.
- *Graphic organizers.* Many teachers now use graphic organizers to tap into students' visual and spatial abilities, strengthening the connection between these ways of knowing and academic tasks. You can use computer-based graphic organizers with whole-class instruction to show the connections among big ideas in the content areas, as well as to demonstrate writing and reading comprehension strategies. Encourage your students to try using graphic organizer programs for annotations during reading or prewriting brainstorming. The ability of most of the software packages to switch between map and outline views supports students' progress through the writing stages.

Technologies will not automatically create success straight out of the box.

- *E-Resources.* Today's Internet contains a plethora of reference and resource material. Encourage all your students to use these resources, which provide "just in time" and "just in case" support to help address vocabulary and background knowledge gaps. For English language learners or students struggling with reading and writing, provide extra training in using e-resources with text-to-speech software. Such support will give these students access to the same powerful knowledge base that their peers enjoy.

Educators Take Note

Accessibility features in common technology applications can help struggling students make important connections—to the content, among ideas, among their own sensory modes of learning, and between their digital competencies and the curriculum. These technologies, however, will not automatically create success straight out of the box. Educators need to strategically integrate these features into sound pedagogy to help struggling learners achieve both academic and technological success.

References

Allinder, R. M., Dunse, L., Brunken, C. D., & Obermiller-Krolikowski, H. J. (2001). Improving fluency in at-risk readers and students with learning disabilities. *Remedial and Special Education, 22*, 48–54.

Hecker, L., Burns, L., Elkind, J., Elkind, K., & Katz, L. (2002). Benefits of assistive reading software for students with attention disorders. *Annals of Dyslexia, 52*, 243–272.

Higgins, E. L., & Raskind, M. H. (1995). Compensatory effectiveness of speech recognition on the written composition performance of postsecondary students with learning disabilities. *Learning Disabilities Quarterly, 18*, 159–174.

Higgins, E. L., & Raskind, M. H. (2000). Speaking to read: The effects of continuous vs. discrete speech recognition systems on the reading and spelling of children with learning disabilities. *Journal of Special Education Technology, 15*, 19–30.

Lewandowski, J., & Montali, L. (1996). Bimodal reading: Benefits of a talking computer for average and less skilled readers. *Journal of Learning Disabilities, 29*(3), 271–279.

Meyer, M. S., & Felton, R. H. (1999). Repeated readings to enhance fluency: Old approaches and new directions. *Annals of Dyslexia, 49*, 283–306.

Silver-Pacuilla, H. (in press). Assistive technology and adult literacy: Access and benefits. *Annual Review of Adult Learning and Literacy, Vol. 7.* Cambridge, MA: National Center for the Study of Adult Learning and Literacy.

Sturm, J. M., & Rankin-Erickson, J. L. (2002). Effects of hand-drawn and computer-generated concept mapping on the expository writing of middle school students with learning disabilities. *Learning Disabilities Research & Practice, 17*(2), 124–139.

Wise, B. W., Ring, J., & Olson, R. K. (2000). Individual differences in gains from computer-assisted remedial reading. *Journal of Experimental Child Psychology, 77*(3), 197–235.

Heidi Silver-Pacuilla is Research Analyst and Deputy Director of the National Center for Technology Innovation at the American Institutes for Research (AIR). **Steve Fleischman,** series editor of this column, is a Principal Research Scientist at AIR; editorair@air.org.

Recognizing Gifted Students

A Practical Guide for Teachers

By watching for certain behaviors and characteristics, teachers in the general education classroom can identify and better understand exceptional students.

SANDRA MANNING

Today, more than ever, student diversity typifies the general education classroom (Tomlinson 2004). In most classrooms, the range of cognitive abilities is vast. Inclusion and legislative mandates challenge general educators to design and implement teaching and behavior management strategies that will ensure success for all student groups—including the gifted and highly able. Research indicates, however, that a majority of teachers have little specific knowledge about this group of children (Archambualt et al. 1993; Robinson 1998; Westberg and Daoust 2003; Whitton 1997).

Lacking awareness of the characteristics and instructional requirements of high ability students, teachers are at a disadvantage. This article explores the characteristics of gifted children and offers the general classroom teacher tips and ideas for understanding the gifted children they teach.

"Gifted students routinely exhibit academic and emotional traits that may be described as intense and, at times, even extreme."

Defining 'Gifted'

High ability students have been labeled in many ways. Currently, the label "gifted" is used to indicate high intellectual or academic ability, and "gifted education" is recognized as the educational field devoted to the study of this student population. However, defining "gifted" is no easy task. The earliest use of this word to identify high ability students was by Lewis Terman in 1925 (Stephens and Karnes 2000; Morelock 1996). This usage came on the heels of the first IQ test developed in the early 1900s by Alfred Binet (Morelock 1996; Morgan 1996; Sarouphim 1999). Terman identified students scoring in the top 2 percent in general intelligence on the Binet test or a similar measure as gifted (Clark 2002).

Over the years, many definitions of this term have been proposed by scholars and researchers. From natural talent awaiting development (Gagne 1995; Tannenbaum 2003) to the ability to use life situations successfully (Sternberg 2003), the common factors in defining giftedness appear to be potential and opportunity.

Clark (2002) defined "gifted" as a label for the biological concepts of superior development of various brain functions. These functions, according to Clark, may be manifested in the areas of cognition, creativity, academics, leadership, or the arts. Clark subtly emphasized the natural aspects of the child's ability, as opposed to learned aspects, and most nearly matched the popular definition of the word gifted—"endowed with a special aptitude or ability" (Webber 1984, 295). Clark (2002, 25), however, went on to say that "Growth of intelligence depends on the interaction between biological inheritance and environmental opportunities." With this phrase, Clark inferred a union of the nature/nurture debate, designating giftedness as partially due to inherited traits of information processing with an integral portion attributed to the environmental experiences the child encounters to develop those traits.

Less formal definitions of the word gifted include those offered by parent groups and gifted students themselves. Russell, Hayes, and Dockery (1988, 2) reported a definition created by a parent group: "Giftedness is that precious endowment of potentially outstanding abilities which allows a person to interact with the environment with remarkably high levels of achievement and creativity." Gifted student Amanda Ashman (2000, 50) defined being gifted as "not something that you can develop. You are born with a capacity for knowledge. Learning and understanding come naturally for the gifted."

These definitions further the meaning of giftedness as an endowment of natural ability apart from learning that takes place in the home or at school. Unfortunately, these types of definitions have given the field of gifted education the reputation of elitism (Morelock 1996) and perhaps have been the impetus of the popular myth that "gifted students will get it on their own." To refute that myth and highlight the need for talent development in all students, growing interest in the idea of multiple intelligences has challenged the singular idea of "general intelligence org" (Gardner 1983; Von Károlyi, Ramos-Ford, and Gardner 2003) and suggested that strengths in many areas more aptly define giftedness in individuals. Further, Sternberg (2003) advocated in his theory of successful intelligence that giftedness is manifested in individuals who are able to take the raw materials of their life situations and transform them into successful experiences. Renzulli (1978; 2003) added that task commitment and creativity must be considered when defining giftedness.

Whether giftedness is inherited, developed, manifested in the ability to manipulate life situations, or a result of some combination of these ideas, it is imperative for the regular classroom teacher to be cognizant of the fact that high ability students are in the classroom. Because these students are present, teachers have a responsibility to create a learning environment conducive to gifted student success.

Characteristics of Gifted Students

One key way classroom teachers can broaden understanding of gifted students is through knowledge of the general characteristics intellectually gifted children exhibit. Characteristics in the cognitive and affective domains most commonly appear in general classroom behavior and, therefore, may be observed by the classroom teacher.

Table 1 highlights general cognitive characteristics of intellectually gifted students. Notice that gifted students often possess an intense desire to learn about their own interests. Their ability to think at abstract levels earlier than same-aged peers and form their own ways of thinking about problems and ideas indicates that intellectually gifted students need advanced content and choice in learning activities. Gifted students' high energy levels and ability to extend the range of projects signify that independent studies may be an option for differentiating instruction for these students.

Varied behaviors and preferences arise from giftedness. An awareness of the social and emotional characteristics of gifted students can further help teachers understand many of the classroom behaviors they observe in these children. For example, the gifted child's desire to share knowledge may be seen by others as an attempt to show off and may lead to peer rejection. Gifted students' high expectations of themselves and others can lead to perfectionism, personal dissatisfaction, or feelings of hopelessness (Clark 2002). Table 2 gives an overview of the characteristics of intellectually gifted students in the affective domain.

Table 1 Cognitive Characteristics of Intellectually Gifted Students

- Process and retain large amounts of information
- Comprehend materials at advanced levels
- Curious and have varied and sometimes intense interests
- High levels of language development and verbal ability
- Possess accelerated and flexible thought processes
- Early ability to delay closure of projects
- See unusual relationships among disciplines or objects
- Adept at generating original ideas and solutions to problems
- Persistent, goal-oriented, and intense on topics of interest
- Form their own ways of thinking about problems and ideas
- Learn things at an earlier age than peers
- Need for freedom and individuality in learning situations
- High desire to learn and seek out their own interests
- Abstract thinkers at an earlier age than peers
- Prefer complex and challenging work
- Transfer knowledge and apply it to new situations
- May prefer to work alone
- May be early readers
- May possess high energy levels and longer attention spans

(Chuska 1989; Clark 2002; Silverman 2000; Winebrenner 2001)

Table 2 Affective Characteristics of Intellectually Gifted Students

- Possess large amounts of information about emotions
- May possess an unusual sensitivity to the feelings of others
- Possess a keen or subtle sense of humor
- Possess a heightened sense of self-awareness
- Idealism and sense of justice appear at an early age
- Develop inner controls early
- Possess unusual emotional depth and intensity
- Exhibit high expectations of self and others
- Display a strong need for consistency in themselves and others
- Possess advanced levels of moral judgment

(Chuska 1989; Clark 2002; Silverman 2000; Winebrenner 2001)

Gifted students routinely exhibit academic and emotional traits that may be described as intense and, at times, even extreme. They are more curious, demanding, and sensitive than their typical developing peers. Gifted children are unique and require parents and educators to modify both home and school environments to meet their strong need to know. Modification is imperative if gifted students are to reach full potential.

Teachers should keep in mind that the traits listed are not exhaustive and that every gifted child will not display each characteristic stated. In fact, intellectually gifted students referred to in the literature as atypical may display their giftedness in other ways. There are many groups to consider when identifying an atypical gifted student, including, but not limited to, non-English speaking students and students from low socioeconomic circumstances. Unfortunately, research has shown that teachers often overlook atypical gifted students and refer a disproportionately high number of European-American children with "teacher-friendly" characteristics such as good behavior and high academic achievement to gifted education programs (Plata and Masten 1998; Bonner 2000). This reality points to the need for additional information on the characteristics of atypical gifted students such as listed in Table 3.

Many traits of atypical gifted students are evident in all intellectually gifted students. However, a strong sense of family, responsibility for adult roles—such as assuming additional tasks in the classroom setting, inner-strength, and self-worth—are key factors for the classroom teacher to look for in recognizing atypical gifted students. These children have the same general abilities as many gifted students. Yet, because of cultural differences or lack of early experiences, they may not display the typical characteristics of intellectually gifted students that often are considered by teachers when making referrals to gifted education programs.

Table 3 Characteristics of Atypical Gifted Students

- Ability to manipulate a symbol system
- Think logically
- Ability to use stored knowledge to solve problems
- Reason by analogy
- Transfer knowledge to new circumstances
- May possess creative and artistic abilities
- Resilient; able to cope with trying family situations
- Take on adult roles in the home
- Strong sense of pride and self-worth
- Exhibit leadership ability and independent thinking
- Possess a strong desire to learn about and understand their culture
- Display a strong inner will
- May display a heightened sensitivity to others and the world around them

(Bonner 2000; Hebert and Reis 1999; Schwartz 1997)

Classroom Behaviors

Because of the unique characteristics gifted students possess, teachers need to be aware of the ways in which these attributes manifest themselves in observable classroom behaviors. Some behaviors can be troubling to the classroom teacher; however, being aware of their root causes will help teachers more fully meet gifted students' needs and build positive relationships vital to meaningful classroom experiences.

The following classroom problem situations (Clark 2002; Winebrenner 2001; Smutny, Walker, and Meckstroth 1997) are offered for consideration.

- Unfinished work may be the result of varied interests and inability to narrow down a topic. Poor work habits might also reveal student feelings that he or she already knows about a particular topic and does not feel the need for practice.
- Poor class work by gifted students is often a sign of disinterest in subject matter. Gifted children may question the appropriateness of classroom activities to their needs, but will work diligently and well on topics of high interest.
- Sensitivity to the attitudes and perceptions of others may cause gifted students to fall into the perfectionism trap or to fear failure. These feelings can lead to unfinished work, procrastination, or underachievement.
- Poor group work often is the result of gifted students' feelings that they will have the burden of the group's work. Gifted students also may prefer to work alone because of feelings that their ideas will be misunderstood or unappreciated by the group.
- Bossiness in group work could be an indicator of younger students practicing their leadership abilities to find the most effective leadership style. Overbearing behavior also may stem from gifted students' desire for control in their lives and their characteristics of independence and nonconformity.
- Slow workers who are gifted may be ensuring that their work is perfect.
- Behavior problems in gifted students could be a result of boredom or the feeling that class work is too easy or beneath them.
- Being the "class clown" may be the result of the gifted student's keen sense of humor being exhibited in unacceptable ways. The behavior also might be an attempt to gain acceptance among peers who may perceive the student negatively because of his or her "gifted" label.
- Emotional outbursts or periods of withdrawal in gifted students may be due to their highly sensitive natures.

Close Observation

Given that gifted students clearly do not always exhibit classroom work, behavior, and dispositions that are "teacher friendly," how can classroom teachers make informed decisions about the children they refer for gifted education programs?

A list of pertinent questions follows. An affirmative and detailed answer to some of these questions regarding a particular student might serve as a signal to begin observing the child more closely and keeping anecdotal records to document patterns of behavior. Such activities not only aid teachers in identifying the student for assessment, but also provide valuable information on the frequency of gifted behaviors to professionals who eventually may assess the student formally for gifted education services.

- Is this student highly verbal in spoken language, written language, or both?
- Does this student use art materials either creatively or uniquely?
- Does this student offer insightful contributions to class discussions that are of interest to him or her?
- Is this student able to comprehend, synthesize, or evaluate story material in unique ways from personal readings or from teacher read-alouds?
- Does this student have unique or varied interests?
- Is this student highly passionate or excited about his or her own interests?
- Does this student have a strong sense of family or interest in family-related topics?
- Does this child get good test grades but often turns in poor class work?

Final Thoughts

This sampling of characteristics and concomitant problems points to the need for classroom teachers to heighten their awareness of issues related to gifted students in their classrooms. Keeping abreast of research and information by reading journals devoted to gifted children and gifted education is a good starting place. Becoming more reflective by asking internal "why" questions to understand the root causes of student behaviors will help teachers as they strive to provide the most meaningful education for all the students they teach.

References

Archambault, F. X., Jr., K. L. Westberg, S. W. Brown, B. W. Hallmark, C. L. Emmons, and W. Zhang. 1993. *Regular classroom practices with gifted students: Results of a national survey of classroom teachers* (Research Monograph 93102). Storrs, CT: University of Connecticut, National Research Center on the Gifted and Talented.

Ashman, A. 2000. Through another's eyes: Amanda's perspective on being gifted. *Gifted Child Today* 23(1): 50–53.

Bonner, F. A., II. 2000. African American giftedness. *Journal of Black Studies* 30(5): 643–63.

Chuska, K. R. 1989. *Gifted learners K–12: A practical guide to effective curriculum and teaching*. Bloomington, IN: National Educational Service.

Clark, B. 2002. *Growing up gifted: Developing the potential of children at home and at school,* 6th ed. Upper Saddle River, NJ: Prentice Hall.

Gagne, F. 1995. From giftedness to talent: A developmental model and its impact on the language of the field. *Roeper Review* 18(2): 103–11.

Gardner, H. 1983. *Frames of mind: The theory of multiple intelligences*. New York: Basic Books.

Hebert, T. P., and S. M. Reis. 1999. Culturally diverse high-achieving students in an urban high school. *Urban Education* 34(4): 428–57.

Morelock, M. J. 1996. On the nature of giftedness and talent: Imposing order on chaos. *Roeper Review* 19(1): 4–12.

Morgan, H. 1996. An analysis of Gardner's theory of multiple intelligence. *Roeper Review* 18(4): 263–69.

Plata, M., and W. G. Masten. 1998. Teacher ratings of Hispanic and Anglo students on a behavior rating scale. *Roeper Review* 21(2): 139–44.

Renzulli, J. S. 1978. What makes giftedness? Re-examining a definition. *Phi Delta Kappan* 60(3): 180–84, 261.

Renzulli, J. S. 2003. A conception of giftedness and its relationship to the development of social capital. In *Handbook of gifted education*, 3rd ed., ed. N. Colangelo and G. A. Davis, 75–87. Boston: Allyn & Bacon.

Robinson, G. J. 1998. Classroom practices with high achieving students: A national survey of middle school teachers. Ph.D. diss., University of Connecticut, Storrs.

Russell, D. W., D. G. Hayes, and L. B. Dockery. 1988. *My child is gifted! Now what do I do?* 2nd ed. Winston-Salem: North Carolina Association for the Gifted and Talented.

Sarouphim, K. M. 1999. Discover: A new promising alternative assessment for the identification of gifted minorities. *Gifted Child Quarterly* 43(4): 244–51.

Schwartz, W. 1997. *Strategies for identifying the talents of diverse students.* New York: ERIC Clearinghouse on Urban Education. ERIC ED 410 323.

Silverman, L. 2000. Characteristics of giftedness scale. Denver, CO: Gifted Development Center. Available at: www.gifteddevelopment.com/Articles/Characteristics_Scale.htm.

Smutny, J. F., S. Y. Walker, and E. A. Meckstroth. 1997. *Teaching young gifted children in the regular classroom: Identifying, nurturing, and challenging ages 4–9.* Minneapolis, MN: Free Spirit Publishing.

Stephens, K. R., and F. A. Karnes. 2000. State definitions for the gifted and talented revisited. *Exceptional Children* 66(2): 219–38.

Sternberg, R. J. 2003. Giftedness according to the theory of successful intelligence. In *Handbook of gifted education*, 3rd ed., ed. N. Colangelo and G. A. Davis, 55–60. Boston: Allyn & Bacon.

Tannenbaum, A. J. 2003. Nature and nurture of giftedness. In *Handbook of gifted education*, 3rd ed., ed. N. Colangelo and G. A. Davis, 45–59. Boston: Allyn & Bacon.

Tomlinson, C. A. 2004. Differentiation in diverse settings. *School Administrator* 61(7): 28–33.

Von Károlyi, C., V. Ramos-Ford, and H. Gardner. 2003. Multiple intelligences: A perspective on giftedness. In *Handbook of gifted education*, 3rd ed., ed. N. Colangelo and G. A. Davis, 100–12. Boston: Allyn & Bacon.

Webber, H., ed. 1984. *Webster's II new Riverside dictionary*. Boston: Houghton Mifflin.

Westberg, K. L., and M. E. Daoust. 2003. The results of the replication of the classroom practices survey replication in two states. *The National Research Center on the Gifted and Talented Newsletter* Fall: 3–8. Available at: www.gifted.uconn.edu/nrcgt/newsletter/fall03/fall032.html.

Whitton, D. 1997. Regular classroom practices with gifted students in grades 3 and 4 in New South Wales, Australia. *Gifted Education International* 12(1): 34–38.

Winebrenner, S. 2001. *Teaching gifted kids in the regular classroom: Strategies and techniques every teacher can use to meet the academic needs of the gifted and talented,* revised, expanded, and updated edition, ed. P. Espeland. Minneapolis, MN: Free Spirit Publishing.

Sandra Manning is Associate Director for The Frances A. Karnes Center for Gifted Studies at The University of Southern Mississippi. Her research interests include young gifted children and differentiating instruction for high ability students. She also holds National Board Teacher Certification.

Raising Expectations for the Gifted

Five teaching strategies allow flexibility in meeting the needs of gifted students in inclusive classrooms.

COLLEEN WILLARD-HOLT

Most gifted students study in regular classrooms for most of their school careers and are taught using the same state standards intended for all students. Most state standards, however, do not provide sufficient intellectual challenge for gifted students.

Neuroscientific research has found that rats in unstimulating environments had thinner cortexes, the part of the brain where higher mental functions reside (Diamond & Hopson, 1998). This effect appeared after just four days!

Education research has shown that gifted students' motivation and performance also declined in the absence of mental stimulation, even leading to underachievement (Purcell, 1993; Whitmore, 1980), but that gifted students exposed to intellectually stimulating content at an accelerated pace outperformed gifted peers not in such programs (Cornell & Delcourt, 1990; Kulik, 1992). It is too great a risk to subject gifted students to a steady diet of unchallenging work.

Standards need not imply standardization of learning activities or expectations. Gifted students may need less time to master a given standard, or they may address the standard in greater depth. Classroom teachers might follow the principle of teaching all students at their optimal level of instruction—what Vygotsky would call their "zone of proximal development" (1978).

How can regular classroom teachers address the needs of their gifted students? The first step in differentiating a standards-based lesson or unit for gifted students is to identify the standards that the lesson will address. An efficient way to accomplish several tasks within one lesson is to combine content, skills, and arts standards. For example, making a poster for National Arbor Day can address science standards in environmental health, language arts standards in research and communication, and standards regarding the elements and principles of visual art.

Teachers can then assess students' grasp of content and skills. They might pretest the students, using an end-of-chapter test that integrates skills with content, or review students' achievement on content and skills that they have previously studied. Perusing student portfolios or assessing interests and multiple intelligences profiles can also provide insight into skills and content knowledge.

Once teachers have determined students' readiness levels, they can execute differentiation strategies. Curriculum compacting, flexible grouping, product choices, tiered assignments, and multilevel learning stations are excellent strategies for differentiating instruction for gifted students in regular classrooms (see Gregory & Chapman, 2002; Maker & Nielson, 1996; Reis, Burns, & Renzulli, 1992; Tomlinson, 1999; Willard-Holt, 1994). Some of these strategies also lend themselves well to meeting the needs of gifted students with disabilities.

Curriculum Compacting

Curriculum compacting is a powerful strategy for ensuring accountability for standards while acknowledging what students already know. Curriculum compacting means streamlining what is taught to students by first assessing their prior knowledge and then modifying or eliminating work that has been partially or fully mastered. After teachers assess student mastery of a particular standard, three groups often emerge: students with poor mastery, students with partial mastery, and students with full mastery who are ready for more advanced work.[1] The first group, usually the largest, proceeds with the planned sequence of instruction; the second group may accomplish the planned sequence more quickly and then proceed to a greater challenge; the third group may begin an independent project immediately.

Consider this math standard for grade 3: "Count, compare, and make change using a collection of coins and one-dollar bills" (PA Std. 2.1.3E).[2] The first group is ready to make several combinations of pennies, nickels, and dimes for given amounts. The second group is confident of these steps and can make change, but they need help using quarters. They will join the rest of the class when the teacher provides information and practice with quarters; the rest of the time they work together on a coin-related project that they will present to the class. The project might entail making a poster of U.S. coinage from colonial times to the present, using drawings, replicas, or actual coins when available. The third group's students, who tested 85 percent or above on the pretest, are making a chart that compares currency systems for different countries. They will defend their choice of the most efficient system at the end of the unit. Such higher-order thinking projects may also satisfy language arts standards, using a similar process for compacting skill standards in reading or writing.

In middle and high school grades, gifted students may not have the technical knowledge to meet a particular content standard and therefore may not show mastery on a pretest. They may be able to learn the content quickly by reading the text and completing application exercises on their own, however, and then successfully complete a criterion-referenced posttest. For example, a life sciences course might focus on the 10th grade standard, "Identify and characterize major life forms by kingdom, phylum, class, and order" (PA Std. 3.3.10A). The teacher invites students who have performed well in previous science units to read the text and work through a packet of exercises at their own pace. This packet consists of activities crucial to understanding the topic and differs from the step-by-step exercises given to the rest of the class. When ready, students take the posttest and, if they demonstrate mastery, undertake an in-depth project, such as creating a three-dimensional clay model of a dissected starfish (Miller & Willard-Holt, 2000). This project addresses skill and arts standards simultaneously.

Teachers can also use compacting with gifted students who have disabilities. If the goal is to master content quickly while circumventing the disability, the teacher can compact in areas of weakness as well as strength. For the standard, "Identify planets in our solar system and their general characteristics" (PA Std. 3.4.4D), the class assignment might be a written report on a planet. A gifted student with a writing disability who demonstrates mastery of the characteristics of the planets on a pretest might instead research current theories about the birth of galaxies and create a PowerPoint presentation.

It is not always necessary to focus on remediation. If the goal is to develop coping strategies for the disability, compacting can focus on the area of strength.

Flexible Grouping

Flexible grouping is particularly effective when students' achievement levels in content and skills differ, as is often the case for gifted students with disabilities. The teacher groups students according to strength, need, or interest, and groups change frequently, sometimes in the course of a single class session. As an illustration, an 11th grade English class might address the standards, "Analyze the relationships, uses, and effectiveness of literary elements used by one or more authors, including characterization, setting, plot, theme, point of view, tone, and style" (PA Std. 1.3.11B) and "Write short stories, poems, and plays" (PA Std. 1.4.11A). The class has read a scene from *Romeo and Juliet*, viewed the corresponding scene from *West Side Story*, and discussed similarities and differences. In groups, students write a contemporary scene in which young people are in love despite their families' differences. Drawing on their knowledge of current events, students research the conflict between the groups that the families represent, such as Israelis versus Palestinians, big business versus environmentalists, or Shiite versus Sunni Muslims. Students could also choose groups that are at odds in their immediate community.

Students initially come together around the specific conflict that most interests them, with groups changing later as needed. Each group has students with mixed levels of ability. The teacher provides mini-lessons to address specific skills—for example, how to research the conflict using print resources, Internet, and interviews of community leaders; write authentic dialogue; punctuate dialogue correctly; or write stage directions. Later, gifted students might meet together to choose a multi-layered conflict, the threads of which they must logically incorporate into the scene.

Product Choices

Another way to plan for gifted students is to allow them choices of what kind of product they will produce. In the *Romeo and Juliet* example, one group might complete a written script (verbal/linguistic intelligence); another, a videotaped dramatization of the scene (bodily/kinesthetic intelligence); and a third, a comic strip (visual/spatial intelligence). In this way, each group addresses the same content standard but uses a different skill or arts standard.

For the 6th grade standard, "Describe the human characteristics of places and regions by their cultural characteristics" (PA Std. 7.3.6B), students studying a unit on Central and South America might choose to create an authentic traditional costume, dance, food, artwork, or model of a home—developing a three-dimensional model, drawing, or verbal description. The projects appeal to different intelligences and address different skills and arts standards.

Product choices are important for gifted students with disabilities, allowing them to demonstrate their understanding of the content without their disability interfering. For example, a student with a learning disability in written expression may conduct research, make the necessary cognitive connections, and demonstrate understanding through art and oral expression, thereby circumventing writing. A blind student may conduct research by using text-to-speech interfaces on the Internet and create a three-dimensional model. In each case, the focus is on content mastery. Assignments in other areas would remediate or develop coping strategies for the disability.

Tiered Assignments

The advantage of this strategy is that the entire class studies the same content, but individual students choose assignments at different levels of complexity, with the teacher's assistance. For example, coupling a 4th grade science standard, "Know basic weather elements" (PA Std. 3.4.4C), with a math standard, "Organize and display data using pictures, tallies, tables, charts, bar graphs, and circle graphs" (PA Std. 2.6.5A), allows students to learn how to gather weather data from various sources and graph the data. Assignment choices might include

- Making a bar graph that shows the average monthly temperatures in two cities (basic level).
- Choosing two appropriate types of graphs to show the proportion of rainy days to sunny days, and the average rainfall by months in a city of your choice (average level).
- Generating two appropriate graphs on the computer to show the ratio of rain to snow, and monthly temperature and precipitation in a city of your choice (advanced level).

Students choose the assignment that sounds most interesting and best stimulates their learning. Gentle nudging might encourage students to accept the appropriate level of challenge.

Multilevel Learning Stations

Multilevel learning stations provide meaningful independent work that extends and enriches class discussions. For example, a learning station can assist 3rd grade students studying ancient civilizations by addressing history, geography, arts, and language arts standards, including the following:

- Compare similarities and differences between the earliest civilizations and life today (PA Std. 8.4.3C).
- Explain the historical, cultural, and social context of an individual work in the arts (PA Std. 9.2.3A).
- Relate works in the arts chronologically to historical events (PA Std. 9.2.3B) or geographic regions (PA Std. 9.2.3G).

Product choices allow gifted students with disabilities to demonstrate their understanding of the content.

Activity cards address such topics as leaders/famous people, arts, structures, ways of life, and location. In addition, the teacher codes the activity cards according to Bloom's thinking levels: red for knowledge/

comprehension, blue for application, green for analysis, yellow for synthesis, and white for evaluation. On the basis of assessment data, each student receives an assignment sheet detailing the number of activities that he or she is to complete at each level. For example, Juan will do one of each color; Sarah will select five activities, all at green, yellow, or white levels; and Randy will choose five red or blue activities.

Teachers often assume that learning stations are appropriate only for the elementary grades, yet secondary students also seem to enjoy them. For example, U.S. history students addressing the Civil War might explore in depth topics relating to battles, leaders, military technology, camp life, civilian life, or the roles of women or African Americans in the war, according to their interests.

Inspiring Extraordinary Achievement

Some gifted students' capabilities and rates of learning are so far beyond their chronological ages that they would spend almost all of their time reviewing what they already knew if they followed the curriculum offered in a regular classroom. These students need a highly individualized program at an advanced level, perhaps through acceleration or mentoring. Other gifted students may be highly advanced in one subject and could benefit from acceleration or mentoring in that subject while remaining in the inclusive classroom for the remainder of the day.

Providing gifted students with instruction at the appropriate level also removes pressure that they might feel in cooperative learning situations within inclusive classrooms. It may be tempting to ask advanced students to tutor others—a strategy that is permissible on occasion, but inappropriate as a regular activity. Gifted students, like all students, come to school to encounter new learning challenges. Depending on gifted students as peer tutors also places them at risk for social isolation if other students come to view them as teacher's pets or know-it-alls (Robinson, 1990).

Teaching to standards need not mean standardization of learning activities or expectations. Simply meeting standards is not an adequate challenge for most gifted students, although that is all the law may require of them. As Tomlinson states in reference to the No Child Left Behind Act of 2001,

> There is no incentive for schools to attend to the growth of students once they attain proficiency . . . and certainly not to inspire those who far exceed proficiency. (2002, p. 36)

Don't we want more than minimal proficiency from our gifted students? By using strategies to challenge all students at their optimal levels of instruction, teachers can meet their responsibilities for accountability while inspiring extraordinary achievement.

Notes

1. A fourth group—those not yet ready to attempt the standard—is beyond the scope of this article.
2. I refer to Pennsylvania standards. The standards are available at www.pde.state.pa.us/stateboard_fed; click Academic Standards.

References

Cornell, D. G., & Delcourt, M. A. B. (1990). Achievement, attitudes, and adjustment. *Communicator, 20*(5), 28.

Diamond, M., & Hopson, J. (1998). *Magic trees of the mind.* New York: Plume Books.

Gregory, G. H., & Chapman, C. (2002). *Differentiated instructional strategies: One size doesn't fit all.* Thousand Oaks, CA: Corwin Press.

Kulik, J. A. (1992). *An analysis of the research on ability grouping* (RBDM 9204). Storrs, CT: University of Connecticut, The National Research Center on the Gifted and Talented.

Maker, C. J., & Nielson, A. B. (1996). *Curriculum development and teaching strategies for gifted learners* (2nd ed.). Austin, TX: Pro-Ed.

Miller, B., & Willard-Holt, C. (2000). *Dare to differentiate: Strategies for enrichment in middle school science.* Manassas, VA: Gifted Education Press.

Purcell, J. H. (1993). The effects of the elimination of gifted and talented programs on participating students and their parents. *Gifted Child Quarterly*, 37(4), 177–187.

Reis, S. M., Burns, D. E., & Renzulli, J. S. (1992). *Curriculum compacting*. Mansfield Center, CT: Creative Learning Press.

Robinson, A. (1990). Cooperation or exploitation? The argument against cooperative learning for talented students. *Journal for the Education of the Gifted*, 14(3), 9–27, 31–36.

Tomlinson, C. A. (1999). *The differentiated classroom: Responding to the needs of all learners.* Alexandria, VA: ASCD.

Tomlinson, C. A. (2002, Nov. 6). Proficiency is not enough. *Education Week*, 22(10), 36, 38.

Vygotsky, L. S. (1978). *Mind in society: The development of higher psychological processes*. Cambridge, MA: Harvard University Press.

Whitmore, J. R. (1980). *Giftedness, conflict, and underachievement*. Boston: Allyn and Bacon.

Willard-Holt, C. (1994). Strategies for individualizing instruction in regular classrooms. *Roeper Review*, 17(1), 43–45.

Colleen Willard-Holt is an associate professor of education in the School of Behavioral Sciences and Education at Penn State—Capital College; cxw20@psu.edu.

From *Educational Leadership*, October 2003, pp. 72–75. Reprinted by permission of the Association for Supervision and Curriculum Development.

Challenging Deficit Thinking

Urban teachers must question unspoken assumptions about the sources of their students' struggles.

LOIS WEINER

Although my research and expertise are in urban teaching, I am now regularly asked to assist schools that are a far cry from the typical urban school. Clearly, teachers and school leaders in suburbs are now grappling with many of the challenges traditionally associated with urban schools, including growing demographic diversity and financial stress. In addition, suburban educators increasingly work in the kind of regulatory environment that has long characterized urban schools, operations and influenced their culture.

We know from research on urban schools that an impersonal, bureaucratic school culture undercuts many of the teaching attitudes and behaviors that draw on student strengths (Weiner, 2000). This bureaucratic culture fosters the pervasive assumption that when students misbehave or achieve poorly, they must be "fixed" because the problem inheres in the students or their families, not in the social ecology of the school, grade, or classroom.

The deficit paradigm that is so deeply embedded in urban schools mirrors a proclivity in national debates about a range of problems. For example, in response to the epidemic of obesity in our youth, public debate and proposed solutions frequently focus on individual behavior and character: If individuals would just say no to french fries or make healthy meals for their children, we could solve the crisis. Of course, many of us would do well to spurn the temptations that await us in supermarket aisles and restaurants. But the social causes of childhood obesity are at least as important as individual failings and choices. Advertising aimed at children, the abundance of cheap fast food, and such school policies as eliminating recess to make time for more literacy and math instruction are powerful influences. A narrow focus on individual weaknesses obscures the importance of these other, more potent, factors.

School practices and assumptions emerging from the deficit paradigm often hide student and teacher abilities. These assumptions are especially powerful because they are unspoken. We overlook our taken-for-granted ideas and practices to an extraordinary degree.

Uncovering Tacit Assumptions and Practices

The graduate program that I coordinate at New Jersey City University provides university-based professional development focusing on teaching and learning in urban schools. The program guides teachers in uncovering, contextualizing, and challenging tacit assumptions about students' weaknesses. Most of the younger teachers are stunned when we question the pervasive diagnoses of student problems. They assume that a "hyperactive" 1st grader requires medication and placement in special education. We challenge them to think about how this explanation makes the teacher a mere referral agent and locates responsibility for student achievement beyond the teachers reach.

School practices and assumptions emerging from the deficit paradigm often hide student and teacher abilities.

In our discussions, I describe the racially segregated elementary school I attended in Wilmington, Delaware, where as a 1st grader I had recess three times a day (10:00 A.M., after lunch, and 2:00 P.M.) and a nap after lunch. Back then, "heterogeneity" consisted of mixing children of upwardly-mobile Jewish, Protestant, and Catholic European-American families. None of the children had disabilities. My blind sister could not attend the school that her siblings attended, and neither could the African American children who lived 10 blocks away.

Looking at this historical context, teachers in our graduate program can readily identify some outdated assumptions and practices, such as legal segregation and the exclusion of students with disabilities. Other changes in assumptions are more difficult for them to see at first. For example, could the definition of "hyperactivity" that their schools take for granted have something to do with today's decreased opportunities for physical activity and rest during the school day?

In one of our online courses, teachers read and analyze research about critical issues in urban education. Most of the teachers work in small suburban or rural districts far away from the university's urban campus. As a result of our readings and discussions they see, often for the first time, that problems they have considered "urban" are present—but hidden—in their communities and schools. For example, one reading helps teachers examine the disproportionate placement of African American males in special education (Civil Rights Project, 2002), and the teachers look at data for their own schools. Almost without exception, the teachers are surprised to discover that their school's special education placements conform to the skewed demographics we see across the United States.

Disrupting the Deficit Paradigm

Educators may become discouraged when they come face-to-face with hitherto unquestioned practices and conditions because they know that they cannot eliminate these practices on their own. What we can all do, however, is acknowledge deficit explanations and examine them critically. Invariably this illuminates possibilities that have eluded us, including strategies that focus on student strengths. In our graduate program, teachers have designed and carried out interventions in their classrooms that have proven remarkably effective in disrupting the deficit paradigm.

Reframing Hyperactivity

One project required teachers to address chronic behavior problems that they had been unable to solve. Using a strategy I have found effective in unearthing and challenging deficit paradigm explanations (Weiner, 2003), I guided the teachers in working to reframe the problem behavior of a student or colleague. As Molnar and Lindquist (1989) explain, the refraining process has four steps:

1. Describe the problem behavior in neutral, observable terms.
2. Identify positive characteristics or contributions the individual makes. This part of the process is often challenging because we are so frustrated and angry that we cannot see the individual's strengths.
3. Create a new, positive perspective on the individual—a frame that you can articulate in a short sentence.
4. State the new frame to the person and act on it. Do not refer back to the previous frame.

Deven, a young white teacher working in a predominantly black school, chose to apply the reframing strategy with April, a student in her kindergarten class. April would not sit still and frequently wandered around during whole-class instruction, disturbing other students. Deven considered April a strong candidate for medication for hyperactivity and referral to special education. In her report, Deven described her original frame—her understanding of April's behavior:

> I spoke with her and modeled the correct way to act. . . . When her misbehavior continued, I believed April was looking for attention. I attempted to ignore her behavior, which made the situation worse. . . . As I became more and more frustrated, I felt April was directly disobeying my instructions, distracting the class, and undermining my lessons.

With support from other teachers in the course, Deven developed and acted on a new explanation of April's behavior:

> I told April that I understood that she had a lot of energy, and that was great! I let her know that lots of people need to move around in order to learn. It was just another thing that made her special. . . . I asked that April please do her exercises on the carpet or by the classroom library. I let her know that whenever she felt she was ready, she could return to the group. I also predicted a relapse. I said that I knew she might forget to move to the carpet or library to do her exercises, but that was OK and I would remind her with our special sign—touching the tip of my nose. She seemed a little surprised, but she said she understood.

Reporting on the results of her intervention, Deven commented,

> The reframing changed my negative, critical altitude toward April's behavior to a positive, supportive outlook. As a result, the exercises and movement no longer upset or distracted me. Once I became comfortable with the reframing, April's behavior really improved. Now, April automatically moves to the carpet or library to exercise. The other students don't seem to mind at all, and there is no more tattling. April is happier and more relaxed during whole-group instruction. My teaching assistant thought that this was a crazy idea. Neither one of us can get over the change. We are already planning to reframe several other behaviors.

Deven's new way of understanding April's behavior—that "lots of people need to move around in order to learn"—drew on Deven's previous knowledge of multiple intelligences. Although Deven had been able to access this previous knowledge in earlier conversations about April, she was unable to *apply* it without the push, from the assignment and her classmates, to reject her negative explanation for Aprils behavior.

An impersonal, bureaucratic school culture undercuts many of the teaching attitudes and behaviors that draw on student strengths.

Reframing Incivility

In another project, teachers applied ideas from Courtney Cazden's classic book *Classroom Discourse* (2001). Teachers identified a problem in achievement connected to discourse practices in their classrooms and designed instructional changes to address the problem. Their analysis of the problem and the changes they planned to make in their instruction were grounded in data they had collected about students' use of language, either through videotaping or audiotaping.

Veronica taught in one of New Jersey's poorest communities. For her project, she chose to address the problems she encountered with the class of 5th graders she met for homeroom and math. She wanted to alter the students' discourse to build a sense of community that would support academic work.

Hired to take over this class in March after the (unsuccessful) teacher had deserted it, Veronica felt overwhelmed. She could not implement her excellent ideas for lessons because students treated one another so disrespectfully, cursing and jeering at any perceived error. A student who answered a question incorrectly or stumbled over a word would he taunted as a "stupid ass." Those who followed instructions and did their work were ridiculed for behaving well.

Although Veronica is the daughter of Hispanic immigrants and is alert to the ways in which deficit paradigms can obscure student strengths, she was dismayed at her students' behavior. When she observed videotapes of her lessons, she was equally stunned at her own unfriendly tone of voice and her incessant nagging. She observed students' increasingly glazed looks as one scolding followed another. Veronica had taught a kindergarten literacy pull-out class in the same school, and in watching the videotape she became aware of her previously unrecognized assumption that older children should already know acceptable norms of behavior and speech.

The other teachers in our class reminded Veronica that her 5th graders had been *mis*educated about acceptable norms of conduct by the previous teacher's failure to clarify, support, and enforce appropriate behavior. I suggested that Veronica include role-playing exercises to help students experience and practice their new language skills. In a subsequent class meeting, Veronica reported delightedly that role-playing had become a highlight of homeroom, especially when normally polite students assumed the role of the person using inappropriate discourse and the usual offenders suddenly became well-mannered.

Changing the class ecology brought out the creativity and leadership of Veronica's most troublesome student, Tyrone. Tyrone proposed, created, and led his classmates in using a remarkably effective tool, which he called the *Helping Hand*—an illustration on a wall chart of a large hand whose fingers contained reminders of words and phrases that students should use. Tyrone foresaw, correctly, that students would need a helping hand when tempted to use familiar but inappropriate language. At this point, they could turn to the chart and find an acceptable substitute. For instance, instead of saying "you stupid," the Helping Hand reminded students to say "I see it differently." Tyrone's role in this venture helped him earn a new reputation, as a class leader and star student.

Teacher Strengths, Student Strengths

Although this discussion has focused so far on deficit thinking as it relates to students, the deficit paradigm actually takes two contradictory forms. The first variation casts *student and family* deficits as the cause of poor achievement. Teachers often find this version seductive because it locates responsibility outside their classrooms. The second variation presents *teacher characteristics and deficits* as the only factor that really counts in undermining student learning. Legislators and parents often find this explanation persuasive because it implies an uncomplicated solution: Fix the teachers we have or hire new and better individuals.

Unfortunately, most professional development, even when the training is aimed to arrest deficit thinking about students, is based on the teacher deficits variant. Like remedial programs for students, professional development programs "fix" teachers by identifying what they don't know or do and telling them how to do it. In my work with teachers in the New Jersey City University graduate program, I have found that both experienced and new teachers already know enough—after learning to challenge their deficit frameworks, scrutinizing qualitative data about their own practice, and working with other teachers who provide support as critical friends—to significantly improve student achievement.

Deven and April, Veronica and Tyrone taught one another. Their learning and growth were synergistic. Assumptions reinforced by school practices, traditions, and political and social conditions initially obscured both teacher and student strengths. Deven and Veronica are urban teachers, but their success in altering their classrooms to capitalize on these strengths has implications far beyond schools that serve primarily poor, minority, or urban students.

As social and political changes alter the face of public education, it becomes increasingly important that all educators scrutinize and challenge tacit assumptions. We can make powerful changes when we break through the pervasive influence of the deficit paradigm and recognize the untapped strengths of students and teachers.

References

Cazden, C. B. (2001). *Classroom discourse: The language of teaching and learning* (2nd ed.). Portsmouth, NH: Heinemann.

Civil Rights Project, Harvard University. (2002, June) *Racial inequity in special education. Executive summary for federal policy makers.* Available; www.civilrightsproject.harvard.edu/research/specialed/IDEA_paper02.php

Molnar, A., & Lindquist, B. (1989). *Changing problem behavior in schools.* San Francisco: Jossey-Bass.

Weiner, L. (2000). Research in the '90s; Implications for urban teacher preparation. *Review of Educational Research, 70,* 369–406.

Weiner, L. (2003). Why is classroom management so vexing to urban teachers? *Theory Into Practice, 42,* 305–312.

LOIS WEINER is Professor of Elementary and Secondary Education at New Jersey City University in Jersey City, New Jersey; lweiner@njcu.edu. She is author of *Urban Teaching: The Essentials,* (Teachers College Press, 2006) and a consultant to schools and districts on teacher development.

From *Educational Leadership,* September 2006, pp. 42–45. Reprinted by permission of the Association for Supervision and Curriculum Development.

The Culturally Responsive Teacher

To engage students from diverse cultural and linguistic backgrounds, we must see them as capable learners.

ANA MARÍA VILLEGAS AND TAMARA LUCAS

Belki Alvarez, a young girl one of us knows, arrived in New York from the Dominican Republic several years ago with her parents and two siblings. After a difficult start in the United States, both parents found jobs; their minimum-wage earnings were barely enough for a family of five to scrape by month to month. As the oldest child in the family, Belki soon had to assume caretaking responsibilities for her younger brother and sister. At only 8 years old, she was responsible for getting her siblings ready for school, taking them there each morning, bringing them back home at the end of the school day, and caring for them until her parents came home from work.

On weekends, she worked with her mother at the community street fair to make extra money for the family by selling products prepared at home. She astutely negotiated prices with customers and expertly handled financial transactions. Belki often spoke enthusiastically about having her own business in the future. She spoke Spanish fluently at home and in the community, and she often served as the English language translator for her parents.

Belki's teachers, however, did not know this competent, responsible, enthusiastic girl. They perceived her as lacking in language and math skills, having little initiative, and being generally disinterested in learning.

Such profound dissonance between her in-school and out-of-school experiences is not unique to Belki. Sadly, this is typical for an increasing number of students in U.S. schools today.

Over the past three decades, the racial, ethnic, and linguistic demographics of the K–12 student population in the United States have changed dramatically. In 1972, 22 percent of all students enrolled in elementary and secondary public schools were of racial/ethnic minority backgrounds (National Center for Education Statistics [NCES], 2002). By 2003, racial/ethnic minority students accounted for 41 percent of total enrollments in U.S. public schools. In six states and the District of Columbia, students of color are already in the majority (NCES, 2005). The immigrant student population has also grown significantly in the past 30 years. Currently, one in five students speaks a language other than English at home, and the majority of these students are learning English as a second language in school (Center on Education Policy, 2006).

A Framework and a Vision

Successfully teaching students from culturally and linguistically diverse backgrounds—especially students from historically marginalized groups—involves more than just applying specialized teaching techniques. It demands a new way of looking at teaching that is grounded in an understanding of the role of culture and language in learning. Six salient qualities (see Villegas & Lucas, 2002) can serve as a coherent framework for professional development initiatives in schools seeking to respond effectively to an increasingly diverse student population.

Understanding How Learners Construct Knowledge

Our conception of culturally and linguistically responsive teaching is grounded in constructivist views of learning (National Research Council, 2000). From this perspective, learners use their prior knowledge and beliefs to make sense of the new ideas and experiences they encounter in school. A central role of the culturally and linguistically responsive teacher is to support students' learning by helping them build bridges between what they already know about a topic and what they need to learn about it.

For example, Belki will learn more from a social studies unit on immigration if her teacher draws on her very real experience as a newcomer to the United States. The teacher might ask her and other immigrant students in the class to describe their experiences learning a new language and compare living in the United States to living in their native countries. The teacher could build on those narratives to introduce relevant concepts, such as factors that lead people to immigrate and phases in the immigration process. The teacher could invite immigrant parents to the class to share their experiences. By involving the students and their parents in these ways, the teacher would not only help students build bridges to learning but also strengthen the connections between home and school. If the teacher does not tap into the experiences of students in the class and instead teaches the unit by focusing solely on the experiences of earlier immigrant groups coming to the United States—such as the Germans and Irish—the material will be much less relevant and engaging.

Learning also involves questioning, interpreting, and analyzing ideas in the context of meaningful issues. With this in mind, an English teacher in a community in the U.S. Southwest that had a large Latino population designed a unit on immigration to the United States. The students were asked to write a letter to the editor of a local newspaper expressing their views on the topic. To write the letter, the students realized that they needed to understand the issues more deeply. So they summarized relevant newspaper articles and developed and administered a questionnaire in their neighborhoods to learn about the community's views on immigration. They debated in class the proposal to build a fence along the United States/Mexico border. Working in groups, they wrote letters to the editor and then assessed their drafts using a rubric that focused on grammar, clarity of position taken, and development of supporting arguments. After receiving the teacher's feedback, the students revised and sent their letters. The students were deeply engaged in a process that helped improve their writing skills.

In embracing constructivist views of learning, we do not mean to suggest that there is no place in schools for direct instruction, memorization, and basic skills instruction. When such transmission-oriented strategies predominate, however, their pedagogical value diminishes, much to the students' disadvantage. Such an approach to teaching does not give students opportunities to actively engage in learning and integrate new ideas and frameworks into their own ways of thinking. Therefore, students are less likely to learn to think critically, become creative problem solvers, and develop skills for working collaboratively—all qualities that are essential for success in life and work.

Learning About Students' Lives

To teach subject matter in meaningful ways and engage students in learning, teachers need to know about their students' lives. We are not suggesting that teachers learn generic information about specific cultural or social groups. Such thinking leads to stereotypes that do not apply to individual students.

Instead, teachers need to know something about their students' family makeup, immigration history, favorite activities, concerns, and strengths. Teachers should also be aware of their students' perceptions of the value of school knowledge, their experiences with the different subject matters in their everyday settings, and their prior knowledge of and experience with specific topics in the curriculum. For example, Belki's teachers would benefit from knowing that she and her family are immigrants, that she often serves as the English language translator for her parents, that she aspires to own a business some day, and that she expertly manages financial transactions at the weekend street fair.

Effective strategies for learning about students' lives outside school include conducting home visits, creating opportunities in the classroom for students to discuss their aspirations for the future, posing problems for students to solve and noting how each student goes about solving them, and talking with parents and other community members. For instance, Belki's teacher might have asked her to give examples of how she uses math outside school. The teacher could have learned even more by visiting the street fair. By observing her animated interactions with customers, the teacher would have seen that Belki is a fluent Spanish speaker with sophisticated negotiation skills and some important math skills.

The vast majority of teachers in the United States are white, middle class, and monolingual English speaking. In most cases, their lives differ profoundly from the lives of their students. Although information-gathering strategies are simple enough to develop, it is more challenging for teachers to learn how to interpret what they discover about students through their data gathering. To make productive instructional use of this information, teachers must possess two fundamental qualities: They must have sociocultural consciousness and hold affirming views toward diversity (Nieto, 1996).

Being Socioculturally Conscious

We define sociocultural consciousness as the awareness that a person's worldview is not universal but is profoundly influenced by life experiences, as mediated by a variety of factors, including race, ethnicity, gender, and social class. Teachers who lack sociocultural consciousness will unconsciously and inevitably rely on their own personal experiences to make sense of students' lives—an unreflective habit that often results in misinterpretations of those students' experiences and leads to miscommunication. For example, students from cultures with a less individualistic and more collectivist worldview than that of mainstream U.S. culture may be overlooked in class and assumed to be less capable than their mainstream peers because, in general, they do not seek individual attention and praise.

Teachers need to know something about their students' family makeup, immigration history, favorite activities, concerns, and strengths.

To develop sociocultural consciousness, teachers need to look beyond individual students and families to understand inequities in society. In all social systems, some positions are accorded greater status than others, and such status differentiation gives rise to differential access to power. Teachers need to be aware of the role that schools play in both perpetuating and challenging those inequities. Professional development carried out in groups and guided by an experienced facilitator who is knowledgeable about multicultural issues can be instructive. Activities might involve reading about the differential distribution of wealth and income in the United States or reflecting on the well-documented fact that a person's social class is the best predictor of academic success and future social standing

(Natriello, McDill, & Pallas, 1990). To see the powerful connections between social and education inequities, participants could read *The Shame of the Nation: The Restoration of Apartheid Schooling in America,* by Jonathan Kozol (2006). By reading and discussing accounts of successful teaching and learning in diverse settings (see Garcia, 1999; Ladson-Billings, 1994; Nieto & Rolón, 1997), teachers can develop a vision of how schools can challenge such inequities.

Holding Affirming Views About Diversity

Unfortunately, evidence suggests that many teachers see students from socially subordinated groups from a deficit perspective (Nieto, 1996). Lacking faith in the students' ability to achieve, these teachers are more likely to have low academic expectations for the students and ultimately treat them in ways that stifle their learning. They are more apt to use drill, practice, and rote-learning activities at the expense of more challenging work that demands the use of higher-order thinking skills. They are also less likely to call on the students in class, give them sufficient wait time to respond thoughtfully to questions, or probe incomplete answers for clarity.

Teaching is an ethical activity, and teachers have an ethical obligation to help all students learn.

By contrast, teachers who see students from an affirming perspective and truly respect cultural differences are more apt to believe that students from nondominant groups are capable learners, even when these students enter school with ways of thinking, talking, and behaving that differ from the dominant cultural norms. Teachers who hold these affirming views about diversity will convey this confidence by providing students with an intellectually rigorous curriculum, teaching students strategies for monitoring their own learning, setting high performance standards and consistently holding students accountable to those standards, and building on the individual and cultural resources that students bring to school. For example, instead of setting out to "correct" students' language through the use of decontextualized drill and worksheet activities, the English teacher who asked her students to write to the newspaper editor helped her students develop their writing skills by involving them in purposeful and intellectually stimulating tasks.

Using Appropriate Instructional Strategies

Teachers can activate students' prior knowledge by asking them to discuss what they know about a given topic, as Belki's teacher could have done by having the immigrant students in the class share their personal experiences with immigration. Teachers can embed new ideas and skills in projects that are meaningful to the students, as the English teacher who helped students improve their writing skills through researching immigration did.

Teachers can also give English language learners access to the curriculum by drawing on the student's native language resources. They can provide students who are literate in their native language with material to read in that language to help them build background knowledge for specific content. They can encourage students to use bilingual dictionaries. They can prepare study guides for instructional units that define relevant vocabulary and outline key concepts in English, using simplified language. They can also use more visual cues and graphic organizers and incorporate more hands-on activities into their lessons.

Using pertinent examples and analogies from students' lives is another instructional strategy that helps students build bridges to learning. For example, one of us recently observed a teacher introducing the concept of rhythm in poetry by having students analyze the rhythm in a well-known hip-hop recording and then engaging the students in a similar analysis of a poem by Robert Frost. In U.S. history classes, teachers can help engage students from historically marginalized groups by having them examine the curriculum to determine whose perspectives are and are not presented. This would work well, for example, with a textbook treatment of slavery. If the students determine through an analysis of the text that they are learning little about the real experiences of slaves, they can read one of the many published slave narratives to deepen their understanding. As these examples suggest, the job of the culturally and linguistically responsive teacher involves engaging all students in learning for understanding.

Advocating for All Students

Numerous practices embedded in the fabric of everyday schooling put students from nonmainstream groups at a disadvantage. These include a school culture of low expectations for students from low-status groups, inadequate general and multicultural learning materials, large class sizes, assignment of the least-experienced teachers to classes in which students need the most help, insensitivity toward cultural differences, questionable testing practices, and a curriculum that does not reflect diverse student perspectives.

To continue to move toward greater cultural and linguistic responsiveness in schools, teachers must see themselves as part of a community of educators working to make schools more equitable for all students. Teaching is an ethical activity, and teachers have an ethical obligation to help all students learn. To meet this obligation, teachers need to serve as advocates for their students, especially those who have been traditionally marginalized in schools.

For example, teachers involved in school- or district-level textbook review committees could ensure that selected textbooks and supplemental materials appropriately reflect the diversity of experiences and perspectives in the student population. Those who have input into the design of professional development activities could identify specific areas in which the faculty might need professional growth. Topics might include how to implement strategies for learning about students' lives, become socioculturally conscious, build on students' interests outside school to advance curriculum goals, and tap community resources in teaching. Responsive classroom teachers could also request common planning time with the English as a second language teacher to coordinate instruction in ways that maximize content learning for their English language learners.

Just Imagine

Certainly, individual teachers can enhance their success with students from diverse backgrounds by working on their own to cultivate these qualities of responsive teaching. However, the framework that we have presented here will have the greatest effect on a school if teachers and school leaders develop a shared vision of the culturally and linguistically responsive teacher.

Teachers need to serve as advocates for their students.

Imagine Belki Alvarez's school life if her teachers had explored these six qualities and shared ideas for applying them in their teaching. They could have capitalized on her entrepreneurial skills to help her learn mathematical concepts. They would have seen her as a capable learner and understood the relevance of her life experiences for her school learning. They might have tapped her experience as the English translator for her family by having her translate for other Spanish-speaking students in the class who spoke minimal English. Approaching a student's education in these culturally and linguistically responsive ways—rather than emphasizing deficits—has the potential to truly engage all students in learning, both in school and beyond.

References

Center on Education Policy. (2006). *A public education primer: Basic (and sometimes surprising) facts about the U.S. education system.* Washington, DC: Author.

Garcia, E. E. (1999). *Student cultural diversity: Understanding and meeting the challenge.* Boston: Houghton Mifflin.

Kozol, J. (2006). *The shame of the nation: The restoration of apartheid schooling in America.* New York: Three Rivers Press.

Ladson-Billings, G. (1994). *The dreamkeepers: Successful teachers of African American children.* San Francisco: Jossey-Bass.

National Center for Education Statistics. (2002). *Digest for education statistics tables and figures.* Washington, DC: U.S. Government Printing Office. Available: http://nces.ed.gov/programs/digest/d02/dt066.asp

National Center for Education Statistics. (2005). *Digest for education statistics tables and figures.* Washington, DC: U.S. Government Printing Office. Available: http://nces.edu.gov/programs/d05/tables/dt05_038.asp

National Research Council. (2000). *How people learn.* Washington, DC: National Academies Press.

Natriello, G., McDill, E. L., & Pallas, A. M. (1990). *Schooling disadvantaged children: Racing against catastrophe.* New York: Teachers College Press.

Nieto, S. (1996). *Affirming diversity: The sociopolitical context of education.* White Plains, NY: Longman.

Nieto, S., & Rolón, C. (1997). Preparation and professional development of teachers: A perspective from two Latinas. In J. J. Irvine (Ed.), *Critical knowledge for diverse teachers and learners* (pp. 89–123). Washington, DC: American Association of Colleges for Teacher Education.

Villegas, A. M., & Lucas, T. (2002). *Educating culturally responsive teachers: A coherent approach.* Albany, NY: SUNY Press.

Ana María Villegas (villegasa@mail.montclair.edu) is Professor of Curriculum and Instruction. **Tamara Lucas** (lucast@mail.montclair.edu) is Associate Dean of the College of Education and Human Services and Professor of Educational Foundations at Montclair State University, Montclair, New Jersey.

Boys and Girls Together

A Case for Creating Gender-Friendly Middle School Classrooms

David Kommer

Are Boys and Girls Really Different?

Close your eyes and picture an average grade school class. Watch the boys and girls as they learn, interact, and deal with problems. Do they look alike in your mind's eye? Do they learn the same way? Do they interact with you and with one another similarly? Do they solve problems—both relationship and academic—in the same ways? Not likely. No, there appears to be a very real difference between boys and girls.

What is the nature of that difference, and from where does it come? Moreover, if there is such a striking difference, are there things we should be doing in the classroom to accommodate for these differences? These are all significant questions that might affect the academic growth of our students.

As young people move into adolescence, they begin to explore gender roles. Finding their way through this potential minefield is complicated and challenging for middle school students. The process of determining the variations in masculinity and femininity is largely a social function, not a biological one (Rice and Dolgin 2002). What it means to be a man, and what it means to be a woman, are communicated to children by all the adults in a child's life, including teachers.

"Peers may play a particularly important role in the development of children's gender identities" (Rice and Dolgin 2002, 195). Boys and girls create very distinct cultures; when they are in same-gender groups they act and play very differently. Girls are talkative and cooperative, boys are competitive and physical (Rice and Dolgin). Teachers need to understand these differences and be purposeful in the treatment of each so as to send the healthiest messages to adolescents.

Looking closely at middle schools, two questions surface: Are boys and girls treated differently from one another? *should* boys and girls be treated differently?

In 1992, the American Association of University Women (AAUW) published a groundbreaking study about how schools were not meeting the needs of young girls. Their schools shortchanged girls in many ways: when questioned in class, girls were less likely to receive a prompt to clarify thinking if they answered incorrectly; boys were more regularly called on, and if not, they were just as likely to shout out an answer, leaving girls to sit quietly; and girls were not encouraged to take advanced math and science classes (AAUW 1992). Perhaps not surprisingly, then, in their middle school years, girls stopped being successful in math and science.

A large concern that must be addressed by middle level educators is the decrease in confidence that girls experience throughout middle school. One recent study shows that just prior to their entry into pre-adolescence, 60 percent of girls had positive feelings about themselves and their ability. Only 29 percent of high school girls felt the same confidence. (This compares with 67 percent of young boys feeling confident, and 46 percent of high school-aged boys having the same confidence.) Confidence fell during middle school (Santrock 2001). I am not suggesting that there is something toxic about middle school, but I am suggesting that while students are on our watch, we can and must do better.

The AAUW (1992) study focused our attention on the issue of educational equity. It was difficult to argue with the findings, and teachers all over the country began to reevaluate their teaching in light of the study. Several years later, the AAUW found that significant progress was made, as evidenced by gains in girls' success in math and science (AAUW 1998). Nevertheless, the story is not yet finished, for it appears now the boys were also often the victims of our educational system. Consider the following gender questions:

1. Who is more likely to drop out of high school?
2. Who is more likely to be sent to the principal's office for a disciplinary referral?
3. Who is more likely to be suspended or expelled?
4. Who is more likely to be identified as a student needing special education?
5. Who is more likely to need reading intervention?

The answer to all of the above questions is "boys" (Taylor and Lorimer 2003). Clearly, the educational system is discouraging some of them. However, even that conclusion is too simple;

this is not a problem that can be solved with a quick fix. Looking again at the questions above, you might also add, "Not all boys are being discouraged/exhibiting behaviors problems." And you would be correct: some girls also show these behaviors and problems. The evidence seems to show that, although there are differences in general, it is not possible to put all the boys on one side and all the girls on the other. In fact, there seems to be some type of spectrum with "maleness" on one end and "femaleness" on the other. Everyone exists somewhere in the spectrum, and generally boys cluster toward one end, and girls toward the other. This, also has ramifications for classrooms. But perhaps there is an effective way to address gender differences.

So what do we do? The first thing is to become aware of the differences between genders. Once these differences are explained and accepted, educators must be proactive in the way boys and girls are treated in schools. This is not a call for separate schools, for we do not live in a gender-segregated world. Indeed, there are distinct advantages to educating boys and girls together appropriately, for in doing so, each gender will begin to see how the other things, feels, responds, and reacts. Such understanding is in itself a major goal for gender-friendly classrooms.

We should also consider the nature of the differences between boys and girls. The question of nature versus nurture is always an intriguing one, but is similarly enigmatic as the one about the chicken and the egg. Most psychologists agree that gender differences may be a function of biological forces, but that they are also shaped by the environments in which our children grow up (Rice and Dolgin 2002). When studying this it is helpful to observe some of the factors and looking more closely at each.

Brain Theory

As you scan the room in which students are supposed to be reading silently, you see that most of the girls are engaged with their books. Because the reading is student selected, the girls have chosen the books that focus on relationships. The boys seem to be more easily distractible and are not, as a rule, focusing their full attention on the text. Some read for a while, then gaze about the room. If they are reading, they are more likely to have selected action books or sports magazines.

Boys and girls have slightly different brain chemistry that may cause each to think differently. While not yet conclusive, research has uncovered many intriguing possibilities that might provide some explanations.

In addition to having slightly different chemistry, the structure of the male and female brain is actually different (Gurian 2001; Sax 2005; Sousa 2001). As most of us have learned, girls mature more quickly than boys, but what does this mean exactly? Gurian suggests that as the individual grows there is an increase in myelin, a coating that transmits electrical impulses through the nervous system. This accumulating coat of myelin occurs earlier in females.

The most striking difference, Gurian and others suggest, is the system of nerves, the corpus callosum, which connect the right and left hemispheres of the brain. In females this structure is, on average, 20 percent larger than it is in males (Gurian, 2001; Sousa 2001; Walsh 2004). Is this why females seem to be able to use both sides of the brain in processing information and are able to multitask more efficiently than males?

Studies on boys and girls also point out some interesting differences in both hearing and seeing (Sax 2005). Studies reported by Sax indicate that girls hear at different levels—in effect, better—than boys. Other studies show that girls are able to read facial expressions more astutely than boys, and this difference is related to a different chemistry in the eye and corresponding receptor in the brain (Sax).

Girls "tend to take in more sensory data than boys" (Gurian 2001, 27). Boys are more likely to engage in physically risky behaviors as a result. Although the effects of testosterone on the adolescent brain spark some controversy, there seems to be wide acceptance of the fact that testosterone leads males into more aggressive and risky actions than estrogen does with girls (Walsh 2004). "Girls and boys assess risk differently, and they differ in their likelihood of engaging in risky behaviors" (Sax 2005, 41). Might there be ramifications for this in the classroom? You bet. Walsh suggests that the initial burst of hormones that come earlier for girls gives their brains a head start in developing the prefrontal cortex, or rational part or the brain. This allows girls to engage in more complex rational thought than boys. By the end of adolescence, boys have caught up with girls.

Girls tend to be less hemisphere dominant than boys, who seem to be largely right hemisphere dominant. As a result, boys are better at spatial tasks, which gives them an advantage in areas such as mathematics, graphs, and maps. Girls seem to use both sides, of the brain and tend to be better at literacy-related activities (Gurian and Stevens 2004; Sax 2005).

In addition to the structural differences, there may be differences caused by the hormones that each gender receives. While this is somewhat more controversial, there is some evidence that the progesterone that girls receive is a bonding hormone, and the testosterone of boys is much more aggressive (Gurian 2001; Sax 2005). It appears that boys receive about a half-dozen spikes of testosterone each day: these spikes may result in boys becoming more anxious, moody, and even aggressive. Estrogen and progesterone, the female hormones, rise and fall throughout the female cycle. Girls experience an increase in mood swings, as well, but they tend to be spread over time rather than the intense change that boys experience. Interestingly, there is evidence that during these hormone infusions in girls, they actually have an increased academic upsurge (Gurian 2001). In short, they are smarter during this peak.

There are many more aspects to this emerging information on brain development and function. However, it should also be noted that although much of what we are learning about the brain is intriguing and may offer keys to helping both genders become more academically successful, perhaps there are other reasons that boys and girls are different.

Social Differences

As the school day begins, students are all congregated in class. They are not really moving to their workplaces as you would like, but are engaged with each other, seemingly oblivious to the fact that you have an educational agenda ready. So what is their agenda, you wonder? The girls all seem to be huddled in groups whispering and looking about to see who might be paying attention to them. The boys are much more physically active as four boys play a game of trying to slap the other's hand before the other moves it away. Others are playing "basketball" with clean sheets of paper rolled up and tossed at the wastebasket.

Perhaps the issue does not lie in nature, but in nurture—that is, in the way we socialize our young people. "Society prescribes how a male ought to look and behave, what type of personality he ought to have, and what roles he should perform" (Rice and Dolgin, 2002, 193). Girls receive these messages equally as strongly. All adolescents receive messages from adults as they grow; from teachers who encourage and discourage in word and deed; from signals sent by peers; and, from the media that also contribute to their developing gender identification.

Boys seem to present the most problems in the academic setting. They often are detached from the learning objective and would prefer to goof off—or so it seems. Why do boys seem ready to respond to any problem by either silence or lashing out? In *Raising Cain: Protecting the Emotional Lives of Boys*, Kindlon and Thompson (2000) argue that boys have been miseducated. Boys get very conflicting messages from everyone: parents, peers, teachers, coaches, and the media. Boys do, in fact, feel they are told not to show emotions; they are told, "Big boys don't cry." And when they hurt, they are told to walk it off. Boys receive strong message that they must be in control and that any show of emotion is unacceptable, with the result that boys are trying to put their feelings someplace where they will not be betrayed by their own emotions.

What we are beginning to see is that boys, like girls, have many of the same feelings of inadequacy. Boys, however, seem ill-prepared to deal with these feelings, and often, the response from those who might guide them is that boys should "suck it up." Pollack refers to this as "boy code" which society teaches all young males as they grow up (1998). Indeed, the feeling that boys can handle the slings and arrows of adolescence with resilience and fortitude is a myth that has come to hurt boys. Given both lack of an emotional vocabulary and permission to deal with their feelings, boys have difficulty understanding and controling their emotions. The result is that we see both stoic and self-destructive behaviors (Kindlon and Thompson 2001; Pollack).

Girls also encounter a constant stream of messages, ones that have a strong influence on the way they succeed in school, deal with others, and feel about themselves as people of worth. As educators we must be mindful of these messages and head off the negative ones as much as we can.

In *Reviving Ophelia: Saving the Selves of Adolescent Girls*, Pipher (1994) relates how young girls have an almost effervescent quality and a feeling that they can do anything. Somewhere in early adolescence, this buoyancy begins to erode. Is it the demands that girls begin to fit into the roles our society has carved for them that extinguishes that exuberance? Those demands are powerful influences.

Girls begin to judge themselves relative to how they are perceived by the opposite gender. In the attempt to become what they feel others expect them to be, girls quickly lose their own. They hide their true selves to their friends and family (Pipher 1994; Powell 2004). Girls are "sugar and spice and everything nice." But during adolescence, this message is lost in a bewildering array of swirling images. They must "[b]e beautiful, but beauty is only skin deep. Be sexy, but not sexual. Be honest, but don't hurt anyone's feelings. Be independent, but be nice. Be smart, but not so smart that you threaten boys" (Pipher, 35–36).

Most girls like being at school, but there is strong evidence that, as a social institution, schools can damage girls at the same time that they educate them (Sax 2005). One reason might be that girls recognize that schools can be male oriented and male dominated; the books they read are most frequently written by men; they know the hierarchy of the school district is dominated by men; science classes frequently focus on male achievements; and math is presented as a male domain. Although our schools are becoming more aware of the sexist nature of education, there is still a great deal to do (AAUW 1998; Pipher 1994).

As a social institution, schools can do a great deal to educate both boys and girls about the messages they receive everyday. For example, media literacy should be taught in all schools, so the culture of appearance is laid bare for all to see. Also, sexual harassment must be eliminated from school hallways and classrooms. Teachers need to be trained in gender issues so they can recognize the features that are detrimental to boys, girls or both genders.

Making Classrooms Appropriate for Both Genders

The students are all in groups and they have projects each group has selected. You have carefully arranged the groups to allow for as much diversity as you can, and you told the students that is why they are placed that way. Within each project are a number of tasks which use several multiple intelligence strategies and learning preferences. It is your hope that each student can contribute to this project using his or her strength.

The goal is not to treat boys and girls equally, but to create equity by purposefully addressing the particular needs of each gender. If you believe that education causes the brain to develop and change, then there are things we can do to offset the gender influences whether they are biological or sociological

(Sousa 2001). In the process, we can encourage students to develop more sensitivity and greater academic character than we are currently seeing. Our goal is not to try to make boys and girls the same; we tried that several decades ago. We might have more success if we teach boys and girls to respond to each other as people (Santock 2001).

Creating a gender-friendly classroom does not mean that you create gender-specific activities, divide your classroom, or even insist on single-sex classes. Remembering that everyone lives in a bigendered world makes it necessary to teach your students ways to be successful in that world. Students should at some times have an opportunity to work in a gender-matched activity, while at other times they should learn to function in a more typical gender-mismatched one. This allows students to experience instructional times that are more comfortable for students when the activities are matched to their nature. But they also learn to function outside that comfort area when they are in a mismatched situation, and thus strengthen weaker areas.

For teachers the imperative is to learn about the differences in gender. Teachers need to accept that learning occurs differently for each gender, and to measure out activities and experiences that favor one some of the time, and the other some of the time. Keep in mind that although some girls may be more linguistically advanced than boys, some boys are just as advanced, although some boys manipulate objects well and see patterns better than girls, some girls are headed toward engineering school. So, to teach only one way for each gender would do a disservice to the boys and girls who do not fit the stereotype.

When teachers plan learning experiences that favor one gender, they are also doing a great thing for the other. For as boys see girls appropriately modeling relationship behaviors, the boys learn how to be more sensitive and open. Likewise, when girls see the appropriate use of assertiveness that boys learn early, the girls see that this can be used to their advantage as well.

Students appreciate knowing the reasons for classroom activities. Teach them the differences between genders and explain why you teach things a certain way (Casky and Ruben 2003). It has amazed me over the last several decades as we learn more about the brain how much we keep from our students. Teachers understand Bloom's Taxonomy, Gardner's Multiple Intelligences, and other theories, but do not let the students in on the secret. Teaching young adolescents about the brain and brain chemistry helps them through these confusing times.

Keep the parents of your students in the information loop as well. By educating them about these differences, they can support your activities at home. This entire concept would make a great parent education evening sponsored by a team.

Begin exploring various gender-friendly strategies in your classrooms. Maintain a balance between competitive and cooperative activities, use gender as a consideration when you regroup, provide movement and energy release activities, build in character education lessons, call on students equally, be aware that some content may be intimidating to one gender or the other, use graphic organizers, provide effective notetaking strategies, provide gender role models, teach students how to be media literate, and provide a positive environment that is gender neutral—these are all ways to make your classroom gender friendly.

Conclusion

In the past decade or so, much progress has been made in understanding the human brain, both physiologically and environmentally. We are now beginning to see that there may even be gender implications in the way the brain receives and uses information. These differences have implications for teachers striving to make learning more effective and efficient for students.

Whether the differences are genetic, or social, or both is not as important to us as the fact that boys and girls do learn in different ways. The quest is not to create classrooms that focus on one or the other gender. Instead, it is to purposefully structure our classroom so that some activities favor one gender's learning style and some favor the other's. Specifically, it is critical that teachers know the differences and structure the learning environment so that the students work sometimes reinforces individuals' stronger area, and sometimes strengthens a weaker one.

We can use this new and exciting information to make students more academically successful and to make classrooms more gender-friendly.

References

AAUW. 1992. *How schools shortchange girls.* New York: American Association of University Women.

_____. 1998. *Gender gaps: Where schools still fail our children.* New York: American Association of University Women.

Caskey, M. M., and B. Ruben. (2003). Awakening adolescent brains. *Middle Matters* 12 (1): 4–5.

Gurian, M. 2001. *Boys and girls learn differently! A guide for teachers and parents.* San Francisco: Jossey-Bass.

Gurian, M., and A. C. Ballew. 2003. *The boys and girls learn differently action guide for teachers.* San Francisco: Jossey-Bass.

Gurian, M., and K. Stevens. 2004. With boys and girls in mind. *Educational Leadership* (62)3:21–26.

Kindlon, D., and M. Thompson. 2000. *Raising Cain: Protecting the emotional life of boys.* New York: Ballantine.

Pipher, M. 1994. *Reviving Ophelia: Saving the selves of adolescent girls.* New York: Ballantine.

Pollack, W. 1998. *Real boys: Rescuing our sons from the myths of boyhood.* New York: Random House.

Powell, K. C. 2004. Developmental psychology of adolescent girls: Conflicts and identity issues. *Education* 125 (1):77–87.

Rice, F. P., and K. G. Dolgin. 2002. *The adolescent: Development, relationships and culture*. 10th ed. Boston: Allyn and Bacon.

Santrock, J. W. 2001. *Adolescence*. 8th ed. Boston. McGraw-Hill.

Sax, L. 2005. *Why gender matters: What parents and teachers need to know about the emerging science of sex differences*. New York: Doubleday.

Sousa, D. A. 2001. *How the brain learns*. 2nd ed. Thousand Oaks, CA: Corwin Press.

Taylor, D., and M. Lorimer. 2003. Helping boys succeed: Which research-based strategies curb negative trends now facing boys? *Educational Leadership* 60 (4):68–70.

Walsh, D. 2004. *Why do they act that way?* New York: Free Press.

David Kommer is an associate professor at Ashland University.

Learning and Gender

By paying attention to the differences between boys and girls, schools can gain new perspectives on teaching all children.

MICHAEL GURIAN

On the day your district administrators look at test scores, grades, and discipline referrals with gender in mind, some stunning patterns quickly will emerge.

Girls, they might find, are behind boys in elementary school math or science scores. They'll find high school girls statistically behind boys in SAT scores. They might find, upon deeper review, that some girls have learning disabilities that are going undiagnosed.

Boys, they'll probably notice, make up 80 to 90 percent of the district's discipline referrals, 70 percent of learning disabled children, and at least two-thirds of the children on behavioral medication. They'll probably find that boys earn two-thirds of the Ds and Fs in the district, but less than half the As. On statewide standardized test scores, they'll probably notice boys behind girls in general. They may be shocked to see how far behind the boys are in literacy skills; nationally, the average is a year and a half.

The moment an administrator sees the disparity of achievement between boys and girls can be liberating. Caring about children's education can now include caring about boys and girls specifically. New training programs and resources for teachers and school districts are opening cash-strapped school boards' eyes, not just to issues girls and boys face but also to ways of addressing gender differences in test scores, discipline referrals, and grades.

In the Edina School District, outside Minneapolis, Superintendent Ken Dragseth and district staff implemented a gender initiative that has helped close achievement gaps and improve overall education for students. In 2002, Dragseth and his staff analyzed district achievement data. They found that girls were doing much better than boys on most academic indicators, showing that they needed to address this achievement gap. They discovered areas of need for girls as well.

Edina officials decided to work on gaining greater knowledge on how boys and girls learn differently. Over the last three years, the district has seen qualitative and quantitative improvement in student performance.

Dragseth says that the gender-specific techniques and gender-friendly instructional theory he and his staff learned at the Gurian Institute helped the district significantly improve student achievement. For example, he says, they have seen higher seventh- and 10th-grade state reading and math mean scores for both boys and girls.

"We have also found that teacher- and parent-heightened awareness of gender differences in learning styles and appropriate strategies has been well received by students themselves," he says.

Brain Research

Gender training and resources used by Edina and other districts rely on information gained from PET, MRI, and other brain scans. This brain-based approach to gender was conceived in the early 1990s when it became clear that teachers were leaving college, graduate school, and teacher certification programs without training in how boys and girls learn differently. Educational culture was struggling to serve the needs of children—the needs of girls were most publicly discussed in the early 1990s—without complete knowledge of the children themselves.

When I wrote *The Wonder of Boys* in 1996, I hoped to bring a brain-based approach to gender issues into a wider public dialogue. In 1998, I joined the Missouri Center for Safe Schools and the University of Missouri-Kansas City in developing a two-year program to academically test the links among brain science, gender, and teacher education.

In six school districts in Missouri, teachers and staff integrated information from various fields and technologies and developed a number of strategies for teaching boys and girls. Gender disparities in achievement began to disappear in these districts. After one year, the pilot elementary school in the St. Joseph School District finished among the top five in the district after testing at the bottom previously. Discipline referrals diminished as well. In Kansas City's Hickman Mills School District, discipline referrals were cut by 35 percent within six months.

In the five years following the Missouri pilot program, more than 20,000 teachers in 800 schools and districts have received training in how boys and girls learn differently. More and more teachers are using this knowledge in the classroom.

Increasingly, universities and teacher certification programs are training young teachers in the learning differences between boys and girls.

Different Learning Styles

As with so many things of value in life, a teacher's innovations on behalf of children begins with an epiphany. A fourth-grade teacher recently told me, "When I saw the brain scans and thought about my class, I just went 'aha.' So much made sense now. The boys and their fidgeting; the girls and their chatting; the girls organizing their binders colorfully; the boys tapping their pencils; the girls writing more words in their essays than the boys; even the way the boys end up in the principal's office so much more frequently than the girls. We were all told long ago that every child should be taught as an individual, so gender didn't matter—but it really matters! Knowing about it has completely changed the way I teach, and the success my students are having."

On your way home this afternoon, stop by your local elementary school and see some of these differences for yourself. Walk down the hallway and find a classroom in which the teacher displays students' written work. Stand for a moment and look at the stories.

With all exceptions noted, you will probably find that the girls on average write:

- More words than the boys,
- Include more complex sensory details like color and texture, and
- Add more emotive and feeling details ("Judy said she liked him" "Timmy frowned").

If you could look with X-ray glasses into the brains of the boys and girls who wrote those stories, you would see:

- More blood flow in the verbal centers (in the cerebral cortex) of the girls' brains;
- More neural connections between the verbal centers and emotive centers in the limbic systems of the girls' brains; and
- More blood flow in sensorial centers (for instance in the occipital lobe), with more linkage between those centers and the verbal centers in the girls' brains.

A Visual Link to Learning

My example of the differences in boys and girls writing has a visual link. The female visual system (optical and neural) relies more greatly than the male on P cells. These are cells that connect color variety and other sensory activity to upper brain functioning. Boys rely more on M cells, which make spatial activity and graphic clues more quickly accessible.

This difference is linked significantly to a gender-different writing process for boys and girls. Boys tend to rely more on pictures and moving objects for word connections than girls. Girls tend to use more words that describe color and other fine, sensory information. Not surprisingly, gender gaps in writing are often "detail" gaps.

Girls use more sensorial detail than boys, receiving better grades in the process. However, when elementary school teachers let boys draw picture panels (with colored pens) during the brainstorming part of story or essay writing, the boys often graphically lay out what their story will be about. After that, they actually write their "word brainstorming" because they can refer to a graphic/spatial tool that stimulates their brains to greater success in writing.

Watch a fourth-grade classroom led by a teacher untrained in male/female brain differences. You'll probably see the teacher tell students to "take an hour to write your brainstorming for your paper." Five to 10 of the boys in a classroom of 30 kids will stare at the blank page.

But when teachers are trained in male/female brain differences, they tell students to draw first and write later. Students who need that strategy will end up writing much more detailed, organized, and just better papers.

The Rest State and Discipline Problems

Another area where you'll see gender differences is classroom behavior. Boys tend to fidget when they are bored. In a boy's brain, less of the "calming chemical," serotonin, moves through the pre-frontal cortex (the executive decision-maker in the brain). Boys thus are more likely to fidget, distract themselves and others, and become the objects of the teacher's reprimands.

Furthermore, the male brain naturally goes into a rest state many times per day and is not engaged in learning. Thus the boy "zones out," "drifts off," or "disappears from the lesson."

Sometimes he begins to tap his pencil loudly or pull the hair of the kid in front of him. He's not trying to cause trouble; in fact, he may be trying to wake up and avoid the rest state. Girls' brains do not go to this severe rest state; their cerebral cortices are always "on." They more rarely need to tap, fidget, or talk out of turn in order to stay focused.

Teachers can learn how to organize classrooms so that any boys (and girls) who need it can physically move while they are learning and keep their brains engaged. The rest state and boredom issues begin to dissolve. Discipline referrals decrease exponentially.

Brains on Math

Both boys and girls can do math and science, of course, but their brains perform these tasks differently. Girls fall behind boys in complex math skills when their lesson plans rely solely or mainly on abstract formulations specified in symbols on the blackboard.

However, when words, essay components, and active group work are added to the toolbox of teacher strategies, girls reach a parity of performance. Brain-based innovations to help girls in math and science over the last decade have brought more verbal elements into math and science teaching and testing: more words, more word-to-formula connections, and more essay answers in math tests.

The results in both math and science achievement have been stunning, with girls closing the math/science gap in many school districts.

Different Reactions to Competition

Because of neural and chemical differences in levels and processing of oxytocin, dopamine, testosterone, and estrogen, boys typically need to do some learning through competition. Girls, of course, are competitive too, but in a given day, they will spend less time in competitive learning and less time relating successfully to one another through "aggression-love"—the playful hitting and dissing by which boys show love.

The current emphasis on cooperative learning is a good thing, and the basis of a diversity-oriented educational culture. However, because they are not schooled in the nature of gender in the brain, teachers generally have deleted competitive learning, and thus de-emphasized a natural learning tool for many boys. We've also robbed girls of practice in the reality of human competitiveness.

When teachers receive training on how competitive learning can be integrated into classrooms (without chaos ensuing) they actually come to enjoy seeing both boys and girls challenge one another to learn better. Many girls who avoided leadership before now step forward to lead.

Learning to Their Potential

Our children are children, of course—but they are also girls and boys. This is something we all know as parents. When a school board makes the decision to focus on how the girls and boys are doing, all children gain. Students learn more, teachers are more productive, test scores and behavior improve, and parents and the community are happier.

A school board member in North Carolina told me, "Ten years ago, it was almost scary to talk about hard-wired gender differences. There were a lot of Title IX concerns, fears of reprisal. Now it's not scary, the brain research has caught up, and now it's so necessary. In fact, it just feels right."

It does indeed feel right to help boys and girls learn to their potential. Ten years ago, our girls were behind our boys in math and science; now, we see that our boys are far behind our girls in literacy. Neither of these gaps need exist anymore, as we engage in best practices on behalf of both boys and girls.

Michael Gurian, co-founder of the Gurian Institute, is author of 21 books, including *The Minds of Boys* (with Kathy Stevens), *The Wonder of Girls*, and *Boys and Girls Learn Differently* (with Patricia Henley and Terry Trueman).

UNIT 4

Learning and Instruction

Unit Selections

Key Points to Consider

- What are some principles for effective teaching that derive from constructivist and social psychological theories of learning?
- How would you go about adapting your instructional methods to teach students who are culturally and linguistically diverse?
- What is "critical thinking"? How does it differ from other types of students? Why is it important to encourage students to think critically?
- What teaching strategies could you use to promote student engagement in the classroom?
- How would you implement cooperative learning in your classrooms?
- What's the difference between *surface* and *deep* learning? How can you support deep learning in your classroom?
- How does project-based learning differ from other instructional strategies? What topics can you think of that could be taught using project-based learning activities?
- If you wanted to create a constructivist classroom in the subject area and/or grade in which you want to teach, what would the classroom look like? What would you emphasize, and how would your actions reflect constructivist principles and research on intelligence.
- How would technology be used in an effective manner with constructivist approaches?

Student Web Site

www.mhcls.com/online

Internet References

Further information regarding these Web sites may be found in this book's preface or online.

The Critical Thinking Community
http://criticalthinking.org

Education Week on the Web
http://www.edweek.org

Online Internet Institute
http://www.oii.org

Teachers Helping Teachers
http://www.pacificnet.net/~mandel/

The Teachers' Network
http://www.teachers.net/

Banana Stock/PunchStock

Although there are many theories of how people learn, learning can be broadly defined as a relatively permanent change in behavior or thinking due to experience. Learning is not a result of change due to maturation or temporary influences. Changes in behavior and thinking of students result from complex interactions between their individual characteristics and environmental factors. A continuing challenge in education is understanding these interactions so that learning can be enhanced. This unit focuses ways of viewing a variety of processes related to learning and instructional strategies that can be supportive to a broad range of learner needs. Each article emphasizes a different set of personal and environmental factors that influence students, with a common theme that learning is an active process requiring students to construct meaning from their interactions with their environment. The articles in this section reflect a recent emphasis research-based strategies the have been applied in schools to improve learning.

Until relatively recently, behaviorism was the best-known theory of learning. Most practicing and prospective teachers are familiar with concepts such as classical conditioning, reinforcement, and punishment, and there is no question that behaviorism has made significant contributions to understanding learning. More recently, educational psychologists have focused on constructivist and social psychological theories to explain how students learn.

According to constructivists, it is important for students to actively create their own understanding and reorganize existing knowledge to incorporate this new knowledge. This emphasizes the importance of providing students with meaningful, authentic contexts so students develop understandings that allow them to connect their learning to real-world applications and existing knowledge. Social psychology is the study of the nature of interpersonal relationships in social situations. Social psychological theories emphasize the affective, social, moral, and personal learning of students. Both constructivist and social psychological theories highlight the importance of social context of learning environments and the need for students to interact with others in order for learning to occur.

The section begins with two articles that focus on improving learning for groups of diverse learners. The first article highlights the importance of using small group instruction and multiple types of scaffolding with English language learners. The second article discusses the importance of differentiating instruction for middle school students in ways that support student autonomy and choice while working within the developmental needs of this age group.

Cognitive psychologists and researchers are continually expanding our knowledge of how the brain works, as well as our understanding of complex cognitive processes. Both areas focus on important procedures related to how we receive, process, and store information, as well as access information for later use that are essential for all learning. Psychologists and educators alike acknowledge that critical thinking and metacognition are cognitive skills essential to student learning. Article #4 in this section argues that critical thinking needs to be viewed as a type of thought that is domain specific rather than a set of skills, which explains why it can be so difficult to teach students. In article #5, the authors suggest that integrating technology in the classroom using principles of constructivist theory and as a metacognitive tool to enhance learning.

Finally, social psychological approaches often look at teacher-pupil relationships and group processes to derive principles of interaction that affect learning. The fifth article, addresses the issue of enhancing meaningful learning by focusing on school culture rather than classroom processes. In the seventh article in this section, the author uses a constructivist framework to examine one teacher's implementation of cooperative learning in his classroom.

Instructional strategies are the teacher behaviors and methods of conveying information that affect learning. Teaching methods or techniques can vary greatly, depending on objectives, group size, types of students, and personality of the teacher. For example, discussion classes are generally more effective for enhancing thinking skills than are individualized sessions or lectures. For the final subsection, five articles have been selected that show how teachers can use principles of educational psychology in their classrooms. In the first article, a framework is presented for teachers to evaluate instruction and assess student learning as a means of fostering deep, as opposed to surface learning. The second article in this section summarizes effective applications of technology in the classroom. The third article highlights how teachers can improve their verbal questioning of students during instruction to support effective higher level thinking.

Recently, more attention has been given to problem- or project-based learning as a method that allows teachers to develop interdisciplinary learning opportunities that foster student motivation and the use of higher level thinking. Article #4 presents the perspectives of a high school teacher and university researcher who collaborated on the implementation of a design-based unit in science.

Finally, student engagement is perhaps one of the more important concepts that is essential for student learning. Successful teachers implement instructional strategies that actively engage students in a variety of ways. In the last article in this unit, the authors identify a number of strategies that can be utilized to foster student engagement; and although they target elementary students, much of what they present can be used by teachers at any grade level.

Differentiating for Tweens

Teaching tweens requires special skills—and the willingness to do whatever it takes to ensure student success.

RICK WORMELI

Effective instruction for 12-year-olds looks different from effective instruction for 8-year-olds or 17-year-olds. Combine the developmental needs of typical tweens and the wildly varying needs of individuals within this age group, and you can see that flourishing as a middle-grades teacher requires special skills.

It's not as overwhelming as it sounds, however. There are some commonsense basics that serve students well. The five strategies described here revolve around the principles of differentiated instruction, which does not always involve individualized instruction. Teachers who differentiate instruction simply do what's fair and developmentally appropriate for students when the "regular" instruction doesn't meet their needs.

Strategy 1: Teach to Developmental Needs

Reports from the Carnegie Corporation (Jackson & Davis, 2000) and the National Middle School Association (2003), as well as the expertise of veteran middle school teachers, point to seven conditions that young adolescents crave: competence and achievement; opportunities for self-definition; creative expression; physical activity; positive social interactions with adults and peers; structure and clear limits; and meaningful participation in family, school, and community. No matter how creatively we teach—and no matter how earnestly we engage in differentiated instruction, authentic assessment, and character education—the effects will be significantly muted if we don't create an environment that responds to students' developmental needs. Different students will require different degrees of attention regarding each of these factors.

Integrating developmental needs into tweens' learning is nonnegotiable.

Take tweens' need for physical movement. It's not enough for tweens to move between classes every 50 minutes (or every 80 minutes on a block schedule). Effective tween instruction incorporates movement every 10 to 15 minutes. So we ask all students to get up and walk across the room to turn in their papers, not just have one student collect the papers while the rest of them sit passively. We let students process information physically from time to time: for example, by using the ceiling as a massive, organizer matrix and asking students to hold cards with information for each matrix cell and stand under the proper location as indicated on the ceiling. We use flexible grouping, which allows students to move about the room to work with different partners.

Every topic in the curriculum can be turned into a physical experience, even if it's very abstract. We can do this for some or all of our students as needed. We can use simulations, manipulatives, body statues (frozen tableau), and finger plays to portray irony, metabolism, chromatic scale, republics, qualitative analysis, grammar, and multiplying binomials (Glynn, 2001; Wormeli, 2005). These aren't "fluff" activities; they result in real learning for this age group.

To address students' need for self-definition, we give them choices in school projects. We help students identify consequences for the academic and personal decisions they make. We also teach students about their own learning styles. We put students in positions of responsibility in our schools and communities that allow them to make positive contributions and earn recognition for doing so. We provide clear rules and enforce them calmly—even if it's the umpteenth time that day that we've needed to enforce the same rule—to help students learn to function as members of a civilized society.

Integrating developmental needs into tweens' learning is nonnegotiable. It's not something teachers do only if we have time in the schedule; it's vital to tween success. As teachers of this age group, we need to apply our adolescent development expertise in every interaction. If we don't, the lesson will fall flat and even worse, students will wither.

Strategy 2: Treat Academic Struggle as Strength

Young adolescents readily identify differences and similarities among themselves, and in their efforts to belong to particular groups, they can be judgmental about classmates' learning styles or progress (Jackson & Davis, 2000). At this junction, then, it's important to show students that not everyone starts at the same point along the learning continuum or learns in the same way. Some classmates learn content by drawing it, others by writing about it, and still others by discussing it—and even the best students are beginners in some things.

Unfortunately, students in nondifferentiated classes often view cultural and academic differences as signs of weakness and inferiority. Good students in these classes often try to protect their reputations as being the kids who always get the problems right or finish first. They rarely take chances and stretch themselves for fear of faltering in front of others. This approach to learning rarely leads to success in high school and beyond.

Educators of tweens need to make academic struggle virtuous. So we model asking difficult questions to which we don't know the answers, and we publicly demonstrate our journey to answer those questions. We affirm positive risk taking in homework as well as the knowledge gained through science experiments that fail. We push students to explore their undeveloped skills without fear of grade repercussions, and we frequently help students see the growth they've made over time.

In one of my classes, Jared was presenting an oral report on Aristotle's rhetorical triangle (*ethos, pathos, logos*), and he was floundering. Embarrassed because he kept forgetting his memorized speech, he begged me to let him take an *F* and sit down. Instead, I asked Jared to take a few deep breaths and try again. He did, but again, he bombed. I explained that an oral report is not just about delivering information; it's also about taking risks and developing confidence. "We're all beginners at one point, Jared," I explained:

> This is your time to be a beginner. The worst that can happen is that you learn from the experience and have to do it again. That's not too bad.

After his classmates offered encouraging comments, Jared tried a third time and got a little farther before stopping his speech. I suggested that he repeat the presentation in short segments, resting between each one. He tried it, and it worked. After Jared finished, he moved to take his seat, but I stopped him and asked him to repeat the entire presentation, this time without rests.

As his classmates grinned and nodded, Jared returned to the front of the room. This time, he made it through his presentation without a mistake. His classmates applauded. Jared bowed, smiled, and took his seat. His eyes watered a bit when he looked at me. Adrenalin can do that to a guy, but I hoped it was more. Everyone learned a lot about tenacity that day, and Jared took his first steps toward greater confidence (Wormeli, 1999).

Strategy 3: Provide Multiple Pathways to Standards

Differentiation requires us to invite individual students to acquire, process, and demonstrate knowledge in ways different from the majority of the class if that's what they need to become proficient. When we embrace this approach, we give more than one example and suggest more than one strategy. We teach students eight different ways to take notes, not just one, and then help them decide when to use each technique. We let students use wide- or college-ruled paper, and we guide them in choosing multiple single-subject folders or one large binder for all subjects—whichever works best for them.

We don't limit students' exposure to sophisticated thinking because they have not yet mastered the basics. Tweens are capable of understanding how to solve for a variable or graph an inequality even if they struggle with the negative/positive signs when multiplying integers. We can teach a global lesson on a sophisticated concept for 15 minutes, and then allow students to process the information in groups tiered for different levels of readiness—or we can present an anchor activity for the whole class to do while we pull out subgroups for minilessons on the basics or on advanced material. Our goal is to respond to the unique students in front of us as we make learning coherent for all.

In the area of assessment, we should never let the test format get in the way of a student's ability to reveal what he or she knows and is able to do. For example, if an assessment on Ben Mikaelsen's novel *Touching Spirit Bear* (Harper Trophy, 2002) required students to create a poster showing the development of characters in the story, it would necessarily assess artistic skill in addition to assessing the students' understanding of the novel. Students with poor artistic skills would be unable to reveal the full extent of what they know. Consequently, we allow students to select alternative assessments through which they can more accurately portray their mastery.

In differentiated classes, grading focuses on clear and consistent evidence of mastery, not on the medium through which the student demonstrates that mastery. For example, we may give students five different choices for showing what they know about the rise of democracy: writing a report, designing a Web site, building a library display, transcribing a "live" interview with a historical figure, or creating a series of podcasts simulating a discussion between John Locke and Thomas Jefferson about where governments get their authority. We can grade all the projects using a common scoring rubric that contains the universal standards for which we're holding students accountable.

Every topic in the curriculum can be turned into a physical experience.

Of course, if the test format *is* the assessment, we don't allow students to opt for something else. For example, when we ask students to write a well-crafted persuasive essay, they can't

The Day I was Caught Plagiarizing

Young adolescents are still learning what is moral and how to act responsibly. I decided to help them along.

One day, I shared a part of an education magazine column with my 7th grade students. I told them that I wrote it and was seeking their critique before submitting it for publishing. In reality, the material I shared was an excerpt from a book written by someone else. I was hiding the book behind a notebook from which I read.

A parent coconspirator was in the classroom for the period, pretending to observe the lesson. While I read the piece that I claimed as my own, the parent acted increasingly uncomfortable. Finally, she interrupted me and said that she just couldn't let me go on. She had read the exact ideas that I claimed as my own in another book. I assured her that she was confused, and I continued.

She interrupted me again, this time angrily. She said she was not confused and named the book from which I was reading, having earlier received the information from me in our pre-class set-up. At this point, I let myself appear more anxious about her words. Her concern grew, and she persisted in her comments until I finally admitted that I hadn't written the material. Acting ashamed, I revealed the book to the class. The kids' mouths opened, some in confused grins, some greatly concerned, not knowing what to believe.

The parent let me have it then. She reminded me that I was in a position of trust as a teacher—how dare I break that trust! She said that I was being a terrible role model and that my students would never again trust my writings or teaching. She declared that this was a breach of professional conduct and that my principal would be informed. Throughout all of this, I countered her points with the excuses that students often make when caught plagiarizing: It's only a small part. The rest of the writing is original; what does it matter that this one part was written by someone else? I've never done it before, and I'm not ever going to do it again, so it's not that bad.

The students' faces dissolved into disbelief, some into anger. Students vicariously experienced the uncomfortable feeling of being trapped in a lie and having one's reputation impugned. At the height of the emotional tension between the parent and me, I paused and asked the students, "Have you had enough?" With a smile and a thank-you to the parent assistant, I asked how many folks would like to learn five ways not to plagiarize material; then I went to the chalkboard.

Students breathed a sigh of relief. Notebooks flew onto desktops, and pens raced across paper to get down everything I taught for the rest of class; they hung on every word. Students wanted to do anything to avoid the "yucky" feelings associated with plagiarism that they had experienced moments ago. I taught them ways to cite sources, how to paraphrase another's words, and how many words from an original source we could use before we were lifting too much. We discussed the legal ramifications of plagiarism. Later, we applauded the acting talent of our parent assistant.

One student in the room that day reflected on this lesson at the end of the year:

> I know I'll never forget when my teacher got "caught" plagiarizing. The sensations were simply too real. . . . Although my teacher is extremely moral, it was frightening how close to home it struck. The moment when my teacher admitted it, the room fell silent. It was awful. All my life, teachers have preached about plagiarism, and it never really sank in. But when you actually experience it, it's a whole different story.

To this day, students visit me from high school and college and say, "I was tempted to plagiarize this one little bit on one of my papers, but I didn't because I remembered how mad I was at you." That's a teacher touchdown.

—Rick Wormeli

instead choose to write a persuasive dialogue or create a poster. Even then, however, we can differentiate the pace of instruction and be flexible about the time required for student mastery. Just as we would never demand that all humans be able to recite the alphabet fluently on the first Monday after their 3rd birthday, it goes against all we know about teaching tweens to mandate that all students master slope and y-intercept during the first week of October in grade 7.

> In 2001, 40.7 percent of students in grades 3–5 and 41.7 percent of students in grades 6–8 participated in after-school activities (such as school sports, religious activities, scouts, and clubs) on a weekly basis.
>
> —NCES, *The Condition of Education 2004*

Thus, we allow tweens to redo work and assessments until they master the content, and we give them full credit for doing so. Our job is to teach students the material, not to document how they've failed. We never want to succumb to what middle-grades expert Nancy Doda calls the "learn or I will hurt you" mentality by demanding that all students learn at the same pace and in the same manner as their classmates and giving them only one chance to succeed.

Strategy 4: Give Formative Feedback

Tweens don't always know when they don't know, and they don't always know when they do. One of the most helpful strategies we can employ is to provide frequent formative feedback. Tween learning tends to be more multilayered and episodic than linear; continual assessment and feedback correct misconceptions before they take root. Tweens learn more when teachers take off the evaluation hat and hold up a mirror to students, helping them compare what they did with what they were supposed to have done.

Because learning and motivation can be fragile at this age, we have to find ways to provide that feedback promptly. We do this by giving students short assignments—such as one-page writings instead of multipage reports—that we can evaluate and return in a timely manner. When we formally assess student writing, we focus on just one or two areas so that students can assimilate our feedback.

To get a quick read on students' understanding of a particular lesson, we can use exit card activities, which are quick products created by students in response to prompts. For example, at the end of a U.S. history lesson, we might ask, "Using what we've learned today, make a Venn diagram that compares and contrasts World Wars I and II." The 3-2-1 exit card format can yield rich information (Wormeli, 2005). Here are two examples:

3—Identify *three* characteristic ways Renaissance art differs from medieval art.
2—List *two* important scientific debates that occurred during the Renaissance.
1—Provide *one* good reason why *rebirth* is an appropriate term to describe the Renaissance.

3—Identify at least *three* differences between acids and bases.
2—List *one* use of an acid and *one* use of a base.
1—State *one* reason why knowledge of acids and bases is important to citizens in our community.

Strategy 5: Dare to Be Unconventional

Curriculum theorists have often referred to early adolescence as the age of romanticism: Tweens are interested in that which is novel, compels them, and appeals to their curiosity about the world (Pinar, Reynolds, Slattery, & Taubman, 2000). To successfully teach tweens, we have to be willing to transcend convention once in a while. It's not a lark; it's essential.

Being unconventional means we occasionally teach math algorithms by giving students the answers to problems and asking them how those answers were derived. We improve student word savvy by asking students to conduct an intelligent conversation without using verbs. (They can't; they sound like Tarzan.) We ask students to teach some lessons, with the principal or a parent as coteacher. Students can make a video for 4th graders on the three branches of government, convey Aristotle's rhetorical triangle by juggling tennis balls, or correspond with adult astronomers about their study of the planets. They can create literary magazines of science, math, or health writing that will end up in local dentist offices and Jiffy Lube shops. They can learn about the Renaissance through a "Meeting of Minds" debate in which they portray Machiavelli, da Vinci, Erasmus, Luther, Calvin, and Henry VIII. The power of such lessons lies in their substance and novelty, and young adolescents are acutely attuned to these qualities.

Ninety percent of what we do with young adolescents is quiet, behind-the-scenes facilitation. Ten percent, however, is an inspired dog and pony show without apologies. At this "I dare you to show me something I don't know" and "Shake me out of my self-absorption" age, being unconventional is key.

Thus, when my students were confusing the concepts of adjective and adverb, I did the most professional thing I could think of: I donned tights, shorts, a cape, and a mask, and became Adverb Man. I moved through the hallways handing out index cards with adverbs written on them. "You need to move quickly," I said, handing a student late to class a card on which the word *quickly* was written. "You need to move now," I said to another, handing him a card with the adverb on it. Once in a while, I'd raise my voice, Superman-style, and declare, "Remember, good citizens of Earth, what Adverb Man always says: 'Up, up, and modify adverbs, verbs, and adjectives!'" The next day, one of the girls on our middle school team came walking down the hallway to my classroom dressed as Pronoun Girl. One of her classmates preceded her—he was dressed as Antecedent Boy. Both wore yellow masks and had long beach towels tucked into the backs of their shirt collars as capes. Pronoun Girl had taped pronouns across her shirt that corresponded with the nouns taped across Antecedent Boy's shirt.

It was better than *Schoolhouse Rock.* And the best part? There wasn't any grade lower than a *B*+ on the adverbs test that Friday (Wormeli, 2001).

Navigating the Tween River

Of all the states of matter in the known universe, tweens most closely resemble liquid. Students at this age have a defined volume, but not a defined shape. They are ever ready to flow, and they are rarely compressible. Although they can spill, freeze, and boil, they can also lift others, do impressive work, take the shape of their environment, and carry multiple ideas within themselves. Some teachers argue that dark matter is a better analogy—but those are teachers trying to keep order during the last period on a Friday.

To successfully teach tweens, we have to be willing to transcend convention once in a while.

Imagine directing the course of a river that flows through a narrow, ever-changing channel toward a greater purpose yet to be discovered, and you have the basics of teaching tweens. To chart this river's course, we must be experts in the craft of guiding young, fluid adolescents in their pressure-filled lives, and we must adjust our methods according to the flow, volume, and substrate within each student. It's a challenging river to navigate, but worth the journey.

References

Glynn, C. (2001). *Learning on their feet*. Shoreham, VT: Discover Writing Press.

Jackson, A., & Davis, G. (2000). *Turning points 2000: Educating adolescents in the 21st century*. New York: Carnegie Corporation.

National Middle School Association. (2003). *This we believe: Successful schools for young adolescents*. Westerville, OH: Author.

Pinar, W. F., Reynolds, W. M., Slattery, P., & Taubman, P. M. (2000). *Understanding curriculum*. New York: Peter Lang Publishing.

Wormeli, R. (1999). The test of accountability in middle school. *Middle Ground, 3*(7), 17–18, 53.

Wormeli, R. (2001). *Meet me in the middle*. Portland, ME: Stenhouse Publishers.

Wormeli, R. (2005). *Summarization in any subject: 50 techniques to improve student learning*. Alexandria, VA: ASCD.

Rick Wormeli (703-620-2447; rwormeli@cox.net) taught young adolescents for 25 years. He is now a consultant who works with administrators and teachers across the United States. He resides in Herndon, Virginia.

Critical Thinking

Why Is It So Hard to Teach?

DANIEL T. WILLINGHAM

Virtually everyone would agree that a primary, yet insufficiently met, goal of schooling is to enable students to think critically. In layperson's terms, critical thinking consists of seeing both sides of an issue, being open to new evidence that disconfirms your ideas, reasoning dispassionately, demanding that claims be backed by evidence, deducing and inferring conclusions from available facts, solving problems, and so forth. Then too, there are specific types of critical thinking that are characteristic of different subject matter: That's what we mean when we refer to "thinking like a scientist" or "thinking like a historian."

This proper and commonsensical goal has very often been translated into calls to teach "critical thinking skills" and "higher-order thinking skills"—and into generic calls for teaching students to make better judgments, reason more logically, and so forth. In a recent survey of human resource officials[1] and in testimony delivered just a few months ago before the Senate Finance Committee,[2] business leaders have repeatedly exhorted schools to do a better job of teaching students to think critically. And they are not alone. Organizations and initiatives involved in education reform, such as the National Center on Education and the Economy, the American Diploma Project, and the Aspen Institute, have pointed out the need for students to think and/or reason critically. The College Board recently revamped the SAT to better assess students' critical thinking. And ACT, Inc. offers a test of critical thinking for college students.

These calls are not new. In 1983, *A Nation At Risk,* a report by the National Commission on Excellence in Education, found that many 17-year-olds did not possess the "'higher-order' intellectual skills" this country needed. It claimed that nearly 40 percent could not draw inferences from written material and only one-fifth could write a persuasive essay.

Following the release of *A Nation At Risk,* programs designed to teach students to think critically across the curriculum became extremely popular. By 1990, most states had initiatives designed to encourage educators to teach critical thinking, and one of the most widely used programs, Tactics for Thinking, sold 70,000 teacher guides.[3] But, for reasons I'll explain, the programs were not very effective—and today we still lament students' lack of critical thinking.

After more than 20 years of lamentation, exhortation, and little improvement, maybe it's time to ask a fundamental question: Can critical thinking actually be taught? Decades of cognitive research point to a disappointing answer: not really. People who have sought to teach critical thinking have assumed that it is a skill, like riding a bicycle, and that, like other skills, once you learn it, you can apply it in any situation. Research from cognitive science shows that thinking is not that sort of skill. The processes of thinking are intertwined with the content of thought (that is, domain knowledge). Thus, if you remind a student to "look at an issue from multiple perspectives" often enough, he will learn that he ought to do so, but if he doesn't know much about an issue, he *can't* think about it from multiple perspectives. You can teach students maxims about how they ought to think, but without background knowledge and practice, they probably will not be able to implement the advice they memorize. Just as it makes no sense to try to teach factual content without giving students opportunities to practice using it, it also makes no sense to try to teach critical thinking devoid of factual content.

Critical thinking is not a set of skills that can be deployed at any time, in any context. It is a type of thought that even 3-year-olds can engage in—and even trained scientists can fail in.

In this article, I will describe the nature of critical thinking, explain why it is so hard to do and to teach, and explore how students acquire a specific type of critical thinking: thinking scientifically. Along the way, we'll see that critical thinking is not a set of skills that can be deployed at any time, in any context. It is a type of thought that even 3-year-olds can engage in—and even trained scientists can fail in. And it is very much dependent on domain knowledge and practice.

Why Is Thinking Critically So Hard?

Educators have long noted that school attendance and even academic success are no guarantee that a student will graduate an effective thinker in all situations. There is an odd tendency for rigorous thinking to cling to particular examples or types of problems. Thus, a student may have learned to estimate the answer to a math problem before beginning calculations as a way of checking the accuracy of his answer, but in the chemistry lab, the same student calculates the components of a compound without noticing that his estimates sum to more than 100 percent. And a student who has learned to thoughtfully discuss the causes of the American Revolution from both the British and American perspectives doesn't even think to question how the Germans viewed World War II. Why are students able to think critically in one situation, but not in another? The brief answer is: Thought processes are intertwined with what is being thought about. Let's explore this in depth by looking at a particular kind of critical thinking that has been studied extensively: problem solving.

Imagine a seventh-grade math class immersed in word problems. How is it that students will be able to answer one problem, but not the next, even though mathematically both word problems are the same, that is, they rely on the same mathematical knowledge? Typically, the students are focusing on the scenario that the word problem describes (its surface structure) instead of on the mathematics required to solve it (its deep structure). So even though students have been taught how to solve a particular type of word problem, when the teacher or textbook changes the scenario, students still struggle to apply the solution because they don't recognize that the problems are mathematically the same.

Thinking Tends to Focus on a Problem's "Surface Structure"

To understand why the surface structure of a problem is so distracting and, as a result, why it's so hard to apply familiar solutions to problems that appear new, let's first consider how you understand what's being asked when you are given a problem. Anything you hear or read is automatically interpreted in light of what you already know about similar subjects. For example, suppose you read these two sentences: "After years of pressure from the film and television industry, the President has filed a formal complaint with China over what U.S. firms say is copyright infringement. These firms assert that the Chinese government sets stringent trade restrictions for U.S. entertainment products, even as it turns a blind eye to Chinese companies that copy American movies and television shows and sell them on the black market." Background knowledge not only allows you to comprehend the sentences, it also has a powerful effect as you continue to read because it narrows the interpretations of new text that you will entertain. For example, if you later read the word "Bush," it would not make you think of a small shrub, nor would you wonder whether it referred to the former President Bush, the rock band, or a term for rural hinterlands. If you read "piracy," you would not think of eye-patched swabbies shouting "shiver me timbers!" The cognitive system gambles that incoming information will be related to what you've just been thinking about. Thus, it significantly narrows the scope of possible interpretations of words, sentences, and ideas. The benefit is that comprehension proceeds faster and more smoothly; the cost is that the deep structure of a problem is harder to recognize.

The narrowing of ideas that occurs while you read (or listen) means that you tend to focus on the surface structure, rather than on the underlying structure of the problem. For example, in one experiment,[4] subjects saw a problem like this one:

> Members of the West High School Band were hard at work practicing for the annual Homecoming Parade. First they tried marching in rows of 12, but Andrew was left by himself to bring up the rear. Then the director told the band members to march in columns of eight, but Andrew was still left to march alone. Even when the band marched in rows of three, Andrew was left out. Finally, in exasperation, Andrew told the band director that they should march

Important

How Do Cognitive Scientists Define Critical Thinking?

From the cognitive scientist's point of view, the mental activities that are typically called critical thinking are actually a subset of three types of thinking: reasoning, making judgments and decisions, and problem solving. I say that critical thinking is a subset of these because we think in these ways all the time, but only sometimes in a critical way. Deciding to read this article, for example, is not critical thinking. But carefully weighing the evidence it presents in order to decide whether or not to believe what it says is. *Critical* reasoning, decision making, and problem solving—which, for brevity's sake, I will refer to as critical thinking—have three key features: effectiveness, novelty, and self-direction. Critical thinking is effective in that it avoids common pitfalls, such as seeing only one side of an issue, discounting new evidence that disconfirms your ideas, reasoning from passion rather than logic, failing to support statements with evidence, and so on. Critical thinking is novel in that you don't simply remember a solution or a situation that is similar enough to guide you. For example, solving a complex but familiar physics problem by applying a multi-step algorithm isn't critical thinking because you are really drawing on memory to solve the problem. But devising a new algorithm is critical thinking. Critical thinking is self-directed in that the thinker must be calling the shots: We wouldn't give a student much credit for critical thinking if the teacher were prompting each step he took.

—D.W.

in rows of five in order to have all the rows filled. He was right. Given that there were at least 45 musicians on the field but fewer than 200 musicians, how many students were there in the West High School Band?

Earlier in the experiment, subjects had read four problems along with detailed explanations of how to solve each one, ostensibly to rate them for the clarity of the writing. One of the four problems concerned the number of vegetables to buy for a garden, and it relied on the same type of solution necessary for the band problem—calculation of the least common multiple. Yet, few subjects—just 19 percent—saw that the band problem was similar and that they could use the garden problem solution. Why?

When a student reads a word problem, her mind interprets the problem in light of her prior knowledge, as happened when you read the two sentences about copyrights and China. The difficulty is that the knowledge that seems relevant relates to the surface structure—in this problem, the reader dredges up knowledge about bands, high school, musicians, and so forth. The student is unlikely to read the problem and think of it in terms of its deep structure—using the least common multiple. The surface structure of the problem is overt, but the deep structure of the problem is not. Thus, people fail to use the first problem to help them solve the second: In their minds, the first was about vegetables in a garden and the second was about rows of band marchers.

With Deep Knowledge, Thinking Can Penetrate Beyond Surface Structure

If knowledge of how to solve a problem never transferred to problems with new surface structures, schooling would be inefficient or even futile—but of course, such transfer does occur. When and why is complex,[5] but two factors are especially relevant for educators: familiarity with a problem's deep structure and the knowledge that one should look for a deep structure. I'll address each in turn.

When one is very familiar with a problem's deep-structure, knowledge about how to solve it transfers well. That familiarity can come from long-term, repeated experience with one problem, or with various manifestations of one type of problem (i.e., many problems that have different surface structures, but the same deep structure). After repeated exposure to either or both, the subject simply perceives the deep structure as part of the problem description. Here's an example:

> A treasure hunter is going to explore a cave up on a hill near a beach. He suspected there might be many paths inside the cave so he was afraid he might get lost. Obviously, he did not have a map of the cave; all he had with him were some common items such as a flashlight and a bag. What could he do to make sure he did not get lost trying to get back out of the cave later?

The solution is to carry some sand with you in the bag, and leave a trail as you go, so you can trace your path back when you're ready to leave the cave. About 75 percent of American college students thought of this solution— but only 25 percent of Chinese students solved it.[6] The experimenters suggested that Americans solved it because most grew up hearing the story of Hansel and Gretel, which includes the idea of leaving a trail as you travel to an unknown place in order to find your way back. The experimenters also gave subjects another puzzle based on a common Chinese folk tale, and the percentage of solvers from each culture reversed. (To read the puzzle based on the Chinese folk tale, and the tale itself, go to www.aft.org/ pubs-reports/ american_educator/index.htm.)

It takes a good deal of practice with a problem type before students know it well enough to immediately recognize its deep structure, irrespective of the surface structure, as Americans did for the Hansel and Gretel problem. American subjects didn't think of the problem in terms of sand, caves, and treasure; they thought of it in terms of finding something with which to leave a trail. The deep structure of the problem is so well represented in their memory, that they immediately saw that structure when they read the problem.

Looking for a Deep Structure Helps, but It Only Takes You So Far

Now let's turn to the second factor that aids in transfer despite distracting differences in surface structure—knowing to look for a deep structure. Consider what would happen if I said to a student working on the band problem, "this one is similar to the garden problem." The student would understand that the problems must share a deep structure and would try to figure out what it is. Students can do something similar without the hint. A student might think "I'm seeing this problem in a math class, so there must be a math formula that will solve this problem." Then he could scan his memory (or textbook) for candidates, and see if one of them helps. This is an example of what psychologists call metacognition, or regulating one's thoughts. In the introduction, I mentioned that you can teach students maxims about how they ought to think. Cognitive scientists refer to these maxims as metacognitive strategies. They are little chunks of knowledge—like "look for a problem's deep structure" or "consider both sides of an issue"—that students can learn and then use to steer their thoughts in more productive directions.

Helping students become better at regulating their thoughts was one of the goals of the critical thinking programs that were popular 20 years ago. As the sidebar below explains, these programs are not very effective. Their modest benefit is likely due to teaching students to effectively use metacognitive strategies. Students learn to avoid biases that most of us are prey to when we think, such as settling on the first conclusion that seems reasonable, only seeking evidence that confirms one's beliefs, ignoring countervailing evidence, overconfidence, and others.[7] Thus, a student who has been encouraged many times to see both sides of an issue, for example, is probably more likely to spontaneously think "I should look at both sides of this issue" when working on a problem.

Unfortunately, metacognitive strategies can only take you so far. Although they suggest what you ought to do, they don't provide the knowledge necessary to implement the strategy. For

Critical Thinking Programs: Lots of Time, Modest Benefit

Since the ability to think critically is a primary goal of education, it's no surprise that people have tried to develop programs that could directly teach students to think critically without immersing them in any particular academic content. But the evidence shows that such programs primarily improve students' thinking with the sort of problems they practiced in the program—not with other types of problems. More generally, it's doubtful that a program that effectively teaches students to think critically in a variety of situations will ever be developed.

As the main article explains, the ability to think critically depends on having adequate content knowledge; you can't think critically about topics you know little about or solve problems that you don't know well enough to recognize and execute the type of solutions they call for.

Nonetheless, these programs do help us better understand what can be taught, so they are worth reviewing briefly.

A large number of programs[1] designed to make students better thinkers are available, and they have some features in common. They are premised on the idea that there is a set of critical thinking skills that can be applied and practiced across content domains. They are designed to supplement regular curricula, not to replace them, and so they are not tied to particular content areas such as language arts, science, or social studies. Many programs are intended to last about three years, with several hours of instruction (delivered in one or two lessons) per week. The programs vary in how they deliver this instruction and practice. Some use abstract problems such as finding patterns in meaningless figures (Reuven Feuerstein's Instrumental Enrichment), some use mystery stories (Martin Covington's Productive Thinking), some use group discussion of interesting problems that one might encounter in daily life (Edward de Bono's Cognitive Research Trust, or CoRT), and so on. However it is implemented, each program introduces students to examples of critical thinking and then requires that the students practice such thinking themselves.

How well do these programs work? Many researchers have tried to answer that question, but their studies tend to have methodological problems.[2] Four limitations of these studies are especially typical, and they make any effects suspect: 1) students are evaluated just once after the program, so it's not known whether any observed effects are enduring; 2) there is not a control group, leaving it unclear whether gains are due to the thinking program, to other aspects of schooling, or to experiences outside the classroom; 3) the control group does not have a comparison intervention, so any positive effects found may be due, for example, to the teacher's enthusiasm for something new, not the program itself; and 4) there is no measure of whether or not students can transfer their new thinking ability to materials that differ from those used in the program. In addition, only a small fraction of the studies have undergone peer review (meaning that they have been impartially evaluated by independent experts). Peer review is crucial because it is known that researchers unconsciously bias the design and analysis of their research to favor the conclusions they hope to see.[3]

Studies of the Philosophy for Children program may be taken as typical. Two researchers[4] identified eight studies that evaluated academic outcomes and met minimal research-design criteria. (Of these eight, only one had been subjected to peer review.) Still, they concluded that three of the eight had identifiable problems that clouded the researchers' conclusions. Among the remaining five studies, three measured reading ability, and one of these reported a significant gain. Three studies measured reasoning ability, and two reported significant gains. And, two studies took more impressionistic measures of student's participation in class (e.g., generating ideas, providing reasons), and both reported a positive effect.

Despite the difficulties and general lack of rigor in evaluation, most researchers reviewing the literature conclude that some critical thinking programs do have some positive effect.[5] But these reviewers offer two important caveats. First, as with almost any educational endeavor, the success of the program depends on the skill of the teacher. Second, thinking programs look good when the outcome measure is quite similar to the material in the program. As one tests for transfer to more and more dissimilar material, the apparent effectiveness of the program rapidly drops.

Knowing that one should think critically is not the same as being able to do so. That requires domain knowledge and practice.

Both the conclusion and the caveats make sense from the cognitive scientist's point of view. It is not surprising that the success of the program depends on the skill of the teacher. The developers of the programs cannot anticipate all of the ideas—right or wrong—that students will generate as they practice thinking critically, so it is up to the teacher to provide the all-important feedback to the students.

It is also reasonable that the programs should lead to gains in abilities that are measured with materials similar to those used in the program. The programs that include puzzles like those found on IQ tests, for instance, report gains in IQ scores. In an earlier column,* I described a bedrock principle of memory: You remember what you think about. The same goes for critical thinking: You learn to think critically in the ways in which you practice thinking critically. If you practice logic puzzles with an effective teacher, you are likely to get better at solving logic puzzles. But substantial improvement requires a great deal of practice. Unfortunately, because critical thinking curricula include many different types of problems, students typically don't get enough practice with any one type of problem. As explained in the main article, the modest benefits that these programs seem to produce are likely due to teaching students metacognitive strategies—like "look at both sides of an issue"—that cue them to try to think critically. But knowing that one should think critically is not the same as being able to do so. That requires domain knowledge and practice.

—D.W.

*See "Students Remember . . . What They Think About" in the Summer 2003 issue of *American Educator;* online at www.aft. org/ pubs-reports/american_educator/ summer2003/cogsci.html.

example, when experimenters told subjects working on the band problem that it was similar to the garden problem, more subjects solved the problem (35 percent compared to 19 percent without the hint), but most subjects, even when told what to do, weren't able to do it. Likewise, you may know that you ought not accept the first reasonable-sounding solution to a problem, but that doesn't mean you know how to come up with alterative solutions or weigh how reasonable each one is. That requires domain knowledge and practice in putting that knowledge to work.

Since critical thinking relies so heavily on domain knowledge, educators may wonder if thinking critically in a particular domain is easier to learn. The quick answer is yes, it's a *little* easier. To understand why, let's focus on one domain, science, and examine the development of scientific thinking.

Teaching students to think critically probably lies in large part in enabling them to deploy the right type of thinking at the right time.

Is Thinking Like a Scientist Easier?

Teaching science has been the focus of intensive study for decades, and the research can be usefully categorized into two strands. The first examines how children acquire scientific concepts; for example, how they come to forgo naive conceptions of motion and replace them with an understanding of physics. The second strand is what we would call thinking scientifically, that is, the mental procedures by which science is conducted: developing a model, deriving a hypothesis from the model, designing an experiment to test the hypothesis, gathering data from the experiment, interpreting the data in light of the model, and so forth.[†] Most researchers believe that scientific thinking is really a subset of reasoning that is not different in kind from other types of reasoning that children and adults do.[8] What makes it *scientific* thinking is knowing when to engage in such reasoning, and having accumulated enough relevant knowledge and spent enough time practicing to do so.

Recognizing *when* to engage in scientific reasoning is so important because the evidence shows that being able to reason is not enough; children and adults use *and* fail to use the proper reasoning processes on problems that seem similar. For example, consider a type of reasoning about cause and effect that is very important in science: conditional probabilities. If two things go together, it's possible that one causes the other. Suppose you start a new medicine and notice that you seem to be getting headaches more often than usual. You would infer that the medication influenced your chances of getting a headache. But it could also be that the medication increases your chances of getting a headache only in certain circumstances or conditions. In conditional probability, the relationship between two things (e.g., medication and headaches) is dependent on a third factor. For example, the medication might increase the probability of a headache *only* when you've had a cup of coffee. The relationship of the medication and headaches is conditional on the presence of coffee.

Understanding and using conditional probabilities is essential to scientific thinking because it is so important in reasoning about what causes what. But people's success in thinking this way depends on the particulars of how the question is presented. Studies show that adults sometimes use conditional probabilities successfully,[9] but fail to do so with many problems that call for it.[10] Even trained scientists are open to pitfalls in reasoning about conditional probabilities (as well as other types of reasoning). Physicians are known to discount or misinterpret new patient data that conflict with a diagnosis they have in mind,[11] and Ph.D.-level scientists are prey to faulty reasoning when faced with a problem embedded in an unfamiliar context.[12]

And yet, young children are sometimes able to reason about conditional probabilities. In one experiment,[13] the researchers showed 3-year-olds a box and told them it was a "blicket detector" that would play music if a blicket were placed on top. The child then saw one of the two sequences shown below in which blocks are placed on the blicket detector. At the end of the sequence, the child was asked whether each block was a blicket. In other words, the child was to use conditional reasoning to infer which block caused the music to play.

Note that the relationship between each individual block (yellow cube and blue cylinder) and the music is the same in sequences 1 and 2. In either sequence, the child sees the yellow cube associated with music three times, and the blue cylinder associated with the absence of music once and the presence of music twice. What differs between the first and second sequence is the relationship between the blue and yellow blocks, and therefore, the conditional probability of each block being a blicket. Three-year-olds understood the importance of conditional probabilities. For sequence 1, they said the yellow cube was a blicket, but the blue cylinder was not; for sequence 2, they chose equally between the two blocks.

"Teaching content alone is not likely to lead to proficiency in science, nor is engaging in inquiry experiences devoid of meaningful science content."

—National Research Council

This body of studies has been summarized simply: Children are not as dumb as you might think, and adults (even trained scientists) are not as smart as you might think. What's going on? One issue is that the common conception of critical thinking or scientific thinking (or historical thinking) as a set of skills is not accurate. Critical thinking does not have certain characteristics normally associated with skills—in particular, being able to use that skill at any time. If I told you that I learned to read music, for

† These two strands are the most often studied, but these two approaches—content and process of science—are incomplete. Underemphasized in U.S. classrooms are the many methods of scientific study, and the role of theories and models in advancing scientific thought.

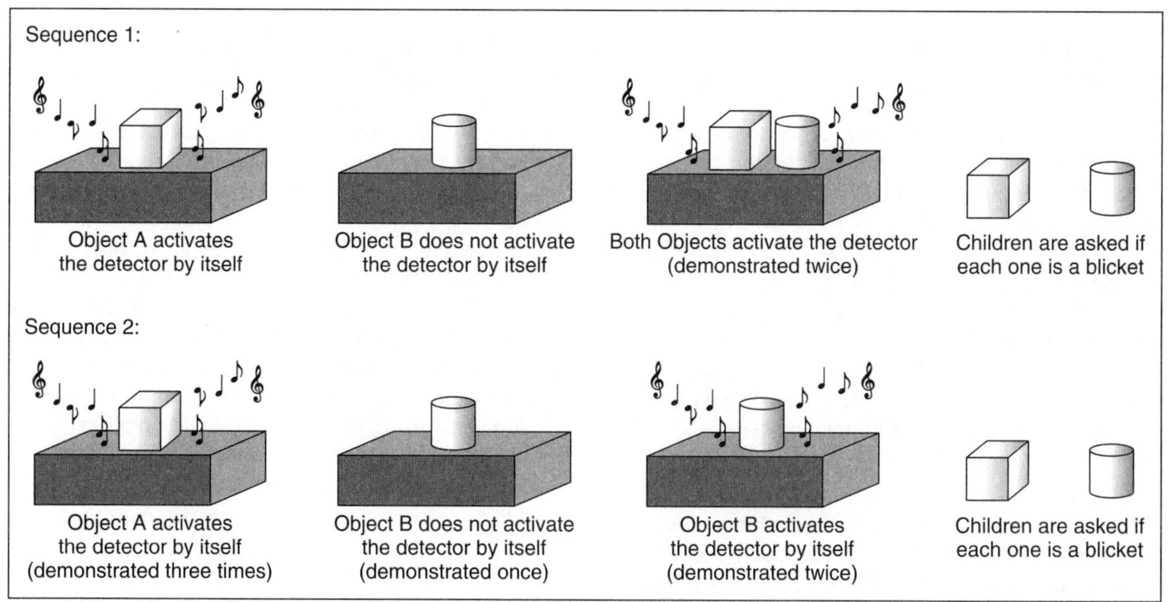

Source: Gopnik, A. and Schulz, L.E. (2004). "Mechanisms of theory formation in young children," *Trends in Cognitive Sciences*, 8, p 373, Elsevier.

example, you would expect, correctly, that I could use my new skill (i.e., read music) whenever I wanted. But critical thinking is very different. As we saw in the discussion of conditional probabilities, people can engage in some types of critical thinking without training, but even with extensive training, they will sometimes fail to think critically. This understanding that critical thinking is not a skill is vital.[‡] It tells us that teaching students to think critically probably lies in small part in showing them new ways of thinking, and in large part in enabling them to deploy the right type of thinking at the right time.

Returning to our focus on science, we're ready to address a key question: Can students be taught when to engage in scientific thinking? Sort of. It is easier than trying to teach general critical thinking, but not as easy as we would like. Recall that when we were discussing problem solving, we found that students can learn metacognitive strategies that help them look past the surface structure of a problem and identify its deep structure, thereby getting them a step closer to figuring out a solution. Essentially the same thing can happen with scientific thinking. Students can learn certain metacognitive strategies that will cue them to think scientifically. But, as with problem solving, the metacognitive strategies only tell the students what they should do—they do not provide the knowledge that students need to actually do it. The good news is that within a content area like science, students have more context cues to help them figure out which metacognitive strategy to use, and teachers have a clearer idea of what domain knowledge they must teach to enable students to do what the strategy calls for.

For example, two researchers[14] taught second-, third-, and fourth-graders the scientific concept behind controlling variables; that is, of keeping everything in two comparison conditions the same, except for the one variable that is the focus of investigation. The experimenters gave explicit instruction about this strategy for conducting experiments and then had students practice with a set of materials (e.g., springs) to answer a specific question (e.g., which of these factors determine how far a spring will stretch: length, coil diameter, wire diameter, or weight?). The experimenters found that students not only understood the concept of controlling variables, they were able to apply it seven months later with different materials and a different experimenter, although the older children showed more robust transfer than the younger children. In this case, the students recognized that they were designing an experiment and that cued them to recall the metacognitive strategy, "When I design experiments, I should try to control variables." Of course, succeeding in controlling all of the relevant variables is another matter—that depends on knowing which variables may matter and how they could vary.

Why Scientific Thinking Depends on Scientific Knowledge

Experts in teaching science recommend that scientific reasoning be taught in the context of rich subject matter knowledge. A committee of prominent science educators brought together by the National Research Council[15] put it plainly: "Teaching content alone is not likely to lead to proficiency in science, nor is engaging in inquiry experiences devoid of meaningful science content."

The committee drew this conclusion based on evidence that background knowledge is necessary to engage in scientific thinking. For example, knowing that one needs a control group in an experiment is important. Like having two comparison conditions, having a control group in addition to an experimental group helps you focus on the variable you want to study. But knowing that you need a control group is not the same as being able to create one. Since it's not always possible to have two

‡ Although this is not highly relevant for K–12 teachers, it is important to note that for people with extensive training, such as Ph.D.-level scientists, critical thinking does have some skill-like characteristics. In particular, they are better able to deploy critical reasoning with a wide variety of content, even that with which they are not very familiar. But, of course, this does not mean that they will never make mistakes.

Did Sherlock Holmes Take a Course in Critical Thinking?

No one better exemplifies the power of broad, deep knowledge in driving critical thinking than Sherlock Holmes. In his famous first encounter with Dr. Watson, Holmes greets him with this observation: "You have been in Afghanistan, I perceive." Watson is astonished—how could Holmes have known? Eventually Holmes explains his insight, which turns not on incredible intelligence or creativity or wild guessing, but on having relevant knowledge. Holmes is told that Watson is a doctor; everything else he deduces by drawing on his knowledge of, among other things, the military, geography, how injuries heal, and current events. Here's how Holmes explains his thought process:

> I knew you came from Afghanistan. From long habit the train of thoughts ran so swiftly through my mind, that I arrived at the conclusion without being conscious of intermediate steps. There were such steps, however. The train of reasoning ran, "Here is a gentleman of a medical type, but with the air of a military man. Clearly an army doctor, then. He has just come from the tropics, for his face is dark, and that is not the natural tint of his skin, for his wrists are fair. He has undergone hardship and sickness, as his haggard face says clearly. His left arm has been injured. He holds it in a stiff and unnatural manner. Where in the tropics could an English army doctor have seen much hardship and got his arm wounded? Clearly in Afghanistan." The whole train of thought did not occupy a second. I then remarked that you came from Afghanistan, and you were astonished.

—Editors

Source: *A Study in Scarlet* by Sir Arthur Conan Doyle.

groups that are *exactly* alike, knowing which factors can vary between groups and which must not vary is one example of necessary background knowledge. In experiments measuring how quickly subjects can respond, for example, control groups must be matched for age, because age affects response speed, but they need not be perfectly matched for gender.

More formal experimental work verifies that background knowledge is necessary to reason scientifically. For example, consider devising a research hypothesis. One could generate multiple hypotheses for any given situation. Suppose you know that car A gets better gas mileage than car B and you'd like to know why. There are many differences between the cars, so which will you investigate first? Engine size? Tire pressure? A key determinant of the hypothesis you select is plausibility. You won't choose to investigate a difference between cars A and B that you think is unlikely to contribute to gas mileage (e.g., paint color), but if someone provides a reason to make this factor more plausible (e.g., the way your teenage son's driving habits changed after he painted his car red), you are more likely to say that this now-plausible factor should be investigated.[16] One's judgment about the plausibility of a factor being important is based on one's knowledge of the domain.

Other data indicate that familiarity with the domain makes it easier to juggle different factors simultaneously, which in turn allows you to construct experiments that simultaneously control for more factors. For example, in one experiment,[17] eighth-graders completed two tasks. In one, they were to manipulate conditions in a computer simulation to keep imaginary creatures alive. In the other, they were told that they had been hired by a swimming pool company to evaluate how the surface area of swimming pools was related to the cooling rate of its water. Students were more adept at designing experiments for the first task than the second, which the researchers interpreted as being due to students' familiarity with the relevant variables. Students are used to thinking about factors that might influence creatures' health (e.g., food, predators), but have less experience working with factors that might influence water temperature (e.g., volume, surface area). Hence, it is not the case that "controlling variables in an experiment" is a pure process that is not affected by subjects' knowledge of those variables.

Subjects who started with more and better integrated knowledge planned more informative experiments and made better use of experimental outcomes.

Prior knowledge and beliefs not only influence which hypotheses one chooses to test, they influence how one interprets data from an experiment. In one experiment,[18] undergraduates were evaluated for their knowledge of electrical circuits. Then they participated in three weekly, 1.5-hour sessions during which they designed and conducted experiments using a computer simulation of circuitry, with the goal of learning how circuitry works. The results showed a strong relationship between subjects' initial knowledge and how much subjects learned in future sessions, in part due to how the subjects interpreted the data from the experiments they had conducted. Subjects who started with more and better integrated knowledge planned more informative experiments and made better use of experimental outcomes.

Other studies have found similar results, and have found that anomalous, or unexpected, outcomes may be particularly important in creating new knowledge—and particularly dependent upon prior knowledge.[19] Data that seem odd because they don't fit one's mental model of the phenomenon under investigation are highly informative. They tell you that your understanding is incomplete, and they guide the development of new hypotheses. But you could only recognize the outcome of an experiment as anomalous if you had some expectation of how it would turn out. And that expectation would be based on domain knowledge, as would your ability to create a new hypothesis that takes the anomalous outcome into account.

The idea that scientific thinking must be taught hand in hand with scientific content is further supported by research on scientific problem solving; that is, when students calculate an answer to a textbook-like problem, rather than design their own experiment. A meta-analysis[20] of 40 experiments investigating methods for teaching scientific problem solving showed that effective approaches were those that focused on building complex, integrated knowledge bases as part of problem solving, for example by including exercises like concept mapping. Ineffective approaches focused exclusively on the strategies to be used in problem solving while ignoring the knowledge necessary for the solution.

What do all these studies boil down to? First, critical thinking (as well as scientific thinking and other domain-based thinking) is not a skill. There is not a set of critical thinking skills that can be acquired and deployed

Teaching Critical Thinking

Teaching students to think critically is high on any teacher's to-do list. So what strategies are consistent with the research?

• ***Special programs aren't worth it.*** In the sidebar, "Critical Thinking Programs: Lots of Time, Modest Benefit," I've mentioned a few of the better known programs. Despite their widespread availability, the evidence that these programs succeed in teaching students to think critically, especially in novel situations, is very limited. The modest boost that such programs may provide should be viewed, as should all claims of educational effectiveness, in light of their opportunity costs. Every hour students spend on the program is an hour they won't be learning something else.

• ***Thinking critically should be taught in the context of subject matter.*** The foregoing does not mean that teachers shouldn't teach students to think critically—it means that critical thinking shouldn't be taught on its own. People do not spontaneously examine assumptions that underlie their thinking, try to consider all sides of an issue, question what they know, etc. These things must be modeled for students, and students must be given opportunities to practice—preferably in the context of normal classroom activity. This is true not only for science (as discussed in the main article), but for other subject matter. For example, an important part of thinking like a historian is considering the source of a document—who wrote it, when, and why. But teaching students to ask that question, independent of subject matter knowledge, won't do much good. Knowing that a letter was written by a Confederate private to his wife in New Orleans just after the Battle of Vicksburg won't help the student interpret the letter unless he knows something of Civil War history.

• ***Critical thinking is not just for advanced students.*** I have sometimes heard teachers and administrators suggest that critical thinking exercises make a good enrichment activity for the best students, but struggling students should just be expected to understand and master more basic material. This argument sells short the less advanced students and conflicts with what cognitive scientists know about thinking. Virtually everyone is capable of critical thinking and uses it all the time—and, as the conditional probabilities research demonstrated, has been capable of doing so since they were very young. The difficulty lies not in thinking critically, but in recognizing when to do so, and in knowing enough to do so successfully.

• ***Student experiences offer entrée to complex concepts.*** Although critical thinking needs to be nested in subject matter, when students don't have much subject matter knowledge, introducing a concept by drawing on student experiences can help. For example, the importance of a source in evaluating a historical document is familiar to even young children; deepening their understanding is a matter of asking questions that they have the knowledge to grapple with. Elementary school teachers could ask: Would a letter to a newspaper editor that criticized the abolishment of recess be viewed differently if written by a school principal versus a thirdgrader? Various concepts that are central to scientific thinking can also be taught with examples that draw on students' everyday knowledge and experience. For example, "correlation does not imply causation" is often illustrated by the robust association between the consumption of ice cream and the number of crimes committed on a given day. With a little prodding, students soon realize that ice cream consumption doesn't cause crime, but high temperatures might cause increases in both.

Knowing that a letter was written by a Confederate private to his wife in New Orleans just after the Battle of Vicksburg won't help the student interpret the letter—unless he knows something of Civil War history.

• ***To teach critical thinking strategies, make them explicit and practice them.*** Critical thinking strategies are abstractions. A plausible approach to teaching them is to make them explicit, and to proceed in stages. The first time (or several times) the concept is introduced, explain it with at least two different examples (possibly examples based on students' experiences, as discussed above), label it so as to identify it as a strategy that can be applied in various contexts, and show how it applies to the course content at hand. In future instances, try naming the appropriate critical thinking strategy to see if students remember it and can figure out how it applies to the material under discussion. With still more practice, students may see which strategy applies without a cue from you.

—D.W.

regardless of context. Second, there are metacognitive strategies that, once learned, make critical thinking more likely. Third, the ability to think critically (to actually do what the metacognitive strategies call for) depends on domain knowledge and practice. For teachers, the situation is not hopeless, but no one should underestimate the difficulty of teaching students to think critically.

Notes

1. Borja, R. R. (2006). "Work Skills of Graduates Seen Lacking," *Education Week, 26,* 9, 10.
2. Green, W. D. (2007). "Accenture Chairman and CEO William D. Green Addresses Senate Finance Committee," Accenture, www.accenture.com.
3. Viadero, D. (1991). "Parents in S.C. Attack Alleged 'New Age' Program." *Education Week,* www.edweek.org.
4. Novick, L. R. and Holyoak, K. J. (1991). "Mathematical problem-solving by analogy," *Journal of Experimental Psychology: Learning, Memory and Cognition, 17,* 398–415.
5. For reviews see: Reeves, L. M. and Weisberg, R. W. (1994), "The role of content and abstract information in analogical transfer," *Psychological Bulletin, 115,* 381–400; Barnett, S. M. and Ceci, S. J. (2002), "When and where do we apply what we learn? A taxonomy for far transfer," *Psychological Bulletin, 128* (4), 612–637.
6. Chen, Z., Mo, L., and Honomichl, R. (2004). "Having the memory of an elephant: Long-term retrieval and the use of analogues in problem solving," *Journal of Experimental Psychology: General, 133,* 415–433.
7. For a readable review see: Baron, J. (2000). *Thinking and Deciding,* Cambridge, UK: Cambridge University Press.
8. For example see: Klahr, D. (2000). *Exploring science: The cognition and development of discovery processes,* Cambridge, Mass.: MIT press.
9. Spellman, B. A. (1996). "Acting as intuitive scientists: Contingency judgments are made while controlling for alternative potential causes," Psychological Science, 7, 337–342
10. For example see: Kuhn, D., Garcia-Mila, M., and Zohar, A. (1995). "Strategies of knowledge acquisition," *Monographs of the Society for Research in Child Development, 60,* 1–128.
11. Groopman, J. (2007). *How Doctors Think,* New York: Houghton Mifflin.
12. Tweney, R. D. and Yachanin, S. A. (1985), "Can scientists rationally assess conditional inferences?" *Social Studies of Science, 15,* 155–173; Mahoney, M. J. and DeMonbreun, B. G. (1981), "Problem-solving bias in scientists," in R. D. Tweney, M. E. Doherty, and C. R. Mynatt (eds.) *On Scientific Thinking,* 139–144, New York:Columbia University Press.
13. Gopnik, A., Sobel, D. M., Schulz, L. E., and Glymour, C. (2001). "Causal learning mechanisms in very young children: Two-, three-, and four-year- olds infer causal relations from patterns of variation and covariation," *Developmental Psychology, 37*(5), 620–629.
14. Chen, Z. and Klahr, D. (1999). "All Other Things Being Equal: Acquisition and Transfer of the Control of Variables Strategy," *Child Development, 70* (5), 1098–1120.
15. National Research Council (2007). *Taking Science to School,* Washington, D.C.: National Academies Press.
16. Koslowski, B. (1996). *Theory and Evidence: The Development of Scientific Reasoning,* Cambridge, Mass.: MIT Press.
17. Friedler, Y., Nachmias, R., and Linn, M. C. (1990). "Learning scientific reasoning skills in microcomputer-based laboratories," *Journal of Research in Science Teaching, 27,* 173–191.
18. Schauble, L., Glaser, R., Raghavan, K., and Reiner, M. (1991). "Causal models and experimentation strategies in scientific reasoning," *The Journal of Learning Sciences, 1,* 201–238.
19. For example see: Dunbar, K. N. and Fugelsang, J. A. (2005), "Causal thinking in science: How scientists and students interpret the unexpected," in M. E. Gorman, R. D. Tweney, D. C. Gooding, and A. P. Kincannon (eds.) *Scientific and Technological Thinking,* 57–79, Mahwah, N.J.: Erlbaum; Echevarria, M. (2003), "Anomalies as a catalyst for middle school students' knowledge construction and scientific reasoning during science inquiry," *Journal of Educational Psychology, 95,* 357–374.
20. Taconis, R., Ferguson-Hessler, M.G.M., and Broekkamp, H., (2001). "Teaching science problem solving: An overview of experimental work," *Journal of Research in Science Teaching, 38*(4), 442–468.

Box Notes

1. Adams, M. J. (1989), "Thinking skills curricula: Their promise and progress," *Educational Psychologist, 24,* 25–77; Nickerson, R. S., Perkins, D. N., and Smith, E. E. (1985), *The Teaching of Thinking,* Hillsdale, N.J.: Erlbaum; Ritchart, R. and Perkins, D. N. (2005), "Learning to think: The challenges of teaching thinking," in K. J. Holyoak and R. G. Morrison (eds.) *The Cambridge Handbook of Thinking and Reasoning,* Cambridge, UK: Cambridge University Press.
2. Sternberg, R. J. and Bhana, K. (1986). "Synthesis of research on the effectiveness of intellectual skills programs: Snake-oil remedies or miracle cures?" *Educational Leadership, 44,* 60–67.
3. Mahoney, M. J. and DeMonbreun, B. G. (1981). "Problem-solving bias in scientists," in R. D. Tweney, M. E. Doherty, and C. R. Mynatt (eds.) *On Scientific Thinking,* 139–144, New York: Columbia University Press.
4. Trickey, S. and Topping, K. J. (2004). "Philosophy for Children: A Systematic Review," *Research Papers in Education 19,* 365–380.
5. Adams, M. J. (1989). "Thinking skills curricula: Their promise and progress." *Educational Psychologist, 24,* 25–77; Nickerson, R. S., Perkins, D. N., and Smith, E. E. (1985), *The Teaching of Thinking,* Hillsdale, N.J.: Erlbaum; Ritchart, R. and Perkins, D. N. (2005), "Learning to think: The challenges of teaching thinking," in K. J. Holyoak and R. G. Morrison (eds.) *The Cambridge Handbook of Thinking and Reasoning,* Cambridge, UK: Cambridge University Press.

DANIEL T. WILLINGHAM is professor of cognitive psychology at the University of Virginia and author of *Cognition: The Thinking Animal* as well as over 50 articles. With Barbara Spellman, he edited *Current Directions in Cognitive Science*. He regularly contributes to *American Educator* by writing the *"Ask the Cognitive Scientist"* column. His research focuses on the role of consciousness in learning.

Constructing Learning

Using Technology to Support Teaching for Understanding

THOMAS M. SHERMAN AND BARBARA L. KURSHAN

A frequent criticism of technology applications in classrooms is that they are little more than extraneous bells and whistles pointlessly tacked onto routine instruction. The flash and splash of a PowerPoint presentation may look good, but many question the value added to student learning. This leads to the question, how can technologies genuinely contribute to enhanced learning? We need to show explicitly how a constructivist perspective can be helpful in planning and delivering instruction and how technologies can significantly support effective and theoretically sound teaching.

We discussed contructivism in depth in our article last month (December–January). Briefly, constructivism is based on the conception that we learn by relating new experiences to our prior knowledge; we construct new understandings based on what we already know. This theory has emerged from research across a broad range of disciplines, but the challenge has been to understand how to promote deeper, more substantive learning. Three principles capture the essence of the challenge. Understanding is:

- the product of actively relating new and prior experiences
- a function of learning facts and core principles of a discipline
- a consequence of using and managing intellectual abilities well

As educators, our challenge is to identify, invent, adopt, and use classroom practices that are consistent with these principles. However, this is no easy quest. For example, one common concern relates to the central role of individual prior knowledge. How can we measure and tailor instruction to each individual's unique experiences? Our response is to identify key characteristics of effective teaching consistent with constructivist theory. Then, for each characteristic we identify ways you can use technology to make these characteristics regular features of your classroom.

Consistency between theoretical conceptions of learning and teaching practice has been shown to support effective applications of technologies to increase achievement. We explore eight teaching characteristics that are consistent with constructivist principles:

- Learner centered
- Interesting
- Real life
- Social
- Active
- Time
- Feedback
- Supportive

Learner Centered

Learner-centered classrooms focus instruction on the intellectual strategies, experiences, culture, and knowledge that students bring into classrooms. The instruction you create uses these experiences as learning paths for students to follow as they examine and transform the new ideas into their own understanding. You can use technology to support this transformation in two important ways.

First, you can use access to extensive libraries of teaching examples and suggestions to tune your instruction to student needs, experiences, and unique situations. For example, Edgate and ProQuestK-12 provide large repertoires of Web-based teaching resources. (***Editor's note:*** Find these URLs and other information in the Resources section on p. 104.) Using online resources such as these, you can search for activities that are consistent with students' learning needs. For example, consider teaching a geography lesson in a classroom where students have limited and extensive experiences with local conditions such as a central business district. You could also use the Edgate site to design language lessons that are related to student cultural experiences from home, such as recipes from Mexico. You can personalize study by using local information resources (e.g., GIS databases, museum records and images online, property records, census data), as a focus for study in science (investigating pollution issues), literature (reading local stories), and social studies (examining the politics of local decisions).

Students can use geographic principles to study data about their own neighborhoods as well as examine other features of interest specifically to them.

Interested students challenge their existing knowledge and are more likely to develop conceptual frameworks that integrate prior knowledge and new information into understanding.

Second, you can teach students to organize their knowledge using computer-based tools and software simulations that model forming and expressing alternate conceptions of concepts and strategies. For example, CSILE (Computer-Supported Intentional Learning Environments) offers several projects and many application examples in which the technology is integrated into curricula so that students' thinking is revealed. With sites such as these, you can help students focus on their thinking as well as look for information. As students develop understandings, you guide them to examine their conclusions based on interactions between their peers, their writing, the information they collect, and their prior knowledge. By trying to explain their ideas to other students and interacting with their peers around academic content, students improve their thinking skills and gain new knowledge. In addition, by reviewing students' CSILE entries, you can find evidence of the kinds of help students provide for each others' thinking and communication skills.

Interesting

Interested students challenge their existing knowledge and are more likely to develop conceptual frameworks that integrate prior knowledge and new information into understanding. Lack of interest is generally the number one reason that students give for not learning to mastery. By focusing on students' current beliefs, you increase the probabilities that students will be intrigued and explore their understandings. Technologies can be an effective tool to promote this interested and active exploration.

Technology-based demonstrations and illustrations such as the math and science animations at ExploreLearning, the Day in the Life Series, and MathMagic stimulate discussions in which students' current beliefs are expressed and tested. By creating classroom environments that encourage manipulating and discussing new ideas, you build opportunities for students to engage their interests and examine the perceptions of others. Although these opportunities can be very rich, it is also important to ensure that students have the skills to interact with each other. Sites such as these usually are open to teacher-led and whole class discussion as well as small and independent group work. Technology enables students to propose an effect and then to test that proposal with a virtual manipulative.

Manipulatives are concrete or symbolic artifacts that students interact with while learning new topics. They are powerful instructional aids because they provide active, hands-on exploration of abstract concepts. Research supports the premise that computer-based manipulatives are often more effective than ones involving physical objects, in part because they can dynamically link multiple representations together.

In addition, because there is a wide range of technology-based materials available on many topics, you can provide opportunities for students to self-select learning activities that are developmentally and topic appropriate as well as capture their personal interests. Thus, rather than a single demonstration of a reaction of chemicals or one perspective on a war battlefield, you can open a broad range of options for students to select those that are most interesting to them.

Real Life

Constructivist teaching incorporates students' communities as the context for learning. Consider the Schools For Thought (SFT) project of the Learning Sciences Institute at Vanderbilt University. In the SFT Jasper Woodbury series, students are presented with computer-based scenarios that involve complex information and sophisticated decisions. You contribute to successful learning by guiding students' inquiry through focused questions and directing students to consider how these principles affect their community-generated questions. As students work through the SFT dilemmas, you can help them recognize the many ways they have used information they learned in math, science, social studies, and literature to address the issues raised.

You can also facilitate depth of understanding by integrating technologies into the fabric of teaching as intellectual tools that students use to study, learn, and communicate with others in their classes as well as others in different locations. Students can respond by using organizing tools, making complex calculations, and employing search engines to mirror the strategies they will use outside of school to seek answers. In this way, real life in school becomes as much a second nature response as real life outside of school. The result should be a much higher potential for transfer in addition to deeper and more meaningful learning.

Social

Constructing meaning comes from interacting with others to explain, defend, discuss, and assess our ideas and challenge, question, and comprehend the ideas of others. Social activities allow students to express and develop their understandings with peers as they pursue projects through conversations that stimulate examining and expanding their understandings.

One increasingly common technology-based strategy is to create online communities of students and adults who collaborate on specific problems. For example, Global Lab and CoVis link students from as many other sites as you choose to monitor, collect, and share scientific data. The Global Lab project was tested in more than 300 schools in 30 countries. These technologies provide opportunities for students to join a large community and analyze data in a very diverse social environment.

Understanding grows from studying difficult concepts several times and in different ways.

As students analyze and share conclusions across different cultures and perspectives, you have the opportunity to help them evaluate the quality and quantity of the evidence on which they build their conceptions. One outcome is that you can demonstrate the effects of cultural and geographical perspectives by discussing the reasons for differences. These technology-based collaborative social classrooms create learning environments in which students can openly express their conclusions, challenge the conclusions of others, and build extensive information resources. Your role is to help students develop standards to judge evidence, lead students as they reflect on and discuss issues, and encourage students to form conceptual frameworks based on social considerations of the ideas they are studying.

Active

The visible learning actions students use to gather and consider information include writing, discussing, and searching. The covert actions that result in monitoring and choosing how to learn are reading, listening, monitoring, reflecting, considering, evaluating, and checking.

Technology-based interactivity can be a tool to facilitate active learning with dialogue between students as well as to evaluate and revise their propositions. WebPals is a collaborative interaction between teacher education students and middle school students in which they jointly read and discuss their interpretations of novels and review implications for their communities and lives. You would moderate these discussions by posing stimulating questions to your students about the novels they read and also about the observations that their Web pals make. By emphasizing thoughtful interpretation of their questions and observations, you show students that how they think is as important as mastering details.

Time

Time and carefully planned experiences are necessary for broad and deep understanding. Two overarching outcomes from in-depth study are essential. First, understanding is the result of well-organized and widely linked concepts. This allows learners to recall and use their knowledge quickly and appropriately in unfamiliar situations. Second, understanding consists of knowing the important questions and cognitive strategies that characterize the disciplines they are studying.

You can employ technology to increase the efficiency and personalization of the time to learn new ideas as well as to rethink and revise existing ideas. Technologies can facilitate these recursive processes in several ways. Word processors and databases can be used to record thoughts and observations so that students can review them regularly and revise as needed. You can embed this individual review in student self-directed routines guided by metacognitive questions such as: Why are you learning this? What do you already know that relates to this information? How interested are you in learning this? How difficult will it be for you to learn? Are you checking your understanding as you study? How should you correct errors? Are there other ways you can study that may be better? These questions focus students to use their time well and to maximize success by selecting and applying the most effective learning strategies.

Supportive scaffolding shows students that you understand their needs and "walk" with them as they work to meet learning goals.

Understanding grows from studying difficult concepts several times and in different ways. You can use technologies to foster these recursive learning processes by providing the same information in different formats and for different situations. For example, presenting math from sites such as Global Grocery List and MathMagic provides variety and maintains students' interest.

Technology can help teachers and students use time more efficiently. Students are empowered to control and organize their learning in programs that respond to their specific needs. Some examples of tutoring programs that use time efficiently are Get A Clue, which provides vocabulary development through stories, and HomeworkSpot, which provides homework help through access to subject-specific links. With sites such as these, you can link students to many help and reference sites. For structured practice, students can be directed to use many available drill and practice programs tailored to independent use. These resources offer students multiple presentations of classroom lessons that use time efficiently and promote greater understanding.

Feedback

Feedback is essential to the process of acquiring and reflecting on the relation between existing knowledge and new information. The feedback you provide is most effective as a continual stream of performance-based observations from which students can revise their thinking as they work on projects. When teachers successfully integrate feedback authentically into projects to support and guide students, learning becomes a journey that is constantly being adjusted as students individually and collectively pursue solving problems or explaining observed phenomena.

Software such as Logal Simulations in Science and Math and Decisions, Decisions in Social Studies and others in nearly all disciplines offer students the opportunity to plug in data or observations and model the results of their efforts. Technology-based feedback is immediate and focused on the learning at hand. Feedback can be presented in graphs that illustrate the effects of the students' propositions and by indicating if a test question has been answered correctly. Test questions can also be put into databases from which practice questions can be generated for students to test their own knowledge. Computer simulations can give students realistic problems to solve for evaluating their use of their knowledge and understanding.

This kind of feedback lets students know what they have and have not learned; students then have the ability to manage their own learning, use their metacognitive skills, and establish personal goals. You can promote this sense of efficacy when students make data-based judgments about what they know and how well they know it. Your models of how to think about using feedback are an important ingredient in students learning to make the most of the feedback they receive.

Supportive

Instructional support provides the right assistance at the right time for learners. You can support or scaffold learning by doing things such as reducing the complexity of a task, limiting the steps needed to solve a problem, providing cues, identifying critical errors, and demonstrating how tasks can be completed.

This kind of supportive scaffolding shows students that you understand their needs and enables you to "walk" with them as they work to meet learning goals. A key part of this support is to determine when students are ready for a nudge and then to provide the scaffold that will support them as they make progress. As learners develop new concepts, the scaffolds are removed.

You can provide opportunities for students to self-select learning activities that are developmentally and topic appropriate as well as capture their personal interests.

When you use technologies such as calculators, spreadsheets, and graphing and modeling programs, you help students as they develop their understandings. In addition, you can use computer programs that serve as mentors to students as they develop their skills and knowledge. Programs with access to experts and tutoring also offer scaffolding for students to question their knowledge and find support for exploring questions with multiple correct answers. For example, the site Smarthinking is designed to increase academic retention and achievement for individual students with interactive mentors and tutors. The Electronic Emissary Project is another site that connects online mentors with K–12 students in collaborative and team projects that are curriculum based.

Conclusion

We have described eight characteristics of effective learning environments consistent with modern constructivist theory. As we see research becoming more interdisciplinary—including not only education but also the physiology of the brain, neurology, psychology, and medicine—the constructivist explanation of how to influence learning and learners appears more and more consistent with the emerging evidence. This research has direct and important implications for what we do in classrooms. Classrooms that are active, interesting, learner centered, focused on real life, and social and provide time to learn, frequent and facilitative feedback, and support both learning to be good learners as well as learning content have consistently been shown to be more effective with all learners.

Creating these environments is a daunting challenge and requires considerable restructuring of classroom routines and teaching practices. Nobody denies the challenge is great, and we do not claim that technologies will make the task easy. But, as we have illustrated, technologies can provide teaching tools that you can genuinely integrate into the instructional fabric of classrooms. In addition, we can teach our students to use technologies to meet their own responsibility to become good learners and also use these technologies as effective tools to teach content. The goal of constructivism—teaching students so they know how and what to learn—is the path to fuller and more relevant understanding of life's important lessons.

Resources

CoVis: http://www.covis.nwu.edu

CSILE: http://www.ed.gov/pubs/EdReform-Studies/EdTech/csile.html

Day in the Life Series: http://www.colonial-williamsburg.com/History/teaching/Day-series/ditl_index.cfm

Decisions, Decisions in Social Studies: http://www.scholastic.com/products/tomsnyder.htm

Edgate: http://www.edgate.com

Electronic Emissary Project: http://emissary.wm.edu

ExploreLearning: http://www.explorelearning.com

Get A Clue: http://www.getaclue.com

Global Grocery List: http://landmark-project.com/ggl/

Global Lab: http://globallab.terc.edu

HomeworkSpot: http://homeworkspot.com

Logal Simulations in Science and Math: http://www.riverdeep.com/products/logal

MathMagic: http://mathforum.org/mathmagic/

ProQuestK-12: http://www.proquestk12.com

Schools For Thought: http://peabody.vanderbilt.edu/projects/funded/sft/general/sfthome.html

Smarthinking: http://www.smarthinking.com

WebPals: http://teacherbridge.cs.vt.edu/public/projects/Web+Pals/Home

---

Thomas M. Sherman is a professor of education in the College of Liberal Arts and Human Sciences at Virginia Tech. He teaches courses in educational psychology, evaluation, and instructional design and has written more than 100 articles for professional publications. Tom works regularly with practicing teachers and students in the areas of learning improvement and teaching strategies. He is also active in civic affairs, serving on local and state committees. **Dr. Barbara Kurshan** is the president of Educorp Consulting Corporation. She has a doctorate in education with an emphasis on computer-based applications. She has written numerous articles and texts and has designed software and networks to meet the needs of learners. She works with investment banking firms and venture groups on companies related to educational technology. She serves on the boards of Fablevision, Headsprout, and Medalis, and on the advisory boards of Pixel, WorldSage, and Tegrity.

Creating a Culture for Learning

SIDNEY TRUBOWITZ

Everywhere we read about efforts to revitalize schools. Such initiatives include restructuring governance by centralizing the power to make decisions, introducing a mandated curriculum for all teachers to follow, and reinforcing an accountability process with a strong focus on test scores. All these school-improvement proposals rely on a belief that change can be imposed from the outside without the participation of teachers, administrators, students, and parents. The likely results of such proposals are the development of learning environments that devote little time to reflection on what constitutes good practice; teachers who function in a mechanical fashion; and, after a momentary flurry of activity, a return to the status quo.

To achieve growth that will be lasting and more than superficial, what is needed are opportunities for public school staffs, parents, students, college faculty, and professional organizations to work together. Their aim must be to build a different kind of school culture, one that develops an exemplary curriculum, identifies effective teaching approaches, and establishes an atmosphere of mutual respect.

Having worked for more than twenty years with the Queens College-Louis Armstrong Middle School collaboration in New York City, I have seen firsthand what helps to establish a different kind of educational tone and what gets in the way of creating a culture promoting learning. Here is what I have learned.

The Elements of a New School Culture

A Thinking Atmosphere

The usual school organization finds the elementary schoolteacher with children all day long and the secondary school instructor seeing 150 students five times a week for a daily forty-five-minute period. The teacher begins each morning by signing in or by punching a time clock. From there it's a walk to a room, a door closed, and a day without peer dialogue. Professional development is restricted to the occasional guru-led workshop. No time is provided for teachers to reflect on the day's happenings with others or by themselves. In other countries "alone time" as part of the teacher's day is considered essential. It is not unusual in the corporate world to provide weekly brainstorming sessions for employees. Recent trends toward extending the school day and year will leave teachers with even less time for reflection.

In our public school-college collaboration, no single event or procedure made up the emotional and intellectual scaffolding that supported a thinking atmosphere. Rather, a day-to-day series of happenings contributed to a climate that encouraged reflection before moving into action. School administrators gave ready approval for teachers to attend professional conferences or visit other schools. A well-publicized professional library to which teachers and parents had easy access was established. Administrators, teachers, and professors who worked in the school recommended articles to each other. Faculty conferences were planned with teachers to demonstrate and discuss what colleagues were doing. At brown-bag luncheons and breakfast meetings with coffee provided, such topics as a favorite children's book or how best to use student teachers were explored. Teacher schedules were organized so that small numbers could meet regularly to discuss topics of mutual interest.

Open Communication

A school culture promoting learning bespeaks an openness of communication in which ideas and feelings are freely expressed and acknowledged. But if that is to occur, there is a need to move through and beyond times of distrust and suspicion. The origin of these negative attitudes is grounded in past experience. There are the years of criticism leveled at public school teachers and administrators by the press, college faculty, the public at large, and even the educational bureaucracy itself. Newspaper headlines highlight the sins of individual instructors and the inadequacies of public education and its personnel. External agencies and professors issue reports describing low levels of student achievement. Central office administrators talk blithely of inferior principals and teachers. It's little wonder that public school personnel experiencing the never-ending onslaught of reprimand view outsiders and often their own school administrators with skepticism and defensiveness. The messages they hear say "This is what you're doing wrong." They never see "This is what you're doing right." In our collaboration we found that only after extensive shared experience did staff feel comfortable enough to express its views without fearing retaliation.

Barriers between people eroded as college faculty and school administrators worked with teachers in their classrooms, as parent-teacher retreats took place at the college environmental center, as parents were invited to shadow their children through a typical day, and as parent-teacher-professor committees explored school concerns. When administrators, teachers, professors, and parents met to discuss educational matters, they interacted not as figures occupying particular roles but as individuals with views to offer. This is not to say that the participants all brought similar levels of expertise and experience to the discussions: only that everyone's contributions received respect. The aim always was to develop an atmosphere of trust in which attitudes of superiority and critical judgments were absent and where opposing stances provided leeway for empathic understanding.

We also recognized the value of social interaction to professional growth. School parties, student-faculty athletic events, theater groups, and book clubs all assisted in getting to the real person, moving past the outer layers of personality, and facilitating authentic communication.

The Value of an Outside Observer

One of the assets school staffs bring to their work is extensive experience within their own institutions. Even the most introspective educators, however, face the dangers of allowing familiarity to influence objectivity and of failing to profit from what others have learned elsewhere. Perceptive observers can ask questions and make comments that broaden understanding and supply insights that may escape those who are immersed in a project.

In our public school-college collaboration, we worked with people of broad backgrounds whose lack of knowledge of bureaucratic strictures proved a boon as they made suggestions free from traditional thinking. For example, at one session dealing with the problem of acclimating students and parents from throughout Queens to a new middle school, Seymour Sarason, a professor emeritus of Yale University and a periodic visitor to thc school, recommended conducting a week-long orientation for newcomers and their families before the beginning of the school year. We were able to persuade the board of education of the value of such an activity despite its departure from usual practice. It has since become a fixture in how the school operates.

In another instance, Clarence Bunch, a professor of art education, proposed installing a school museum. After consultation with the principal, teachers, and colleagues, it too has become an integral part of how the Louis Armstrong Middle School functions. It is now the scene of displays of student work, shows by neighborhood artists, and exhibitions of artifacts produced by children from other countries.

The Need to Develop a Common Language

A healthy educational community needs to avoid jargon and to use words and phrases that have shared meaning. The list of terms bandied about in discussions of education without clear definition is long. For example, there is much support for the idea of parental involvement, but there is little talk about how parents are to participate in a school. Are they to help set goals? To be used only as resource people? To evaluate teachers? To establish budgetary priorities? To select texts?

Other ideas needing clarification include accountability, curriculum, staff development, and leadership. To create a culture in which the participants communicate with clarity, there is a need to reach common understanding of these terms and others.

In our collaboration, the effort to ensure that people used mutually understood terms was supported by weekly preschool meetings attended by the principal, teachers, parents, and college faculty. Teachers and professors joining with parents at the monthly Parent-Teachers Association (PTA) meetings also helped to bridge language barriers.

Respecting Teacher Autonomy

In many schools, teachers are besieged by external impositions on instructional time. Public-address announcements interrupt the day. Directives from the district office insist on participation in citywide contests. A steady stream of messages emanating from the school's main office, administrators, colleagues, and others fragments the flow of teacher-student interaction. Test scores become the single measure of teacher effectiveness, with the result that teaching to the test becomes the norm and occupies much of the school day. Teachers are mandated to teach in a prescribed manner. A one-size-fits-all approach views teaching as a robotic endeavor rather than one demanding thoughtful analysis of student needs.

At the Louis Armstrong Middle School, curriculum exploration and experimentation are the norm, undergirded by a belief that a rich educational program will result in good student test scores. That has been the case over the years. It has also become a cardinal rule that the public-address system is used only for the direst of emergencies; that for the first hour at least, messages to classrooms are forbidden; and that demands for written reports are to be kept to a minimum. If time for instruction is to be valued, then the teacher's domain, the classroom, needs respect and not indiscriminate intrusion.

Obstacles to Building a Positive School Culture

The task of building a school culture that promotes learning is ongoing with the constant struggle to overcome obstacles. For example, the traditional way in which schools function inhibits an easy exchange of ideas among professionals. Schools have a hierarchical organization headed by a principal aided by assistant principals, chairpeople, and deans. The teacher group alone is seen as the target for improvement. A common method for achieving instructional growth is the supervisory observation, with classroom visits followed by a discussion in which the principal, after an initial listing of strengths, outlines areas in need of improvement. Rarely is this process viewed as a conversation in which ideas are shared. Rarely are questions asked that might encourage reflection. Rarely are plans made to pursue issues in greater depth. The subordinate position of the teacher is reinforced by requiring that planbooks gain administrative approval and letters sent home are first screened by the principal.

If thinking is to become part of the school culture, there should be a different conception of how people in different roles are to operate. The hierarchical nature of schools, with communication flowing only one way, leaves little opportunity for groups to dialogue about instructional issues.

The limitations of professional preparation present another problem. Cooperation and collegiality are characteristics of a school culture promoting group exploration of ideas. When educators have had little experience in working together, the attempt to collaborate is likely to meet strong obstacles. The education of teachers, administrators, and such specialists as reading instructors, school psychologists, and special education staff takes place in separate courses. With other faculty I arranged to bring graduate classes of special education teachers, prospective school psychologists, and potential administrators together for a few sessions. The initial inability of the participants to listen to the point of view of the others was startling. It is clear that if school professionals are to work effectively with one another, teacher-preparation programs must help future educators become aware of how roles shape behavior and learn ways of dealing with conflict.

The culture prevailing in the society outside schools also impacts the task of creating a thoughtful school community. We live in an environment filled with demands for immediate solutions to complex problems. Profound political issues are presented in sound bites. Popular television programs appeal to instincts removed from any need to think. The speed of e-mail and fax machines obliterates the opportunity for considered contemplation before making a response. To build a culture supportive of learning, schools must resist external pressures pushing for precipitous action unsupported by prior thinking.

Another obstacle to establishing a culture for learning is the inevitability of resistance to new ideas. The teaching profession draws people who are hard workers, who are committed to service, and who place a high value on stability. Attempts to alter customary work patterns will encounter resistance. The desire for the security of the status quo will serve to reinforce customary modes of behavior and to block out ideas that are different. The challenge for those trying to create a new school culture is to empathize with the reluctance to change and, at the same time, to support those ready to explore new approaches to education.

To develop schools that are not simply institutions responding to the external pressures prevailing at a particular time but rather are centers of ongoing exploration, learning, thinking, and adapting to the needs of students, we need to look more closely at how schools are organized, how people interact with one another, how change occurs, and how we view the role of the teacher.

SIDNEY TRUBOWITZ is a professor emeritus at Queens College of the City University of New York.

Reprinted with permission of the author from *Educational Horizons*, quarterly journal of Pi Lambda Theta Inc., International Honor Society and Professional Association in Education, P O Box 6626, Bloomington, IN 47401, Spring 2005, pp. 171–176.

Teaching for Deep Learning

The authors have been engaged in research focused on students' depth of learning as well as teachers' efforts to foster deep learning. Findings from a study examining the teaching practices and student learning outcomes of sixty-four teachers in seventeen different states (Smith et al. 2005) indicated that most of the learning in these classrooms was characterized by reproduction, categorizing of information, or replication of a simple procedure. In addition to these and other findings, in this article, the authors provide a definition of surface and deep learning and describe the structure of the observed learning outcome taxonomy, which was used to evaluate depth of learning. The authors also provide implications for practitioners interested in fostering deep student learning.

TRACY WILSON SMITH AND SUSAN A. COLBY

In public education and in a democratic society, few could question the spirit and intention of the moral imperative to provide all children the opportunity to learn and meet high standards. However, in recent years, our approaches to help all students meet higher standards have resulted in the establishment of a system in which we equate high standards with high test scores. At times, it seems such a system limits students' prospects for moving beyond superficial thinking (Kohn 2000). As educators, we must advocate for a focus on learning that fosters students' opportunities to reach for deeper levels of understanding. Evidence has shown that teachers can adopt a surface or deep approach to teaching, which has consequential effects on what and how students learn (Boulton-Lewis et al. 2001).

Recently, we completed a study examining the teaching practices and student learning outcomes of sixty-four teachers in seventeen states (Smith, Gordon, Colby, and Wang 2005). The sample included elementary, middle, and high school teachers. Thirty-five (55 percent) of the participants had achieved National Board Certification, and twenty-nine (45 percent) had attempted but had not achieved National Board Certification. Specifically, we designed the study to answer two research questions: (*a*) Do students taught by National Board Certified teachers produce deeper responses (to class assignments and standardized writing assessments) than students of teachers who attempted National Board Certification but were not certified? (*b*) Do National Board Certified teachers develop instruction and structure class assignments designed to produce deeper responses than teachers who attempted National Board Certification but were not certified?

The findings of our study yielded statistically significant differences between the comparison groups; however, some of the most interesting results of the study were related to teachers' efforts to elicit and obtain deep learning outcomes with their students, regardless of their National Board Certification status. We assessed teachers' instructional aims through qualitative and quantitative analyses of work samples submitted based on a unit of instruction. The findings indicated that a majority of the teachers (64 percent), regardless of certification status, aimed instruction and assignments toward surface learning outcomes. Additionally, analysis of student work samples collected in the study suggested that the student outcomes in most of the teachers' classrooms were at the surface level (78 percent). These findings suggest that most of the learning in these classrooms was characterized by reproduction or categorizing of information or replication of a simple procedure.

In our study, we learned that our teacher participants tended to teach at surface levels; therefore, their students generated surface responses. Furthermore, we suspect that this finding is not uncommon among the general population of teachers and students. To reverse this trend, we propose that teachers need to understand, value, and foster deep approaches to learning in their students.

Defining Surface and Deep Learning

Although the distinction between surface and deep learning seems intuitive to most educators, it has also been well documented. Marton and Säljö (1976) completed the original work related to deep and surface approaches to learning. Their study examined students' approaches to a particular task. They instructed students participating in the study to read a text and told them that they would later be asked questions about it. Students adopted two differing approaches to this task. The first approach was to try to understand the big ideas in the passage; their focus was on comprehending and understanding the text. The researchers characterized students using this approach as adopting a deep approach to learning. The second approach involved an attempt to remember the facts and details from the text and a focus on what they thought they would be asked later. This group demonstrated rote learning, or a superficial, surface approach to the task.

According to Marton's framework, a surface approach involves minimum engagement with the task, typically a focus on memorization or applying procedures that do not involve reflection, and usually an intention to gain a passing grade. In contrast, a deep approach to learning involves an intention to understand and impose meaning. Here, the student focuses on relationships between various aspects of the content, formulates hypotheses or beliefs about the structure of the problem or concept, and relates more to obtaining an intrinsic interest in learning and understanding. High-quality learning outcomes are associated with deep approaches whereas low-quality outcomes are associated with surface approaches (Biggs 1987; Entwistle 2001; Marton and Säljö 1984). Teachers who are more likely to lead students to deep learning structure lessons, set tasks, and provide feedback and challenge that encourage the development of deep processing (Hattie 1998, 2002).

The SOLO Taxonomy

In our study, we used a research-based framework to assess teachers' instructional approaches and students' learning outcomes. This framework, the structure of the observed learning outcome (SOLO) taxonomy, is a promising tool that educators can use to understand and examine the depth of teaching and learning. Informed by the work of Marton (1976, 1984) and his colleagues, Biggs and Collis (1982) created the SOLO taxonomy that illustrates a continuum from surface to deep learning. The SOLO taxonomy is structured into five major hierarchical levels that reflect the quality of learning of a particular episode or task. In his most recent book, Biggs (1999) represented the SOLO taxonomy graphically, as shown in figure 1.

The first level, prestructural, represents a response that is irrelevant or misses the point. The next two levels, unistructural and multistructural, correspond to surface learning, and the final two (relational and extended abstract) correspond to deep learning. An advantage and unique distinction of the SOLO model is that it can be used to reliably analyze and interpret classroom lessons and assignments, and the student work produced in response to those assignments (Bond et al. 2000; Boulton-Lewis et al. 2001; Boulton-Lewis, Wilss, and Mutch 1996; Burnett 1999; Chan et al. 2002; Hattie 1998, 2002; Hattie et al. 1996).

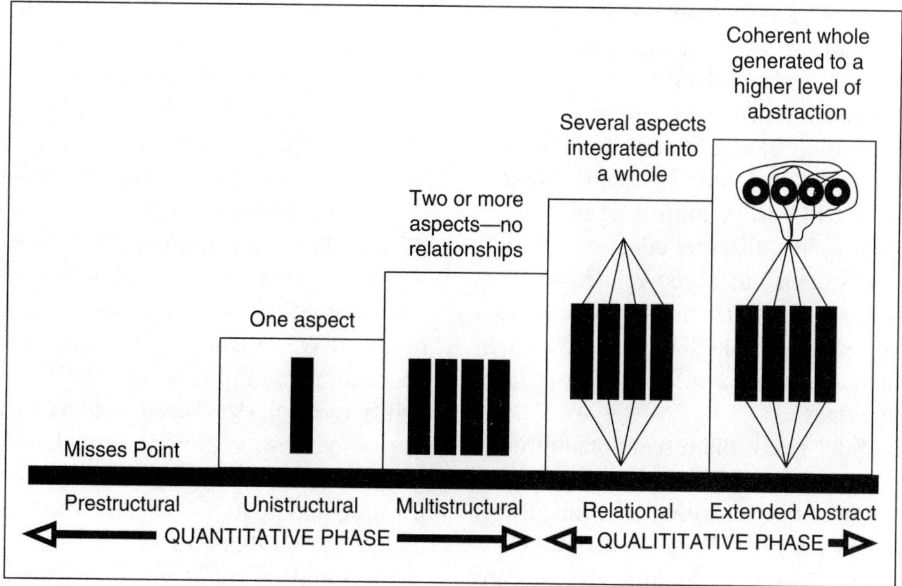

Figure 1 Graphic representation of the structure of the observed learning outcome (SOLO) taxonomy (Biggs 1999).

A Call to Action: Implications for Practitioners

What prevented the teachers in our study from fostering deep learning outcomes among their students? One possibility is that these teachers had not been given the training, tools, and time to engage in practices that contribute to these outcomes. Educators must engage in intentional efforts to foster deep learning in their students. This section gives recommendations for promoting deep learning among students. We have also used a high school world history class scenario to illustrate how the SOLO taxonomy can be translated into practice.

Engage in Dialogue about Deep Learning

A critical first step in the effort to foster deep student learning is to raise and cultivate awareness regarding the characteristics of deep and surface learning. One way to accomplish this is to engage all members of the learning community in intentional, substantive, and inclusive dialogue about student learning. Some of these conversations should take place as part of formal professional development sessions focused on understanding what deep learning looks like. Other conversations, although more informal, should occur more frequently among teams of colleagues. For example, in a typical ninth grade world history course, students might be asked to analyze the causes and results of twentieth-century conflicts among nations (North Carolina standard course of study). Prior to developing this set of lessons, world history teachers might engage in collegial dialogue focused on the following questions: (*a*) What does a deep understanding of twentieth-century conflicts look like? (*b*) How will we know that students have a deep understanding of these conflicts? A deep level of learning related to this outcome might be characterized by a response that uses multiple independent details about the causes and effects of specific conflicts to support a general understanding of how conflicts have affected our nation and our world. If a student is able to construct such a sophisticated response, that student will be more able to develop and support generalizations in a different context (e.g., current global conflicts). Collegial dialogue related to deep learning outcomes is essential as teachers progress from identifying what deep learning looks like in their content area to developing activities and assessments correlated with deep learning outcomes.

In the early stages of our study, the research team found our dialogue about learning to be particularly helpful as we worked collaboratively to design a writing assessment that would elicit deep student learning. Prior to designing the writing assessment, we engaged in multiple discussions focused on the question: What is depth of knowledge of writing? As we began to formulate our thoughts, we realized how important our dialogue was to our understanding of what deep learning looks like in the area of writing. We then envisioned how helpful similar conversations would be to students engaged in the learning process. From our experiences, we discovered that students who move beyond a surface approach to learning consider any given task as a series of internal rhetorical questions: What do I know about this subject? How does this information relate to what I already know? What is the broader implication or significance of what I've learned? If students do not naturally ask these questions, their teachers must model aloud thought processes that lead to deep outcomes and support students as they are engaged in reflecting about the quality of their own learning. Our goal as teachers should be to help students ask questions of themselves as they are learning and to help them establish habits for continually using a deep approach to learning.

Examine Teaching and Learning

In addition to raising awareness and understanding about the quality of student learning through dialogue, educators must engage in purposeful, systematic examinations of their teaching and the resultant student learning. Teachers must critically examine the teaching resources they are using, the types of questions they are asking students, the assignments they are developing and requiring of students, and their methods of assessing the quality of student learning. One repeating pattern in the teachers' artifacts was that the teachers' expectations or the design of the instructional materials seemed to limit students. It was often difficult to determine students' actual depth of learning because the tasks and questions assigned to them aimed only at surface outcomes. Students rarely demonstrated a deep understanding when the tasks were not aimed at fostering deep learning outcomes.

The SOLO taxonomy is particularly helpful as a tool for examining the quality of teaching and learning. Teachers can use the SOLO taxonomy to construct and categorize questions and assignments (Hattie and Purdie 1998) and to determine whether their instructional goals and tasks will promote deep student learning. Returning to our world history class scenario, a high school world history teacher adopting a surface approach to learning may teach about the causes and results of World War II by lecturing, assigning readings, and conducting multiple-choice tests that evaluate a student's ability to memorize, recall, and even categorize the specific causes and results previously reviewed. In contrast, a high school world history teacher adopting a deep approach to learning may require students to develop a more conceptual understanding about war. The teacher may require students to use this understanding when proposing solutions to current conflicts around the world. Using the SOLO taxonomy in content-specific instruction and assessment allows teachers to determine whether they are facilitating a surface or deep approach to learning.

The usefulness of the taxonomy was evident in our study. When we evaluated the teachers' materials, we realized that many of the resources were commercially made. We worked with our scorers to defuse the bias that often accompanies the observation of worksheet-driven instruction. We trained scorers to assess the value and intent of materials for eliciting deep student learning based on the SOLO taxonomy rubrics created for this study. Even when teachers had not created the materials, we assumed that they purposely selected them for the particular lessons. If the teaching resources were designed to elicit surface responses, usually students responded in like manner. If, however, the instructional materials were designed to foster the understanding of concepts, relationships, and other deep outcomes, students made connections among the facts and details presented to arrive at more sophisticated understandings. By examining the learning goals, resources, content, and sequence of instruction with the SOLO taxonomy in mind, teachers can ascertain if their instructional materials and approaches have potential to move students beyond surface into deep learning.

Likewise, teachers can use the SOLO taxonomy to evaluate the work and responses of students. Examining student learning is essential if we are to understand the results of our efforts to support students in achieving deep learning. Our analyses of student work should be collaborative and independent. Collaborative examinations of student work help teachers determine the concepts, principles, and generalizations they value in their respective content areas. By examining student work samples collaboratively, with others who teach the same course or content, teachers can identify student work at different levels of the continuum and analyze how and why particular work samples represent various levels. More important, what practitioners learn from this process can inform discussions about how they might help students in achieving deep learning outcomes.

Equally as important are independent examinations of student work that, conducted regularly, allow teachers to determine their own effectiveness in helping students achieve deep learning outcomes. Using the SOLO taxonomy as a framework when examining work produced by their students, teachers can begin to understand what type of learning their instructional methods are yielding and how well their students are performing. They can then use this information to support students in achieving deep learning outcomes related to specific content. Because the SOLO taxonomy represents a learning cycle, we must continually support students as we introduce new ideas. We cannot assume that because a student has reached a deep level of understanding with one idea, the student will understand other ideas at the same level. One simple method for supporting students in the attainment of deep learning outcomes is to assist them in reaching for the next level on the SOLO taxonomy. Our experiences as researchers and classroom teachers indicate that the taxonomy is so straightforward that students in upper elementary, high school, and college can understand its value for evaluating their own learning.

Rethink Classroom Assessment

One of the greatest values of the SOLO taxonomy is that it provides a framework for accomplishing a critical aim of classroom assessment: improving student understanding and performance. Wiggins (1998) suggested, "the aim of assessment is primarily to *educate and improve* student performance, not merely to *audit* it" (original emphasis, 7). Wiggins contended that when we test what is easy to test, we sacrifice our aims, our children's intellectual needs, and information regarding what we truly want to assess. Instead, we settle for score accuracy and efficiency. If we do not study how students learn and demonstrate their learning, we can never understand how to help them learn better. Similarly, Hattie and Jaeger (1998) argued for an approach to assessment that acknowledges its importance in the learning process. They contend "assessment needs to be an integral part of a model of teaching and learning if it is to change from its present status as an adjunct to 'see' if learning has occurred, to a new status of being part of the teaching and learning process" (111). The SOLO taxonomy has potential for helping practitioners assess student learning in process. It not only acknowledges the importance of facts and information, but also provides a way to think about the progression of student learning to higher levels.

For example, the SOLO taxonomy has practical benefits when used as the framework for communicating expectations and creating rubrics to evaluate student work. If the teacher of the world history course asked students to describe the relationships between the causes and effects of twentieth-century conflicts among nations, the responses he or she might receive are likely to represent a range of complexity. If the teacher wants to evaluate students' depth of learning relative to the curriculum goal, the task must be open enough that students have flexibility in their responses. She can provide feedback to students who provided surface responses and guide them to deeper levels of learning. In this way, SOLO is used as an instructional and an evaluative tool. Table 1 provides characteristics of possible responses for each level of the SOLO taxonomy.

Our study provides evidence that although deep learning can happen, most often, it does not. Promising steps along the way to helping students achieve deep learning include (*a*) supporting teachers as they engage in dialogue about surface and deep learning, (*b*) examining teaching practices and the resultant student learning, and (*c*) rethinking classroom

Table 1 Characteristics of Possible Student Responses Corresponding to Structure of the Observed Learning Outcome (SOLO) Levels

	SOLO Level	Characteristics of Possible Student Response	Rationale for SOLO Rating
Surface	Prestructural	The student response indicates that there were many causes and effects of conflicts in the twentieth century.	The student misses the point and generates a response that merely repeats the question.
	Unistructural	The student response provides one cause and effect pair related to World War II.	The response focuses on only one aspect of the task. The student has defined the task in a limited way, focusing only on one specific twentieth-century conflict.
	Mulistructural	The student response provides multiple cause and effect pairs related to World War II.	The student has provided multiple relevant details but has not discussed the relationship among those details. The teacher knows that the student used a recall strategy to generate the response because all cause and effect pairs had been discussed in class.
Deep	Relational	The student response provides multiple cause and effect pairs related to multiple twentieth-century conflicts. Additionally, the student discusses the relationships between the causes and effects and uses examples from various conflicts as support.	The student has identified multiple relevant details and has discussed the relationship between these details.
	Extended abstract	The student response provides multiple cause and effect pairs related to multiple twentieth-century conflicts. Additionally, the student discusses the relationships between the causes and effects and uses examples from various conflicts as support. Finally, the student hypothesizes how similar cause and effect pairs might play out in specific current conflicts (or in conflicts in regions of the world not previously discussed).	The student has identified multiple relevant details, discussed the relationships among these details, and has constructed principles about conflict that he or she has used to develop hypotheses about global conflicts that might not have been explicitly studied in the twentieth-century conflicts unit.

assessment with deep learning approaches in mind. Abigail Adams stated, "learning is not attained by chance; it must be sought for with ardor and attended to with diligence" (Howe 2003). Our research has shown that teachers' efforts to foster deep learning outcomes do make a difference. As educators, we must devote ourselves to intentional rather than happenstance efforts to teach for deep student learning.

References

Biggs, J. 1987. *Student approaches to learning and studying.* Melbourne: Australian Council for Educational Research.

———. 1999. *Teaching for quality learning at university.* England: Society for Research into Higher Education and Open University Press.

Biggs, J., and K. F. Collis. 1982. *Evaluating the quality of learning: The SOLO taxonomy.* New York: Academic.

Bond, L., T. W. Smith, W. K. Baker, and J. A. C. Hattie. 2000. *The certification system of the national board for professional teaching standards: A construct and consequential validity study.* http://www.nbpts.org/research/research_archive.cfm (accessed October 1, 2000).

Boulton-Lewis, G. M., D. Smith, A. R. McCrindle, P. C. Burnett, and K. J. Campbell. 2001. Secondary teachers' conceptions of teaching and learning. *Learning and Instruction* 11 (1): 35–51.

Boulton-Lewis, G. M., L. Wilss, and S. Mutch. 1996. Teachers as adult learners: Their knowledge of their own learning and implications for teaching. *Higher Education* 32 (1): 89–106.

Burnett, P. C. 1999. *Assessing the outcomes of counseling within a learning framework.* Paper presented at the annual conference of the American Educational Research Association, Montreal, Canada.

Chan, C. C., M. Tsui, M. Y. C. Chan, and J. H. Hong. 2002. Applying the structure of the observed learning outcomes (SOLO) taxonomy on student's learning outcomes: An empirical study. *Assessment and Evaluation in Higher Education* 27 (6): 511–17.

Entwistle, N. 2001. Conceptions, styles and approaches within higher education: Analytic abstractions and everyday experience. In *Perspectives on cognitive, learning, and thinking styles,* ed. R. Sternberg and L. F. Zhang, 103–36. Mahwah, NJ: Erlbaum.

Hattie, J. A. C. 1998. *Evaluating the Paideia program in Guilford County schools: First year report: 1997–1998.* Greensboro: Center for Educational Research and Evaluation, University of North Carolina, Greensboro.

———. 2002. What are the attributes of excellent teachers? In *Teachers make a difference: What is the research evidence?,* ed. Bev Webber, 1–17. Wellington: New Zealand Council for Educational Research.

Hattie, J. A. C., J. C. Clinton, M. Thompson, and H. Schmitt-Davis. 1996. *Identifying expert teachers.* Technical report presented to the National Board for Professional Standards, Detroit, MI.

Hattie, J. A. C., and R. Jaeger. 1998. Assessment and classroom learning: A deductive approach. *Assessment in Education* 5 (1): 111–21.

Hattie, J. A. C., and N. Purdie. 1998. The SOLO model: Addressing fundamental measurement issues. In *Teaching and learning in higher education,* ed. B. Dart and G. Boulton-Lewis, 72–101. Melbourne: ACER Press.

Howe, R., ed. 2003. *The quotable teacher.* Guilford, CT: Lyons.

Kohn, A. 2000. Standardized testing and its victims. *Education Week.* http://www.alfiekohn.org/teaching/edweek/staiv.htm (accessed September 27, 2000).

Marton, F., and R. Säljö. 1976. On qualitative differences in learning: Outcome as a function of learners' conception of task. *British Journal of Educational Psychology* 46: 115–27.

———. 1984. Approaches to learning. In *The experience of learning,* ed. F. Marton, D. Hounsell, and D. N. Entwistle, 39–58. Edinburgh: Scottish Academic Press.

Smith, T. W., B. Gordon, S. A. Colby, and J. Wang. 2005. *An examination of the relationship between depth of student learning and national board certification status.* http://www.nbpts.org/UserFiles/File/Applachian_State_study_D_-_Smith.pdf (accessed January 8, 2007).

Wiggins, G. 1998. *Educative assessment: Designing assessments to inform and improve student performance.* San Francisco: Josey-Bass.

Tracy Wilson Smith, PhD, is an associate professor in the Department of Curriculum and Instruction at Appalachian State University in Boone, North Carolina, where she also serves as assistant middle grades education program coordinator. Susan A. Colby, EdD, is assistant professor in the Department of Curriculum and Instruction at Appalachian State University in Boone, North Carolina.

The Changing Classroom: Challenges for Teachers

DOUGLAS KELLNER, PHD

Since the emergence of the Internet and the dramatic expansion of PCs in education, business and everyday life, there have been fierce debates about whether and how to employ computers in K–12 education. At first, there was a generational divide with younger teachers and some students putting computers to use in the classroom and discovering along the way how information technology could contribute to learning. However, for many educators comfortably conditioned by traditional teaching methods, the advent of technology was not a welcomed change. Yet with the explosive development of the Internet in the '90s and the enthusiastic embrace of the "information superhighway" by the Clinton administration, many educators noticed that computers could play a critical role in teaching. As the classroom began to change with the integration of technology, the role of the teacher has inevitably changed too. With technology delivering an ever-accelerating learning curve which everyone must keep up with, teachers have begun to see that they must learn to work differently with their students in order for education to remain relevant and effective.

Changing the Learning Process

In the late '90s, many in the education field and government, as well as in the media and public, recognized a "digital divide" in which some school districts and classrooms were "wired" and had up-to-date computer technology, while others did not. Accordingly, there were efforts undertaken by government, business and educators to wire classrooms and make computer technology available to a greater number of students and teachers.

While many teachers and students are engaging in innovative forms of research and novel projects, there are still many traditional teachers who resist learning new computer skills and do not want to bring computer-based technologies into their classrooms. Yet, these technologies carry a transformative power, and many schools recognizing this are now requiring that teachers make use of computer-mediated instruction. Students today are exposed to a barrage of new technologies outside of the classroom, including home computers, e-mail and text messaging, and many possess greater technological skills than their teachers. This has shifted a dynamic between teachers and their students, forcing teachers to engage in the learning process themselves.

Teachers have to develop the ability to demonstrate how these technologies can be used for academic purposes and convey the educational advantages of computers and the Internet to their students. This means acquiring and teaching new literacies involving teachers and students in innovative types of research projects, and interacting in novel ways as everyone learns to use new technology and media.

Indeed, to meet the challenges of an always-evolving high-tech society, teachers today need to develop multiple forms of computer and information literacy to help improve education. This means using technology in the classroom to illustrate lesson topics; teaching students how to use the Internet and information technology to research topics; and using technology to enhance education outside the classroom, ideally in ways that involve students in the learning process.

Cultivating Information Literacy Skills

While computer literacy concerning how to use different computer programs is usually interpreted in narrow, technical terms, a broader conception would involve learning how to access and evaluate information, using the technology for research and discussion of issues, and even producing Web sites, Weblogs or other forms of Internet culture. In order to achieve these goals, teachers need to involve students in hands-on projects that make them active participants in the learning process rather than passive receptacles of information. Group projects can also spark curiosity, making the learning experience fun.

Merely putting computers in a lab or classroom will not necessarily have beneficial effects; there are important preconditions that must be met before technology can enhance learning. At the most basic level, many schools lack adequate technical support and expertise that will enable teachers to make effective use of information technology. Some teachers simply do not have a clear idea of how they can actually use information technology to better teach their subject matter and their students.

Many teachers are developing highly promising projects that make productive use of information technology, and in some cases students are taking the lead and helping produce instructive educational material. However, some students may be more computer literate than their teachers. These students are often willing and able to share their skills with their teachers and their classmates. The result is a changing classroom and learning environment that promises to re-involve students in the learning process while cultivating multiple literacies that will be of use in further education, future job endeavors and everyday life.

To begin, it is useful for teachers to start with assignments that do not require specialized computer skills and knowledge. Teachers can take a topic from current events or an issue from an existing course, and assign students to use a search engine such as Google to search for three or four items on a specific topic. They can then ask their students how useful the material was for clarifying the topic or issue at hand. A further exercise might explore what limitations students encountered while using Internet materials as opposed to textbooks or library resources. Teachers must advance their own "information literacy" skills and learn to discern the quality of material their students are accessing through this process. Teachers, along with students, will quickly learn that some Internet sites may contain misinformation and be highly biased, while others will be educational and instructive. Just as students need to learn how to use the library to access the most relevant and sound print material, both teachers and students must also become Internet literate and learn to critically evaluate the online information they access.

Providing Participatory Learning Projects

When using technology in the classroom, teachers must become open-minded and recognize that learning new processes and skills is an ongoing necessity. Although this involves added work, there are many imaginative ways of using technology to engage students in the learning process. High school students, for example, can learn a more advanced use of information technology that would include developing a course Web site. Here, students could put in hyperlinks to relevant course material from reputable Internet sources on the topic being taught. Obviously, developing a Web site involves some technical skill, although there is often someone in the school computer lab who is able to undertake the project. In some cases, students also might be able to do the development themselves. The teacher can then have students do research to add to the site, which is an ideal way for everyone, teachers included, to develop Web site construction skills and learn to publish online. An additional plus this exercise provides is that classes can expand upon the site from year to year in order to provide important teaching resources that makes materials available to an Internet-wide audience around the globe.

Another shift for teachers comes with adopting a more flexible mindset about how the lesson plan should flow. This means that teachers must get comfortable with the idea of not teaching all their students the same information at the same time. Since most classrooms do not have enough computers to enable everybody in class to use them simultaneously, teachers can rotate students to different projects so that while some work on computers, others can utilize textbooks and other materials.

Next, if there is access to computer labs and technical support, teachers can also set up a class bulletin board or discussion forum on a Web site and have students log in to discuss a certain topic. Students can be assigned to make comments on topics studied in the classroom, share information or ideas, and comment on other students' postings. Also, students could be assigned to search and post Internet addresses (i.e., URLs) of interesting sites on the topic discussed, as well as given the task of commenting on what they learned from the site and why they think it is reliable and educationally useful.

A more advanced use of the Internet for high school students would be to have students develop Weblogs, or blogs, which consist of student postings on specific topics. (For a detailed look at the use of blogs in the classroom from a 2004 issue of *T.H.E. Journal,* visit http://www.thejournal.com/magazine/vault/A4677.cfm.) Blogs can range from personal diaries discussing what students are reading, learning and doing in relation to the course, to posting hyperlinks for useful Internet sites to debate over issues being discussed in class or of other topical interests.

There are several Weblog sites such as SchoolBlogs.com or Blogger.com that provide free Weblog technology. There have been recent articles on how students are taking to blogging, as well as making it a highly involving and interesting cultural forum as well (Nussbaum 2004).

Such participatory learning projects not only provide real-life experience of Internet research, production or discussion, but help prepare students for activities later in life, ranging from preparation for jobs to giving them the social and communicative skills necessary to be a good citizen. Therefore, teachers face the challenge of transforming their classrooms to make learning more relevant for the contemporary era, as well as preparing their students to actively engage and participate in the learning process and the society of tomorrow.

Reference

Nussbaum, E. 2004. "My So-Called Blog." *New York Times* 11 January (D1). Online: http://www.nytimes.com/2004/01/11/magazine/11BLOG.html.

Douglas Kellner, PhD, serves as the 2003–2004 Fellow of The Sudikoff Family Institute for Education & New Media and holds the distinguished George F. Kneller Chair in the Philosophy of Education at UCLA's Graduate School of Education & Information Studies. His work explores cultural studies, the philosophy of education, and the relationship between technology, education and society.

Improve Your Verbal Questioning

KENNETH E. VOGLER

Most teachers are well aware that verbal questioning can aid student learning. Asking questions can stimulate students to think about the content being studied (Carlson 1997; Good and Brophy 2000; Graesser and Person 1994; Wilen 2004; Wilen 2001), connect it to prior knowledge (Good and Brophy 2000; Graesser and Person 1994; Wilen 2001), consider its meanings and implications (Carlson 1997; Good and Brophy 2000; Graesser and Person 1994; Seymour and Osana 2003; Wilen 2004), and explore its applications (Carlson 1997; Good and Brophy 2000; Graesser and Person 1994; Wilen 2001). Researchers have found that teachers ask about 300–400 questions per day (Levin and Long 1981), and depending on the type of lesson, as many as 120 questions per hour (Carlson 1991; Carlson 1997; Graesser and Person 1994). With teachers asking this many questions, it is essential that they be skilled in using verbal questioning. Unfortunately, research on teachers' use of verbal questioning has shown that this skill is typically less effective than it could be (Anderson and Burns 1989; Dantonio 1990; Graesser and Person 1994; Seymour and Osana 2003).

A common problem with many teachers' use of verbal questioning is a lack of knowledge about questioning taxonomies and sequencing, knowledge essential for productive verbal questioning (Barnes 1979; Good and Brophy 2000; Lucking 1978; Pollack 1988; Rice 1977; Wilen 2001). Without an understanding of the different cognitive levels of questions, teachers could quite possibly be asking questions at only one or two cognitive levels, probably asking low cognitive level questions that require students to merely recall knowledge or information, rather than asking high cognitive level questions that require students to perform higher order thinking (see Martin 1979; Redfield and Rousseau 1981; Wilen and Clegg 1986; Wilen 2001; Wimer et al. 2001). Without an understanding of the sequence to ask questions, delivery techniques such as the use of wait time, prompting, probing, and refocusing become less effective. And if the questions are poorly worded or the sequence is haphazard, even skillfully used delivery techniques will not prevent student confusion and frustration (Good and Brophy 2000). This article will begin by comparing different question taxonomies, recognizing the importance of knowing the right question to ask and when to ask it, as well as understanding that verbal questioning is a skill that must be practiced before it can be effectively used. Next, it will review relevant research on question sequencing and patterns. Finally, it will present an activity using colleague classroom observations to improve teachers' verbal question sequencing.

Question Taxonomies

Taxonomies are human constructs used to classify questions based on the intellectual behavior or mental activity needed to formulate an answer (Morgan and Schreiber 1969). They are very similar to a continuum. Questions that may have only one "correct" answer and require only minimal mental activity are at one end of the continuum. More complex questions requiring greater mental activity are at the other end of the continuum.

Arguably, the most well-known question taxonomy was created by Benjamin Bloom and his associates—known formally as Bloom's Taxonomy of the Cognitive Domain, or more commonly, Bloom's Taxonomy. Bloom's Taxonomy is comprised of six levels of intellectual behavior (Bloom 1956).

1. *Knowledge.* The knowledge level is the lowest level. At this level, students are only asked to recall information.
2. *Comprehension.* At the comprehension level, students are asked only to put information in another form.
3. *Application.* At this level, students are asked to apply known facts, principles, and/or generalizations to solve a problem.
4. *Analysis.* A question at the analysis level asks students to identify and comprehend elements of a process, communication, or series of events.
5. *Synthesis.* At this level, students are asked to engage in original creative thinking.
6. *Evaluation.* This is the highest questioning level. Students are asked to determine how closely a concept or idea is consistent with standards or values.

Bloom's Taxonomy is just one of a number of questioning taxonomies. Table 1 compares Bloom's Taxonomy with the questioning taxonomies of Krathwohl (2002) and Gallagher and Ascher (1963).

As shown in table 1, Krathwohl's Taxonomy, sometimes referred to as "the revised Bloom's Taxonomy" or simply "the revised Taxonomy"

Table 1 Comparison of Different Questioning Taxonomies

Bloom	Krathwohl	Gallagher and Ascher
Knowledge	Remember	Cognitive-memory
Comprehension	Understand	Convergent thinking
Application	Apply	
Analysis	Analyze	Divergent thinking
Synthesis	Evaluate	
Evaluation	Create	Evaluative thinking

Sources. Airasian, P. W., K. A. Cruikshank, R. E. Mayer, P. R. Pintrich, J. Raths, and M. C. Wittrock. 2001. *A taxonumy for learning, teaching, and assessing: A revision of Bloom's taxonomy of educational objectives.* Ed. L. W. Anderson and D. R. Krathwohl. New York: Longman, Bloom, B. S. 1956. *Taxonomy of educational objectives, handbook I: Cognitive domain.* New York: David McKay. Gallagher, J. J., and M. J. Ascher, 1963. A preliminary report on analyses of classroom interaction. *Merrill-Palmer Quarterly* 9 (1): 183–94.

(see Airasian and Miranda 2002; Byrd 2002; Krathwohl 2002), uses the same number of categories as Bloom's Taxonomy, but there are some differences. Knowledge, the first category in Bloom's Taxonomy, was renamed Remember, and Comprehension was renamed Understand. These category changes do not reflect a difference in the cognitive level of the questions between the two taxonomies, but in their description. The terms "Remember" and "Understand" were chosen because they are commonly used by teachers to describe their work (Krathwohl 2002). For example, a question from the Remember category would be, "What is a noun?" An example of a question from the Understand category is, "What is another way of stating the results of your experiment?" Of the remaining categories, Application, Analysis, and Evaluation were changed to Apply, Analyze, and Evaluate. And finally, Synthesis switched places with Evaluation and was renamed Create.

Gallagher and Ascher (1963) use memory, and three different types of thinking, to describe the question levels in their taxonomy. The lowest question level is Cognitive-Memory. A Cognitive-Memory question only requires simple processes such as recognition, rote memory, and selective recall. For example, "What do you call the angle of elevation of a roof?" Convergent Thinking is the next level, and is a combination of Bloom's Application and Analysis levels. It is convergent because there is only one expected answer, but it requires an analysis and integration of given or remembered data. An example from this category would be, "How would you sum up in one sentence why the main character decided to leave home?" Divergent Thinking, the next level in this taxonomy, requires using independently generated data or a new direction or perspective on a given topic. For example, "Suppose the United States had won the Vietnam War. What impact would that have on foreign policy in Southeast Asia?" Evaluative Thinking is the highest level in this taxonomy. This level requires dealing with matters of judgment, value, and choice. An example from this category would be, "Should an applicant's race be a factor in college admissions decisions? Explain."

Question Sequencing and Patterns

Being a skillful questioner requires not only an understanding of the cognitive levels of individual questions, but also an understanding of question sequencing and patterns (Barnes 1979; Good and Brophy 2000). Question sequencing is a series of questions designed so that each question builds on the answer to the previous one (Wragg and Brown 2001). Wragg and Brown analyzed more than a thousand questions asked by teachers during classroom discussions. They found that 53 percent of questions stood alone and 47 percent were part of a sequence of two or more questions. But of the questions that were part of a sequence, only 10 percent were part of a sequence of more than four questions (Wragg and Brown 2001).

Researchers have noted six patterns of questions (Brown and Edmondson 1989; Good and Brophy 2000; Taba 1971; Wilen and White 1991; Wilen 2001; Wragg and Brown 2001). The first pattern is called extending and lifting (Taba 1971). This questioning pattern involves asking a number of questions at the same cognitive level, or extending, before lifting the level of questions to the next higher level. For example, a science teacher reviewing a chapter on cell division could ask the following series of questions: "What four events must occur in order for any cell to divide?" "What is mitosis?" "What are the five phase of mitosis division?" "What is meiosis?" "What are the five phases of meiotic division?" "How is cell division different in prokaryotic cells and eukaryotic cells?" In this pattern, the first five questions are all at the same cognitive level—extending. Finally, the sixth question requires students to think at a higher level to answer.

The circular path is the second questioning pattern (Brown and Edmondson 1989). This pattern involves asking a series of questions that eventually lead back to the initial position or question. A humorous example of this pattern begins with the question, "Which came first, the chicken or the egg?" After a number of subsequent questions based on responses, the discussion will inevitably lead back to the initial question—a circular path.

The third pattern is called same path, or extending (Brown and Edmondson 1989). This involves asking questions all at the same cognitive level. For example, a teacher questioning students about the sun and the energy it produces could ask the following: "How far away is the sun from the earth?" "What is the temperature of the sun in degrees Fahrenheit?" "What is the diameter of the sun in miles?" "What is the process that causes the sun to release energy as light and heat?" "How does the energy of the sun reach the earth?" This pattern uses all lower level, specific questions.

Narrow to broad is the fourth questioning pattern (Brown and Edmondson 1989; Good and Brophy 2000; Taba 1971; Wilen and White 1991; Wilen 2001). This pattern involves asking lower level, specific questions followed by higher level, general questions. For example, a history teacher discussing the American Revolution could ask the following series of questions: "Why is there a statue of Benedict Arnold's boot in Saratoga, New York?" "Why was the Battle of Saratoga considered a major turning point in the American Revolutionary War?" "Why did 'Americans' feel a revolution was necessary?" "Should rights be given or earned? Explain." In this pattern, the questions start with a lower level, specific question, and progress to higher level, general questions.

The fifth questioning pattern is called broad to narrow, or funneling (Brown and Edmondson 1989; Good and Brophy 2000; Wilen and White 1991, Wilen 2001). This question sequence begins with low level, general questions followed by higher level, specific questions. For example, a teacher could ask the following questions about ecology and the environment: "What is ecology?" "What are ecosystems?" "What are some ways ecosystems can change due to nature?" "Explain how 'succession' affects an ecosystem." "How did Rachel Carson's *Silent Spring* impact perceptions about the relationship between environment and ecosystem?" This pattern, the exact opposite of the narrow to broad questioning pattern, begins with low level, general questions followed by increasingly higher level, specific questions.

The last questioning pattern is called a backbone of questions with relevant digressions (Brown and Edmondson 1989). In this sequence, the focus is not on the cognitive level of the questions but on how closely they relate to the central theme, issue, or subject of the discussion. For example, in a lesson on creative writing and imagery, an English teacher could ask the following sequence of questions about a television commercial: "Who is being targeted?" "What kind of lifestyle is presented?" "How old are the characters?" What is the literal meaning of the message?" "What is the underlying message?" "How does the way the characters are dressed add to the message?" "If you could create another commercial about this subject, what would you say and how would you say it?" The focus of this pattern has nothing to do with the cognitive level of the questions but how they relate to the theme of script writing and imagery in a television commercial.

Colleague Classroom Observations

Obviously, merely understanding the cognitive level of individual questions and question sequencing and patterns will not, by themselves, make teachers skilled in using verbal questioning. The key to developing and mastering any skill is practicing. Teachers must use their knowledge of cognitive levels of individual questions to practice question sequencing and patterns.

Teacher's Name ______________________ Date __________

Observer's Name ______________________ Date __________

Front of Room

Symbols for this observation:

Question Cognitive Level
CM = Cognitive-memory question
CT = Convergent thinking question
DT = Divergent thinking question
ET = Evaluative thinking question

N = Non-volunteering student
V = Volunteering student

Question Sequence
EL = Extending and lifting
CP = Curcular path
SP = Same path
NB = Narrow to broad
F = Funneling
B = Backbone

Figure 1 Classroom observation instrument.

An effective activity to help teachers develop verbal questioning skills is colleague classroom observations. Working in pairs, teachers observe their partner, as well as are observed, leading classroom discussions. A classroom observation instrument (see figure 1) adapted from Sadker and Sadker (1997) can be used to record these observations. Note that the instrument shown in figure 1 employs a traditional classroom seating configuration. For actual use, the instrument must accurately represent the seating arrangement of the classroom to be observed. The classroom observation instrument utilizes Gallagher and Ascher's (1963) questioning taxonomy because there are just enough categories in this taxonomy for even a novice observer to recognize different levels of questions without having difficulty identifying which category questions belong (see Riley 1980). For each classroom observation, the observer must identify the number of each question, the level (category) of each question asked, the student (whether volunteering or non-volunteering) who answered the question, and the question sequence used. For instance, if the first question asked was a cognitive-memory question answered by a volunteering student, the observer would write "1CMV" in the space on the instrument that corresponds to where the student who answered the question sat. If the next question was a convergent thinking question answered by a non-volunteering student, it would be labeled "2CTN." Once question sequences are recognized, they are also labeled. For example, if the first question sequence was funneling, it would be labeled "1F." At a pre-observation conference, a review can be made of questions that will be asked during the lesson, otherwise known as a question script. After the lesson, during a post-observation conference, a completed classroom observation instrument can provide valuable feedback on the cognitive level of individual questions asked and question sequences used.

I have used this activity for the past six years with a number of colleagues. At first glance, it seems like a very demanding and intimidating activity. The teacher being observed must write out, or at least accurately describe, the individual questions and question sequences they will be using during the observation. The teacher doing the observing is responsible for keeping track of the number of questions asked, making a quick judgment on the cognitive level of each question, locating who answered the question and if they volunteered the answer, and recognizing the question pattern used—things that only someone confident in their ability to recognize cognitive levels and patterns would feel comfortable doing. But a lot can and should be done during the pre-observation conference to alleviate any apprehension about participating in the activity. For instance, colleagues can agree on a "formal" observation for a limited number of question patterns. This allows the teacher being observed not to have to write or describe all the questions they plan to ask during the observation. This also allows the observer, after the agreed-on number of question patterns have been completed, to listen and ideally recognize cognitive levels of questions and question patterns without feeling compelled to write it all out. Sometimes, observations made during this time lead to wonderful post-observation discussions.

Speaking of post-observation discussions, there are a number of topics a new team can focus on to begin their post-observation conference. The first topic has to do with the use of a question script. A discussion about this topic usually can be started by asking questions such as: Did the question script work as planned? Was there a need to ask more questions than originally scripted? Were students able to follow your line of questioning? Why or why not? Often, answers include an acknowledgment that a few more questions were needed than anticipated. Sometimes, this can lead to a discussion about the cognitive level of questions students seem to respond to the best and possible reasons why. Another interesting topic is question transition—whether it is question level to another question level, or question sequence to another question sequence. This discussion could begin with a question such as: Was the transition from ______ to ______ as smooth as you anticipated? Why or why not? Finally, a discussion about question sequences is another good way to begin a post-observation conference. In many instances a teacher may have only used one or two types of question sequences during the observation—question sequences the teacher often used in the past. In this situation, the discussion should focus on getting the teacher out of his or her "comfort zone" and trying other question sequences. Remember, practice builds confidence and competence.

Conclusion

Asking questions and leading classroom discussions can have a positive impact on student learning. They can monitor student comprehension, help make connections to prior knowledge, and stimulate cognitive growth. But good questions and classroom discussions don't just happen. Verbal questioning is a skill, and like any skill, it must be practiced before it is mastered. It is hoped that this knowledge about sequencing and patterns, as well as the classroom observation activity, will help teachers become skilled in using verbal questioning effectively and productively.

References

Airasian, P. W., and H. Miranda. 2002. The role of assessment in the revised taxonomy. *Theory into Practice* 41 (4): 249–54.

Anderson, L., and R. Burns. 1989. *Research in classrooms: The study of teachers, teaching and instruction.* New York: Pergamon.

Barnes, C. P. 1979. Questioning strategies to develop critical thinking skills. Paper presented at the 46th annual meeting of the Claremont Reading Conference, California. ERIC, ED 169486.

Bloom, B. S. 1956. *Taxonomy of educational objectives, handbook I: Cognitive domain.* New York: David McKay.

Brown, G. A., and R. Edmondson. 1989. Asking questions. In *Classroom teaching skills*, ed. E. C. Wragg, 97–120. New York: Nichols.

Byrd, P. A. 2002. The revised taxonomy and prospective teachers. *Theory into Practice* 41 (4): 244–48.

Carlson, W. S. 1991. Questioning in classrooms: A sociolinguistic perspective. *Review of Educational Research* 61 (2): 157–78.

———. 1997. Never ask a question if you don't know the answer. *Journal of Classroom Interaction* 32 (2): 14–23.

Dantonio, M. 1990. *How can we create thinkers? Questioning strategies that work for teachers.* Bloomington, IN: National Education Service.

Gallagher, J. J., and M. J. Ascher. 1963. A preliminary report on analyses of classroom interaction. *Merrill-Palmer Quarterly* 9 (1): 183–94.

Good, T. J., and J. Brophy. 2000. *Looking in classrooms.* 8th ed. New York: Longman.

Graesser, A. C., and N. K. Person. 1994. Question asking during tutoring. *American Educational Research Journal* 31 (2): 104–37.

Krathwohl, D. R. 2002. A revision of Bloom's taxonomy: An overview. *Theory into Practice* 41 (4): 212–18.

Levin, T., and R. Long. 1981. *Effectiveness instruction.* Alexandria, VA: Association for Supervision and Curriculum Development.

Lucking, R. A. 1978. Developing question-conscious language arts teachers. *Language Arts* 55 (5): 578–82.

Martin, J. 1979. Effects of teacher higher-order questions on student process and product variables in a single-classroom study. *Journal of Educational Research* 72 (2): 183–87.

Morgan, J. C., and J. E. Schreiber. 1969. *How to ask questions.* Washington, DC: National Council for the Social Studies. ERIC, ED 033887.

Pollack, H. 1988. *Questioning strategies to encourage critical thinking.* ERIC, ED 297210.

Redfield, D. L., and E. W. Rousseau. 1981. A meta-analysis of experimental research on teacher questioning behavior. *Review of Educational Research* 51 (3): 237–45.

Rice, D. R. 1977. The effect of question-asking instruction on preservice elementary science teachers. *Journal of Research in Science Teaching* 14 (4): 353–59.

Riley, J. P. 1980. A comparison of three methods of improving preservice science teachers' questioning knowledge and attitudes toward questioning. *Journal of Research in Science Teaching* 17 (5): 419–24.

Sadker, M., and D. Sadker. 1997. *Teachers, schools and society.* Boston: McGraw-Hill.

Seymour, J. R., and H. P. Osana. 2003. Reciprocal teaching procedures and principles: Two teachers' developing understanding. *Teaching and Teacher Education* 19 (3): 325–44.

Taba, H. 1971. *Teaching strategies and cognitive function in elementary school children.* San Francisco: San Francisco State College.

Wilen, W. W. 2001. Exploring myths about teacher questioning in the social studies classroom. *Social Studies* 92 (1): 26–32.

———. 2004. Refuting misconceptions about classroom discussion. *Social Studies* 95 (1): 33–39.

Wilen, W. W., and A. Clegg. 1986. Effective questions and questioning: A research review. *Theory and Research in Social Education* 14 (2): 53–62.

Wilen, W. W., and J. White. 1991. Interaction and discourse in social studies classrooms. In *Handbook of research in social studies teaching and learning,* ed. J. P. Shaver, 483–95. New York: Macmillan.

Wimer, J. W., C. S. Ridenour, K. Thomas, and A. W. Place. 2001. Higher order teacher questioning of boys and girls in elementary mathematics classrooms. *Journal of Educational Research* 95 (2): 84–92.

Wragg, E. C., and G. Brown. 2001. *Questioning in the primary school.* London: Routledge Falmer.

Kenneth E. Vogler is an assistant professor in the Department of Instruction and Teacher Education at the University of South Carolina.

Designing Learning Through Learning to Design

This paper represents a conversation between a high school science teacher and a university researcher as they found common ground in the theory and experiences of designing powerful learning experiences. The teacher describes an instructional unit in which students designed a complex, interactive display showing what life may have been like during the Mesozoic Era. The researcher offers analysis of that activity through the lens of design and design-based learning. Their voices intentionally co-mingle as they illuminate aspects of one another's work—the pedagogical work of the teacher, and the theoretical analysis of the researcher. The conversation provides useful insight for teachers wishing to employ design-based learning in their classrooms and an important analytic lens for researchers to view teaching and learning.

PUNYA MISHRA AND MARK GIROD

Introduction

Much is written today about design-based learning (Author, Zhao, & Tan, 1999; Author & Koehler, in press; Kafai & Resnick, 1996;). Design, as a pedagogical activity, has come to be perceived as forward-looking, reform-oriented, and progressive (Roth, 1998). Reformers and writers commonly support design-based learning for its authentic outcomes and activities, and collaborative and cross-curricular nature (Brown, 1992). These, however, are only surface-level characteristics of design-based learning that fail to capture three, much deeper, psychologically-based characteristics, that illuminate the efficacy and potential of design-based learning.

This paper provides one teacher's account of a unique design-based learning situation in which 40 high school students worked to represent life during the Mesozoic age. Students' design projects had to: a) communicate (teach) a particular element related to life during the Mesozoic period such as plant and animal life, climate, or physiographic features of the earth's surface; b) provide something for both children and adults to do to help them learn or understand the point being made by the representation, and; c) be scientifically accurate and artistically crafted to provide a unique experience to those viewing the representations. Projects were displayed in a community open-house referred to as the Mesozoic Resource Center (MRC). Woven throughout an extended pedagogical description of the MRC, as told by the teacher (in italics), is a parallel, theoretical analysis through the lens of design, as told by the university researcher (in plain text). The intent is to illuminate salient features of both the pedagogical description and the theoretical analysis in ways educative to both teachers and researchers.

The Case of the Mesozoic Resource Center[1]

As I looked around my classroom I saw Reuben, a known gang member, reading a story he had written and illustrated about a young Pachycephalosaurus to five first graders. Chris, an eighteen-year-old sophomore labeled severely emotionally disturbed, was smiling and enthusiastically debating the feasibility of the asteroid impact theory with our school superintendent. Linda and Becky, both of whom had failed other science classes, were surrounded by several parents as they described the nesting behavior of hadrosaurs.

This was the scene at the opening of my classes' Mesozoic Resource Center. Forty high school science students and I had been working diligently for ten weeks in preparation for this evening. We had set up displays on both floors of our unusual two-story classroom. Downstairs visitors browsed through student constructed displays ranging from the diversity of pterosaurs to a debate over whether dinosaurs were warm or cold-blooded. Students manned their displays clarifying ideas and offering additional information to visitors as they passed.

In one corner, elementary children were invited to excavate dinosaur toys from a simulated paleontological dig, pour resin over insects to simulate the famous mosquito stuck in amber from Jurassic Park, or use a rubber stamp kit to construct their own dinosaurs. Each group was closely supervised by my students.

Upstairs, another group was conducting tours of a lost age. Guides assigned to each period, Triassic, Jurassic, and Cretaceous, led visitors through their respective age describing the plants, animals, and climate of that time. Visitors stood stunned at the bleakness of the dry, sandy, desert-like surroundings in the Triassic, marveled at the 8 meter long Apatosaurus model being eyed by the head of a Parasaurolophus peering through ferns and lush greenery, and were amazed by the 3 meter tall Tyrannosaurus Rex model glaring down at them as the first flowering plants appeared in the Cretaceous Period. The sights and conversation were academic, enthusiastic, and engaging for everyone involved.

What started as a trial in self-directed learning exploded in both size and scope. Before I knew it, these students, most previously characterized as disinterested, unmotivated, and apathetic, were tearing down the walls of traditional learning. In its place they built a community of scholars each working toward understanding and communicating what life was like millions of years ago in the Mesozoic Era. As their teacher, I could barely keep up.

New to teaching about dinosaurs and the era in which they lived, I had few resources and even less personal knowledge about these topics. I chose to involve my students, as well as myself, with a book called Dinosaur! (Norman, 1991). It is filled with information about current thinking regarding dinosaurs and is richly illustrated. We supplemented our reading with the four-part A&E television series by the same name. In areas where these two sources were insufficient in providing enough information, students consulted our school library, the internet, local experts, university libraries, and even college professors. Just learning how to gather information was a worthwhile experience for many of my students.

We soon realized that to get a complete picture of life in the Mesozoic Era we needed to split up and become experts in many different areas. With a little guidance, my students were able to focus their inquiry into very specific topics. With their topic in mind, they had one goal. Each student was to become an expert in a particular area. I challenged each student to develop their knowledge of the subject far beyond mine or anyone else's in our school. These were empowering words for largely disenfranchised students. They eagerly accepted the challenge! As students' knowledge grew it became clear that I had to find a way to showcase their work. Our simple dinosaur projects became the Mesozoic Resource Center described above.

Ready to show off their products, my students suggested that I call the local newspaper and television station. To our surprise, both agencies were eager to come and do short stories. Everyone was thrilled to be on television but the pressure to look and sound impressive was mounting. The television crew arrived a couple hours before the grand opening as my high school students were hosting groups of second and third graders from our local elementary school. One of the requirements for each student display was that it must have something for both child and adult visitors to do. In this case, the elementary teachers examined the computer-generated overlays describing dinosaur anatomy while children distinguished Ornithischians from Saurischians using very realistic plastic models.

By far, the biggest hit of the Mesozoic Resource Center was the walk-through-diorama showing how life might have been during the each of the three periods of the Mesozoic. Together with my students and our school janitors, we had built fake walls of black plastic to separate the ages. Across several days we hauled in 500 gallons of sand and rocks to spread across the floor. Students working on the diorama spent two Saturdays hauling brush, driftwood, and small shrubbery to "plant" in our 200 million-year-old setting. Our local florist donated several large boxes of ferns to add to the realism. With back lighting and sound effects piped in through a hidden stereo system, our diorama became very impressive.

The highlights of the diorama were two very large dinosaur models built and assembled by my students. We ordered balsa wood snap-together models from a supply house and traced each of the pieces. Using an opaque projector and very steady hands, six students made patterns of dinosaur bones approximately 1/4 normal scale. The students traced the patterns onto sheets of plywood, and using jigsaws, cut them out. After sanding and painting all the pieces and using a few bolts and clamps, we assembled these massive dinosaur models in their appropriate time periods.

Second only to the huge dinosaur models in impressiveness were two dinosaur heads painted in exquisite detail. A student who was an avid hunter found a taxidermy magazine that sold closed-cell styrofoam forms of dinosaur heads. Taxidermists buy and display them on their wall in jest like any other trophy animal. But this student imagined the heads mounted on the wall peering out of bushes that would be planted in front. After airbrushing the forms to amazing realism, the effect was quite startling. Imagine walking through a darkened classroom, marveling at the magnitude of the dinosaur models in front of you, listening intently as students explained the hunting habits of small, carnivorous dinosaurs, and then suddenly eyeing one, head sticking out of some bushes lit by a soft green glow. The effect was fantastic. In fact, one first grader wet his pants!

A Researchers Conceptualization of "Design"

Design activities are one class of activities that fall under the broader rubric of project-based activities. In such activities, students design complex interactive artifacts to be used by other students for learning about a particular subject (Harel, 1991). Design-based projects have involved the development of presentations, instructional software, simulations, publications, journals, and games (Carver, 1991; Guzdial, 1993; Kafai, 1995, 1996; Lehrer, 1991; Vyas & Author, 2002). With such projects, students learn both about design—through the process of developing complex artifacts—and a variety of academic disciplines, such as programming, social studies, language arts, etc.

Research and theory suggest that design-based activities provide a rich context for learning (Willet 1992). Within the context of social constructivism (Cole, 1997; Vygotsky, 1978) or constructionism (Papert, 1991), design projects lend themselves to sustained inquiry and revision of ideas. Other scholars have emphasized the value of complex, self-directed, personally motivated and meaningful design projects for students (Blumenfeld, Soloway, Marx, Krajcik, Guzdial, & Palinscar, 1991; Collins, Brown & Newman, 1990, Harel & Papert, 1990, Kafai, 1996).

Such design-based, informal learning environments offer a sharp contrast to regular classroom instruction, the effectiveness of which has been questioned by many scholars (Papert, 1991, 1993; Pea, 1993; Lave & Wenger, 1991). As one might imagine, adapting such open-ended problem solving situations into the structure and organization of the conventional classroom is often difficult to manage logistically.

Design, broadly speaking, can be seen as "structure adapted to a purpose" (Perkins, 1986, p. 2). Perkins' definition captures elegantly an essential quality of design: it is a process of constructing artifacts that exhibit "goodness of fit." Design can be seen both in material artifacts, such as a hammer or a piece of software, as well as in non-material artifacts, such as a poem, a theory or a scientific experiment. This conceptualization of design can play itself out within multiple contexts. In the MRC project, for instance, students designed complex educational artifacts based on their understanding of important ideas in science and art. Further, they acted as social scientists designing usability studies and evaluation tools to test how their exhibits were used by exhibit visitors.

At another level, design applies to educational researchers attempting to better understand the pragmatic and theoretical aspects of developing design-based activities. In essence, our perspective sees design as being both "an object of study as well as context for a study of learning" (Author, Zhao, & Tan, 1999; Kafai 1996, pg. 72; Koehler, Author, Hershey & Peruski, under review). This view of design as adaptation generates several significant implications that can help us understand the pedagogical value of design-based learning activities. These implications are discussed in terms of the MRC.

Design in Analysis of the Mesozoic Resource Center

One of the most interesting aspects of the MRC project is the multiple levels of understanding that were required for completing the design task. Students surely gained a deep understanding of the core ideas of deep-time and evolutionary biology, and the manner in which they play out in different domains. Students also developed strategies and techniques to help others learn these concepts through their exhibit. This required them to think beyond the science concepts to consider ways in which others would generate their own understandings of these ideas. Further, students needed to develop technological skills in order to construct the artifacts that embodied their ideas. To understand this, we can apply the design experiment approach (Brown, 1992), focusing on the following social and cognitive aspects of the design activities to help interpret what was observed:

- The role of knowledge in design, technology, and subject matter content in learning to design, the patterns of interaction among knowledge in different domains
- The role of audience, mentors, leaders, collaborators, and peers in learning and design; patterns of interaction, both face-to-face and online and their effects on learning and design
- The role of artifacts and ideas as tools for construction, expression, communication and inquiry
- The nature of representation and manipulation of symbols in the process of design

As these aspects of the design experiment approach suggest, design works at multiple levels; thus, understanding what happened in this classroom requires analysis at multiple levels as well. The unit of analysis is not merely the individual, but rather the interaction of the learner, the practices, the resources being used, the community within which these practices are nested and the constraints of the situation—i.e. the intersection of individual, activity, and context (Lave & Wenger, 1991; Roth, 1998).

Three themes emerge from this juxtaposition of the pedagogical instantiation of the Mesozoic Resource Center and the psychological analysis via design. Each theme is illustrated by a brief vignette drawn from the teacher's account of experiences during production of the Mesozoic Resource Center. The vignettes are designed to be broadly representative of the experiences of students' learning in this design-based setting. They should not be considered atypical or unusual. Three different stories could have been easily selected to illustrate these same three design themes. As with the intertwining of voices used previously, these themes, as offered by the researcher appear, in plain text, and their corresponding illustrative stories, supplied by the teacher, appear in italics.

Theme I: Design as a Transformative Experience

Vygotsky (1978) and Dewey (1933) emphasize the role of dialogue or interplay in learning. As the individual acts on the environment, the environment also acts upon the individual. Inquiry and learning, like design, are not simply about understanding and assembling materials. They are fundamentally about ideas and transforming oneself and the world through the process of working with those ideas.

At the heart of design is an interplay between theory and practice, between constraints and trade-offs, between designer and materials, and between designer and user/learner. Through this dialogue, meanings and artifacts are defined and understood (Dewey, 1934). The interaction is bi-directional and open-ended.

Design also requires that learners discern the essential qualities of an idea and represent it in a compelling manner. To have new ideas is more than simply labeling or thinking about the world differently; rather, it is to have a new way of *being* in the world. To have an idea is to be more fully alive with thought, feeling, and action (Dewey, 1934; Jackson, 1998). It is to have an "energy-for-action" that is directed by thought and fueled by emotion. The having of a new idea is more than the acquisition or application of information. It is, therefore, critical to have students work with ideas that are inherently empowering and generative.

Story I: Seeing the World Differently

Oscar was particularly captivated by the debate over the warm or cold-bloodedness of dinosaurs. After much research on predator to prey ratios, body mass to energy expenditure ratios, and heat dissipation and conservation anatomy and strategies, Oscar literally began to see the world through the eyes of this debate. Oscar told a story about seeing a mouse in his mother's kitchen to illustrate his new-found worldview, "See how it moves in quick, darting motions. I bet it needs to eat all the time because it expends so much energy moving in that jerking way." At our open-house, I overheard him explain to his mother, "Scientists believe these fin-backed dinosaurs actually pumped blood up in this sail-like thing to help cool off or warm up." This uniquely energizing idea had transformed Oscar's world from static observations of nature to more alive and dynamic ways of seeing and experiencing the world. In fact, Oscar enrolled in zoology class the next semester because he said he found animals interesting for the first time in his life. Design put Oscar in contact with powerful, transformative ideas in ways that led him into further inquiry and further educative experiences.

Theme II: Design as Inquiry

Design activities create opportunities to learn about the nature of inquiry itself. First, design forces students to pay attention to the process and consequences of their actions. Second, students learn to appreciate the nonlinear, often messy nature of inquiry. Design tasks are often ill-structured and afford many viable solutions. This perspective on knowledge and inquiry is quite different from the epistemological illusion typically found in classrooms, where problems are well-defined with clear-cut solutions. Additionally, to design is to engage in a fundamentally social activity. Students learn the value of communicating effectively and of attending to the experience of others. The design process requires building and negotiating ideas in a community of practice, just as ideas are generated and validated among practicing scientists. Students become experts in specific domains and share their knowledge with one another. Data gathering, validation, and accurate representation of those data force students to move beyond the constraints of their classroom, and school.

Story II: Imagining the Past

The guiding task was to present life in the Mesozoic in as much reality and detail as possible. Rachel, Heather, and Desiree thought deeply about the climate and plant life of the Mesozoic as they were assigned the task of making scenery for the walk-through diorama. They assumed their task would be to examine, and try to reproduce, artwork that portrayed dinosaurs, plant and animal life, and climate in the Mesozoic. However, after some research, they discovered that flowering plants did not appear until the Cretaceous period—no where near the Triassic period in which so many flowers appeared in our textbook! After a few more discoveries of inconsistencies, the three girls embarked on an all-out study of flora, fauna, and climate in the Mesozoic. They wanted their contribution to the MRC to be as scientifically accurate as possible to provide the most authentic experience to visitors. Gradually, their understanding of the period developed and the scenery they produced was stunning in its accuracy and attention to detail. The opportunity to design had forced them to investigate best and most accurate ways to represent their ideas.

Theme III: Design is Expression

Design is the process of exploring new ways of being in the world, and hence a deeply personal and expressive act. Design is an inner idea expressed outwardly—it is a private possibility acted upon publicly. Design-based activities, therefore, give students opportunities to bring their own unique interpretations to subject matter ideas. We contend that this idea stands in significant contrast with conventional schooling, where ideas are impressed rather then expressed and where, too often, artistic activity is seen as separate from scientific activity. Too often learning in science is viewed as solely cognitive. We believe the power and beauty of ideas to move and inspire is often disregarded. By allowing students to construct artifacts that are personally meaningful and communicative we allow students to tap into the aesthetic aspects of learning ideas. It allows students to develop their artistic potential as well, all within the overarching goal of developing expressive and engaging artifacts that communicate to an audience.

Story III: The Art of Science

Ruben had an incredible talent for art. Typically pensive and brooding, he wasn't interested in the difficult and academic tasks with which the rest of the class was engaged. After a few days considering options, halfhearted attempts, and dead-ends, Ruben remembered one of our goals was to share our findings with the community—in particular K–3 students from our local elementary school. Ruben posed to me his plan to author and illustrate a scientifically accurate story about a dinosaur as it moved through a day in the Cretaceous period. Ruben was able to couch his academic learning in the personal expression of his developing story. The end result was a well-written, conceptually faithful, wildly personalized and expressive story about Packy—a young Pachycephalosaur living and learning 80 million years ago. He joyfully read his story several times to different groups of young, enthusiastic MRC visitors. Ruben, who had been in trouble with the law, drugs, and violence, was newly perceived as a teacher, explorer, and artist by these young children and their parents. Ruben was clearly proud of his accomplishment and through this design process changed both his perceptions of himself and the world in ways that possibly no other school related experience had before.

Discussion

It is clear that not all design (or project based) activities have equal educational value. Merely giving students "something to construct" may keep them busy but it is unclear as to what pedagogical value exists in doing so. Elucidation of the pedagogical and psychological elements of design offer educators a framework useful in developing project-based experiences for students that can motivate, challenge and teach as well as researchers a framework for thinking more clearly about powerful classroom teaching and learning.

In this vein, valuable design based projects will be centered on important subject matter ideas that are powerful, generative, and expansive; ideas that move students to see the world in different ways. Powerful ideas lie at heart of all disciplines, though too often obscured by terminology and shallow understandings. Design based activities allow students to engage with these powerful ideas in a serious manner, and, most importantly, to act on them in ways that move students into the world engaged, curious, and poised to learn more.

Design based learning centers learning on this goal of "acting on" an idea, both intellectually and physically. Intellectually, the designer engages with the ideas and concepts and attempts to learn more. Physically the designer works with the artifact, modifying, manipulating objects to fit the desired ends. This is essentially a dialogue between ideas and world, between theory and its application, a concept and its realization, tools and goals. This dialogue is at the heart of inquiry, involving as it does the construction of meaning and the evolution of understanding through a dialogic, transactional process. Thus, sound design-based projects carefully incorporate opportunities for inquiry within them.

Finally, design based activities hold the artistic/aesthetic aspects of learning as of equal value to the cognitive. Notions of the aesthetic are fundamental to both the intellectual and physical aspects of the design process. Intellectually, students learn to appreciate the beauty of ideas; physically, they learn the beauty of constructing an aesthetically pleasing artifact. In this view, design based projects offer students opportunities to explore affective aspects of learning and should be rewarded for doing so successfully.

Pedagogy centered on design raises important issues that effectively "raise the bar" on what a powerful, constructivist education entails. As a psychological lens, design expands definitions of teaching and learning in ways that bring other outcomes to bear on educational problems. In this way, we hope design and design-based learning enrich the work of both teachers and researchers.

Note

1. Some of the text describing the Mesozoic Resource Center has appeared previously as Author (1998). Educational Leadership.

References

Author (1998). *Educational Leadership.*

Author, & Koehler, M. J. (in press). In Y. Zhao (Ed.). *What teachers should know about technology: Perspectives and practices.*

Author, Yong, Z., & Tan, S. (1999). *Journal of Research on Computing in Education.*

Blumenfeld, P. C., Soloway, E., Marx, R. W., Krajcik, J. S., Guzdial, M., & Palincsar, A. (1991). Motivating project-based learning: Sustaining the doing, supporting the learning. *Educational Psychologist, 26* (2 & 4), 369–398.

Brown, A. L. (1992). Design experiments: theoretical and methodological challenges in creating complex interventions in classroom settings. *The Journal of the Learning Sciences 2:* 141–178.

Carver, S. (1991). *Interdisciplinary problem solving.* Paper presented at the American Educational Research Association, Chicago, IL.

Cole, M. (1997). *Cultural psychology: A once and future discipline.* Cambridge: Harvard University Press.

Collins, A. S., Brown, J. S., & Newman, S. (1990). Cognitive apprenticeship: Teaching the craft of reading, writing, and mathematics. In L. B. Resnick (Ed.), *Cognition and instruction: Issues and agendas* (p. 453–434). Hillsdale, NJ: Lawrence Erlbaum Associates.

Dewey, J. (1933). *How we think: A restatement of the relation of reflective thinking to the educative process.* Boston, MA: Heath.

Dewey, J. (1934). *Art as experience.* New York: Perigree.

Guzdial, M. (1993). *Emile: Software-realized scaffolding for science learners programming in mixed media.* Unpublished doctoral dissertation, Ann Arbor, MI: University of Michigan.

Harel, I. (1991). *Children designers.* Norwood, NJ: Ablex.

Harel, I., & Papert, S. (1990). Software design as a learning environment. *Interactive Learning Environment, 1* (1), 1–32.

Jackson, P. W. (1998). *John Dewey and the lessons of art.* New Haven: Yale University Press.

Kafai, Y., & Resnick, M. (Eds.)(1996). *Constructionism in practice: Designing, thinking and learning in a digital world.* Mahwah, NJ: Lawrence Erlbaum Associates.

Kafai, Y. (1995). *Minds in play: Computer game design as a context for children's learning.* Hillsdale NJ: Lawrence Erlbaum Associates.

Kafai, Y. (1996). Learning design by making games: Children's development of design strategies in the creation of a complex computational artifact. In Y. Kafai & M. Resnick, (Eds.), (pp. 71–96). *Constructionism in practice: Designing, thinking and learning in a digital world.* Mahwah, NJ: Lawrence Erlbaum Associates.

Koehler, M. J., Author, Hershey, K., & Peruski, L. (under review). With a little help from your students: A new model for faculty development and online course design. *Journal of Technology and Teacher Education.*

Lave, J. & Wenger, E. (1991). *Situated learning: Legitimate peripheral participation.* New York: Cambridge University Press.

Lehrer, R. (1991). *Knowledge as design.* Paper presented at the American Educational Research Association, Chicago, IL.

Norman, D. (1991). *Dinosaur!* Upper Saddle River,New Jersey Prentice Hall.

Papert, S. (1991). Situating constructionism. In I. Harel & S. Papert. (Ed.) *Constructionism.* Norwood. NJ: Ablex.

Papert, S. (1993). *The children's machine: Rethinking school in the age of the computer.* New York: Basic Books.

Pea, R. (1993). Practices of distributed intelligence and designs for education. In G. Salomon (Ed.), *Distributed cognitions: Psychological and educational considerations.* (pp. 47–87). Cambridge, UK: Cambridge University Press.

Perkins, D. N. (1986). *Knowledge as design.* Hillsdale, NJ: Lawrence Erlbaum Associates.

Roth, W.-M. (1998). *Designing communities.* Dordrecht: Kluwer Academic Publishers.

Vyas, S., & Author (2002). Experiments with design in an after-school Asian literature club. In R. Garner, M. Gillingham, Y. Zhao (Eds.). *Hanging out: After-school community based programs for children.* Greenwood Publishing Group: CT. 75–92.

Vygotsky, L. S. (1978). *Mind in society: The development of higher psychological processes.* Cambridge: Harvard University Press.

Willett, L. V. (1992). *The efficacy of using the visual arts to teach math and reading concepts.* Paper presented at the annual meeting of the American Educational Research Association, San Francisco, CA.

Using Engagement Strategies to Facilitate Children's Learning and Success

JUDY R. JABLON AND MICHAEL WILKINSON

The third-graders in Ms. Neil's classroom begin a lesson on dictionaries with a whole-group discussion about what the children already know about the purpose and organization of these resources. Ms. Neil then explains to the children that they will work in small groups to examine the dictionary carefully; make observations about the book's organization, structure, and format; and record their group's findings on a chart. After ensuring that everyone is clear about the task, she posts a chart showing six teams of four children and sends them off with a task sheet to begin work.

The teams disperse to get the necessary materials: chart paper, dictionaries, and a basket with markers, pencils, and sticky notes. A few minutes later, a buzz of activity and conversation fills the room as all six teams pore over dictionary pages, discuss their observations, collaborate, and debate how to keep track of the information on their charts. Ms. Neil circulates around the room talking with each group, posing questions to promote thinking, responding to children's questions, and noting to individual children what she observes about their work. Within the groups, laughter is interspersed with argument as children comment on humorous or unfamiliar words, multiple meanings, and unusual punctuation. Twenty minutes into the work period, the six charts are filling up with lots of information.

Picture your classroom. Are there moments like this one when children are fully involved, curious about finding answers to real questions, taking initiative, enthusiastic? The room hums with positive energy and children are deeply engaged in their learning. You step back with a deep sense of satisfaction and think, "Wow! They are working well together. I wish it were always like this." You recognize that the children are a community of learners.

In this article we define what engagement is and why it is important to children's success as learners. We offer strategies for facilitating children's engagement in learning and provide some tips for implementing them.

Defining Engagement

Children begin life eager to explore the world around them. Watching a baby fascinated by the hands she has just discovered as hers or a toddler as he carefully lifts a shovel full of sand, spills it into the colander, then watches, eyes wide open, as the sand flows through the tiny holes—for the fifth time—is seeing engagement at its best!

Research about engagement in the classroom describes both psychological and behavioral characteristics (Finn & Rock 1997; Brewster & Fager 2000; Marks 2000). Psychologically, engaged learners are intrinsically motivated by curiosity, interest, and enjoyment, and are likely to want to achieve their own intellectual or personal goals. In addition, the engaged child demonstrates the behaviors of concentration, investment, enthusiasm, and effort.

In the opening example the children demonstrate engagement through their curiosity, effort, and persistence. They can be described as busy and on task. But they are also using their minds, hearts, and even their bodies to learn. In his book *Shaking Up the School House,* Schlechty captures the difference between being engaged and being on task:

> Engagement is active. It requires that students be attentive as well as in attendance; it requires the student to be committed to the task and find some inherent value in what he or she is being asked to do. The engaged student not only does the task assigned but also does it with enthusiasm and diligence. Moreover, the student performs the task because he or she perceives the task to be associated with a near-term end that he or she values. (2001, 64)

What Does Research Tell Us about Engagement in the Classroom?

Not surprisingly, research shows a significant correlation between high levels of engagement and improved attendance and achievement as measured through direct observations and interviews with and questionnaires to children and teachers (Finn & Rock 1997; Marks 2000; Roderick & Engle 2001; Willingham, Pollack, & Lewis 2002). After children enter school, their natural motivation and interest in learning do not always persist. Research also tells us that disengagement increases as children progress from elementary to middle to high school (Graham & Weiner 1996; Felner et al. 1997; Brewster & Fager 2000). Children may lose interest in classroom activities, respond poorly to teacher direction and classroom interaction, and perform significantly lower on tests. Studies have shown that patterns of educational disengagement begin as early as third grade (Rossi & Montgomery 1994).

Research shows a significant correlation between high levels of engagement and improved attendance and achievement as measured through direct observations and interviews with and questionnaires to children and teachers.

As important as engagement is for children's success as learners, strategies for promoting engagement are not emphasized or even present in the vast majority of school settings (Marks 2000; McDermott, Mordell, & Stolzfus 2001). Instruction that promotes passivity, rote learning, and routine tends to be the rule rather than the exception (Yair 2000; Goodlad 2004). Because children with low levels of engagement are at risk for disruptive behavior, absenteeism, and eventually dropping out of school (Roderick & Engle 2001), the need to increase engagement is critical to children's success in school.

Engaging Children in the Classroom

Educators of young children tend to share the goal of fostering children's successful learning and achievement. As the pressure to emphasize academic standards increases, it is all the more essential to reflect on the most effective practices for ensuring that children are actually learning what is being taught. Some factors related to children's achievement are not in teachers' control, but creating a climate of engagement in the classroom is. The use of engagement strategies is a powerful teaching tool critical in promoting children's achievement because it

- focuses children on learning;
- supports learning specific skills and concepts; and
- provides children positive associations with learning.

The authors' experiences observing in classrooms and talking with teachers show that many teachers use strategies throughout the day to engage children in learning. In a recent conversation with a group of K–3 teachers, one teacher remarked, "I care a lot about engaging my kids. But it just comes naturally to me. I'm not sure I actually use strategies." Another teacher added, "It's just part of the culture of my classroom." These teachers work hard to foster positive relationships with children and create a learning community. But the more we talked, they gradually began to analyze the little things they do and concluded collectively that they do use strategies to facilitate engagement.

Some teachers use engagement strategies to introduce children to new ideas or bring a topic of study to conclusion. Others use them to keep children focused, energize the group, manage behavior, and avoid chaos during transitions. Engagement strategies can be used for different purposes and in different settings.

Below are some engagement strategies for use with whole groups, small groups, and individual learners:

KWL—To begin a new study or theme, teachers ask children, "What do you already k*now,* what do you w*onder* about, and what do you want to l*earn?*" Use of this strategy tells children that their prior knowledge and interests are valued.

How many ways can you do this?—Teachers pose this question or organize an activity with this as the opener in various situations. For example, how many ways can you create shapes on a geoboard? or how many ways can you sort bottle caps? As soon as you ask children to come up with many different ways to use a material, answer a question, or end a story, their desire to make choices and be inventive comes into play and leads to engagement.

Think, pair, share—This strategy works well at group time to ensure that each child has an opportunity to respond to questions. After posing a question, the teacher tells children to take a moment to think of an answer and then turn to a partner to talk. After everyone has had a chance to talk with their partners, volunteers share a few ideas with the whole group.

Dramatic touch—Teachers can use drama and humor to enhance child interest. For example, to encourage children to use other words for *said* in their writing, a teacher darkened the room, lit a flashlight, and attached a card with the word *said* written on it to a make-believe tombstone. Then the class brainstormed other words they could use.

See what you can find out—The primary purpose of this approach is to introduce children to a new topic, material, book, or tool. Ms. Neil used it to encourage children to further explore a valuable resource tool.

Characteristics of Engaging Experiences

- activate prior knowledge
- foster active investigation
- promote group interaction
- encourage collaboration
- allow for choice
- include games and humor
- support mastery
- nurture independent thinking
- do not make children wait

Quick games—Twenty Questions, I'm Thinking of a Number, and other games that capture children's interest can be applied to different subject areas and often work especially well to keep children engaged during transition times.

Understanding Why Engagement Strategies Work

Think back to the story of Ms. Neil's classroom at the beginning of the article. Amidst an atmosphere of energy, enthusiasm, and productivity, the children are actively acquiring and applying skills related to using a dictionary. They are purposeful while investigating how to understand and use an important reference tool. They are researchers working in teams to discover, share, and organize information. Ms. Neil carefully selected the engagement strategy See What You Can Find Out because it addresses the purposes of her lesson:

- **to expose children to new information**—Ms. Neil is teaching how to learn about and use reference materials. She also addresses a third grade state literacy standard: determine the meanings and other features of words (for example, pronunciation, syllabication, synonyms, parts of speech) using the dictionary and thesaurus (and CD-ROM and Internet when available).
- **to promote excitement through discovery**—In this lesson Ms. Neil exposes children to all that the dictionary offers as a research tool.

See What You Can Find Out engages children because it includes instructional methods that fit well with how children learn. This approach

- **activates prior knowledge**—Children answer "What do you already know about [in our example, the dictionary]?"
- **requires active investigation**—Children answer "What can you find out about_____?"
- **encourages collaboration**—Children work in teams of four, divide responsibilities, and share information and knowledge with peers.
- **allows choice**—Children determine how to go about the task, what information they will gather, and how to record it on their chart.

Teachers tell us that they themselves are energized by the children's increased enthusiasm and success.

Using this strategy gives children greater responsibility for their learning, a prerequisite for high achievement.

As stated earlier, research tells us that teacher awareness and the use of engagement strategies benefit children tremendously. Their interest in learning and their confidence as learners will increase, and hopefully those children who are engaged learners in the early grades will bring this characteristic with them as they continue in school. What's more, teachers tell us that they themselves are energized by the children's increased enthusiasm and success.

Facilitating Engagement Strategies

The engagement strategies you choose depend on your purpose, teaching style, and the children in your classroom. Regardless of the strategies selected, effective facilitation is a key to making them work. By facilitation we mean the techniques used to execute a strategy.

When Ms. Neil uses the See What You Can Find Out strategy to encourage children to explore the dictionary, she facilitates the lesson by providing

- **a clearly stated purpose**—She lets children know the overall purpose of the task and why they are being asked to do it: they are researchers finding out about how to use a powerful tool.
- **explicit directions**—Ms. Neil provides directions about the what and how of the task at each step, both verbally and in writing.
- **needed materials**—Children have dictionaries, chart paper, and baskets with pencils, markers, and sticky notes.
- **guidance**—Ms. Neil circulates among groups, asking and answering questions as well as giving feedback.

Conclusion

Ideally, teachers should use a wide range of engagement strategies and then masterfully facilitate their implementation. Not only do engagement strategies enable teachers to capture the interest of children as they learn the skills and concepts necessary for success in school, but children also experience what it feels like to be engaged in learning—a lifelong gift.

References

Brewster, C., & J. Fager. 2000. *Increasing student engagement and motivation: From time on task to homework.* Portland, OR: Northwest Regional Educational Laboratory. Online: www.nwrel.org/request/oct00/textonly.html.

Felner, R. D., A.W. Jackson, D. Kasak, P. Mulhall, S. Brand, & N. Flowers. 1997. The impact of school reform for the middle years: Longitudinal study of a network engaged in *Turning Points*-based comprehensive school transformation. Phi Delta Kappan 78 (March): 528–32; 541–50.

Finn, J. D., & D. A. Rock. 1997. Academic success among students at risk for school failure. *Journal of Applied Psychology* 82 (2): 221–34.

Goodlad, J. I. 2004. *A place called school: Prospects for the future.* 20th anniversary ed. New York: McGraw-Hill.

Graham, S., & B. Weiner. 1996. Theories and principles of motivation. In *Handbook of educational psychology,* eds. D. Berliner & R.C. Calfee, 62–84. Mahwah, NJ: Erlbaum.

Marks, H. M. 2000. Student engagement in instructional activity: Patterns in the elementary, middle and high school years. *American Educational Research Journal* 37 (1): 153–84.

McDermott, P. A., M. Mordell, & J. C. Stolzfus. 2001. The organization of student performance in American schools: Discipline, motivation, verbal and non-verbal learning. *Journal of Educational Psychology* 93 (1): 65–76.

Roderick, M., & M. Engle. 2001. The grasshopper and the ant: Motivational responses of low-achieving students to high-stakes testing. *Educational Evaluation Policy Analysis* 23 (3): 197–227.

Rossi, R., & A. Montgomery. 1994. *Education reforms and students at risk: A review of the current state of the art.* Washington, DC: U.S. Department of Education.

Schlechty, P. 2001. *Shaking up the school house: How to support and sustain educational innovation:* San Francisco: Jossey-Bass.

Willingham, W. W., J. M. Pollack, & C. Lewis. 2002. Grades and test scores: Accounting for observed differences. *Journal of Educational Measurement* 39 (1): 1–37.

Yair, G. 2000. Reforming motivation: How the structure of instruction affects students' learning experiences. *British Educational Journal* 26 (2): 191–210.

Judy R. Jablon, MS, is a consultant, facilitator, and author who works with teachers and administrators in a variety of settings serving children ages 3 through 11. Books she has coauthored about instruction and assessment include *The Power of Observation* and *Building the Primary Classroom.* **Michael Wilkinson** is managing director of Atlanta-based Leadership Strategies–The Facilitation Company and is a certified master facilitator (CMF). He is author of *The Secrets of Facilitation* and *The Secrets of Masterful Meetings* and has served as a consultant for school systems in Florida, Tennessee, and Georgia.

UNIT 5

Motivation and Classroom Management

Unit Selections

Key Points to Consider

- Discuss several ways to motivate both at-risk and typical students. What difference is there?
- Why should motivational style be consistent with instructional techniques?
- How are motivation and classroom management related?
- Discuss several ways to discipline both typical students and those with exceptionalities.
- How are classroom management and discipline different? Discuss whether discipline can be developed within students, or whether it must be imposed by teachers, supporting your argument with data derived from your reading.

Student Web Site

www.mhcls.com/online

Internet References

Further information regarding these Web sites may be found in this book's preface or online.

I Love Teaching
http://www.iloveteaching.com

The Jigsaw Classroom
http://jigsaw.org

North Central Educational Regional Laboratory
http://www.ncrel.org/sdrs/

Teaching Helping Teachers
http://www.pacificnet.net/~mandel/

Several theories of motivation, each highlighting different reasons for sustained goal-oriented behavior, have been proposed. We will discuss three of them: behavioral, humanistic, and cognitive. The behavioral theory of motivation suggests that an important reason for engaging in behavior is that reinforcement follows the action. When reinforcement is controlled by someone else and is arbitrarily related to the behavior (such as money, a token, or a smile), then the motivation is extrinsic. In contrast, behavior may also be initiated and sustained for intrinsic reasons, such as curiosity or mastery.

Humanistic approaches to motivation are concerned with the social and psychological needs of individuals. Humans are motivated to engage in behavior to meet these needs. Abraham Maslow, a founder of humanistic psychology, proposes that there is a hierarchy of needs that directs behavior, beginning with physiological and safety needs and progressing to self-actualization. Some other important needs that influence motivation are affiliation and belonging with others, love, self-esteem, influence with others, recognition, status, competence, achievement, and autonomy.

The dominant view of motivation in the educational psychology literature is the cognitive approach. This set of theories proposes that our beliefs about our successes and failures affect our expectations and goals concerning future performance. Students who believe that their success is due to their abilities and efforts are motivated toward mastery of skills. Students who blame their failures on inadequate abilities have low self-efficacy and tend to set ability and performance goals that protect their self-image.

In the first article about motivation, Patrick McCabe shows the presents the relationship between learning and self-efficacy. He suggests that the prompts and feedback teachers give to students during tasks play an important role in their self-efficacy and subsequent learning. The second article on motivation focuses on the negative consequences of academic pressure, particularly among highly-motivated students, and what teachers can do to reduce academic stress that may de-motivate students and impede learning. In, "Why We Can't Always Get What We Want," Barbara Bartholomew illustrates the importance of intrinsic motivation as an essential precondition for learning. The next two articles focus on fostering student success through engaging students in activities they find meaningful and encouraging self-regulation and goal-setting. The final article on motivation returns to a discussion of behaviorist principles addressing how praising students can have both positive and negative consequences for student motivation.

Regardless of how motivated students are to learn, or the teacher's attempts to create lessons that will engage and

Tim Pannell/CORBIS

motivate students, teachers also need to be effective managers of their classrooms. Classroom management is more than controlling the behavior of students or disciplining them following misbehavior. In addition, teachers need to initiate and maintain a classroom environment that supports successful teaching and learning. The skills that effective teachers use include preplanning, deliberate introduction of rules and procedures, assertiveness, continual monitoring, consistent feedback to students, and specific consequences.

The next six articles address specific classroom management issues facing teachers today. The first article, "When Children Make the Rules," shows how constructivism extends to classroom management. The next article by Robert and Jana Marzano emphasizes the importance of quality student-teacher relationships as a basis for classroom management. The third article presents proactive strategies for handling the particular dynamics related to classroom management in secondary settings. The final three articles focus effective strategies for addressing the behaviors of students with more challenging needs. The fourth article, "No! I Won't!" presents characteristics of students with Oppositional Defiant Disorder (ODD) and how positive behavior supports and functional behavioral assessment can help teachers understand these students. In the fifth article, the subject of bullying in school as an increasingly important issue for teachers and presents strategies for intervention and prevention in the classroom in addressed. The final article in this section proposes a practical approach with steps for teachers to assist them in working with students with behavioral problems.

Convincing Students They Can Learn to Read

Crafting Self-Efficacy Prompts

PATRICK P. MCCABE

It is lunchtime at Anytown Middle School, and Ms. Williams, a seventh-grade teacher, is telling Mr. Rodriguez, a sixth-grade teacher, about one of her students. Ms. Williams says:

> Maybe you can help me. You know Ezekiel. You had him last year, right? Well, I can't get him to attempt to read words longer than one syllable. He just gives up. He can read small words and syllables in isolation, but those longer words intimidate him. I have tried to teach him word-recognition strategies such as using context clues, breaking up big words into smaller parts, thinking about the topic in which he is reading, and looking at any accompanying pictures and illustrations, but all to no avail. I even bought a book on baseball, and you know he loves baseball. I then gave him a preview of the story and thought he would use this information to make reasonable guesses when he encountered big words in the story. I even previewed two or three of the longer words with him, showing him how to divide them into syllables. He was able to read the words that I broke up for him, but he did not even try others of the same length, even though he could read each syllable when I showed them in isolation to him. I also try to be positive with him. On the rare occasion when he does try and is successful, I tell him that he is doing a great job and give him a high five! Once, after I congratulated him for decoding a three-syllable word, he said, "Aw, that was just luck. I just guessed and it was right! Everyone knows that I am special ed, and that I am dumb. Everyone in my family is like that." With that, he shrugged his shoulders. He has such a self-defeating attitude; it is really starting to bother me. I have tried everything. He is just unreachable. Oh, well! I guess there is nothing else I can do. All I can say is that I have tried my best and must spend my energy where I can really make a difference. I hate doing it, but I do have other students. Maybe Ezekiel will wake up one day!

Discouraged and frustrated with her inability to motivate Ezekiel, Ms. Williams has decided to focus on other students because, in her words, "Ezekiel is unreachable." Ezekiel, convinced of his inability to read multisyllabic words, has decided instead to skip them and thus avoid personal frustration and embarrassment. Although Ms. Williams's words of encouragement were well-intentioned, they apparently did not help Ezekiel recognize his ability to sound out long words. Evident in Ezekiel's comments is a strong belief that he is incapable of learning, and unless his "can't-do" attitude changes, he has doomed himself to fail in school. This is especially unfortunate for Ezekiel because, according to Ms. Williams, he does have the ability to sound out the isolated syllables in multisyllabic words. As May and Rizzardi stated, "Half the battle in teaching is just getting children to take a chance with their self-esteem and try new tasks. If students feel they cannot be successful, the result will typically be what is termed 'work avoidance' " (2002, 331).

Ms. Williams's instruction regarding the use of a repertoire of word-recognition strategies ranging from the use of personal schema and textual context to wordbound strategies was pedagogically sound. However, although her verbal feedback when Ezekiel was successful was encouraging, well-intentioned, and sincere, it failed to help him attribute his success to personal effort and was not as effective as it could have been in developing and maintaining motivation. Her conclusion that Ezekiel was "unreachable" resulted—at least in part—from a lack of understanding of how to affect a learner's motivation. Therefore, the purpose of this article is to explain and provide a research-based rationale for the use of teacher verbal feedback prompts that convince students of their ability to succeed on a task.

Understanding Ezekiel's Behavior

Bandura's (1986) social-cognitive theory of motivation provides a framework for understanding Ezekiel's behavior and attitude, and suggests a practical solution to help Ms. Williams. In this theory, an individual's beliefs about him- or herself are a strong influence on behavior. Thus, if Ezekiel believes he does not have the skills to decode long words, he is not likely to become involved in that task. In Bandura's theory, belief about one's competence on a prospective task is called self-efficacy: it is a perception of one's ability that is not necessarily accurate; self-efficacy and perceived self-efficacy are often used synonymously. "Perceived self-efficacy is defined as people's judgments of their capabilities to organize and execute courses of action required to attain designated types of performances" (Bandura, 391). A self-efficacy belief is task specific, exists prior to attempting a task, predicts how well a person thinks he or she will do, and may vary within the same individual according to the task. Self-efficacy is a relative concept that can be applied generally or specifically. For example, it is possible to have high self-efficacy for math and low self-efficacy for reading, or high self-efficacy for multiplying two-digit numbers and low self-efficacy for multiplying three-digit numbers. Furthermore, self-efficacy differs from self-concept, which is defined as "one's collective self-perceptions" (Schunk 2004, 373); it is possible to have a strong self-concept and simultaneously have low self-efficacy for math, science, or playing golf.

If self-efficacy is positive and strong, and if the goal of a task has value to the individual, he or she will be likely to make the decision to become involved. A student might be able to multiply two-place digits, for example, but not wish to do so because the reward for success may not have value to him or her. However, the same student might quickly become involved in two-digit multiplication to figure out the amount of money he or she might earn from an after-school job in a two-week period.

Self-efficacy beliefs are a powerful influence on motivation. A recent study by Bogner, Raphael, and Pressley (2002) reported a decline in elementary students' motivation to read that correlated with a decline in belief in their ability to read. "People's level of motivation, affective states, and actions are based more on what they believe than on what is objectively the case" (Bandura 1995, 2). Although classroom variables such as appropriate material, tasks, instructional procedures, and teacher affect also influence student motivation and engagement in learning (Alderman 2004; Brophy 1981; Dolezalt et al. 2003; Mastropieri and Scruggs 2004; Pintrich and Schunk 2002; Stipek 2001; Turner 1995), Ezekiel's low self-efficacy for reading multisyllabic words was the critical and most influential factor resulting in his lack of motivation to read.

In describing human fear, Bandura stated, "Persons who judge themselves as lacking coping capabilities, whether the self-appraisal is objectively warranted or not, will perceive all kinds of dangers in situations and exaggerate their potential harmfulness" (1986, 220). Individuals such as Ezekiel, who feel they cannot read well, will often avoid reading rather than experience failure and frustration. Therefore, Ms. Williams's positive feedback comments to Ezekiel should help him recognize evidence that he does, in fact, have the ability to accomplish the task.

"For learners to evaluate their progress, it is essential that they receive goal progress feedback, especially when they cannot derive reliable information on their own" (Schunk 2003, 164). "These progress indicators convey that students are capable of learning and performing well, which enhances their self-efficacy for further learning" (Pintrich and Schunk 2002, 148). The learner's awareness of indicators of his or her progress is critical to the development of self-efficacy and, thus, to sustaining motivation.

Verbal feedback that makes the learner aware of his or her advancement is one type of progress indicator that, if used correctly, can become a prompt for sustaining learner behavior (Atkinson, Renkl, and Merrill 2003; Ernsbarger 2002; Ormrod 2004). Such prompts "include clues, cues, hints, or reminders that facilitate the occurrence of a particular behavior" (Ernsbarger, 280).

Below I suggest exemplary phrases, consistent with Bandura's framework, that convince students of their ability to learn. (The key word in the previous sentence is "convince" because the words and phrases suggested below are directed toward not just telling but persuading students to have a positive belief about themselves.) Skill level will of course differ among students, so it is important that feedback from teachers is appropriate and credible. Brophy (1981) developed guidelines for effective praise that included being contingent on success and not gratuitous, being specific, demonstrating the value of the task, and attributing success to effort. Telling a student that he or she was successful when that was not the case is disingenuous, unlikely to have value to the learner, and affects the credibility of the teacher. Celebrating student success on a task that was too easy will also have little value to the learner, because he or she may feel the teacher has low expectations of him or her or that he or she is capable of only simple tasks.

What to Say to Ezekiel

Brophy noted that students' interpretation of praise was most valuable when it helped them "make attributions about their abilities and about the linkages between their efforts and the outcomes of those efforts" (1981, 27). While seemingly intuitive, there is also evidence that "teacher feedback can affect self-efficacy. Persuasive statements (e.g., 'I know that you can do this') can raise self-efficacy" (Schunk 2001, 127). Therefore, verbal feedback from the teacher is especially critical and needs to be crafted to convince the learner that he or she possesses the ability to complete a given task. Recently, Brown (2003) and Clark (2004) outlined useful reading instruction prompts to help students decode words. Brown suggested prompts based on developmental stage of reading, and Clark (2004) suggested prompts based on (1) "general cues to prompt thought" (metacognition) and (2) "cues to prompt specific action" (explicit instruction to use word bound and contextual cues). In concluding her article, Brown posed a critical question for teachers: "What kind of prompt should I be using with this reader at this point in development?" (728). To that, I add the following: "What kind of prompt should I be using with this reader at this point in his or her motivational development?"

When prompts such as those suggested by Brown (2003) and Clarke (2004) are used in conjunction with prompts directed toward building self-efficacy, there is an increased probability that students will be successful in reading tasks. Words of encouragement such as "good job," "you can do it," and "fantastic work, keep it up!" are too global and do not address the motivational needs of Ezekiel and students like him because they fail to draw attention to evidence of success. Therefore, they do not adequately convince Ezekiel that he has the ability to sound out multisyllabic words. Just as many students need explicit instruction to learn an academic skill, students like Ezekiel need explicit teacher verbal feedback crafted to enhance their self-efficacy.

In the following paragraphs, I provide a rationale for exemplary words and phrases that can be used to convince students like Ezekiel they have the ability to succeed on a given task. Consistent with Bandura's (1986) theory, the italicized words and phrases embedded within a larger sentence context are critical because they focus learners' attention on important feedback information about their progress and contribute to enhancing their self-efficacy. Other words and phrases that are consistent with the rationale presented here may be equally effective with students such as Ezekiel.

According to Bandura (1997), there are four sources through which an individual can acquire information about his or her competence and, thus, develop selfefficacy beliefs: enactive mastery, vicarious experiences, verbal persuasion, and physiological/affective state (see table 1). Each source is explained below, accompanied by relevant exemplary words and phrases. Although these comments are presented below in separate categories according to the sources of self-efficacy, "[a]ny given influence, depending on its form, may operate through one or more of these sources of efficacy information" (Bandura, 79). Therefore, teachers should think of them as complementary and mutually reinforcing.

Enactive Mastery

A student's recognition that he has mastered a task as a result of expending personal effort provides strong feedback that he possesses the ability to succeed. This knowledge, in turn, has a significant effect on the development of self-efficacy. "Enactive mastery experiences are the most influential source of efficacy information because they provide the most authentic evidence of whether one can muster whatever it takes to succeed" (Bandura 1997, 80).

Table 1 Teacher Feedback

Category	Example
Enactive master (accomplishment)	*"You were able to"*
	"You got"
	"You now have the idea"
	"Now you have the knack of"
	"You have the skill to"
Vicarious experience (modeling)	*"Watch me (Oscar) as I (he). . . . You can also do this, just as I (Oscar) did."*
	"Did you see what I (Oscar) did? You can do the same thing, just as I (Oscar) did."
	"Notice how I (Oscar). . . . You have the ability to do this, just as I have (Oscar has)."
	"Listen while I (Oscar). . . . You can also do this, just as I (Oscar) can."
	"Try to remember what I am (Oscar is) about to do. You will also be able to do the same thing."
Verbal persuasion (attribution)	*"Because you"*
	"And that helped you"
	"As a result of . . . you were able to"
	"Remembering helped you"
Physiological/affective state (feeling)	*"You must feel great"*
	"Did you realize you smiled to yourself?"
	"Do you know you did not fidget?"
	"How did you feel when?"
	"You must feel proud"

The following phrases could direct Ezekiel's attention to evidence of success during mastery in decoding multisyllabic words. They specify the particular accomplishment and would make Ezekiel aware of success by explicitly drawing his attention to his accomplishment. These phrases would clearly tell him that he has achieved a noteworthy accomplishment.

> "You were able to sound out all the parts of that long word."
> "You got all the sounds in the word correct."
> "You now have the idea of how to sound out long words."
> "Now you have the knack of sounding out long words."
> "You have the skill to sound out long words."

Vicarious Experiences

"Efficacy appraisals are partly influenced by vicarious experiences mediated through modeled attainments" (Bandura 1997, 86). Being vicarious means taking part in the feeling and experience of another, so vicarious experiences—observations and comparison to others' actions or skills—provide an individual with useful information about his personal competence to the degree that the observer can relate to the model unique to each person. When the observer feels that characteristics of the model, such as age, gender, personal affinity, interests, or ethnicity, are similar to his own characteristics, the vicarious experience of watching a model is an effective learning tool. Such experiences provide a template and help the learner judge the degree to which he can expect to possess a particular skill. The observer might think, "Hey, he is like me, and if he can do it, so can I." Models which the learner cannot relate to are less effective, and peer models can be as effective or more so than adult models. For example, if Ms. Williams used a peer model, she should select someone to whom Ezekiel can easily relate in terms of one or a combination of the characteristics mentioned above. Two categories of models are a mastery model who successfully completes the task, and a coping model who struggles to some degree but eventually implements a strategy or strategies that lead to success.

Expanding on Ezekiel's situation, suppose that Ms. Williams chose Oscar, a classmate of Ezekiel's, as a peer model. Here are some phrases that Oscar could use to increase the probability that Ezekiel will benefit from Oscar's achievement.

> "Watch me (Oscar) as I (he) sound(s) out this word. You can also do this, just as I (Oscar) did."
> "Did you see what I (Oscar) did? You can do the same thing, just as I (Oscar) did. "
> "Notice how I am (Oscar is) dividing the word into parts. You have the ability to do this, just as I have (Oscar has)."
> "Listen while I (Oscar) tell(s) you what I am thinking as I read. You can also do this, just as I (Oscar) can."
> "Try to remember what I am (Oscar is) about to do. You will also be able to do the same thing."

Verbal Persuasion

The goal of verbal persuasion is to convince an individual that success is achieved through his efforts. This is called attribution, "a perceived cause of an outcome" (Pintrich and Schunk 2002, 402). "Research indicates that some students struggle unnecessarily because they incorrectly attribute failure to ability rather than to lack of effort or undirected effort" (Bruning et al. 2004, 125). Students can attribute success on a task to any number of factors; however, students with low self-efficacy tend to attribute their success to luck or happenstance and students with high self-efficacy tend to attribute their success to personal effort (Bruning et al.). Further, Bruning et al. and Pintrich and Schunk reported that students who made attributions in which they recognized themselves as the reason for their success strengthened their self-efficacy and learning. Bruning et al. stated, "For this reason, we believe that teachers should discuss the role of attributions in learning and provide some degree of retraining for students who make inappropriate attributions" (125).

Although there is some evidence that praise for just ability is less motivational than praise for effort (Craven, Marsh, and Debus 1991; Mueller and Dweck 1998), "people who are persuaded verbally that they possess the capabilities to master given activities are likely to mobilize greater sustained effort and sustain it than if they harbor self-doubts and dwell on personal deficiencies when problems arise" (Bandura 1986, 400). Therefore, both effort feedback and ability feedback should be used by teachers in what Burnett (2003) called a "balanced and strategic" (13) manner. Coupled with successful enactive mastery experiences, verbal persuasion that focuses on attribution retraining can bolster feelings of self-efficacy. However, according to Robertson (2000), although attribution training has been advocated for many years, it has not been practiced in the schools. I encourage teachers to use the following words and phrases (and others similar to them) to enhance student self-efficacy by helping students attribute their success to personal effort and ability.

> "You were able to divide the word into parts because you remembered the rule."
> "You remembered the rule and that helped you to divide the word into parts."
> "As a result of studying the rule, you were able to divide the word into parts."
> "Because you studied, you were able to divide the word into parts."
> "Remembering the rule helped you divide the word into parts."

Physiological/Affective State

Physiological and affective reactions can occur concurrently with one or all of the three other sources of efficacy information. For example, success on a new and moderately challenging task is likely to lower anxiety levels and increase positive feelings when confronted with the same or a similar task in the future. However, "by conjuring up aversive thoughts about their ineptitude and stress reactions, people can rouse themselves to elevated levels of distress that produce the very dysfunction they fear" (Bandura 1997, 107). "Bodily symptoms serve as physiological cues. Sweating and trembling may signal that students are not capable of learning. Students who notice they are reacting in a less-agitated fashion to tasks feel more efficacious about learning" (Pintrich and Schunk 2002, 172). Therefore, "parents and teachers can do students a great service by helping them understand their emotional reactions to success and failure" (Bruning et al. 2004, 125). By directing Ezekiel's attention to his physiological or affective state, Ms. Williams can help him recognize such feedback as additional information about his ability to learn. The following direct student attention to physiological and affect reaction.

> "You must feel great that you sounded out that long word."
> "Did you realize you smiled to yourself after you sounded out that long word?"
> "Do you know you did not fidget so much when you sounded out that long word?"
> "How did you feel when you were able to sound out that long word?"
> "You must feel proud now that you have sounded out that word."

A Final Few Words

In his discussion of teachers' praise to students, Brophy stated, "rather than just assume its effectiveness, teachers who wish to praise effectively will have to assess how individual students respond to praise" (1981, 27). Therefore, it is important for teachers to monitor students' reactions to self-efficacy comments and make necessary adjustments. Studies have identified a number of situational and personal variables that may individually or in combination affect how students perceive verbal feedback prompts. Teachers should be aware of these variables when assessing the results of their efforts, especially when working with struggling readers with low self-efficacy.

One variable is the difficulty level of the task. Tasks that are too easy or too difficult will likely negate the value of the self-efficacy prompts suggested here; prompts accompanying a task that is perceived by the learner as too easy may engender a counterproductive response in which the learner assigns little or no value to the teacher's comments (Pintrich and Schunk 2002). In such a case, the learner may think, "That was so easy. Why is Ms. Williams telling me how great this was? Is that all she thinks I can do? I must really be dumb!" Assignments that are frustrating to the learner because of the difficulty of material or the nature of the task are equally undesirable because they result in further weakening self-efficacy and motivation and contribute to a reinforced feeling of learned helplessness. A useful concept when designing instructional tasks is Vygotsky's "Zone of Proximal Development," described by May and Rizzardi as "the difference between what a child can already do alone and what he or she can do with assistance from a more competent person" (2002, 19), and by Pintrich and Schunk as, "the amount of learning possible by a student given proper instructional support" (160). Therefore, prior to assigning a task and providing self-efficacy prompts, the teacher should decide if the student is likely to be successful, and the tasks should be moderately challenging.

Another variable that may affect the impact of self-efficacy prompts is the setting. Some students may be embarrassed when they receive prompts in front of their peers, while others may conclude that they have not received the same feedback from the teacher because they lack the ability or potential (Robertson 2000). Individual and private feedback may be more effective for some children, especially those who struggle with, and have low self-efficacy for, reading but are in a class or group in which the majority of students read better than they do.

Teacher credibility is also a critical variable for selfefficacy prompts to be successful. Such prompts should not be used with all students indiscriminately, but only with those who have both the ability and low self-efficacy for a specific task. The teacher's credibility suffers when he gives these prompts to a student who does not have the ability to successfully complete a given task, and this may result in the student ignoring or doubting the teacher in the future.

Additionally, Pintrich and Schunk (2002) and Alderman (2004) reported a host of personal variables, includingage, developmental level, gender, ethnicity, and economic background, that can affect students' perceptions of the cause of success or failure on a task. These variables may interact in various combinations and permutations and affect self-efficacy and motivation in different and unexpected ways. Age and gender may affect strength of influence of verbal self-efficacy feedback prompts because "young children see ability as more modifiable than do older students," and "overall, the attributions of girls reflect a lower expectancy pattern" (Alderman, 41). According to Pintrich and Schunk, the relationship and effect of ethnicity to self-efficacy development has been difficult to determine; this area requires additional research. In many of the studies conducted, economic level may have interacted with ethnicity and confounded the explanation of student attributions as due to effort or ability (Alderman; Pintrich and Schunk). In one study reported by Alderman, fifth and sixth graders of various ethnicities from low economic backgrounds rated ability as the cause of success or failure in math; however, in another study, both middle-class African American and white students attributed failure to lack of effort (Alderman).

Alderman (2004) and Pintrich and Schunk (2004) describe the developmental change in attributions in children at about age ten. At this time, children begin to differentiate between effort and ability as the cause of success, but prior to that age they believe that effort and ability are the same. Therefore, the younger student who has tried but has not succeeded on a task may conclude that she does not have the ability and may no longer attempt that or similar tasks. Teachers of young children should take care to ensure that their students are given tasks on which they can succeed in order to avoid starting a young child on a self-defeating path of self-doubt and learned helplessness regarding school tasks.

The exemplary verbal feedback prompts I have suggested should not be limited to middle school students such as Ezekiel, but should be applied throughout the grades. As children become members of the community of learners and are enculturated into the school society in the early grades, teachers should provide them with positive, informative, and credible feedback about their ability to learn. This is especially true for children whose parents or caretakers may have done little to build, and may even have eroded, the child's self-efficacy and even her self-concept. The result of comments such as, "Your sister could read when she was your age. Why can't you?" or "How many times will it take for you to get it?" are deleterious to the young child's beliefs about himself as a learner, will carry over to the formal school environment and, if not immediately addressed by teachers, will become entrenched within the learner's psyche. Other children may be aware of their abilities thanks to nurturing parents or caretakers, but have learned from the formal school experience they are not as good as others and are not achieving according to school standards. This may result from poor or inconsistent instruction, including inappropriate material and pacing, lack of the teacher's individual attention, or classroom environmental issues such as noise level, lighting, overcrowding, or the seating arrangement. Ezekiel may have experienced either or a combination of these scenarios. When the verbal feedback I have suggested is consistently applied throughout the grades and is part of a schoolwide philosophy for learning, students will be much less likely to develop negative or weak self-efficacy beliefs such as those held by Ezekiel.

Although change in self-efficacy perceptions may occur in a relatively short period of time for some children, it is more likely that the results of these verbal prompts will occur gradually over a longer period of time, especially for children who have a painful history of failure and frustration in school. When the prompts I suggest are combined with the instructional prompts suggested by Brown (2003) and Clark (2004) and used in conjunction with sound literacy development practices that include appropriate tasks, materials, and instructional procedures, teachers will have a much better chance of reaching, and teaching, students such as Ezekiel.

References

Alderman, M. K. 2004. *Motivation for achievement: Possibilities for teaching and learning*. 2nd ed. Mahwah, NJ: Erlbaum.

Atkinson, R. K., A. Renkl, and M. M. Merrill. 2003. Transitioning from studying examples to solving problems: Effects of self-explanation prompts and fading worked-out steps. *Journal of Educational Psychology* 95 (4): 774–84.

Bandura, A. 1986. *Social foundations of thought and action*. Englewood Cliffs, NJ: Prentice-Hall.

———. 1995. Exercise of personal and collective efficacy in changing societies. In *Self-efficacy in changing societies*, ed. A. Bandura, 1–45. New York: Cambridge University Press.

———. 1997. *Self-efficacy: The exercise of control*. New York: Longman.

Bogner, K., L. Raphael, and M. Pressley. 2002. How grade 1 teachers motivate literacy activity by their students. *Scientific Studies of Reading* 6 (2): 135–65.

Brophy, J. 1981. Teacher praise: A functional analysis. *Review of Educational Research*, no. 51:5–32.

Brown, K. J. 2003. What do I say when they get stuck on a word? Aligning teachers' prompts with students' development. *Reading Teacher* 56 (8): 720–33.

Bruning, R. H., G. J. Schraw, M. M. Norby, and R. R. Ronning. 2004. *Cognitive psychology and instruction*. 4th ed. Upper Saddle River, NJ: Pearson.

Burnett, P. C. 2003. The impact of teacher feedback on student selftalk and self-concept in reading and mathematics. *Journal of Classroom Interaction* 38 (1): 11–16.

Clark, K. F. 2004. What can I say besides "sound it out"? Coaching word recognition in beginning reading. *Reading Teacher* 57 (4): 440–49.

Craven, R. G., H. W. Marsh, and R. L. Debus. 1991. Effects of internally focused feedback and attributional feedback on the enhancement of academic self-concept. *Journal of Educational Psychology*, no. 83:17–27.

Dolezal, S. E., L. M. Welsh, M. Pressley, and M. M. Vincent. 2003. How nine third grade teachers motivate student academic engagement. *Elementary School Journal* 103 (3): 240–67.

Ernsbarger, S. C. 2002. Simple, affordable, and effective strategies for prompting reading behavior. *Reading and Writing Quarterly* 18 (3): 279–84.

Mastropieri, M. A., and T. E. Scruggs. 2004. *The inclusive classroom: Strategies for effective instruction*. Upper Saddle River, NJ: Merrill Prentice-Hall.

May, F., and L. Rizzardi. 2002. *Reading as communication*. 6th ed. Upper Saddle River, NJ: Merrill Prentice-Hall.

Mueller, C. M., and C. S. Dweck. 1998. Praise for intelligence can undermine children's motivation and performance. *Journal of Personality and Psychology* 75 (1): 33–52.

Ormrod, J. E. 2004. *Human learning*. Upper Saddle River, NJ: Merrill.

Pintrich P. R., and D. H. Schunk. 2002. *Motivation in education: Theory, research, and applications*. Upper Saddle River, NJ: Merrill.

Robertson, J. S. 2000. Is attribution training a worthwhile classroom intervention for K–12 students with learning difficulties? *Educational Psychology Review* 12 (1): 111–34.

Schunk, D. H. 2001. Social cognitive theory and self-regulated learning. In *Self-regulated learning and academic achievement: Theoretical perspectives*, 2nd ed., ed. B. Zimmerman, 125–52. Mahwah, NJ: Lawrence Erlbaum.

———. 2003. Self-efficacy for reading and writing: Influence of modeling, goal setting, and self-evaluation. *Reading and Writing Quarterly* 19 (2): 159–72.

———. 2004. *Learning theories: An educational perspective*. 4th ed. New York: Pearson.

Stipek, D. J. 2001. *Motivation to learn: Integrating theory and practice*. Needham Heights, MA: Allyn and Bacon.

Patrick P. McCabe is an associate professor of education and reading at St. Johns University in Queens.

Why We Can't Always Get What We Want

BARBARA BARTHOLOMEW

He was the new reading teacher's greatest challenge—a sixth-grader reading at roughly the first-grade level. Sometimes he acted out, but mostly he just daydreamed, talked, or slept while his classmates worked. No one, including his guardian, knew how to motivate him to want to succeed.

As she was leaving the building one afternoon, the teacher happened upon a rambunctious game of basketball. She entered the nearly empty gym, sat in the bleachers, and immediately noticed the boy playing with his team. She returned his frantic wave. As the game drew to a close, he dashed up to her, and they launched into an excited conversation about the game.

After that, she made a point of going to almost every practice for the rest of the season. There, she would often study the coach, focusing on how attentive the team was to him. They responded to his intensity, his knowledge of the game and the players, his planning, and his single-minded commitment to winning.

Taking this cue, she set a small number of attainable short- and long-term classroom goals for the boy, simultaneously adjusting her own demeanor, expectations, and responses to more closely match her colleague's. Progress toward reading goals was measured on a hand-drawn schematic of a basketball court in the boy's folder; each movement toward his "basket" was noted with a ball drawn on the paper court. Soon she and the boy began listening and responding carefully to each other.

The note of exasperation on which the year had begun quietly gave way to a fragile optimism shared by the student and teacher, now learners together. The boy began to believe he could make learning connections off the court, and the teacher began to understand that effective teaching depends a great deal on the efforts of the students themselves. After just five months of uneven yet steady progress, the boy's reading score had risen by more than a grade.

The year was 1995. The teacher was me.

Context First

What I had stumbled on in my first year of teaching would take years to implement consistently as a way to drive instruction. It was, in a word, *motivation*. Motivation involves creating the inspiration *to do* or *to achieve*. Some students arrive at school fully motivated. Often, though, the opposite is the case.

As a new teacher, I had assumed what most in the field of education believe to be true: motivation springs from effective curriculum and instruction. If we have some perfect blend of elements—direct instruction, whole-language instruction, a new trade book or textbook, an intervention, a new set of standards—students will become deeply involved and interested learners. Everything circled back to effective curriculum and instruction. It had been the focus of my college course-work, of every professional development session I had ever attended, and of every piece of advice I had ever received from a principal. But it was clear to me from that first experience that the most vexing issues I faced as a teacher stemmed less from the content that I knew and could control than from the context of things I did not know and could not control.

Chief among these things was what made my students tick. Human thought processes are not directly observable. Because we see others behaving in a way that is consistent with our efforts to influence their actions, we deduce that we have succeeded in our attempts to motivate them. But for every teacher who has run a "token" society, rewarded those who comply with candy, phoned a parent to gain a student's cooperation, changed seating charts in the hope of ending chatter, or flashed classroom lights as a signal for silence, it remains unclear exactly what is motivating the students. It is easy to confuse behavioral cueing with motivational change.

The Star Story

A principal I knew had once been a teacher at an alternative high school. Many of his pupils were returning from stints in jail or in drug treatment programs. Most were in their late teens and quickly bonded with him as a strong and important male presence in their lives. His dream for them was that they would be able to defy the odds of repeated failure and, as he had done, forge independent paths of success for themselves.

He placed a motivational chart in his classroom. As students reached important milestones, he would reward them with a gold star on the chart. One day, with only a few minutes until class was to begin, he realized that it was reward day and that he had run out of gold stars. He dashed across the street to a local grocery, only to find it was sold out of the tiny gold stars. He settled for silver stars instead.

When award time rolled around, he began posting the silver stars that he had purchased as substitutes. Almost immediately furious shouts erupted from his normally quiet group, and within moments the class had dissolved into a chaotic mix of fist fighting and chair throwing. The police were summoned. As the students were being questioned, virtually every one, some in tears, expressed frustration that their teacher had disrespected them by demoting them from the level of gold stars to the lesser status of silver.

With no background in either the power or the shortcomings of behavioral motivation models, he had missed important pieces of the context in which he was working. He failed to account for how much value his students had placed on the public recognition of individual accomplishment played out in front of the entire group. Other contextual issues might have affected their motivation as well. Had fair and equitable rules been set for earning the rewards? Could he have anticipated that an all-male class would see the stars as designations of merit similar to gold and silver medals?

It is well established in the literature of motivation that successful motivational models do not necessarily rely on extrinsically controlled rewards and punishments. Rather, the best motivational models take advantage of those "satisfiers" and "valuations" chosen and controlled by an individual. Without knowing of alternative ways of developing autonomous learners, the teacher had simply resorted to the carrot-and-stick model that was actually least likely to bring him the results he wanted.

Classroom Management or Motivation?

A common confusion of teachers and school leaders alike is that classroom management and motivation are basically one and the same. Teachers continue to focus on tight control of the environment and curriculum in the closely held belief that doing so will eventually create motivated students and positive learning outcomes. Since it sometimes does, they are encouraged to keep trying whatever occasionally successful system brings them the result they seek. Because a quiet classroom where students are busy is equated with good teaching, it is an ideal for which most teachers strive. The paradox, of course, is that such successful behavior management does not create motivation to learn, any more than work completed with little care for learning demonstrates student progress.

What classroom management can provide is the space to create motivating opportunities for students to engage in a level of self-determination about their own learning.[1] But if the chance is not seized, teachers will find themselves very quickly painted into a corner of endlessly distributing rewards and punishments, with little opportunity to focus on mastery in content areas.

A number of studies, including the government's own, have established the correlation between teacher attrition and lack of classroom control.[2] These same data suggest that more than 50% of teachers leave the profession because of poor student behavior.

What we have failed to provide in the professional training of teachers is a realistic understanding that control and compliance will not in themselves create a climate for academic attainment. Indeed, in some cases, they may actually prove to be a disincentive to learning. Causes of disengagement vary, from boredom and frustration to anger and depression. So long as we continue to focus on the symptoms of the uninspired rather than on the problem itself, we will persist in overlooking the root causes of why students fail to thrive.

A Misunderstood Precondition

The education community has not done a good job of articulating the idea that student motivation is a necessary precondition to learning that teachers need to create and foster. And teachers must do this nurturing from their diagnostic and practical knowledge of human behavior, not from a knowledge of subject matter. Not one of the top 10 schools of education in the *U.S. News and World Report* rankings requires students seeking credentials as teachers or pursuing graduate degrees in leadership to complete a dedicated class in educational motivation. Typically, the study of motivation has been located in graduate schools of psychology or in departments of educational psychology. Students in these areas are not very likely to become the professionals who interact with students daily in a school setting.

If motivation is covered at all in most schools of education, it is folded into the subject matter of another class, such as organizational management or learning theory, rather than studied as an essential stand-alone subject. In the endless parsing of "best practices" in training programs for teachers and school leaders—both preservice and inservice—learning to foster student motivation, the most obvious of all best practices, is conspicuously absent.

There exists an entrenched belief in American education that student learning will spring from the right alchemic brew of macro components: firm direction from state and local departments of education, strong district- and school-based leadership, a good teacher, the right curriculum, and appropriate books.[3] However, such matters as the steady increase in the number of students whose families face grave economic stresses and the need for common touchstones in a multicultural society argue that the time is right to examine carefully the framework of human variables involved in teaching and learning.

The best place to start is the field of educational motivation, which encompasses a well-developed and compelling body of knowledge from such fields as psychology, sociology, linguistic and speech studies, and organizational management. In this knowledge base we are sure to find at least part of what we need to help us create classrooms that will appeal to those who teach and those who learn.

Higher up the policy ladder, state and local administrators are beginning to reassess the effect on student achievement of micromanaged schools and scripted curricula. They will need to consider what elements and training will be necessary to create motivational classrooms. It is also essential that they take a hard look at the impact of factory-model educational designs of the kind encouraged by the No Child Left Behind (NCLB) Act on school personnel's morale and, in turn, on student achievement.[4]

As the reauthorization of NCLB looms in 2007, we would be wise to ask ourselves how we can do better at preparing highly qualified professionals for the jobs they will face. It is widely acknowledged that something monumental has shifted beneath our feet, and teachers have been saying for years that they are social workers and psychologists first. Yet we continue to prepare them as content specialists and to evaluate their teaching proficiency on how well they meet subject content standards. What is our plan, then, for the human content standard?

Rethinking Preparation and Practice

One reason schools, offices of education, and even university departments of education have ignored motivational theory and practice is doubtless the difficulty of identifying generalizable and effective courses of action for teachers, given the endless variety of challenging conditions educators face. It is unlikely that there will ever be a single program to address all possibilities, but some relevant universals can be found.

It is in education that behaviorism has probably come closest to achieving mass popularity, and it has done so in part because of the simplicity of its basic stance and its appeal to commonsense ideas about control and reward. However, as the "star story" illustrates, behaviorism is not always an easy tool to use. Nevertheless, it would be foolish and impractical to dismiss thoughtful behavioral reward systems altogether simply because they do not draw on intrinsic motivation or because they violate an ideological ideal. Those programs that provide meaningful, noncontrolling feedback or those in which students themselves determine how they wish to be rewarded are clearly worth examining.[5]

Programs that have proved useful in enhancing student learning should not be dismissed simply because they do not conform to today's trends in practice. What is important is that both instructional and motivational programs demonstrate a justifiable probability of success. Moreover, whatever the theoretical underpinnings of a program, those who would apply it must learn both the theory and the ways it plays out in practice.

Both teacher preparation programs and educational leadership programs should require a minimum of a one-term class dedicated to the topic of motivation. Indeed, a full-year sequence would be best. Such a program should provide its students with broad preparation in the cross-disciplinary cornerstones of motivational theory and in the details of practice. Case study analyses, combined with opportunities for clinical observation, practice, and reflection, would give all educators a far better chance of success.

Motivation in Action

One of the great puzzles of education is how to take a successful innovative program, transfer it to a new setting, and obtain equally good results. Though we don't always like to acknowledge it, classroom and school cultures are created at the local level. Successful instructional motivation programs must therefore be able to take account of the context of individual communities and of the students in specific classrooms. What drives people of all ages to make choices about where to exert themselves is, to some degree at least, relevance to their lives. If we perceive that something is relevant, we will choose to participate in learning it even if it does not interest us or even if we feel we don't have the ability to learn it easily. Following a similar line of thought, psychologist Gordon Paul posed a classic question for clinical researchers: "*What* treatment, by *whom*, is most effective for *this* individual with *that* specific problem, and under *which* set of circumstances?"[6] These are sage words for anyone wondering where to begin a discussion of motivation.

While there is no universal framework to follow, there are a number of fundamentals that apply broadly and can be used as a foundation for building models of classroom excellence. When they are ignored or violated, we decrease our chances of fostering the personally meaningful satisfaction and enrichment of lives that education has always sought.

One such general principle of "satisfaction" could be stated this way: we are drawn to do what gratifies us and avoid doing what pains us—especially when we see no clear benefit from the undesirable experience. Below, I mention briefly several other considerations that would have both broad applicability and individual relevance for creating a classroom where intrinsic motivation rules.

- *Sustainability must be considered.* Good practices get better as routines are established and weaknesses identified and weeded out. No program or component of a program should be kept if it is not working.
- *Age determines course of action.* Opportunities for students to achieve success at every level of schooling are crucial to establishing and maintaining motivation. Younger children are generally more confident that they will succeed in school—probably because their perceptions have not yet been firmly shaped with regard to their abilities and achievement history.[7] From grades 3 through 8, studies have shown that intrinsic motivation falls off steadily.

Older students—like those in the star story—present complex personal histories and problems. Those who have accepted failure and those who have learned helplessness may not believe that they possess the ability to change their learning outcomes. Others seek to avoid failure in a variety of unsatisfactory ways, including not challenging themselves to learn and even lapsing into plagiarism and other forms of cheating.[8]

Standardized assessments may not accurately determine how prepared students are in content areas. And uncovering the strengths students bring to the classroom and the relevance to their lives of classroom learning is key to remediation and engagement, especially for older students.

• *Teachers set expectations and establish routines.* Classroom management will not be the focal point of efforts to increase student motivation. Instead, a well-managed classroom will be the result of good organization, clear expectations, positive teacher communication, and valuing student input and engagement. Teachers must model and enforce the kind of respectful interchange they expect. Praise is an appropriate reward when it is specific and deserved; it should never be used when students have performed work without effort or care. And once again, consistency is essential in establishing an effective classroom and in maintaining a classroom culture of trust and equality.

• *Students, with guidance from teachers, establish goals, strategies, and achievement plans.* Allowing students to set goals is probably the most effective means of having them begin to take charge of their learning. How this process is arranged can vary, but students' plans should incorporate short- and long-term goals and an explicit outline of what will be needed to achieve them. So as not to overwhelm students, the goals can be broken down into smaller units of daily or weekly goals. Some students may wish to work with partners to brainstorm, to gauge their progress, and to obtain feedback on their work. Student-maintained records of individual progress can provide incentives for self-monitoring.

• *Providing students with choices can be motivating.* In general, we should allow students to participate in class decision making and should give them as many choices as possible about the topics and work they will pursue. Class-constructed rubrics can establish group norms for how work will be evaluated. Students will perceive evaluation systems into which they have had input as fairer than those from which they have been excluded.

• *Teachers set class tone; students set their individual tone.* In the classrooms I have observed, minds at rest have a tendency to stay at rest until an outside force acts on them. Once in motion, if they're encouraged and supported, they tend to stay in motion and continue to move forward independently. Building students' intrinsic motivation involves a seemingly contradictory degree of stage setting, coaching, and feedback from the teacher, especially as routines are being set. And even as the students "take over," teachers must still be comfortable with a wide variety of teaching strategies in order to accommodate the range of subjects and the range of student learners.

Two components that help set the tone are likely to play key roles in the degree to which students engage themselves independently as learners. The first is respecting the power of listening. The simple act of listening carefully to others while holding their gaze conveys attentiveness, interest, respect for (though not necessarily agreement with) the speaker's views, and a range of other nonverbal messages. By combining attentive listening with such conversational guidelines as turn-taking, gauging understanding, and conveying empathy, the teacher can both build and help monitor engagement.[9] Creating opportunities to teach and practice listening is a frequently overlooked element in establishing a mutually motivational environment for both teacher and student. Listening is also an important aspect of relationship building, the most obvious of all motivational strategies.

The second component that helps foster a tone that supports motivation is building and expanding on positives. The expanding field of positive psychology has yielded insights into the phenomenon of "learned optimism," or the theory that positive thinking patterns can be acquired.[10] In one classic experiment, researchers paired animated, happy individuals with nonexpressive partners in a conversational setting. In a short time, the mood of the nonexpressive individuals began to lighten and approached that of the more positive individuals.[11] Such positive emotions as joy, pride, and contentment have been shown to lead to physiological and psychological changes that cause individuals—at least momentarily—to broaden their cognitive perceptions, to become more open to change, and to increase their emotional well-being.

Barbara Fredrickson has proposed a "broaden and build" theory that suggests that positive moments create opportunities for mental expansiveness. Seizing on these moments when the potential for growth is at its peak can lead to greater classroom learning.[12] Humor, celebrations, trips, visual reminders, and games fall under the umbrella of building intrinsic motivation through positive approaches.[13]

The Satisfaction Principle

Educators are not all that different from students. They also thrive in climates where they feel their input is viewed as important, where they can engage in daily curricular and instructional choices, and where they feel valued and respected.[14] Like older students, they will avoid the pain of working in environments over which they have little control and in which they meet daily failure. When they are unable to find satisfaction in their work environment, the data show that they will leave.

One failing that has been noted about standards-based systems is that, when externally mandated goals are not met, blame enters the picture. In such work climates, teachers are unlikely to experiment with any classroom technique that could cause them to be targeted for blame should students fail to achieve.[15] In the present national environment of rigid adherence to lockstep formulas, following standard practice is the equivalent of job insurance. If students fail because of policies made higher up the chain of command, then schools and teachers can say that they did as they were told, and culpability will be pushed back up the ladder. Teachers are a well-educated group and will, when they have had enough, move on. Students, lacking this option, will be the ones who will lose the most.

It is within our power, as a profession, to reshape what exists into what could be. We have misplaced the knowledge that hope and dreams are the mortar of our business. We now define and justify our actions through the accountability sweepstakes, but until we reset our direction, we will remain disappointed, like the students racing for gold stars and inexplicably receiving silver ones. The star chart has replaced the satisfaction principle.

Notes

1. Edward L. Deci and Richard M. Ryan, "The Paradox of Achievement: The Harder You Push, the Worse It Gets," in Joshua Aronson, ed., *Improving Academic Achievement: Contribution of Social Psychology* (New York: Academic Press, 2002), pp. 59–85.
2. "The Condition of Education, 2005, Special Analysis: Mobility in the Teacher Workforce," U.S. Department of Education, http://nces.ed. gov/programs/coe/2005/analysis/index.asp; and New York City Council, "A Staff Report of the New York City Council Division on Teacher Attrition and Retention," Eric Goia, Chair, 2004.
3. Michael J. Feuer, "Better Than Best," *Harvard Education Letter,* May/June, 2006.
4. Barbara Bartholomew, "Transforming New York City's Public Schools," *Educational Leadership,* May 2006, pp. 61–65.
5. Martin V. Covington and Kimberly J. Mueller, "Intrinsic Versus Extrinsic Motivation: An Approach/Avoidance Reformulation," *Educational Psychology Review,* vol 13, 2001, pp. 157–76.
6. Gordon L. Paul, "Strategy of Outcome Research in Psychotherapy," *Journal of Consulting Psychology,* vol. 31, 1967, p. 111.
7. Deborah J. Stipek, *Motivation to Learn* (Boston: Allyn and Bacon, 1993), p. 14.
8. Ibid.; and Covington and Mueller, pp. 169–70.
9. Lyn S. Turkstra, "Looking While Listening and Speaking: Eye-to-Face Gaze in Adolescents with and Without Brain Injury," *Journal of Speech, Language, and Hearing Research,* December 2005, pp. 1429–41.
10. Martin E. P. Seligman, *Learned Optimism* (New York: Simon and Schuster, 1998).
11. Howard S. Friedman and Ronald E. Riggio, "Effect of Individual Differences in Nonverbal Expressiveness on Transmission of Emotion," *Journal of Nonverbal Behavior,* December 1981, pp. 96–104.
12. Barbara L. Fredrickson, "The Role of Positive Emotions in Positive Psychology: The Broaden and Build Theory of Positive Emotions," *American Psychologist,* vol. 56, 2001, pp. 218–26.
13. Paula Milligan, "Bringing Fun into Organization," *Teaching Pre-K–8,* August/September 2006, available at www.teaching-k-8.com/archives/articles/bringing_fun_into_organization_by_paula_milligan.html.
14. Catherine Scott, Stephen Dinham, and Robert Brooks, "The Development of Scales to Measure Teacher and School Executive Operational Satisfaction," paper presented at the annual meeting of AARE-NAARE, 1999, Melbourne, Aus.
15. Nona Tollefson, "Classroom Applications of Cognitive Theories of Motivation," *Educational Psychology Review,* March 2000, pp. 63–83.

Barbara Bartholomew is an assistant professor of reading and literacy at California State University, Bakersfield.

How to Produce a High-Achieving Child

Frantic parents trying to ensure that their children can maintain an edge throughout their school careers have become a fixture of today's society. But Ms, Kuhn suggests that we are focusing on the wrong side of the equation. Instead of dwelling on what students bring with them to school, we should be considering whether school offers children and young adults sufficiently meaningful experiences to engage them.

DEANNA KUHN

Any lingering pleasant associations parents might entertain in connection with their children's schooling are increasingly being edged out by anxiety. Have I done all I can to ensure my child is on the right track? Perhaps even ahead of the pack? Did I arrange the best summer activities? The right social connections? Or have my efforts been too little or, worse, too late? Is my child already in danger of being "left behind"?

Especially poignant is the fact that in many cases the children of parents harboring these anxieties are no more than a few years old. And these anxieties are not particular to the privileged. They lurk in the minds of parents from one end of the socioeconomic continuum to the other. Among parents at the high end, "average" has become a disappointing outcome, and a large proportion of parents—and their children along with them—are destined to find themselves disappointed.

It is worrying, then, that recent research appears to justify this parental angst. The NICHD Early Child Care Research Network offers this summary in a recent report: "The early childhood years are increasingly seen as a crucial period for the growth and consolidation of important . . . skills necessary for successful school transition and later academic functioning. Major individual differences in these skills emerge well before children arrive at school."[1]

A recent study by Angela Duckworth and Martin Seligman, published in a major academic journal and noted in the *Washington Post,* supports this conclusion. Their study claims that the personal trait of "self-discipline" is the most powerful determinant of young adolescents' academic achievement.[2] The authors asked teens to choose between receiving $1 immediately or $2 next week. Better students were more likely to opt for the $2. Even more notable, related studies have suggested that this ability to delay gratification can be identified in preschoolers and remains stable at least into adolescence. Similarly, Stanford psychologist Carol Dweck reports that people show stability from early childhood on in their beliefs about ability (that it is fixed or can be developed), and she claims that this characteristic significantly affects academic performance.[3]

Is a child's fate determined even before his or her school career has begun? Or are there reasons to doubt that the race to success is won or lost in these earliest years? Among the reasons for doubt is the fact that the formulas for success that focus on traits students bring with them to school leave unexamined the other half of this transaction: what the setting offers the student.

This latter component is critical because it is the student (at any age) who makes what meaning he or she can out of the school experience. We can interpret educational settings only through the lens of how students experience them. And in the end, it is students themselves who select what and when they want to learn. By early adolescence, they begin wanting reasons for investing time and effort in any activity, and they begin to exercise greater autonomy in deciding what is worthwhile.

How I'm Doing Versus What I'm Doing

Why do some children come to value the activities they are asked to engage in at school while others do not? The answer seems likely to lie in the meaning they are able to attribute to these activities. How do children go about constructing authentic meaning out of what they do in school? And is such productive meaning-making critical to academic achievement?

The extensive research on psychological factors affecting school performance contains few answers to these questions. The reason is that most research has been focused not on what children think about school activities but rather on what they think about their own abilities and standing with respect to schoolwork. Only as a secondary effect have researchers considered how these self-evaluation factors affect the value students assign to academic activities themselves.

Thus Dweck reports that whether a student has a performance orientation toward school (believing that ability is fixed) or a learning orientation (believing that ability can be developed) does not predict self-esteem in elementary school but does predict self-esteem by the beginning of junior high school.[4] Self-esteem has been found to decline at this time, especially for girls and for those with a performance orientation. So does professed interest in academic subjects.[5] The causal scenario is not hard to imagine. A performance orientation heightens fear that ones incompetence may be exposed, especially once a young person has experienced failure. An unflattering evaluation lowers self-esteem, and as a self-protective mechanism, the value attached to the activity is reduced. "I'm not interested in it" is more protective of self-esteem than "I'm no good at it."

To the extent that a student is ego-involved rather than task-involved, academic activities come to serve primarily as occasions for evaluating one's competence relative to others.[6] In addition to the danger this orientation poses to children's vulnerable self-esteem, it has a further serious downside. With attention focused on evaluating *how* one is doing relative to others, little attention is left to contemplate *what* one is doing. Every occasion becomes an occasion for social comparison, and the results of these comparisons dictate whether one will continue to invest in and value the activity that is the basis for comparison. Highly privileged, pressured children, especially, feel that they can afford to invest time and effort only in those activities at which they excel. Just when children and adolescents might ideally explore and expand their interests, they begin instead to narrow them.

Suppose, instead, we were able to redirect students' attention to the meanings they attach to their schoolwork, rather than to their ability. What do we know about such meanings? Very little, it turns out.[7] Neither parents nor teachers often elicit children's ideas about why it is they study what they study. It's considered enough that the adults in charge have a sound rationale for what they ask children to do and for the goals these activities will meet. But what evidence we do have suggests that students' understanding is not all we might like it to be. When I asked one young teen whether the world history he was studying would be of value to him in the future, he replied, "Only if you were trying to impress somebody in a conversation." Perhaps we shouldn't be surprised, for the value of much of what students do in school is not immediately apparent—least of all to students themselves.

The New York Story

With increasing age, students do become more likely to question what they are asked to do—a fact that New York City Mayor Michael Bloomberg seems to have overlooked. The mayor has declared creation of "a public education system second to none" as a mission of his second term. If he is to fulfill this mission, he and his associates are going to have to think deeply about what makes a school successful.

Following promising improvements in fourth-graders' test scores in response to a tough new no-automatic-promotion policy, Mayor Bloomberg has extended the policy to students in middle schools and high schools. But in so doing, he neglects an important difference between younger and older children. By the preteen years, children have become less pliable and eager to please adults and so less likely to accept parents' and teachers' admonitions that they must work hard in school or suffer negative consequences. They may become skeptical of the message they've been given that school is the path to success and begin to ask themselves, "What's the point? Why are we doing these things?"

In a society increasingly divided into haves and have-nots, it is the youths in the latter group who most often lack answers. Indeed, they might eventually stop asking questions and simply give up on making sense of much of what their elders ask them to do. Their basic literacy skills are likely to have plateaued at this point, and these young people are sizing up what else it is they're supposed to be getting out of school. Close personal relationships with teachers have largely been sacrificed in the transition from elementary to departmentalized junior high schools, and the students' self-esteem has become even more fragile.[8] If students are going to work any harder, they'll need to find a reason. Complying with the goals adults have for them won't do. For these at-risk youths—who are the primary targets of Mayor Bloomberg's (and many others') effort—the most likely effect of not being promoted is confirmation of a growing sense that "whatever education is about, it's not for me."

Socially advantaged children, in striking contrast, soon develop a ready answer to the "Why are we doing this?" question: to get into a top college. And the competition to do so is stiff enough that they have little time to ponder *why* they're studying what they study ("Will I ever need to know this?"). They've accepted that this is what you need to do to get into college and that getting into college is the path to success. Once there, they'll continue working to fulfill a set of requirements of others' making. And again, the point is to get a degree—and then start a life.

When they do get out into the real world, privileged youths encounter a world in which a markedly different set of norms prevails. All that is done is done for a purpose, most often monetary, and to achieve their purposes people must interact. Both of these characteristics of adult work life—its purposeful and collaborative nature—are largely absent during the school years that precede them. And so, especially in a tight, no-nonsense economy, even the most privileged young people often have a hard time making the transition from school to the working world of adults.

Making School Make Sense

Perhaps one key to the puzzle of academic motivation is to make school make sense, not just to those who structure our school systems or rely on them to educate their children, but to the young people for whom they are designed. Certainly, children's developing self-understanding and the influence of family and community on their development deserve examination, but so does school itself—in particular, the meaning children make of it.

How can we increase the likelihood that school will make sense to students? I suggest two ways. One is to center the curriculum on educational activities whose purpose and value are readily apparent to those who partake in them.[9] This means to a large extent focusing education on intellectual tools—the ones I stress are inquiry and argument—whose purpose and value are easily recognized and whose broad utility and power are evident. Second, and closely related, we need to make schooling more connected to the adult life it is intended to prepare students for.[10] We cannot predict exactly what students will need to know in the

21st century, but we can help them develop the intellectual skills that will enable them to construct this knowledge. Both efforts would serve the haves and have-nots equally well.

Students need to experience for themselves the value of the intellectual activities they engage in and the intellectual tools they acquire. They should become able to make use of them for their own purposes and to see the fruits of their labors, recognizing that intellectual skills, such as inquiry and argument, give them a most productive path for answering questions, solving problems, resolving conflicts, and participating in a democratic society. These are achievements that come about only as the endpoint of a long developmental course, one in which the student is the key player, the meaning-maker. Students do not learn the power of inquiry and argument merely by being told.

Before saying more about how such objectives might be met, I should note that developing sound intellectual motivation depends on students' own intellectual development. This does not mean children are at the mercy of fate, with only some happening to be born to parents who will give them the right recipe to ensure their intellectual development. Rather, the intellectual development of concern here requires only intellectual engagement, and it can take a variety of forms. It is development that is not concentrated in the first few years of life and is within the potential of all children.

Such development encompasses not only the capacity for meaning-making in general, but the ability to make meaning out of ones own life—to find a purpose and to identify goals that can influence actions. We do know that the requisite self-awareness and self-management—what cognitive psychologists are more likely to refer to as self-regulation or "executive control"—do increase in the years between middle childhood and mid-adolescence.[11]

This development is critical because self-regulation is necessary if students are to become active in their own learning and to develop and pursue their own goals.[12] By the time children enter adolescence, they have more discretion than before over how they will spend their time and energy. They are likely to have become more aware of, and highly judgmental about, their own performance. And so their interests will begin to narrow as they make judgments about what they're good at and what they're not good at. And they will have considerable freedom to act on these judgments.

If we want the young people navigating the challenges of this period to decide that the life of the mind is something they are disposed to pursue, we need to consider what they take an intellectual life to be. What is knowledge, and why would one want to invest the effort to acquire it? Researchers studying cognitive development have identified a predictable sequence in students' ideas about the nature of knowledge and knowing, one worth taking into consideration in seeking to understand their academic motivations.[13]

Early in their school lives, children are uniformly naive objectivists. In elementary school, children regard knowledge as something that exists out in the world, independent of the knower. If you and I disagree, it's simply a matter of accessing the information that will determine which of us is right and which wrong. To these young absolutists, there are no shades of gray.

By some time during adolescence, though, fueled by the troubling discovery that reasonable people—even experts—disagree, most young people undergo a dramatic shift and come to embrace, at least for a time, a radical relativism with regard to knowledge and knowing. In a word, everyone is now right. If no one knows for certain, everyone must be accorded the right to believe as he or she chooses. Like pieces of clothing, beliefs are the personal possessions of the believer and not to be questioned. The subjective knower thus enters the equation but eclipses the objective known. Moreover, because everyone has a right to individual beliefs, one belief cannot be said to be any more right than another. Tolerance for multiple views is equated with the impossibility of discriminating among them.

Only some young people will make the transition to the next level of development, one in which the subjective and objective components of knowledge are coordinated. They come to understand that, although all have a right to their own views, some views are nonetheless more right than others, to the extent that they are better supported by evidence. Justification for a belief becomes more than personal preference. The adolescent "whatever" is no longer the automatic response to every assertion. There are now legitimate discriminations and choices to be made.

Until students reach this level of understanding, their motivation for intellectual pursuits remains on shaky ground. If facts can be ascertained with certainty and if they are readily available to anyone who seeks them, as the absolutist conceives, or if any claim is as valid as any other, as the relativist conceives, there is little point in expending the mental effort that intellectual inquiry and the evaluation of claims entail. Only at the third, "evaluativist" level of epistemological understanding are thinking and reason recognized as essential to support beliefs and actions. Thinking enables us to make informed choices between conflicting claims, and understanding this fact leads students to value thinking and to be willing to expend the serious effort it requires.

By the time students reach college, differences in their levels of epistemological understanding correlate with how they process new information and also serve to predict academic achievement.[14] While they are still in high school, students' levels of epistemological understanding predict the degree to which they have identified future academic and career plans and goals. Those who have reached an evaluativist level of understanding are more likely to have specific plans and goals than are those who remain relativists or absolutists.[15]

When looking at the connection between intellectual development and intellectual values, it is interesting to make comparisons across cultural and subcultural groups. Ironically, Asian and Asian American students, despite their reputation for academic achievement, do not show accelerated development of epistemological understanding or intellectual values. My associates and I have asked questions such as the following of middle-schoolers and high-schoolers and their parents in several American communities; in Israel; in Cyprus; and in Japanese, Korean, Korean American, and Taiwanese American communities: "Many social issues, like the death penalty, gun control, or medical care, are pretty much matters of personal opinion, and there is no basis for saying that one person's opinion is any better than another's. So there's not much point in people having discussions about these kinds of issues. Do you strongly agree, sort of agree, or disagree? (If disagree) What do you think?" A majority of American parents and teens disagreed with such statements, claiming that it was worthwhile to discuss these issues. The percentages of those who disagreed among the Asian and Asian American groups ranged from 0% to a high of 38%.[16]

These findings are perhaps not entirely surprising. The Asian distaste for disagreement and desire to maintain harmony are well known—a cultural stereotype almost. Should these values be cause for concern? "To each his own" and "Live and let live" are stances we arguably need more of in every part of the world.

Yet there is a less apparent but real cost. When asked hypothetical questions about two discrepant views (e.g., whether one musical composition could be judged better than another or one scientific theory more correct than another), Asian and Asian American respondents more often espoused the absolutist belief in certain knowledge that would yield a single right answer or the relativist position that one alternative cannot be judged any more right than the other and that disagreeing parties have a right to their respective views. Thus tolerance and indiscriminability are equated.

Asian education experts in high-performing nations like Singapore have begun to ask themselves whether the development of the skills and disposition to engage ideas and examine them critically (and creatively) has been shortchanged in their education systems. Perhaps developing these skills is an important part of what it means to become educated. The best thinking is very often collaborative rather than solitary. But collaborative intellectual engagement comes with what may be a high cost from the Asian perspective—the risk of at least temporarily sacrificing agreement and harmony.

How Do We Help Children Buy into Education?

Parents can push and pull their children to bring home those A's, but in the end, it is the children who need to find sound reasons for wanting to do so. And the most important thing we can do to help them find those reasons may be to make school an endeavor that makes sense. In early adolescence, as children acquire more freedom to choose how to invest their time and energy and as their skills in self-management increase, cognitive support for achievement motivation becomes crucial. Affective factors should not be eliminated from the equation.[17] But it is arguably the cognitive factors—both within the child and within the setting—that have not been given sufficient attention. For too long we have relied on much the same curriculum for secondary schools that these students' parents and grandparents plodded their way through, and we have simply expected today's students to recognize how it meets their needs.

Prominent among such cognitive factors is students' own intellectual development. The intellectual development that occurs in the second decade of life—not just during those early years that receive the lion's share of attention—is enormously important. The die is far from cast in the first years of life. One of the most important things adults can do for older children may be to make sure that their school experience is the kind that they can readily make sense of instead of having to depend on reassurances from teachers or parents that "this is what you need to know." Such efforts are surely as important in promoting a child's future success as anything a parent does, or fails to do, in the early years.

What makes school experiences easy for students to make meaning of? It's entirely possible to engage secondary students in highly educational activities whose purpose and value become apparent in the process of engaging in them—activities that do not require young people to accept adult pronouncements about the "need to know." As one concrete example, suppose high school students were asked to work together to investigate one of the problems plaguing their city, say, a scarcity of potable water. They would examine causes and potential solutions and in so doing research how other cities, past and present, had dealt with the matter. They would appreciate both what they were doing and why. In the process, they would learn a good deal and learn how to learn—both individually and collaboratively. They would be less likely to ask, "Why do we need to know this?"

They might also escape the norm that prevails in school culture: sit down, be quiet, and wait for instructions. I was struck to learn from my son who graduated this past year from the U.S. Air Force Academy about one bit of educational wisdom that has evolved there. Cadets are being prepared to assume a certain kind of well-delineated leadership role. As part of their education, inside the classroom and out, they are taught not to seek or await instructions (as one might suppose at a military academy), but instead to approach any new situation by identifying the problem and then proceeding to make themselves useful in addressing it. In a word, figure out what needs to be done and get to work doing it.

Problem-based learning is far from new—it can be traced back to John Dewey—and modern evidence for its effectiveness continues to accumulate. The intellectual skills that develop when engaging in problem-based learning aren't tapped by multiple-choice tests. We need new kinds of assessments. Some might lament the diminished command of knowledge measured by conventional tests that students would forgo in pursuing problem-based learning. But if we asked any college to choose between an applicant well versed in biological or historical knowledge and one well versed in analytical thinking, there would be little contest. Colleges are presumptuous enough to believe they can readily impart knowledge. It is students who have learned to use their minds well that they seek. Yet, for now, selective colleges have no choice but to make their increasingly fine admission discriminations primarily on the basis of how well applicants have mastered traditional high school subject matter.

For some time it has been unclear whose needs even well-functioning middle and high schools are serving. And, of course, it's quite possible that they are serving no one's needs very well—not those of young people or those of their future employers or those of institutions of higher learning.

As we continue to pour more effort and resources into schools that aren't working, perhaps the time is finally here to make real change, rather than to simply "get tougher" about what we've already been doing for so long. The "raising standards" approach reflected in Mayor Bloomberg's "no-automatic-promotion" policies and in the myriad regulations of No Child Left Behind represent more of the same. In response to the provocative claim Bill Gates made last year to a coalition of state governors that American high schools were obsolete, the governors responded by pledging to adopt "higher standards, more rigorous courses, and tougher examinations."

We need to be clearer about just where we'd like all the children we're not going to leave behind to be headed. Setting our sights on even one objective might take us a long way. Let's give students in our middle and secondary schools good reasons—ones that readily make sense to them—to invest themselves in school. That means thinking carefully about what we ask them to do there and making sure that it makes sense—to them and to us.

Indeed, if we took the idea of education as an extended meaning-making endeavor seriously, it could change everything. Instead of a contest with winners and losers that is won or lost early in life, school could become a path for development where everyone wins.

Notes

1. NICHD Early Child Care Research Network, "Multiple Pathways to Early Academic Achievement," *Harvard Educational Review,* vol. 74, 2004, pp. 1–29.
2. Angela Duckworth and Martin Seligman, "Self-Discipline Outdoes I.Q. in Predicting Academic Performance of Adolescents," *Psychological Science,* vol. 16, 2005, pp. 939–44.
3. Carol Dweck, "The Development of Ability Conceptions," in Allan Wigfield and Jacquelynne S. Eccles, eds., *Development of Achievement Motivation* (San Diego: Academic Press, 2002), pp. 57–91.
4. Ibid.
5. Allan Wigfield et al., "Development of Achievement Motivation," in Nancy Eisenberg, ed., *Handbook of Child Psychology, Vol. 3: Social Development,* 6th ed. (Hoboken, N.J.: Wiley, 2006), pp. 933–1002; and Allan Wigfield and A. Laurel Wagner, "Competence, Motivation, and Identity Development During Adolescence," in Andrew J. Elliot and Carol S. Dweck, eds., *Handbook of Competence and Motivation* (New York: Guilford Press, 2005), pp. 222–39.
6. John G. Nicholls, *The Competitive Ethos and Democratic Education* (Cambridge, Mass.: Harvard University Press, 1989).
7. Janine Bempechat and Eleanor Drago-Severson, "Cross-National Differences in Academic Achievement: Beyond Etic Conceptions of Children's Understandings," *Review of Educational Research,* vol. 69, 1999, pp. 287–314.
8. Wigfield et al., op. cit.
9. Deanna Kuhn, *Education for Thinking* (Cambridge, Mass.: Harvard University Press, 2005).
10. John Anderson et al., "Perspectives on Learning, Thinking, and Activity," *Educational Researcher,* May 2000, pp. 11–13.
11. Deanna Kuhn, "Do Cognitive Changes Accompany Developments in the Adolescent Brain?," *Perspectives on Psychological Science,* March 2006, pp. 59–67.
12. Barry J. Zimmerman, "A Social Cognitive View of Self-Regulated Learning," *Journal of Educational Psychology,* September 1989, pp. 329–39; and Albert Bandura, *Self-Efficacy: The Exercise of Control* (New York: Freeman, 1994).
13. William Perry, *Forms of Intellectual and Ethical Development in the College Years* (New York: Holt, Rinehart & Winston, 1970); Barbara K. Hofer and Paul R Pintrich, "The Development of Epistemological Theories: Beliefs About Knowledge and Knowing and Their Relation to Learning," *Review of Educational Research,* Spring 1997, pp. 88–140; and Deanna Kuhn and Sam Franklin, "The Second Decade: What Develops (and How)?," in Deanna Kuhn and Robert S. Siegler, eds., *Handbook of Child Psychology, Vol. 2: Cognition, Perception, and Language,* 6th ed. (Hoboken, N.J.: Wiley, 2006), pp. 953–93.
14. Lucia Mason and Pietro Boscolo, "Role of Epistemological Understanding and Interest in Interpreting a Controversy and in Topic-Specific Belief Change," *Contemporary Educational Psychology,* April 2004, pp. 103–28; Michael Weinstock, Yair Neuman, and Amnon Glassner, "Identification of Informal Reasoning Fallacies as a Function of Epistemological Level, Grade Level, and Cognitive Ability," *Journal of Educational Psychology,* vol. 98, 2006, pp. 327–41; and Michelle M. Buehl and Patricia A. Alexander, "Motivation and Performance Differences in Students' Domain-Specific Epistemological Belief Profiles," *American Educational Research Journal,* vol. 42, 2005, pp. 697–726.
15. Sari Locker, "Influences of Adolescents' Developing Epistemological Understanding and Theories of Intelligence on Their Aspirations" (Doctoral dissertation, Teachers College, Columbia University, 2006). Interestingly, high school-aged students who believed ability is fixed were more likely than those who believed it is developed to have made the transition to evaluativist thinking and to have specific future plans. Those who believed that ability develops over time were more likely to remain open with respect to possibilities for their personal futures.
16. Deanna Kuhn and Seung-Ho Park, "Epistemological Understanding and the Development of Intellectual Values," *International Journal of Educational Research,* vol. 43, 2005, pp. 111–24.
17. Suzanne Hidi and Judith M. Harackiewicz, "Motivating the Academically Unmotivated: A Critical Issue for the 21st Century," *Review of Educational Research,* Summer 2000, pp. 151–79.

Deanna Kuhn is a professor of psychology and education at Teachers College, Columbia University, New York, N. Y.

"If Only They Would Do Their Homework"

Promoting Self-Regulation in High School English Classes

This study examined ways that seven high school English teachers attempted to promote higher levels of self-regulation and students' responses to their efforts. Researchers met with teachers once a week for three months to design higher-order reasoning questions for assignments and quizzes, review student responses and plan instructional strategies. They functioned as participant observers in these sessions examined student homework logs, and interviewed students and teachers. Teachers' responses emphasized the value of collaboration and asking higher-order reasoning questions. Although students continued to articulate performance goals that focused on grades and rewards, their responses demonstrated greater awareness of self-regulation and goal setting. Most students were able to use the language of self-regulation to describe relations among goals, effort, and outcomes. Results of this case study suggest that efforts to promote self-regulation more explicitly within the fabric of lessons might be productive, especially if offered for an extended amount of time.

JEWELL E. COOPER, SUZANNE HORN, AND DAVID B. STRAHAN

Among the frustrations often expressed by high school English teachers are that "these students are just not motivated" and "if only they would do their home-work." These familiar laments represent a common assumption—that when students do not perform as well as they might, they should just try harder. Most teachers want students to accept more responsibility for their own learning. High school students, in contrast, often suggest that if assignments were more challenging or if the expectations were more explicit, they would invest more effort in their work. Interestingly, research suggests that teachers and students are both correct. Students perform better when they take more responsibility for their work and when assignments are more challenging (Hagen & Weinstein, 1995; Pintrich, 1995; Zimmerman, 2000).

This study examined the responses of students and teachers to an intervention designed to improve the quality of assignments and enhance student motivation in seven English classes. As part of a comprehensive school reform initiative at one southern high school, teachers and technical assistants decided to address these issues in a connected fashion. They began by reviewing the available research on student motivation. Encouraged by studies showing the benefits of promoting "self regulation," they developed an intervention to promote higher levels of student involvement in lessons and homework assignments. This research report chronicles the ways they developed this intervention and presents the results of their efforts.

Theoretical Framework

Grounded in social cognitive theory, self-regulation is self-generated thoughts, feelings, and actions used to attain goals (Zimmerman, 2000). According to social cognitive theorists, the interdependent relationship among cognitive, behavioral, and environmental factors helps to improve self-regulation. In a cognitive sense, students must examine goals, self-efficacy, metacognition, strategic knowledge, perceptions of value, and affect. As behavioral factors, self-monitoring, self-judgment, and self-reactions must be considered. The environmental factors that also must be considered within selfregulation are found within the classroom environment or in the student's outside study environment (Schunk, 2000). With recognition of these factors, learning becomes an "open-ended process that requires cyclical activity on the part of the learner" (Zimmerman, 1998, p. 2). This cyclical activity occurs in three phases. Forethought is the beliefs that students have about learning. Volitional control is the processes that affect concentration during the learning process, and self-reflection requires that students examine thoughts and the process of learning after completing an activity.

How Goals Impact Self-Regulation

Setting and meeting goals are particularly vital to the secondary education classroom. Students who are skilled at self-regulation report having mastery goals rather than performance goals. According to Zimmerman (1998), the self-regulated learner sees the intrinsic value of learning and feels more confident in accomplishing learning goals than students who lack skills in self-regulation. Attaining these goals becomes intrinsically motivating for students (Zimmerman, 2000). Students with mastery goals in mind regularly choose challenging tasks for themselves, regardless of their ability levels. They demonstrate a high level of persistence when faced with difficult tasks, and have a much higher rate of using effective learning strategies. They master course material often because they focus on learning the content well and they value the importance of the learning process (Hagen & Weinstein, 1995). On the other hand, students who value performance goals over mastery goals focus on the outcome; the process is not relevant. These students choose not to spend as much time choosing, developing, and practicing effective learning strategies and accompanying tasks. Their chief goal is to make a good grade or to avoid failure (Hagen & Weinstein, 1995).

When students are self-regulating, they analyze an activity for its goals and relate them to their personal goals for learning. Afterwards, they devise a strategy on how to complete the task, determine which methods to use, and monitor how effective the methods are while they are using them. Methods that are not effective are discarded and replaced with those considered to be more effective. Important to note is the difficulty that students may experience in mastering goal setting and strategy implementation. Practice and reinforcement are key to successful strategy refinement. Once students recognize the impact of their learning methods, they begin taking more responsibility for their learning (Zimmerman et al., 1996).

Crucial to successful goal-setting by students is the realism of the goal. Students who have realistic goals and refine them as they gain feedback from self-monitoring become more aware of their feelings of efficacy (confidence in ability). They can examine areas of their studies with low self-efficacy as they point to areas in which they need to work. As students become more successful, self-confidence builds and becomes a motivator (Zimmerman et al. 1996).

Students and Self-Regulation

Students who self-regulate are generally interested in the topic at hand, prepared for class, and participate in class by asking questions and generating ideas and insights in the class discussion (Zimmerman & Paulsen, 1995). They conduct some of the following activities: keeping a study calendar, having a specific study location, setting up regular study periods, setting realistic goals, prioritizing tasks, saying no to distractions, and self-rewarding success. When completing homework and assignments, self-regulating students: clarify difficulties, self-question so that they can deeply understand assignments, make predictions about what will happen next, find main ideas, summarize readings, and relate work to prior knowledge and experiences (Zimmerman et al., 1996).

The Teacher's Role in Helping Students Self-Regulate

Teachers can help students acquire self-regulation skills by structuring their courses and practicing instructional methods that aid students in becoming self-regulators (Pintrich, 1995). In other words, self-regulation skills can be taught. By reflecting on what the coursework is, determining what skills students need to gain concepts, and assumptions that are tacit to the field, teachers assist students in learning (Zimmerman et al., 1996). Students need direct instruction about the processes that help them learn content area information independently. By teachers applying self-regulation models and teaching and practicing study skills, students will grow in their ability and confidence while self-regulating (Zimmerman et al., 1996). Furthermore, by modeling skills, teachers visually provide students who do not independently practice self-regulation skills correct procedures in doing so (Zimmerman, 1998). Teachers can also model thoughts about content and strategies so that students become knowledgeable of the learning requirements of the coursework and how students can self-regulate the content information (Pintrich, 1995; Zimmerman et al., 1996). On the other hand, while teachers can facilitate the acquisition of self-regulation skills (Zimmerman, Bonner & Kovach, 1996), most parents and students are unaware that these skills can indeed be taught; moreover, teachers may be so overwhelmed by the increasing demands of accountability that they do not consciously teach students the skills (Schunk & Zimmerman, 1998).

Teachers help students to become self-regulated learners by offering challenging tasks. Tasks that are challenging and interesting to students will stimulate student engagement. Beginning with tasks that students can accomplish, teachers immediately provide students with opportunities of success. Therefore, students are more likely to be persistent in their efforts while completing increasingly difficult tasks. Another way to assist students with challenging tasks is to identify methods students can use in problem solving. For instance, modeling skills in comparing/contrasting, using analogies, and paraphrasing can encourage students to take responsibility for their own learning. Once students feel that their efforts are not in vain, they become more likely to attempt learning (Hagen & Weinstein, 1995). Additionally, by effectively instructing students in challenging curriculum and promoting self-management during difficult tasks, students learn self-regulation skills that benefit them across varied content areas (Belfiore & Hornyak, 1998).

Keeping records of students' progress is another method by which students can determine if their self-regulation skills are effective. Grades are not necessarily the best record because they are global and inconsistent. An "A" on an essay, homework assignment, or test can have different meanings to a variety of people. Teachers need to help students see their absolute performance; they should establish the level of proficiency to be reached and explain how to reach the objectives. With such practice, teachers can assist students in shifting from performance goals to mastery goals. Teachers' feedback can be provided to students to help determine if their self-monitoring is accurate (Schunk, 2000; Zimmerman et al., 1996). More specifically, teachers can give students a set of organizational questions for a new task. As an example, they can give students questions to guide comprehension monitoring. When students are comfortable with structured self-monitoring, they can begin to develop their own protocol. Teachers can gauge students comfort levels with self-monitoring as they will be able to generalize the information from topic to topic (Pintrich, 1995). Teachers can also help students make connections in various tasks that are routinely used in the classroom. By giving daily assignments and weekly quizzes, students can monitor their self-regulation development before taking an exam that largely affects their grade (Zimmerman et al., 1996).

Operalization of Terms

Throughout this study cognitive skill is examined by students making better predictions on their actual quiz grades, a raise in quiz grade scores, and spending more time on task in enriched classroom discussion. Motivation is examined as students' ability to express personal goals, higher expectations in their work and the raised self-efficacy, or belief that they can complete the work given to them by teachers.

The Case Study

Seven English teachers and 42 of their students participated in the study. Each teacher implemented the intervention in one class of their choosing. The school, located in a medium-sized city in the Piedmont Triad of the Carolinas, had at the time of the study 1075 students enrolled with 777 (72%) of them categorized as minority descent (System Statistics). The school was organized by a four-by-four block schedule.

As a part of the Comprehensive School Reform Grant, the technical assistance team for school improvement invited all teachers to participate in a self-regulation project. The researchers worked with English Department teachers who expressed initial interest. Of those teachers, seven made a commitment to participate in the research project. These teachers agreed to meet for three half-day inservice workshops where research team members introduced the framework for the project (self-regulation model) (Zimmerman et al., 1996 and Marzano's et al., *Dimensions of Thinking*, CROP 2001). Committed teachers met in groups of two or three according to planning periods for three months for formal planned meetings. However, research members met individually with participants weekly to identify needs for resources, answer questions, and discuss questioning strategies.

Participants

A new teacher to the school, Teacher A had previous experience in teaching middle school. Though she accepted a job at the high school, she missed the team teacher planning that was in the fabric of the middle school schedule. Teacher A viewed working in the project as an opportunity to work toward a common goal with other English teachers. She also came from a school with strong staff development programs and considered continuing professional development for teachers as an opportunity to challenge herself and improve her teaching skills. Her opinion was that without these opportunities to reflect, teachers become stagnant. She was also interested particularly in how to help motivate her freshmen students in reading.

Teacher B was an experienced teacher who had spent eight years teaching at the school. She taught both Spanish and English courses. In the semester that the study was implemented, she taught only Spanish. The researchers had originally assigned her to another group, but she believed in the project so strongly that she wanted to continue with the group. Teacher B was not concerned as much about getting students to read, but she wanted them to more successfully comprehend so that they would have the ability to elaborate when answering questions. Her students were a mixture of juniors and seniors.

Teacher C worked several years at the school and was looking for a way to motivate her freshmen students. She was frustrated by her students' lack of effort and felt their abilities could not be improved with the apathy they possessed. Teacher C engaged her students in group projects as a means of motivating them.

Teacher D was an experienced teacher who had spent eight years teaching at the school. This vibrant, comical woman used humor and enthusiasm to will her students into working hard. Her concern was that her students had tremendous apathy and hoped that the project would help them to attempt their reading assignments. She felt that if the project could help motivate them to pick up their work, she could help them with their reading skills.

Teacher E was a career teacher with 29 years of experience. He taught both English and drama. He wanted his students to gain skills in self-monitoring so that they would be aware of their progress. It was important to him that his students were conscious of their performance in reading and of their comprehension of the content. He was greatly concerned that his students were seniors. The next year they would enter college or the world of work and would need self-awareness and self-monitoring to be successful in the future.

Teacher F taught ninth grade students participating in the AVID (Advancement Via Individual Determination) Program. He was very interested in helping students to monitor their ability to answer challenging questions and to describe what they discovered about themselves as students through the homework log. His concern was that students were lacking skills to monitor their performance and then make choices about changes in strategies.

Teacher G, a 20-year veteran, was concerned that her students did not comprehend the reading assignments. She was enthusiastic that challenging questions would help their reading comprehension. Teacher G also preferred the social components of the plan, where students discussed their findings in small groups and then shared them with the class. She felt this strategy would strengthen students' resolve in meeting their academic goals.

Research Methods

The researchers conducted a case study based on Yin's (1994) model of case study. Data collection included a review of archival records, student and teacher interviews, direct observation, participant-observation, student homework logs, and teacher instructional information (i.e., higher-order thinking skills questions used in lessons).

Observations

Three classroom observations were made during the nine-week period of each participating class. Anecdotal notes were taken of the class in session. The purpose of the observations was to see how teachers were using the higher-order thinking skills questions designed in half-day professional development sessions and to see if and how they were instituting the agreed upon plan. Observations also served as discussion points between the teachers and researchers.

Anecdotal Notes

Notes were taken during all planning sessions with teachers. Three half-day professional development sessions were held throughout the year as well as bi-weekly meetings until the nine-week implementation of the intervention started. Once the intervention began, teachers met one-on-one with a researcher monthly for the purpose of interviewing, giving feedback, and providing consultation. These notes served to help researchers remember important points in conversation and what objectives were decided upon for meetings.

Interviews

Four to six students from each class were randomly selected for a round of three interviews. Interviews were conducted with teachers and students at the beginning, middle, and end of the project implementation. Students and teachers were interviewed with an open-ended interview sheet. Questions were formed based on the propositions that emerged in the literature and changes in both instruction and learning that occurred in the classroom. Informal interviews were held weekly with teachers to problem solve, identify needs and discuss questioning strategies. Teachers also met informally to discuss the process. Team members conducted focus group interviews with participants to assess the validity of the preliminary report and to add insights and illustrations that might enhance the study.

Data Analysis

Researchers analyzed data in three phases. First, we clustered interview responses by question and identified patterns and variations among responses of teachers and students. We established categories to capture these patterns and variations. For example, in the teacher interview, we asked, "What are the challenges you faced in writing questions for your class?" We then listed all of the responses. Examples are "Trying to get the appropriate level of questioning . . ." and "I have had no problem writing them, it is just finding the time to sit down and plan . . .". We then categorized these responses by patterns. The first response was placed in the category of "Finding an Appropriate Student Level" where as the second was placed in a category labeled "Time". We used these categories to code the data, and tallied responses. In the second phase, we examined observations and field notes to identify ways that teachers implemented self-regulation strategies in their classroom. Specifically, we explored ways that they promoted reading comprehension through higher order questions and encouraged student awareness of tasks. Finally, we examined all of the data in reference to our two primary research questions and reported the results accordingly:

1. How did participating teachers promote self-regulation and higher level reasoning?
2. How did students respond to teachers' effort of promoting self-regulation and higher level reasoning?

Results

Teachers' Efforts to Promote Self-Regulation

Participants met with a researcher on a weekly basis for a period of three months for informal meetings where their discussions shaped the strategies used. From these formal and informal meetings, the research team and participating teachers designed the practices of the study based on individual teachers' needs. These practices included designing higher-order reasoning questions for assignments and quizzes, an introduction to the use of study logs, and feedback on discussions with students using small group and/or whole class formats.

Teachers worked collaboratively on higher-order thinking questions and personalized them based on students' levels of understanding. They met for half-day in-service service sessions to work on higher-order thinking questions for class. Teachers worked together in teams by class area. For example, Teachers A, E, and G, all of whom taught British literature, worked together to form questions. At first, they worked together on each piece as they were learning how to develop higher-order questions. They also worked on rephrasing the reading questions into quiz questions. Then, as they became more familiar and comfortable with the process, they divided the assignments that they would be covering in the upcoming weeks. Each would work on a separate story and then share the questions. Researchers assisted by being a sounding board for teachers as they grappled with how to infuse higher-order vocabulary into their questions. Researchers also attended classes to observe teachers using the questions with their students.

Teachers used a homework log to assess students' perspective of their ability to complete assignments. Students answered several questions about their assignments such as: date that the assignment was completed, the assignment, the time started, the time spent on the assignment, the study context that included where, with whom, and distractions. Students were also asked to rate their self-efficacy in the assignment. Questions were also asked with answers determined through a Likert scale. These questions included thoughts about the type of thinking students had to do in order to complete the assignment. The design of the homework log was tailored to each teacher's needs. Some teachers wanted students to write out a detailed explanation of their self-efficacy, while others used the Likert scale form. Still others required students to write the letter grade they thought they would receive on the assignment. Another way of tailoring the log was the time in which students filled out the log. Some teachers used it as a daily class starter, while others required students to keep the log in their notebook and complete it as they were doing their work.

The plan that all agreed upon was as follows.

- Teachers handed out permission slips to all students for the one class that teachers selected.
- Students were divided by ability level based on their last End-of-Course English scores. Six students from each class were randomly chosen from those who returned permission slips.
- Teachers initially met weekly to work as a group on writing quiz and homework questions. For the last two months of the study researchers and teachers met informally for consultation and for instructional task clarification.
- Students received higher-order thinking questions (based on the Bloom and Marzano models of thinking) developed earlier by their teachers that were used as guiding questions through independent reading.
- Students completed a homework log after completing their assignments cataloging their successes and struggles.
- Teachers had students meet in small groups or had full class discussions of reading questions.
- Students were given a weekly quiz based on the reading assignments that were developed by the teacher. The quiz was comprised of rewritten guided reading questions.
- Students were asked to estimate how well they thought they had done on their quizzes and then compare their estimate to their actual grades.
- Students recorded their estimated quiz grades versus their actual quiz grades on their homework logs.
- Researchers interviewed the selected students and the teachers.

Teachers' Responses to the Initiative

Six of seven teachers interviewed for the study found writing higher-order thinking skills' questions for reading assignments and quizzes to be initially challenging in that they had been used to preparing questions on the literal level of comprehension. One teacher noted,

> The greatest challenge I faced was maintaining the higher-order thinking skills notion when writing the questions. We've become so accustomed to asking literal questions and emphasizing the meaning of certain vocabulary words. Teachers regress just as well as students. Since students are more successful and comfortable with the literal interpretation of readings, teachers have become comfortable in asking literal questions" (Teacher G).

They found that verbal elaboration was needed for students to understand the vocabulary of the questions. "I had to thoroughly discuss the question before students attempted to answer questions independently. Over time, however, the writing of questions became 'simpler' " (Teacher C). Teacher G recognized that a change in students' practice was necessary. She said,

> I had to change their mindset of 'what page is the answer on' to actually searching for the answer themselves. I noticed that they ignore the language and move on to the meat of the questions. They still look in the test for the 'right there' answer."

All of the teachers noticed that students became more comfortable in answering the questions; nonetheless, some students, particularly those in the exceptional children's program, continued to struggle with them.

Teachers' own goals included consistently integrating vocabulary needed for higher-order thinking skills questions as well as introducing students to vocabulary that would be seen on their end-of-course test. Six teachers agreed that most students predicted their scores accurately. For those who predicted their scores lower, they transferred the difficulty of the reading and the quizzes to the test.

The higher-order thinking skills impacted the seven teachers' practice. It helped them change their own routines of questioning for comprehension. They were focusing more, and becoming more aware of students' learning and how students perceived their own skill and motivation to succeed. Teachers believed that the questioning helped students to think about their own responsibility in student learning. One teacher said, "This pointed out that we are creatures of habit and you need to break that habit for students to succeed. If you do things different ways, it helps students to be successful and not give up. This [higher-order questioning] makes me more aware" (Teacher E). Teacher A commented, "It changed my way of planning. It also made me reflect a lot. I thought about my ability to ask questions and it gave me a better understanding of where students were with their higher level thinking." Lastly, another said, "Asking questions ahead of time and rephrasing them in quizzes helps to focus in on what you are interested in them [students] learning" (Teacher F). Though two teachers did not think the questioning strategy impacted their professional development, four noted their growth as teachers and in their beliefs about what students can and can not do. In fact, one teacher was challenged not to "cave in" to her students. She said,

> I must not cave in and believe that they can't do it. For the past three–four years, I chose not to believe that they can't do. My challenge is not to cave into the kids. They realize that they aren't challenging themselves. They are not utilizing all they have to be successful. They have been told too long that they can't do it; therefore they believe it." (Teacher G)

Recognized as important to their development as teachers was the ability to collaboratively plan instruction together as a group. All of the English teachers noted that they had never been given an opportunity to come together as a department for instructional planning purposes. "It's been great. We've never planned together before" (Teacher G). Another replied, "Team planning takes the weight off that I'm not doing anything outside the box. I feel stronger as a unit. I get creative ideas [when planning together]" (Teacher D). Each of them stated that they learned from each other different ways of planning, organizing and presenting instructional content to students.

Two of the seven teachers noted that some students filled out homework logs without prompting. For the other teachers in the study, the logs became a chore at times for both teachers and students; however, the logs did serve to help students self-monitor, assess, and improve their grades. One teacher noted that setting and implementing goals require skills not yet fully developed by some of their students. Nonetheless, four teachers felt that the teaching of self-regulation strategies had a positive effect on their students. Teacher A revealed that "they [the students] know they have to complete class work and they have to study those questions. They have to ask me a lot more questions before a quiz" (Teacher A). Teacher B discovered that her classroom "feels more like a place of higher learning; students are more enthusiastic. I feel more a part [of the discussion] rather than a leader of the discussion and they [students] are forced to think outside the box."

Student's responses to teachers' effort of promoting self-regulation and higher level reasoning.

Note: A total of 42 students participated in the project; however, on the days of the interviews, 32–42 students answered interview questions. (For the first round of interviews, 32 students participated. During the second round of interviews 42 students responded to questions. On the third round, 38 students responded).

Goal Setting

In setting goals for themselves, performance goals, such as getting a good grade and doing well enough to be exempt from the examination were cited most often. "To strive for an A" (Student of Teacher A), "to get an A or a B" (Student of Teacher D), and "to be exempt from the exam and to study vocabulary" (Student of Teacher B) were examples of responses made. However, seven of 42 students wanted more lasting goals. They desired to be exposed to new material that they would not have chosen themselves, pay attention, not get distracted, and become better readers. One student desired to "read books that I probably would never think of reading" (Student of Teacher F). Cited by another student as a goal was "to become a better reader and understand what I read" (Student of Teacher G). Weekly and semester goal setting also included performance and mastery goals. Twenty-eight students acknowledged reaching the goals that they had set for themselves. Thirty students noted that their teachers helped them to set the goals and recognized that their teachers contributed to their learning.

When questioned about personal interest in reading assignments, 12 students found the reading assignments interesting. One mentioned that "I find my reading assignments interesting because I love to read and enjoy participating in our reading assignments because it give[s] me a chance to read new things and experience new things" (Student of Teacher A). Another said, "yes, because I like the way my teacher teaches us how to br[e]ak things down" (Student of Teacher C). Eleven students thought that the readings were somewhat interesting. A student of Teacher E revealed that "whenever we read as a class out loud I think it's interesting, but to me, it's pretty boring when I read individually." Another student said, "some of them are if I like what the story is about and if it is a 'page turner' " (Student of Teacher B). Eight students did not find the readings interesting at all. One student shared that the readings "are boring and you have to stop every few words to look up a word" (Student of Teacher B). Another student admitted that because the readings were somewhat interesting "most times I don't read. I just look at the question and find the answer in the reading" (Student of Teacher D). Dislike of reading, lack of understanding vocabulary, and difficulty in following the story were cited as reasons.

Perceptions of Tasks

Students found quizzes were easy if they studied and could connect the prior assignment questions to the actual quiz. Students also acknowledged that reading, listening to discussions in class, studying, and reviewing notes more would improve their quiz grades. Their responses indicated that they were now more aware of relationships among goals, efforts, and outcomes. One student stated that he would improve his quiz grade in reading if he would "start reading the whole story instead of just answering questions" (Student of Teacher D). Two other students would "study harder and take my time to read the question over if necessary" (Student of Teacher C) and "review homework questions before the quiz" (Student of Teacher B).

Students were asked to describe their reading assignments and how they could improve their written assignments and quiz performance. Of the 32 respondents, seven described reading assignments as "difficult". They made comments like "Our reading assignments are challenging because we are asked questions that require us to understand the deepness of the reading materials. [The] majority of our reading requires us to be able to read in between the lines" (Student of Teacher G). Another student said, "I usually just read during class, because when I go home it [the reading] is difficult for me to understand. So I just wait until I get back to school so the teacher can explain" (Student of Teacher E). For those students who believed their assignments to be "difficult", teacher assistance in interpreting the reading was required. Fifteen students noted that readings were "somewhat difficult". One student mentioned, "It's not that difficult. It's just sometime[s] hard to understand how to work out problems" (Student of Teacher A). Another said, "I think that they are on the 12th grade level. And they are pretty much easy. Some things I have to ask about but most of the time I make the assignment out" (Student of Teacher A). Other students who believed that their reading assignments were "somewhat difficult" could answer the questions after considerable thought. Seven stated that their reading assignments were "easy". One student believed that the readings "are not difficult. They don't really present a challenge to me. I think that they should be more challenging" (Student of Teacher D).

The wording of the questions was challenging for 11 students, especially when attempting to understand what the questions were asking. However, teacher explanations helped students to understand the questions better. One student said, "the questions are confusing, but when you think about it, it becomes clear" (Student of Teacher A). Another student felt that the questions "make you think more" (Student of Teacher E). A third student admitted, "I just think about the story and [use] a dictionary to help me find the word that I can't understand" (Student of Teacher D). On the other hand, 10 students thought the wording was "understandable." One student said, "They [the readings] are easy because she makes sure she goes over it and explains what it means" (Student of Teacher C). Eleven students noted that the wording of the questions was "somewhat difficult." Some students' comments included items such as "They are easy to understand, but [for] some I may have to ask questions" (Student of Teacher C) and "the wording of the questions are OK but some times they ask for too much elaboration on things unnecessary" (Student of Teacher B).

Strategies Used

When completing reading assignments, 26 students answered most of the questions. While 15 students completed their assignments alone, 16 of them preferred teacher-assisted instruction, small group discussion, or whole class reading and answering questions. Six students stated that they did not complete reading assignments that accompanied the questions. These students tended to complete reading questions in class, after school, or at night as homework. One student did not do assignments at all. The television, radio, talking to friends and family and the telephone were named as distractions to reading and completing assignments.

In preparation for reading, the process students used to answer questions included reviewing the questions first and then reading the story (15) or reading the story first and later looking at the questions (26). One student did not attempt to read or answer questions. Of the 26 who read the story first, some students took notes as they read; others depended on group discussions to help them answer questions. Forty students went back to the text to find the answers. Two of them did not go back to the text in search for answers. While reading, students visualized the text, thought about the events of the story and possible questions the teacher would ask. A few of them daydreamed and thought about other things because they considered the reading boring.

Students used prediction of quiz grades and material on the quizzes as a learning tool. Thirty-eight students reported to have accurately predicted their quizzes and course grades. Only four students responded that they usually predict inaccurately or not at all. Forty of 42 students stated that their predictions provided revelations about their own learning with two students admitting that their predictions told them "nothing" about their learning.

Thirty-three students also recognized that their teachers assisted them with the reading assignments by having the class read aloud, explaining passages, having discussions, offering after school help, and giving students time to work on the assignments in class. They stated that their teachers helped them to identify distractions while reading, encouraged them to practice better time management skills, exposed them to new vocabulary in the reading and in the questions for reading assignments and quizzes, and taught them a different method by which questions can be asked.

Conclusions

This exploratory study investigated students' and teachers' responses to an intervention designed to improve the quality of assignments and enhance student motivation in seven English classes. Participants promoted student self-regulation and higher level reasoning in several ways. Teachers offered challenging questions based on Marzano's Core Dimensions of Thinking Skills (C.R.O.P., 2001). Teachers structured classroom activities to introduce students to the language of self-regulation and to encourage them to monitor the effort they invested in their assignments. They also modeled appropriate ways to thoroughly answer questions and to chart their progress in reading. Teachers reported that students needed a lot of support and modeling at the beginning of the project, which ultimately ameliorated students' frustration about engaging in more challenging tasks.

At the conclusion of the project, teachers reported that the major benefit of this initiative was the opportunity to collaborate more intensively with their colleagues. Teachers stated that participating in this intervention was a positive experience. They particularly liked working together to plan questions for students. They thought that the homework logs helped students to think about their work and the quality of the job they were doing. However, the log required about five minutes of daily class time and teachers needed to monitor students to ensure they were not doing a superficial job. Participants agreed that the higher level questions helped students read more closely. Teachers suggested that one of the major outcomes of this project was that it encouraged them to think more about what they assigned students in class.

Students' responses to these interventions were generally positive. In their task interviews, students described several ways they had improved their reading strategies. Forty of them reported specifically that they looked back to the text to find answers. Thus, they were able to detect that a first reading was not enough to help them glean needed information from the text and they needed to revisit the text to reread. Fifteen respondents discussed using skills such as previewing question and taking notes while reading. Some students also reported visualizing reading. Students also recognized their teachers' efforts to help them define clearer goals for studying. Thirty students noted that teachers were trying to help them set goals. Most of them reported setting performance goals. Their comments indicated that classroom discussion was not enough to help them develop the level of mastery goals that their teachers hoped they would develop.

This study illustrated many of the results of previous investigations. Earlier studies showed that keeping records of their progress helps students to be successful in self-regulation (Zimmerman et al., 1996; Covington & Beery, 1976; Schunk, 2000). In this study, teachers facilitated record keeping by having students keep logs of their reading. Students commented on their study atmosphere, ability to complete assignments, and how much they actually did through the logs. This intervention helped teachers discover how students responded to their efforts. Hagen and Weinstein (1995) found that offering more challenging tasks assists students in their self-regulation. In this study, teachers hoped that their revised assignments would encourage students to learn the material at a deeper level for the purpose of gaining important concepts, thus promoting a stronger mastery orientation (Schunk, 2000; Zimmerman et al., 1996). Instead, students continued to articulate performance goals that focused on grades and rewards.

This study also demonstrated the complexity of efforts to improve motivation and enhance higher levels of reasoning. Teachers struggled with offering tasks that were challenging but not overwhelming. Students responded to the fact that their teachers were working to help them be successful in their reading, yet six students skimmed assignments for answers and one refused to complete any assignments or read the material. Teachers were encouraged that the majority of students were reading and emphasized that class discussions were deeper as a consequence. Students also reported that the class discussions about reading helped them to clear misconceptions and understand material.

Implications for Research and Practice

This study suggests a number of implications for research and practice through its limitations. The study did not run the entire semester. Ideally, the self-regulation skills teaching and modeling approach should be woven into the fabric of the entire course. The findings reveal that high school students can learn the language of self-regulation and can communicate it. However, though students became aware of relationships among goals, efforts, and outcomes, they did not have enough time to internalize them. Therefore, given block scheduling, a study of this kind should be actively conducted with students engaged in the skills of self-regulation for the full semester.

While the teacher participants in this study were experienced, some of them were not initially familiar with the vocabulary of higher-order thinking skills language. This may be particularly true for lateral entry or emergency licensure persons who frequently are found teaching in high schools today given the national teacher shortage. An assessment of teachers' knowledge of higher-order thinking skills and self-regulation practices should be made and ongoing professional development offered at the beginning of the academic year with the actual study including students commencing during the second half of the year. Teachers would have an opportunity to practice modeling the skills with first semester students as well as second semester students who are participating in the actual study. Specific to this study, future studies should include a goal sheet where students set goals for their learning in addition to a homework log. Such an addition will assist teachers and students in thinking about goals.

References

Belfore, P. J., & Hornyak, R. S. (1998). Operant theory and application to self-monitoring in adolescents. In D. H. Schunk & B. J. Zimmerman (Eds.), *Self-regulated learning: From teaching to self-reflective practice* (pp. 184–202). New York: Guilford Publications.

Cooper, H., & Valentine, J. C. (2001). Using research to answer practical questions about homework. *Educational Psychologist, 36*, 143–153.

Covington, M. V., & Beery, R. G. (1976). *Self-worth and school learning.* London: International Thomson Publishing.

C.R.O.P. (Communities Resolving Our Problems) (2001). *Core thinking skills within the dimensions of thinking framework of Robert Marzano.* Retrieved November 27, 2001 from http://www.ceap.wcu.edu/Houghton/Learner/Think94/NcmarzanoThink.html.

Epstein, J. L., & Van Voorhis, F. L. (2001). More than minutes: Teachers' roles in designing homework. *Educational Psychologist, 36*, 181–193.

Garcia, T. (1995). The role of motivational strategies in self-regulated learning. In P. R. Pintrich (Ed.), *New directions for teaching and learning, understanding self-regulated learning 63*, 29–42. San Francisco: Jossey-Bass.

Hagen, A. S., & Weinstein, C. E. (1995). Achievement goals, self-regulatedlearning, and the role of classroom context. In P. R. Pintrich (Ed.), *New directions for teaching and learning, 63*, 43–56. San Francisco: Jossey-Bass.

Ormrod, J. E. (2000). *Educational psychology: Developing learners.* Upper Saddle River, NJ: Prentice Hall.

Pintrich, P. R. (1995). Understanding self-regulated learning. In P. R. Pintrich (Ed.), *New Directions for Teaching and Learning, 63*, 3–12. San Francisco: Jossey-Bass.

Schunk, D. H. (2000). *Learning theories: An educational perspective* (3rd ed.). Upper Saddle River, NJ: Prentice-Hall. (Original work published 1996).

Schunk, D. H., & Zimmerman, B. J. (1998). Preface. In D. H. Schunk, & B. J. Zimmerman (Eds.), *Self-regulated learning: From teaching to self-reflective practice* (pp. viii–x). New York: Guilford Publications.

System Statistics of Local Education Agency (2001). *10 day membership.* Retrieved April 25, 2002 from http://wsfcs.k12.nc.us/about/10day01h.html.

Trawick, L., & Corno, L. (1995). Expanding the volitional resources of urban community college students. In P. R. Pintrich (Ed.), *New directions for teaching and learning, 63*, 57–70. San Francisco: Jossey-Bass.

Warton, P. M. (2001). The forgotten voices in homework: Views of students. *Educational Psychologist, 36*, 155–165.

Yin, R. K. (1994). *Case study research design and methods* (2nd ed.). Thousand Oaks, CA: Sage. (Original work published in 1984).

Zimmerman, B. J. (1998). Developing self-fulfilling cycles of academic regulation: An analysis of exemplary instructional models. In D. H. Schunk, & B. J. Zimmerman (Eds.) , *Self-regulated learning: From teaching to self-reflective practice* (pp. 1–19). New York: Guilford Publications.

Zimmerman, B. J. (2000). Attaining self-regulation: A social cognitive perspective. In M. Boekaerts, P. R. Pintrich, & M. Zeidner (Eds.), *Handbook of self-regulation* (pp. 13–39). San Diego, CA: Academic Press.

Zimmerman, B. J., & Paulsen, A. S. (1995). Self-monitoring during collegiate studying: An invaluable tool for academic self-regulation. In P. R. Pintrich (Ed.), *New directions for teaching and learning, 63*, 13–28. San Francisco, CA: Jossey-Bass.

Zimmerman, B. J., Bonner, S., & Kovach, R. (1996). *Developing self-regulated learners*. Washington, DC: American Psychological Association.

Protocol I

1) How difficult are your reading assignments to complete?
2) Do you find your reading assignments interesting? Why or why not?
3) What do you think about the wording of the questions for your reading assignments?
4) How difficult are your quizzes based on your reading assignments?
5) What would you do to improve your quiz grades in reading?
6) How would you do that?
7) What could the teacher do to help you?
8) How do you think you will do on the next reading quiz?
9) How accurate are your predictions of what you will receive on your quizzes?
10) How do you prepare for your reading quizzes?
11) Did you complete your reading and answer the assigned questions for each assignment?
12) When did you complete your reading assignments for this week in English?
13) Where did you complete your reading assignments?
14) Did you complete assignments with someone else? (If yes, how did that go?)
15) Did you have any distractions while you were reading? (If yes, what were they?)

Protocol II

1) When you have a reading assignment with questions, describe the process you go through to answer the questions.
2) Do you often go back to the text when looking for answers to reading questions? (If yes, what do you look for? If no, what do you do instead)?
3) How do you complete reading assignments for this class (describe the steps you take)?
4) What do you think about when reading for this class?
5) What goals have you set for yourself in this class?
6) Have you set goals in this class for this week? (If yes, please list).
7) Have you set goals for this semester in this class? (If yes, please list).
8) Are you reaching goals that you have set for yourself in this class? (Why or why not—please include the goal in your description).
9) Has your teacher helped you with setting goals for this class? (Explain)
10) Has your teacher helped you with your reading assignments in this class? (Explain)
11) How well have you done in predicting your grades for this class?
12) How has your teacher helped you in making predictions for this class?
13) What do your predictions tell you about your own learning?

Protocol III

1) What has your teacher discussed with you about distractions while reading?
2) What distractions have you identified in your study environment? (Give examples)
3) How have you eliminated distractions? (Give examples)
4) What goals have you reached in this class?
5) How has your teacher helped you to reach your goals?
6) Have you found that your teacher has used more difficult vocabulary in reading questions?
7) How have you found out what these words mean?
8) Has your teacher asked you questions where the answers cannot be easily found in the reading? (Give examples)
9) Has the teacher asked you questions that make you think about how the reading is similar to real life?
10) During the semester has your teacher helped you manage your time?

Figure 1 Appendix A. Student interviews.

Protocol I

1) What are the challenges you faced. . .
   – In writing questions for your class?
   – In student responses to questions?
   – In goal setting (teacher and student)?
2) How well did the students predict their scores?
3) What did you infer from this information?
4) How do you feel that questioning impacted. . .
   – your teaching?
   – student learning?
   – your professional development?
5) Did students fill our their logs willingly, or did they need teacher prompting?
6) How did the student logs impact learning?
7) Did you see patterns of student monitoring their own learning? If so, how did you see them emerge?
8) What have you looked for in students' reading to assess patterns?
9) How do you think the study impacted the amount of reading that students completed?
10) How do you think group-work impacted students' learning?
11) How do you think that this project has impacted students' studying?

Protocol II

1) How comfortable are you with:
   – writing questions for your class
   – are students answering questions with greater ease
   – are students benefiting from goal setting (refer to chart)
2) How well did students predict their scores?
   – What did you infer from this information?
3) How do you feel goal setting strategy impacted:
   – your teaching;
   – student learning;
   – professional development?
4) Did students fill out log and goal sheets or did they need prompting?
5) How did goal sheet impact student learning?
6) Did you see patterns of student monitoring of their own learning?
   – If so, how did you see them emerge?
7) How do you think group discussions of goals has impacted student learning?
8) How do you think this project has impacted student learning?

Protocol III

1) How have you incorporated goal setting into your class?
2) What discussions have you had about students reaching goals?
3) How do you determine if students meet their goals?
4) How has consistently asking higher-order questions affected. . .
   – your class atmosphere;
   – your view of yourself as a teacher;
   – individual student learning?
5) Have you noticed any "aha" moments where higher-order thinking has clicked?
6) How has you development as a teacher been impacted by this project?
7) Has exposure to any of the various topics of this project motivated you to look deeper into any of the subjects (higher-order thinking, goal setting, student self-monitoring)?
8) Have students brought learning conflicts or problems with class work to your attention?
9) In what way have you mentioned your students' abilities to:
   – set goals;
   – answer higher-order questions;
   – monitor their time?
10) Did you discover any problems they were having, and how did you help them?
11) What portion of this project will you use next year in your teaching?
12) How dedicated were you to this project?
13) How do you think that this project effect school culture, in what ways?

Figure 2 Appendix B. Teacher interviews.

1) How does the 4th passage on p. 171 present Arthur as a romantic hero?
2) "Welcome, my sister's son, I weened ye had been dead! And now I see thee on live, much am I behoden unto Almighty Jesu." What context clues might you use to figure out the meaning of the word weened?
3) "Never since that time has there been a more doleful battle in any Christian land." How would this be phrased today?
4) On the second column of p. 174, what do the details help you see and hear? (Imagery)
5) How does Arthur, a hero out of the medieval romance, compare and contrast with Beowulf, a hero form a different, and much older society? (Consider each hero's quest, powers, feelings, enemies, and allies.)
6) Many people have hunted for Arthur's tomb. According to this story, what should archeologists look for in their search for Arthur's grave?

Corresponding Quiz

1) Apply the mysterious circumstances surrounding Arthur's death to an important persons death in our society.
2) How is Arthur portrayed as a romantic hero in the legendary story?
3) "Welcome, my sister's son, I weened ye had been dead!" Explain what word we might use in our own "slang" today to replace the word "weened".
4) Compare and contrast the Arthur and Beowulf using three examples.
5) Create a sentence that is an example of imagery.

Figure 3 Appendix C. Guided reading questions for Le Morte D' Arthur developed cooperatively by three teachers.

Date	Assignment	Time Started	Time Spent	Study Context Where?	With Whom?	Distractions	Self-Efficacy

It really made me think?

Not at All			Somewhat		Quite a Bit	
1	2	3	4	5	6	7

I had to read really well.

Not at All			Somewhat		Quite a Bit	
1	2	3	4	5	6	7

I had to write really well.

Not at All			Somewhat		Quite a Bit	
1	2	3	4	5	6	7

I had to think about what I was doing from day to day.

Not at All			Somewhat		Quite a Bit	
1	2	3	4	5	6	7

I really wanted to do my work.

Not at All			Somewhat		Quite a Bit	
1	2	3	4	5	6	7

Figure 4 Appendix D. Student study log.

The Perils and Promises of Praise

The wrong kind of praise creates self-defeating behavior. The right kind motivates students to learn.

Carol S. Dweck

We often hear these days that we've produced a generation of young people who can't get through the day without an award. They expect success because they're special, not because they've worked hard.

Is this true? Have we inadvertently done something to hold back our students?

I think educators commonly hold two beliefs that do just that. Many believe that (1) praising students' intelligence builds their confidence and motivation to learn, and (2) students' inherent intelligence is the major cause of their achievement in school. Our research has shown that the first belief is false and that the second can be harmful—even for the most competent students.

As a psychologist, I have studied student motivation for more than 35 years. My graduate students and I have looked at thousands of children, asking why some enjoy learning, even when it's hard, and why they are resilient in the face of obstacles. We have learned a great deal. Research shows us how to praise students in ways that yield motivation and resilience. In addition, specific interventions can reverse a student's slide into failure during the vulnerable period of adolescence.

Fixed or Malleable?

Praise is intricately connected to how students view their intelligence. Some students believe that their intellectual ability is a fixed trait. They have a certain amount of intelligence, and that's that. Students with this fixed mind-set become excessively concerned with how smart they are, seeking tasks that will prove their intelligence and avoiding ones that might not (Dweck, 1999, 2006). The desire to learn takes a backseat.

Other students believe that their intellectual ability is something they can develop through effort and education. They don't necessarily believe that anyone can become an Einstein or a Mozart, but they do understand that even Einstein and Mozart had to put in years of effort to become who they were. When students believe that they can develop their intelligence, they focus on doing just that. Not worrying about how smart they will appear, they take on challenges and stick to them (Dweck, 1999, 2006).

More and more research in psychology and neuroscience supports the growth mind-set. We are discovering that the brain has more plasticity over time than we ever imagined (Doidge, 2007); that fundamental aspects of intelligence can be enhanced through learning (Sternberg, 2005); and that dedication and persistence in the face of obstacles are key ingredients in outstanding achievement (Ericsson, Charness, Feltovich, & Hoffman, 2006).

Alfred Binet (1909/1973), the inventor of the IQ test, had a strong growth mind-set. He believed that education could transform the basic capacity to learn. Far from intending to measure fixed intelligence, he meant his test to be a tool for identifying students who were not profiting from the public school curriculum so that other courses of study could be devised to foster their intellectual growth.

The Two Faces of Effort

The fixed and growth mind-sets create two different psychological worlds. In the fixed mind-set, students care first and foremost about how they'll be judged: smart or not smart. Repeatedly, students with this mind-set reject opportunities to learn if they might make mistakes (Hong, Chiu, Dweck, Lin, & Wan, 1999; Mueller & Dweck, 1998). When they do make mistakes or reveal deficiencies, rather than correct them, they try to hide them (Nussbaum & Dweck, 2007).

They are also afraid of effort because effort makes them feel dumb. They believe that if you have the ability, you shouldn't need effort (Blackwell, Trzesniewski, & Dweck, 2007), that ability should bring success all by itself. This is one of the worst beliefs that students can hold. It can cause many bright students to stop working in school when the curriculum becomes challenging.

Finally, students in the fixed mind-set don't recover well from setbacks. When they hit a setback in school, they *decrease* their efforts and consider cheating (Blackwell et al., 2007). The idea of fixed intelligence does not offer them viable ways to improve.

Let's get inside the head of a student with a fixed mind-set as he sits in his classroom, confronted with algebra for the first time. Up until then, he has breezed through math. Even when he barely paid attention in class and skimped on his homework, he always got *A*s. But this is different. It's hard. The student feels anxious and thinks, "What if I'm not as good at math as I thought? What if other kids understand it and I don't?" At some level, he realizes that he has two choices: try hard, or turn off. His interest in math begins to wane, and his attention wanders. He tells himself, "Who cares about this stuff? It's for nerds. I could do it if I wanted to, but it's so boring. You don't see CEOs and sports stars solving for *x* and *y*."

By contrast, in the growth mind-set, students care about learning. When they make a mistake or exhibit a deficiency, they correct it (Blackwell et al., 2007; Nussbaum & Dweck, 2007). For them, effort is a *positive* thing: It ignites their intelligence and causes it to grow. In the face of failure, these students escalate their efforts and look for new learning strategies.

Let's look at another student—one who has a growth mind-set—having her first encounter with algebra. She finds it new, hard, and confusing, unlike anything else she has ever learned. But she's determined to understand it. She listens to everything the teacher says, asks the teacher questions after class, and takes her textbook home and reads the chapter over twice. As she begins to get it, she feels exhilarated. A new world of math opens up for her.

It is not surprising, then, that when we have followed students over challenging school transitions or courses, we find that those with growth mind-sets outperform their classmates with fixed mind-sets—even when they entered with equal skills and knowledge. A growth mind-set fosters the growth of ability over time (Blackwell et al., 2007; Mangels, Butterfield, Lamb, Good, & Dweck, 2006; see also Grant & Dweck, 2003).

The Effects of Praise

Many educators have hoped to maximize students' confidence in their abilities, their enjoyment of learning, and their ability to thrive in school by praising their intelligence. We've studied the effects of this kind of praise in children as young as 4 years old and as old as adolescence, in students in inner-city and rural settings, and in students of different ethnicities—and we've consistently found the same thing (Cimpian, Arce, Markman, & Dweck, 2007; Kamins & Dweck, 1999; Mueller & Dweck, 1998): Praising students' intelligence gives them a short burst of pride, followed by a long string of negative consequences.

In many of our studies (see Mueller & Dweck, 1998), 5th grade students worked on a task, and after the first set of problems, the teacher praised some of them for their intelligence ("You must be smart at these problems") and others for their effort ("You must have worked hard at these problems"). We then assessed the students' mind-sets. In one study, we asked students to agree or disagree with mind-set statements, such as, "Your intelligence is something basic about you that you can't really change." Students praised for intelligence agreed with statements like these more than students praised for effort did. In another study, we asked students to define intelligence. Students praised for intelligence made significantly more references to innate, fixed capacity, whereas the students praised for effort made more references to skills, knowledge, and areas they could change through effort and learning. Thus, we found that praise for intelligence tended to put students in a fixed mind-set (intelligence is fixed, and you have it), whereas praise for effort tended to put them in a growth mind-set (you're developing these skills because you're working hard).

We then offered students a chance to work on either a challenging task that they could learn from or an easy one that ensured error-free performance. Most of those praised for intelligence wanted the easy task, whereas most of those praised for effort wanted the challenging task and the opportunity to learn.

Next, the students worked on some challenging problems. As a group, students who had been praised for their intelligence *lost* their confidence in their ability and their enjoyment of the task as soon as they began to struggle with the problem. If success meant they were smart, then struggling meant they were not. The whole point of intelligence praise is to boost confidence and motivation, but both were gone in a flash. Only the effort-praised kids remained, on the whole, confident and eager.

When the problems were made somewhat easier again, students praised for intelligence did poorly, having lost their confidence and motivation. As a group, they did worse than they had done initially on these same types of problems. The students praised for effort showed excellent performance and continued to improve.

Finally, when asked to report their scores (anonymously), almost 40 percent of the intelligence-praised students lied. Apparently, their egos were so wrapped up in their performance that they couldn't admit mistakes. Only about 10 percent of the effort-praised students saw fit to falsify their results.

Praising students for their intelligence, then, hands them not motivation and resilience but a fixed mind-set with all its vulnerability. In contrast, effort or "process" praise (praise for engagement, perseverance, strategies, improvement, and the like) fosters hardy motivation. It tells students what they've done to be successful and what they need to do to be successful again in the future. Process praise sounds like this:

- You really studied for your English test, and your improvement shows it. You read the material over several times, outlined it, and tested yourself on it. That really worked!
- I like the way you tried all kinds of strategies on that math problem until you finally got it.
- It was a long, hard assignment, but you stuck to it and got it done. You stayed at your desk, kept up your concentration, and kept working. That's great!
- I like that you took on that challenging project for your science class. It will take a lot of work—doing the research, designing the machine, buying the parts, and building it. You're going to learn a lot of great things.

What about a student who gets an *A* without trying? I would say, "All right, that was too easy for you. Let's do something more challenging that you can learn from." We don't want to make something done quickly and easily the basis for our admiration.

What about a student who works hard and *doesn't* do well? I would say, "I liked the effort you put in. Let's work together some more and figure out what you don't understand." Process praise keeps students focused, not on something called ability that they may or may not have and that magically creates success or failure, but on processes they can all engage in to learn.

Motivated to Learn

Finding that a growth mind-set creates motivation and resilience—and leads to higher achievement—we sought to develop an intervention that would teach this mind-set to students. We decided to aim our intervention at students who were making the transition to 7th grade because this is a time of great vulnerability. School often gets more difficult in 7th grade, grading becomes more stringent, and the environment becomes more impersonal. Many students take stock of themselves and their intellectual abilities at this time and decide whether they want to be involved with school. Not surprisingly, it is often a time of disengagement and plunging achievement.

We performed our intervention in a New York City junior high school in which many students were struggling with the transition and were showing plummeting grades. If students learned a growth mind-set, we reasoned, they might be able to meet this challenge with increased, rather than decreased, effort. We therefore developed an eight-session workshop in which both the control group and the growth-mind-set group learned study skills, time management techniques, and memory strategies (Blackwell et al., 2007). However, in the growth-mind-set intervention, students also learned about their brains and what they could do to make their intelligence grow.

They learned that the brain is like a muscle—the more they exercise it, the stronger it becomes. They learned that every time they try hard and learn something new, their brain forms new connections that, over time, make them smarter. They learned that intellectual development is not the natural unfolding of intelligence, but rather the formation of new connections brought about through effort and learning.

Students were riveted by this information. The idea that their intellectual growth was largely in their hands fascinated them. In fact, even the most disruptive students suddenly sat still and took notice, with the most unruly boy of the lot looking up at us and saying, "You mean I don't have to be dumb?"

Indeed, the growth-mind-set message appeared to unleash students' motivation. Although both groups had experienced a steep decline in their math grades during their first months of junior high, those receiving the growth-mind-set intervention showed a significant rebound. Their math grades improved. Those in the control group, despite their excellent study skills intervention, continued their decline.

What's more, the teachers—who were unaware that the intervention workshops differed—singled out three times as many students in the growth-mindset intervention as showing marked changes in motivation. These students had a heightened desire to work hard and learn. One striking example was the boy who thought he was dumb. Before this experience, he had never put in any extra effort and often didn't turn his homework in on time. As a result of the training, he worked for hours one evening to finish an assignment early so that his teacher could review it and give him a chance to revise it. He earned a *B+* on the assignment (he had been getting *C*s and lower previously).

Other researchers have obtained similar findings with a growth-mind-set intervention. Working with junior high school students, Good, Aronson, and Inzlicht (2003) found an increase in math and English achievement test scores; working with college students, Aronson, Fried, and Good (2002) found an increase in students' valuing of academics, their enjoyment of schoolwork, and their grade point averages.

To facilitate delivery of the growth-mind-set workshop to students, we developed an interactive computer-based version of the intervention called *Brainology.* Students work through six modules, learning about the brain, visiting virtual brain labs, doing virtual brain experiments, seeing how the brain changes with learning, and learning how they can make their brains work better and grow smarter.

When students believe that they can develop their intelligence, they focus on doing just that.

We tested our initial version in 20 New York City schools, with encouraging results. Almost all students (anonymously polled) reported changes in their study habits and motivation to learn resulting directly from their learning of the growth mind-set. One student noted that as a result of the animation she had seen about the brain, she could actually "picture the neurons growing bigger as they make more connections." One student referred to the value of effort: "If you do not give up and you keep studying, you can find your way through."

Adolescents often see school as a place where they perform for teachers who then judge them. The growth mind-set changes that perspective and makes school a place where students vigorously engage in learning for their own benefit.

Going Forward

Our research shows that educators cannot hand students confidence on a silver platter by praising their intelligence. Instead, we can help them gain the tools they need to maintain their confidence in learning by keeping them focused on the *process* of achievement.

Maybe we have produced a generation of students who are more dependent, fragile, and entitled than previous generations. If so, it's time for us to adopt a growth mind-set and learn from our mistakes. It's time to deliver interventions that will truly boost students' motivation, resilience, and learning.

References

Aronson, J., Fried, C., & Good, C. (2002). Reducing the effects of stereotype threat on African American college students by shaping theories of intelligence. *Journal of Experimental Social Psychology, 38,* 113–125.

Binet, A. (1909/1973). *Les idées modernes sur les enfants* [Modern ideas on children]. Paris: Flamarion. (Original work published 1909)

Blackwell, L., Trzesniewski, K., & Dweck, C. S. (2007). Implicit theories of intelligence predict achievement across an adolescent transition: A longitudinal study and an intervention. *Child Development, 78,* 246–263.

Cimpian, A., Arce, H., Markman, E. M., & Dweck, C. S. (2007). Subtle linguistic cues impact children's motivation. *Psychological Science, 18,* 314–316.

Doidge, N. (2007). *The brain that changes itself: Stories of personal triumph from the frontiers of brain science.* New York: Viking.

Dweck, C. S. (1999). *Self-theories: Their role in motivation, personality and development.* Philadelphia: Taylor and Francis/Psychology Press.

Dweck, C. S. (2006). *Mindset: The new psychology of success.* New York: Random House.

Ericsson, K. A., Charness, N., Feltovich, P. J., & Hoffman, R. R. (Eds.). (2006). *The Cambridge handbook of expertise and expert performance.* New York: Cambridge University Press.

Good, C., Aronson, J., & Inzlicht, M. (2003). Improving adolescents' standardized test performance: An intervention to reduce the effects of stereotype threat. *Journal of Applied Developmental Psychology, 24,* 645–662.

Grant, H., & Dweck, C. S. (2003). Clarifying achievement goals and their impact. *Journal of Personality and Social Psychology, 85,* 541–553.

Hong, Y. Y., Chiu, C., Dweck, C. S., Lin, D., & Wan, W. (1999). Implicit theories, attributions, and coping: A meaning system approach. *Journal of Personality and Social Psychology, 77,* 588–599.

Kamins, M., & Dweck, C. S. (1999). Person vs. process praise and criticism: Implications for contingent self-worth and coping. *Developmental Psychology, 35,* 835–847.

Mangels, J. A., Butterfield, B., Lamb, J., Good, C. D., & Dweck, C. S. (2006). Why do beliefs about intelligence influence learning success? A social-cognitive-neuroscience model. *Social, Cognitive, and Affective Neuroscience, 1,* 75–86.

Mueller, C. M., & Dweck, C. S. (1998). Intelligence praise can undermine motivation and performance. *Journal of Personality and Social Psychology, 75,* 33–52.

Nussbaum, A. D., & Dweck, C. S. (2007). Defensiveness vs. remediation: Self-theories and modes of self-esteem maintenance. *Personality and Social Psychology Bulletin.*

Sternberg, R. (2005). Intelligence, competence, and expertise. In A. Elliot & C. S. Dweck (Eds.), *The handbook of competence and motivation* (pp. 15–30). New York: Guilford Press.

Carol S. Dweck is the Lewis and Virginia Eaton Professor of Psychology at Stanford University and the author of *Mindset: The New Psychology of Success* (Random House, 2006).

When Children Make Rules

In constructivist classrooms, young children's participation in rule making promotes their moral development.

RHETA DEVRIES AND BETTY ZAN

Sherice Hetrick-Ortman's kindergartners were passionate about block building. These children at the Freeburg Early Childhood Program in Waterloo, Iowa, lavished care on their complex structures and felt justly proud of their creations. Some of the children were concerned, however, about problems in the block area. They discussed the matter at group time and came up with some new rules to post in the block-building area:

- Keep hands off other people's structures.
- No knocking people's structures down.
- Four friends in the block area at one time.

When children care about a classroom problem such as this one and take part in solving it, they are more likely to view the resulting rules as fair. Having *made* the rules, they are more likely to observe them. Just as important, participating in the process of rule making supports children's growth as moral, self-regulating human beings.

Rules in schools have traditionally been made by teachers and given to children. Today, many teachers see the benefits of allowing children to have a voice in developing classroom rules. But if we are not careful, this involvement can be superficial and meaningless. How can we best involve children in making classroom rules?

Morality and Adult-Child Relationships

We speak from a constructivist point of view, inspired by the research and theory of Jean Piaget. In constructivist education, rule making is part of the general atmosphere of mutual respect, and the goal is children's moral and intellectual development (DeVries & Zan, 1994).

Piaget (1932/1965) identified two types of morality that parallel two types of adult-child relationships: one that promotes optimal moral and intellectual development, and one that retards it. *Heteronomous* morality consists of conformity to external rules without question. Overly coercive relationships with adults foster this type of morality and can impede children's development of self-regulation. *Autonomous* morality, by contrast, derives from an internal need to relate to other people in moral ways. Cooperative relationships with adults foster this type of morality and help children develop high levels of self-regulation.

Obviously, children and adults are not equals. However, when the adult respects the child as a person with a right to exercise his or her will, their relationship has a certain psychological equality that promotes autonomy.

Piaget, of course, did not advocate complete freedom, and neither do we. Although constructivist teachers minimize the exercise of adult authority or coercion in relation to children, *minimize* does not mean *eliminate* (DeVries, 1999; DeVries & Edmiaston, 1999; DeVries & Kohlberg, 1987/1990). Rather, we strive for a balance that steadily builds the child's regulation of his or her own behavior.

Norms and Rules in Constructivist Classrooms

To investigate how constructivist teachers use external control and how they develop classroom norms and rules, we interviewed the teachers at the Freeburg Early Childhood Program, a laboratory school serving children ages 3–7 in a predominantly low-income neighborhood. The school's aim is to demonstrate constructivist practices.

Norms Established by Teachers

We define *norms* as specific expectations that teachers establish for children's behavior—ways of behaving that everyone takes for granted as part of the culture of the classroom. A norm is usually unwritten and sometimes unspoken until someone violates it and the teacher takes corrective action. The Freeburg teachers' reflections revealed three kinds of norms that existed in their classrooms:

- *Safety and health norms* ensure children's well-being. Our teachers articulated these as non-negotiables. Examples include "No hurting others," "Lie down at rest time," "Keep shoes on outside," "No crashing trikes or other vehicles," and "Don't throw sand."

- *Moral norms* pertain to respect for people and animals. They often relate to fair treatment or distribution of goods. Examples of these are "Take fair turns," "Talk through a conflict until there is a resolution," "If you bring a live animal into the classroom, try to make it comfortable," and "No hurting animals."
- *Discretionary norms* consist of routines and procedures to make the classroom run smoothly and make learning possible. Kathy Morris, the teacher in the 3-year-olds' class, pointed out that young children do not like chaos, and they need adults to figure out routines that work so that events run smoothly. Discretionary norms also include societal norms for politeness and individual responsibility that children need to know. Examples include "Sit with the group at group time," "Wait until all are seated at lunch before eating," and "Clean up your place after lunch."

All teachers must sometimes exert external control.

All teachers have safety and health norms, moral norms, and discretionary norms. These norms are acceptable and necessary uses of external authority in a constructivist classroom. But constructivist teachers carefully evaluate their reasons for norms and attempt to minimize the use of external control as much as possible.

Rules Made by Children

We define rules as formal agreements among teachers and children. Constructivist teachers often conduct discussions of problems that relate to their norms and engage children in making classroom rules that arise from these norms.

When teachers first suggest that children make rules, children often parrot such adult admonitions as "Never talk to strangers" or "Raise your hand and wait to be called on." This occurs especially when children are unaccustomed to a sociomoral atmosphere in which they feel free to express their honest opinions. Children may view rule making as another exercise in trying to figure out the right answer or say what they think the teacher wants to hear. The rules that they suggest may not reflect a real understanding of the need to treat others in moral ways. When children only mindlessly restate adults' rules, they have not engaged in true rule making.

Children who engage in true rule making sometimes reinvent rules that elaborate on already established norms. Although these elaborations are not entirely original, they still give the children feelings of autonomy in their power to create rules. For example, Gwen Harmon's 4-year-olds, working within the classroom norm "Don't hurt animals," developed the following practical and concrete rules regarding the chicks that they hatched in the classroom:

- Pick them up safely.
- Don't push them.
- Don't squeeze them.
- Don't put things in their box.
- Don't punch them.
- Don't put them on the light bulb.
- Don't drop them.
- Don't throw them.
- Don't pick them up by their wings.
- Don't color on them.
- Don't pull their heads off.

Reinvented rules demonstrate children's understanding of the moral norm because they translate the norm into children's own words and provide elaborations that make sense to them. Sometimes the elaborations are novel, dealing with situations that the teacher had not considered discussing. For example, in Beth Van Meeteren's 1st grade classroom, where the norm is to treat others with respect, children made the rule, "When people pass gas, do not laugh, or they will be upset or embarrassed."

Sometimes children develop entirely original rules. Unlike reinvented rules, invented rules reflect children's power to make decisions in the classroom. For example, Dora Chen's class of 4-year-olds invented a new rule in response to a problem they saw during one of their classroom routines. One day during clean-up, a child saw another child finishing a snack and felt that no one should eat snacks during clean-up time. He told the teacher, who raised the issue at group time. She asked, "What should our rule be?" After a 17-minute discussion in which the children suggested various possibilities, the teacher clarified the choice between "No snack during clean-up: throw it away" or "Finish snack before going outdoors." The children voted to throw away their unfinished snacks when clean-up started.

The new rule, driven by children's interest and concern, went beyond the teacher's concerns. Although the teacher preferred giving the children more time to finish their snacks, she believed that the children's solution was fair given the one-hour activity time in which to eat snacks.

Guidelines for Exerting External Control

Some people have the misconception that constructivist teachers are permissive and that external control never occurs in constructivist classrooms. In fact, all teachers must exert external control sometimes. From our discussions with teachers and our understanding of research and theory, we have derived four general guidelines for the use of external control.

Provide a general and pervasive context of warmth, cooperation, and community. We draw inspiration for this guideline from the work of Jean Piaget, especially from *The Moral Judgment of the Child* (1932/1965). Many others, however, have come to this same conclusion starting from different theoretical perspectives (Nelson, 1996; Watson, 2003). In fact, almost all of the recent classroom management programs on the market, with the exception of Assertive Discipline, stress the importance of cooperation and community (Charles, 2002).

Act with the goal of students' self-regulation. A developmental perspective leads us to focus on the long term. We want to contribute to the development of autonomous, self-regulating human beings who can make decisions based on the perspectives of all involved. Therefore, compliance is not our primary goal. Of course, we all wish sometimes that children would be more compliant. But we constantly remind ourselves and one another that developing self-regulation takes time, and we celebrate significant events, such as when an aggressive child actually uses words for the first time to tell another child what he wants instead of slugging him.

Minimize unnecessary external control as much as is possible and practical. Constructivist teachers do use external control; in fact, they use it quite a bit. As Piaget states, "However delicately one may put the matter, there have to be commands and therefore duties" (1932/1965, p. 180). Teachers in constructivist classrooms, however, use external control of children consciously and deliberately, not impulsively or automatically. The teachers with whom we work constantly ask themselves whether the external regulation is absolutely necessary.

Through discussions with teachers Gwen Harmon, Shari McGhee, and Christie Sales, we have identified several situations that can lead to unnecessary control of children. Avoidable control-inducing situations occur when

- The classroom arrangement invites rowdy behavior.
- Children do not know the classroom routine.
- Too many transitions lead to too much waiting time.
- Crowding in a part of the classroom leads to conflicts.
- Group time goes on for too long; children become restless, and some act out.
- Activities are not sufficiently engaging to appeal to children's purposes, and children become aimless.
- The classroom does not contain enough materials, and children compete for what is available.
- Clean-up is poorly organized, and children resist cleaning up after activity time.
- A mismatch exists between the teacher's expectations and the children's competencies.
- The teacher attributes a character flaw to a child who misbehaves.

When external control is necessary, use the least amount necessary to secure compliance. Ideally, the constructivist teacher uses external control judiciously to make sure that the child's experience overall is a mixture increasingly in favor of the child's self-regulation. When external regulation becomes necessary, the teacher must preserve the child's dignity and autonomy—for example, by giving the child a choice and thus returning a degree of autonomy as soon as possible.

Meaningful Rule Making

For many years, we have advocated allowing young children to make classroom rules, arguing that such opportunities are part and parcel of a constructivist, democratic classroom. By encouraging children to make classroom rules, the teacher minimizes unnecessary external control and promotes the development of children's moral and intellectual autonomy.

To genuinely think for themselves and exercise autonomy, children must be given the power to make rules and decisions that both elaborate on classroom norms and break new ground. By actively seeking out appropriate opportunities and recognizing them when they arise in the daily life of the classroom, teachers can create classrooms that are fair and democratic.

References

Charles, C. (2002). *Building classroom discipline* (7th ed.). Boston: Allyn and Bacon.

DeVries, R. (1999). Implications of Piaget's constructivist theory for character education. In M. Williams & E. Schaps (Eds.), *Character education.* Washington, DC: Character Education Partnership.

DeVries, R., & Edmiaston, R. (1999). Misconceptions about constructivist education. *The Constructivist, 13*(3), 12–19.

DeVries, R., & Kohlberg, L. (1987/1990). *Constructivist early education.* Washington, DC: National Association for the Education of Young Children.

DeVries, R., & Zan, B. (1994). *Moral classrooms, moral children: Creating a constructivist atmosphere in early education.* New York: Teachers College Press.

Nelson, J. (1996). *Positive discipline.* New York: Ballantine Books.

Piaget, J. (1932/1965). *The moral judgment of the child.* London: Free Press.

Watson, M. (2003). L*earning to trust.* San Francisco: Jossey-Bass.

Rheta DeVries is a professor and Director of the Regents' Center for Early Developmental Education, University of Northern Iowa, 107 Schindler Education Center, Cedar Falls, IA 50701; (391) 273–2101; rheta.devries@uni.edu. **Betty Zan** is an assistant professor and Research Fellow at the Regents' Center for Early Developmental Education; (319) 273–2101; betty.zan@uni.edu.

Strategies for Effective Classroom Management in the Secondary Setting

Over the years, researchers have written many books and articles about the lack of discipline or lack of respect students have toward their teachers. This image is enhanced by the daily accounts in movies, newspapers, television, and radio or in speaking to students, their teachers, or parents. In this article, the author provides working strategies that can be used by new and veteran teachers that will provide educators with procedures to maximize classroom instruction by incorporating effective classroom management techniques into their daily routines.

PAUL PEDOTA

Everyone concedes that there is a severe shortage of qualified teachers in the United States and that one of the most frequent reasons cited in the literature regarding the problem of staffing and retaining qualified individuals is the lack of student discipline (Macdonald 1999; Tye and O'Brien 2002). In speaking to new and veteran teachers who have left the profession primarily due to discipline problems in the classroom, many have commented that although they felt that during the preteaching training period sufficient time was spent on classroom management, they were not truly prepared for the realities of the classroom, which contributed to feelings of frustration, anger, and helplessness (Miech and Elder 1996).

In reviewing the research, one can see that effective teachers—those who have fewer discipline problems in the classroom—spend a good deal of time on planning (Brown 1998); take into account diversity as well as the preference of individual learning styles (Daniels, Bizar, and Zemelman 2001; Dunn and Dunn 1993; Sleeter and Grant 2003); provide activities that get students to begin work immediately and ensure there is a sufficient amount of work that will have students working the entire period (Ornstein and Lasley 2004); and are consistent in classroom management techniques with ". . . a healthy balance between rewards and punishment" (Miller, Ferguson, and Simpson 1998, 56).

Establishing, explaining, reviewing, and modifying (as needed) rules, routines, and procedures that are clearly understood to handle the daily recurring activities as well as developing procedures for unpredictable events that may occur, will help you to devote the maximum amount of time available for instruction and enhance classroom management (Marshall 2001).

The following is based on my beliefs, my personality, and thirty-seven years of experience as an educator. Individuals should use this article as a guide and not as a complete list of strategies or techniques that can be used for effective classroom management. Your personality and philosophy of education will dictate those ideas you will or will not use in dealing with developing, setting up, and using an effective strategy to ensure maximum instruction with few classroom discipline problems.

First Things First

As a teacher, ensuring that all students can learn in a safe environment is your prime objective. Before you can begin to teach, you must devote time to preparing your classroom and developing procedures that will help you maximize instruction in a positive climate, such as the following:

Seating Plans

Permanent seating arrangements will help you to learn students' names quickly, take attendance, and perform any other administrative task while students are involved in some instructional activity. The use of a Delaney book or seating chart can help to make this task a simple one. In addition, you should think about how your seating arrangements can be modified to support different types of instruction, such as whole group instruction, small group instruction, or students working individually.

Physical Surroundings

The room should be arranged to ensure that all students can see well, there are no obstructions, the lighting is adequate, and if and when students move around, they do not interfere with other students. Your desk should be positioned so that you can monitor the activities of all students as well as not interfere with movement within the class.

Housekeeping Procedures

Procedures for the storing of equipment and other material, the distribution and collection of student material, keeping the chalkboard clean, the location of the wastepaper basket, using the pencil sharpener, and so on, must also be developed.

Displays

The classroom should be a showcase for student work, as well as posters, magazine covers, charts, maps, and pictures. It is important to let students know that their work is important as well as let others know what students are learning. Your material, as well as student work, should be changed, at least every month or when you begin a new unit. This will allow for all students to have the opportunity to have their work displayed, which will give them a sense of ownership. School and class rules should also be posted as a reminder to students of the code of behavior.

Instruction

Plan for a variety of instructional experiences and keep students actively involved. You will find that by avoiding the sameness of daily classes, you will help prevent discipline problems. One way that this can be accomplished is by allowing students to be active participants in learning rather than passive listeners.

Setting Classroom Standards for Behavior and Work

Students, just like adults, prefer to be in an environment that is structured and predictable. In school, where students have individual teachers who hold different beliefs as to how to handle certain situations, it is important that you make your expectations perfectly clear. To this end, it is extremely important that procedures are in place that are consistent with schoolwide policy and that both students and their parents know what is expected in terms of behavior and class work. If rules are firm, fair, and followed consistently, you will be able to handle most situations that may infringe on the use of instructional time. Developing a written syllabus or contract that includes the subject material, subject class requirements, and class and individual code of conduct helps all to understand their responsibilities (Brophy 1986; Curwin and Mendler 1988).

The following provides some examples of what should be included in a code of conduct:

Student attendance: The importance of daily class attendance must be emphasized. Students should know what are considered legitimate reasons for being absent, procedures to follow when absent as well as when returning from an absence, and the impact recurring absences will have on grades.

Student lateness and dismissal: Students must understand the importance for being on time for class. Being late causes students to not only interrupt instruction for others, but also causes them to miss work. In addition, procedures for dismissal should be in place at the end of the instructional period and students should be reminded that only you dismiss the class.

Classroom interruptions: Procedures should be developed to handle classroom interruptions—such as intercom announcements, visitors, and fire drills. In all of these situations, students must know that you alone give direction on student actions.

Students leaving classroom: What are the procedures for leaving the room? Are you going to use a sign-out book, issue a pass, write the names of students on the chalkboard, or restrict the pass at certain times?

Student work: You should make students aware of the subject manner to be studied; instructional objectives you hope that students will obtain; skills that will be developed; their responsibility regarding class work, homework, or any other assignments; the number and types of tests; and a review of how you will arrive at a grade for each student.

Recognizing students in class: Students should not shout out questions, answers, or comments without first being recognized by you. Moving around the room as you call on volunteers as well as nonvolunteers will ensure that all students are on task as you build a climate for learning.

Instruction: Policies should also be developed to take into account how students should act and interact with each other during different types of instruction. For example, when working in groups what is the expected behavior of students? How is this behavior different from behavior exhibited during other types of instruction? If during group work students are speaking to one another, how do you control the volume?

Recognition of accomplishments: It is important to see the glass as half full not half empty, that is, try to accentuate the positive over the negative. To establish a positive classroom environment, students must feel that you recognize their accomplishments.

Inappropriate behavior: Ignoring inappropriate behavior until it reaches a point that you have no choice but to give a harsh punishment should be avoided. In deciding on the appropriate course to be taken, you must ensure that you are reacting to what took place and not the individual.

It is imperative to realize that once classroom rules and procedures have been developed, the worst thing that you can do is act hastily, not enforce a rule, or enforce it sporadically. In addition, you may not have thought of everything and may have to revise, modify, add, or disregard a rule. Do not be afraid to talk to a colleague or school official if you are having a problem or to change something if what you had originally planned is not working.

You must model the behavior that you expect from your students. You must avoid the use of insulting, abusive, or threatening language. Although it may be hard at times, you must learn to control your temper. Your words and/or actions can upset others and may even instigate physical actions, which can cause harm to the student, other students, or adults. To get respect, you must earn it, and by setting a good example and by treating others as you would like to be treated, this can be accomplished.

Communication

Communication can be verbal and nonverbal and just as in everyday life, poor communication can cause unnecessary problems. Table 1 displays some simple "Dos" and "Do nots" in using communication efficiently and effectively.

If you must reprimand students, use a normal tone of voice, look at the student, do not use gestures such as pointing your finger, and do not insist on the last word (Kerr and Nelson 2002).

Good communication skills and being a good listener, as well as a good speaker, can help in preventing problems in the classroom. When students feel that they are welcomed into a nonthreatening environment where learning is encouraged, they usually come ready, willing, and able to learn.

Table 1 Dos and Do Nots in Communication

DO	DO NOT
Think before you speak	Say you will do something you cannot do
Speak only when you have everyone's attention	Speak to individuals and not pay attention to the class
Give students the opportunity to ask questions	Be close minded
Be specific in your statements, directions, questions, and so on	Take silence as knowing

Table 2 Top Ten List for Classroom Management

10. Develop a philosophy of "we" rather than "I" and use a personal approach in working with your students.
9. Class rules should be reasonable, fair, equitable, and used in a consistent manner.
8. Your actions, words, and deeds should model the behavior that you expect from your students.
7. Remember self-esteem is as important for adolescences as it is for you—avoid sarcasm or actions that belittle an individual in front of classmates.
6. Be proactive. Move around the room and keep your eyes moving.
5. Before you speak, get everyone's attention and say what you mean and mean what you say.
4. Keep parents informed. Parent involvement will support your role as a teacher.
3. Always give students hope—make them feel that they can accomplish anything.
2. Treat your students as you yourself would like to be treated.
1. Be yourself. Do not be an imitation of someone else. Success will follow if you allow your own personality to show.

Strategies to Help Manage Your Classroom

By now you should be asking yourself, how can I build an environment in my classroom where there is trust and mutual respect among all, as well as have rules that are firm, fair, consistent, and followed? Table 2 outlines ten rules to help manage a classroom.

Combining structure and fairness with clear expectations in a caring, nonthreatening environment are the major elements of good teaching and effective classroom management. Students who believe that you really care about them as individuals, that is, academically, socially, and emotionally, will gain status and recognition and a sense of self-worth and belonging (Dreikurs, Grunwald, and Pepper 1971; Glasser 1990) as well as establish your authority and credibility.

Conclusion

By following these simple strategies, you can have an orderly classroom environment that will improve students' learning outcomes while providing for an atmosphere that is structured and consistent and shows that you are serious about teaching and learning. Motivating, challenging, and engaging students as you strive for high expectations will not only help to improve student behavior in school and academic accomplishments but will also provide the key for students to understand how to act in a moral and ethical way in society.

References

Brophy, J. 1986. Classroom management techniques. *Education and Urban Society* 18 (2): 182–94.

Brown, T. 1998. *Effective school research and student behavior.* Southeast/South Central Educational Cooperative Fourth Retreat Making a difference in student behavior. Lexington, KY.

Curwin, R. L., and A N. Mendler. 1988. *Discipline with dignity.* Alexandria, VA: Association for Supervision and Curriculum Development.

Daniels, H., M. Bizar, and S. Zemelman. 2001. *Rethinking high school: Best practice in teaching, learning and leadership.* Portsmouth, NH: Heinemann.

Dreikurs, R., B. Grunwald, and F. Pepper. 1971. *Maintaining sanity in the classroom: Classroom management techniques.* New York: Harper and Row.

Dunn, R., and K. Dunn. 1993. *Teaching secondary students through their individual learning styles: Practical approaches for grades 7–12.* Boston: Allyn and Bacon.

Glasser, W. 1990. *The quality school: Managing students without coercion.* New York: Harper and Row.

Kerr, M. M., and C. M. Nelson. 2002. *Strategies for managing behavior problems in the classroom.* 4th ed. Upper Saddle River, NJ: Merrill/Prentice Hall.

Macdonald, D. 1999. Teacher attrition: A review of the literature. *Teaching and Teacher Education* 15:839–48.

Marshall, M. 2001. *Discipline without stress, punishments, or rewards: How teachers and parents promote responsibility and learning.* Los Alamitos, CA: Piper.

Miech, R. J., and G. H. Elder. 1996. The service ethic and teaching. *Sociology of Education* 69:237–53.

Miller, A., E. Ferguson, and R. Simpson. 1998. The perceived effectiveness of rewards and sanctions in primary schools: Adding in the parental perspective. *Educational Psychology* 18 (1): 55–64.

Ornstein, A., and T. Lasley. 2004. *Strategies for Effective Teaching.* 4th ed. Boston: McGraw Hill.

Sleeter, C, and C. Grant. 2003. *Turning on learning: Five approaches for multicultural teaching plans for race, class, gender, and disability.* 3rd ed. New York: Wiley.

Tye, B. B., and L. O'Brien. 2002. Why are experienced teachers leaving the profession? *Phi Delta Kappan* 84 (1): 24–32.

Paul Pedota is a former principal in a New York City secondary school and is currently the director of alternative certification programs at St. John's University, New York.

From *The Clearing House,* March/April 2007, pp. 163–166. Reprinted by permission of the Helen Dwight Reid Educational Foundation. Published by Heldref Publications, 1319 Eighteenth St., NW, Washington, DC 20036-1802.

"No! I Won't!"
Understanding and Responding to Student Defiance

ANDREA SMITH AND ELIZABETH BONDY

> Ms. Jackson was at her wit's end. For the past two months it was the same routine. Taking a deep breath, she crossed her fingers and hoped that today would be different as she asked the students to join her on the rug for a story. Jon, a wide-eyed 8-year-old, remained motionless.
>
> "Jon, please come join us for a story." Silence. "Jon . . . come on over so you can listen to the story." The small boy's eyes narrowed as his jaw tightened. "No! I won't!"

Student defiance, or resisting the authority of the teacher, is commonplace. In fact, some researchers have reported that the vast majority of discipline referrals are due to defiance (Gregory, 2005; Kohl, 1994). Due to the prevalence of childhood defiance and its potential for bringing instruction to a grinding halt, it is essential for educators to be prepared to understand it and respond to students who exhibit it. The authors will examine defiant behavior and the strategies that can minimize and manage it effectively.

Understanding Defiant Behavior

Defiance ranges from minor, easily defused incidents to highly disruptive and dangerous events. Sometimes a student's defiance is so extreme and persistent that the student is identified as having oppositional defiant disorder (ODD). According to the Diagnostic and Statistical Manual of Mental Disorders, fourth edition (DSM-1V), ODD is characterized by a

> pattern of negativistic, hostile, and deviant behavior lasting at least six months, during which four (or more) of the following are present. The student (1) often loses his or her temper (2) often argues with adults (3) often actively defies or refuses to comply with adults' requests or rules (4) often deliberately annoys people (5) often blames others for his or her mistakes or misbehaviors (6) is touchy or easily annoyed by others (7) is often angry and resentful (8) is often spiteful or vindictive. (BehaveNet® Clinical Capsule™)

Students with ODD are at an increased likelihood of having problems with substance abuse or juvenile delinquency, developing a mental disorder, and committing violent crimes (van Lier, Muthen, & van der Sar, 2004). This extreme kind of defiance appears to be caused by a variety of factors, including genetics (Eaves, Rutter, Silberg, & Shillady, 2000), chemical imbalance (Jensen, 2001), either excessively authoritarian or *laissez-faire* parenting (Levy, O'Hanlon, & Goode, 2001), and social factors, such the experience of racial discrimination and poverty that can cause severe social stress in a family (Barkley, 1997). In addition, challenging behavior can be related to the quality of the mother's prenatal care and nutrition; the child's prenatal exposure to alcohol, drugs, and/or lead; poor nutrition; inadequate health care; and maltreatment, in the form of negligence and/or physical and emotional injury (Zirpoli & Melloy, 2001). Although these factors are presented as distinct, it is likely that they intermingle, creating a complex system of causation. Because the prevalence of ODD is less common than milder forms of defiance, we turn our attention to the more moderate and commonly observed forms of defiant behavior in elementary classrooms.

A pattern of defiant behavior, as illustrated by Jon in the vignette to the right, often indicates that a student is trying to accomplish something. The defiance serves a particular function. Researchers who study functional behavior assessment (e.g., Day, Horner, & O'Neill, 1994; Scott & Nelson, 1999) note that behavior tends to serve one of two (and sometimes both!) kinds of functions: to acquire and/or to avoid. Specifically, a student who behaves defiantly might be trying to get something, such as power, autonomy, status, attention, or a sense of belonging. The student also might be trying to avoid something, such as an aversive task or person.

Sometimes teachers and peers can trigger defiant behavior. Zirpoli and Melloy (2001) point out that teachers promote noncompliant behavior when they allow themselves to be lured into power struggles with students, react to inappropriate behavior rather than give students attention for their positive behavior, and respond inconsistently so that students are unsure what teachers expect of them. The strategies of functional behavior assessment, summarized later, provide educators with insights into the functions served by a particular behavior as well as environmental triggers for the behavior and consequences in the environment that could be reinforcing the behavior. With insights into the functions served by the defiant behavior and the conditions that support that behavior, educators can learn to intervene productively.

Some scholars remind us that defiance is not necessarily a "disease" (Diamond, 2003). Instead, it could be viewed as a social behavior that students should learn to use effectively. In fact, Kohl (1994) referred to defiance as a form of "creative maladjustment" that students use to resist adults' negative labels (e.g., "troublemaker," "slow learner"). Nevertheless, patterns of defiance in a classroom indicate that something is amiss. Given these insights into student defiance, what strategies might educators use to intervene productively?

Creating a Psychologically Supportive Environment

The old saying "An ounce of prevention is worth a pound of cure" rings true for many aspects of classroom management, and student defiance is no exception. A fundamental strategy in working with defiant behavior is to establish and maintain a psychologically supportive classroom environment (Patrick, Turner, Meyer, & Midgley, 2003). This kind of classroom features caring relationships between adults and students and among students, clear and high expectations for academic performance and behavior, and opportunities for meaningful participation in learning. In this kind of environment, students can develop social competence, a sense of purpose, problem-solving skills, and autonomy—all of which form a core of resilience in young people (Benard, 2004; Henderson & Milstein, 1996). Classroom Morning Meetings (Bondy & Ketts, 2001; Kriete, 2002), the use of positive behavior supports (U.S. Office of Special Education Programs, 1999), and the avoidance of common classroom management traps (Alderman, 1999) all contribute to the development of a psychologically supportive environment for students.

Conducting Morning Meetings

Morning Meeting, articulated and promoted by the Northeast Foundation for Children (Kriete, 2002), is a structure for beginning the school day. Before coming to the Morning Meeting circle, students read and interact with a message board or chart that will become part of the meeting. They then participate in the four elements of the meeting: Greeting, Sharing, Group Activity, and News and Announcements. The entire meeting can last between 15 and 30 minutes.

The Greeting enables students to say "hello" to one another in any number of traditional and nontraditional ways. After the Greeting, a student will start the Sharing portion of Morning Meeting by stating, in one sentence, something he or she would like to tell the group. Classmates are encouraged to listen during the sharing, then ask a predetermined number of questions in response to the sharer's invitation ("I'm ready for questions and comments"). The third component of Morning Meeting is a Group Activity, which usually involves a game, such as those often played in camps, scouts, and other social groups. The final part of Morning Meeting is News and Announcements. The class's attention is focused once again on the message board. Students read the board and discuss the interactive portion before transitioning into the school day.

As Kriete (2002) explains, Morning Meeting teaches a variety of skills and makes important contributions to the tone and content of a classroom. She notes that Morning Meeting establishes a climate of trust and helps students to believe that they are valued. In short, Morning Meeting helps to establish a psychologically supportive environment in which students are less likely to behave defiantly.

Using Positive Behavior Supports

Special educators have recognized for years the power of positive behavior supports in enabling students to optimally participate in school (e.g., U.S. Office of Special Education Programs, 1999). Unlike traditional approaches to behavior management, which view the individual student as a "problem" that must be "fixed," a positive behavior support approach views the individual in context to understand why the behavior occurs. Although positive behavior supports can be implemented in response to a student's difficulties, many teachers recognize them as powerful proactive strategies. Like Morning Meeting, positive behavior supports contribute to a psychologically supportive environment in which students feel valued and are able to succeed. In this kind of climate, defiant behavior is less likely to occur.

Ruef, Higgins, Glaeser, and Patnode (1998) summarized five teacher-recommended, proactive, proven positive behavior support strategies: altering the physical environment, maintaining predictability and scheduling, increasing choice making, making curriculum responsive to students, and appreciating positive behaviors. Paying attention to these areas enables all students—not only those prone to defiance—to participate successfully in classroom life.

Altering the Physical Environment. Room arrangement and the use of space can influence student behavior. Teachers can avoid overcrowding students at desks, in workstations, and in high-traffic areas of the classroom. Crowds and noise can trigger problem behavior, as can an over- or under-stimulating physical space. Teachers also may need to consider accommodating individual students' environmental needs. For instance, distractible students can benefit from a well-defined workspace located away from high-traffic areas and an identified spot on the carpet when sitting on the floor.

Maintaining Predictability in the Schedule. Predictable classroom schedules and routines help students feel secure and decrease anxieties, frustration, and challenging behaviors, such as defiance. Students should be made aware of the schedule and be prompted to refer to it throughout the day. When changes occur to the daily schedule, such as a fire drill or absence of a teacher, students should be prepared and informed about what the day will look like. Related to maintaining a predictable schedule is preparing students for transitions during the school day. If teachers make students aware of upcoming transitions, students will have time to finish their work and prepare for a change.

Increasing Choice Making. Many have argued that due to high-stakes accountability, teachers have narrowed curriculum and instruction to focus on test preparation (Abrams, Pedulla, & Madaus, 2003; Barksdale-Ladd & Thomas, 2000). In an attempt to comply with local, state, and national mandates, teachers may have reduced the choices available to students and thereby increased the likelihood of defiance. Ruef et al. (1998) asserted that students need opportunities to make choices in order to believe that they have some control over their environment. Of course, adults can develop lists of acceptable choices, perhaps in conjunction with students.

Making Curriculum Responsive to Students. Teachers who adjust the substance and process of instruction to be responsive to a particular group of students are likely to experience less challenging behavior than those who do not (Ruef et al., 1998). In fact, Ruef and his colleagues noted that tasks reflecting students' interests and developmental levels were associated with positive behavior, whereas tasks that did not reflect these characteristics were associated with challenging behaviors. They also noted that the difficulty level length, and pace of an activity influenced students' behavior. Given these findings, the authors recommended that teachers think carefully about the nature of the task (e.g., High or low interest? Too easy or too difficult?) and the way in which it is presented (e.g., Use of different modalities? Pace? Tight teacher control or more student-centered?). When students believe they can be successful, they feel supported and are less likely to behave defiantly.

Appreciating Positive Behaviors. Although teachers want to avoid bribing and manipulating students through contrived reinforcement systems, making positive comments in the classroom will contribute to a psychologically supportive environment more readily than will negative, punitive comments. In addition, positive, encouraging comments can help students develop behaviors that serve them well in and out of the classroom. Punitive comments, on the other hand, can intensify defiance and trigger other challenging behaviors. Ruef et al. (1998) encourage teachers to use words of encouragement, appreciation, and affection as well as hugs, pats, and smiles to signal to students that they are, indeed, on "the right track." In fact, Walker, Colvin, and Ramsey (1995) encouraged teachers to praise students for exhibiting behaviors that are close to, or necessary for reaching, the desired goal recognizing that it could take a while before students have perfected a new, complex behavior. Students who do not have the social, learning, or behavioral skills that will help them thrive in the classroom require coaching and feedback as they develop those skills. When teachers approach students' behavior proactively, they establish an expectation of success and communicate their confidence in students' ability to succeed.

Avoiding Classroom Management Traps

In the crush of activity and on-the-spot decision making in elementary classrooms, teachers can slip into responses that can exacerbate rather than minimize defiant behavior. Alderman (1999) provided useful warnings to teachers about common classroom management traps. By steering clear of these common pitfalls, teachers can preserve a psychologically supportive environment.

The Too-General Trap. When teachers give instruction or direction to students, they must choose their words carefully. Effective directions are specific and stated once in 10 words or less (Bloomquist, 1996). Ineffective directions include vague directions, question directions, rationale directions, frequent directions, and multiple directions. Vague directions use imprecise language (e.g., "Cut it out") that does not communicate clear expectations. If a student does not know what behavior is desired, he or she will be unable to do it. Question directions are stated as a question, such as, "Would you stop tapping your pencil?" This invites a student to provide an answer, either with or without behavioral compliance. Rationale directions are those that include an explanation as to why the student should follow the directions. For example, Ms. Jackson, from the introductory vignette, asked Jon to join the group so he could "listen to the story." Students can perceive this to be a lecture, and may resist by arguing against the teacher's rationale. A typical response could be, "I don't need to come to the rug because I don't want to listen to the story!" (Bloomquist, 1996). Furthermore, rationale directions sometimes become too lengthy. This technique is ineffective, because students will usually quickly stop listening and then focus on the teacher's body language rather than the words (Alderman, 1999). Another form of ineffective direction is one that is repeated frequently, thereby eliciting a cycle of giving directions and obtaining defiant responses. Finally, one should avoid giving directions that include multiple steps in one statement (Bloomquist, 1996), a format that easily confuses and/or frustrates some students.

The "I Must Win Them Over" Trap. Often, the students who struggle the most inspire teachers to dedicate themselves to helping those strugglers to succeed. Teachers hope to see sweeping changes in student behavior and dream of being the one who visibly turns the child's life around. Visible, sweeping changes, however, are not always common, and many of the greatest changes are not readily observable; for instance, it may not be until many years later that a teacher learns of the impact he or she had on a student. Therefore, Alderman (1999) advises teachers not to expect or demand immediate changes. Instead, he recommends that teachers focus on achieving small steps toward the desired goal and celebrating that progress with students and their families. For example, if Jon, the boy from the introductory vignette, were to say "No! I won't!" but then stomp over to the rug, his behavior could be viewed as improved. Although his language is the same, his actions have shifted toward group participation, and this is better than complete refusal to participate. Ms. Jackson might say, in a matter-of-fact tone, "It's good to have you with us, Jon," and proceed quickly to the story.

The Passionate Discipline Trap. Pleading or getting angry while disciplining students is an easy trap to fall into that can trigger student defiance. Often, with the best intentions, a teacher might say something like "Could you PLEASE, just this once, do as I ask?!" or "My goodness! If you do that ONE MORE TIME I'll . . . " These kinds of responses are likely to elicit further undesirable behaviors from students who enjoy exerting power over adults. Alderman (1999) suggests several strategies for avoiding this trap. First, use a matter-of-fact approach to discipline. This includes controlling facial expressions, vocal intonations, and body language. Next, point to or quote a classroom rule that the student is neglecting to follow. Finally, consider writing on a small piece of paper or a sticky note to clarify for the student what he or she should be doing. Each of these strategies can help the teacher avoid an overly emotional response.

Responding to Defiant Behavior

Despite a supportive classroom climate and impeccable avoidance of management traps, some students will continue defiant behavior. This section covers options for responding to such defiant behavior. Although teachers may understandably prefer to avoid thinking about a student who defies their authority and disrupts lessons, avoiding the problem will not resolve it. Kohn (1996) recommends that teachers think of defiance as an opportunity to teach students something new.

Consider the Function of the Defiance

A Functional Behavior Assessment (FBA) is a systematic, seven-step way of determining the function, or purpose, a behavior serves. The Individuals With Disabilities Education Act Amendments of 1997 require that an FBA be conducted under certain circumstances. However, the less formal use of an FBA by a classroom teacher can help that teacher understand the function of the student's behavior and lead to effective intervention. For example, the appropriate intervention for Jon's defiance will vary, based on what function his behavior serves. If he is defiant because he wants to avoid rug time, the intervention should be different than if he is defiant because he wants attention.

There are seven steps in an FBA (see Figure 1). First, one must observe the student's behavior in context to determine what external factors cause and maintain the behavior. This step entails describing the behaviors in observable terms, noting the antecedents that appear to trigger the behavior, and identifying the consequences that appear to reinforce the behavior. Second, a hypothesis should be formed about the function a behavior serves in a particular context. As stated earlier, many behaviors are directed toward acquiring something, avoiding something, or both. Third, the validity of this hypothesis should be assessed through monitoring the behavior, including when it occurs in both the presence and absence of the predicted antecedents and consequences. Fourth, an intervention should be designed that allows the student to achieve the desired function of the behavior by performing a behavior the teacher finds more desirable. This may require teaching the student a "replacement behavior." The goal is to create a win-win situation wherein both the student and the teacher get what they want. Fifth, the teacher may need to alter the environment in order to help the student replace the old behavior with the new. For example, if a student's disruptive behavior stems from a particular classmate sitting next to him or her, then the seating arrangement should be modified. Or, if the defiance is related to the student's frustration over assignments he or she finds difficult, the teacher should modify instruction and perhaps assignments so the student can participate more appropriately. Sixth, the effectiveness of the intervention must be considered by monitoring its impact on the student. Finally, if ineffective in supporting behavior change, the intervention should be altered.

Ideally, the functional behavior assessment will provide adequate insight into the student's defiance to enable the teacher to intervene and support positive behavior. Perhaps, for example, Jon's teacher discovers that Jon's defiance is related to his anxiety about the student who sits next to him on the rug. Jon seeks to avoid contact with his peer through his defiance, and the teacher reinforces his behavior by allowing him to remain in his seat. By helping Jon get to know the other student, the teacher may resolve the defiant behavior.

Further Interventions

Although teachers can resolve student defiance and many other troublesome behaviors with insights gained through an FBA, some behaviors are so ingrained that more direct, assertive approaches need to be considered. We review some of them here.

Use the Premack Principle. When applicable, teachers should use the Premack Principle (Warner & Lynch, 2002). As applied to teacher commands, the principle produces a directive followed by an incentive statement, reflecting a "When . . . then . . . " format. For example, the person making the command could say, "When you put away your markers, then we will take a game break," or "Once all chairs are pushed under the desks, we can go to recess." This strategy is beneficial in that it pairs a non- or less-preferred activity with a preferred activity (Warner & Lynch, 2002), thereby encouraging the student to comply with the request.

Steps
Observe behavior in context to determine its triggers and reinforcers.
Formulate a hypothesis about the function the behavior serves.
Assess the validity of the hypothesis through further observation.
Plan an intervention that enables student to achieve the same function through a desirable behavior. (Teach a replacement behavior, if necessary.)
Alter the environment to help student replace the old behavior with the new.
Monitor the effectiveness of the intervention by observing and recording its impact on student.
Alter intervention if it has not had the desired impact on student behavior.

Figure 1 Steps in a Functional Behavior Assessment.

Provide Consequences. Teachers may need to provide students with consequences for defiant actions. Consequences should be mild, with the intention of informing the student that the behavior is not appropriate. Consequences can be very effective when used appropriately (Bloomquist, 1996). However, students probably will be unhappy with the consequences, and some might express this displeasure. If students do express their unhappiness, the teacher should listen to the student's point of view and avoid getting into a power struggle. If the teacher is unsure how to respond to the student's displeasure or to an explanation the student provides, the teacher can tell the student that he or she will think about the situation and get back to the student at a designated time. The consequence should still be administered (Evertson, Emmer, & Worsham, 2006) in order to avoid providing reinforcement for the student's behavior.

Teachers may want to consider the two main types of consequences—natural consequences and logical consequences when planning consequences for defiant behavior. Natural consequences are those that occur directly as a result of the action, and include emotional responses. For example, if one falls off a bicycle, one might hurt oneself, or if one trips in front of the whole class, one might feel embarrassed. This form of consequence often proves to be the most effective, but it is difficult to administer. In Jon's case, a natural consequence of his refusal to join the group could be disappointment at missing an exciting group activity. The other main form of consequence, a logical consequence, is imposed by someone. In order to be effective, logical consequences should be "relevant," or directly related to the problem behavior. An effective way to develop relevant consequences is to think about what the student should be doing and design the consequence based on that desired behavior. For example, if Jon refuses to participate in a group activity, perhaps he will have to finish it during another period of the day. When consequences are logically connected to the misbehavior, they are likely to discourage the misbehavior. Still, it is important for teachers to gain insight into the function of the student's defiance in order to know what kind of consequence might be effective. Irrelevant consequences are likely to elicit anger and further defiance.

Use Time-Out. Although some researchers suggest that time-out is not always the ideal consequence, it does have the advantage of giving both the teacher and the student a chance to get away from the situation, think, and calm down (Evertson, Emmer, & Worsham, 2006). It also allows students to test their boundaries for autonomy and control while still remaining in a supportive environment (Charney, 2002). If a teacher decides to use time-out, he or she must have a plan for how it will be used. This includes knowing where time-out will occur and deciding ahead of time what actions will warrant time-out.

Some important things must be considered when planning where time-out will occur. Time-out should occur in a quiet place where there will be little to no mental stimulation. Often, teachers send the student to a desk in the hall, where the student has opportunities to chat with friends who pass by. Under these conditions, time-out can be an experience that reinforces the student's undesirable behavior. A teacher also must consider the purpose of the student's defiant behavior. In order for time-out to be effective, the teacher must be confident that the student is not exhibiting the defiant behavior to escape an aversive situation, such as an assignment or class activity that he or she dislikes. If avoidance is the function of the student's defiance, putting the student in time-out will only reinforce the defiance by helping the student escape. Students should understand, as part of time-out, that their feelings are never inappropriate; however, the actions used to convey these feelings (the actions that might have elicited their placement in time-out) can be inappropriate (Nelsen, Lott, & Glenn, 2000). Many resources are available to help teachers implement time-out (e.g., Brady, Forton, & Porter, 2003; Charney, 2002; Nelsen, 1999). Teachers considering time-out should research the strategy in order to develop a system likely to help their particular group of students.

Try Behavior Charts. Behavior charts are a management tool that can be used for many different forms of misbehavior, including defiance. They come in many forms. For example, Barkley (1997) suggests the use of a daily report card. The advantage of the daily report card is that it involves the family in teaching the desired behavior. As implied by the name, this process involves the teacher filling out a form each day to record and rate the student's behavior. This form should be reviewed nightly by the student's guardian, who then acknowledges the positive remarks and gives points and rewards for the positive behaviors. Guardians should discuss the positive and negative behaviors with the child each night, along with possible strategies for avoiding the negative behaviors and maintaining positive behaviors in the future. A second form of behavior chart is a contingency contract. This contract should outline the behaviors the student should exhibit and the rewards or punishments that will be implemented if the behavior is or is not displayed. The student and teacher come to an agreement on the behavior, rewards, and punishments. Both the student and teacher sign and date the contract (Blendinger, Devlin, & Elrod, 1995). Levy et al. (2001), however, suggest proceeding with caution when using behavior charts, especially those similar to the daily report card. They argue that charts should be implemented for only three to six weeks; after this time period, the children acclimate to them and do not work as hard to gain the rewards. Therefore, behavior charts are not effective for long-term use. Figure 2 provides an illustration of a behavior contract that teacher and student (and parent) can develop collaboratively to target specific behavioral expectations and rewards. The form encourages teacher and student to identify a time period after which progress can be assessed and decisions can be made about next steps.

Collaborate With Other Adults. Teachers who work with defiant students must use several key resources. The first resource is the parent(s) or guardian(s) of the student who exhibits defiance. It is likely that these adults encounter the same difficult behaviors from the child at home and know of a strategy that works for the child. If not, or if their strategy is ineffective, it might be beneficial to collaboratively create a plan for preventing and responding to the behaviors. A collaborative plan ensures that the adults approach the problem in the same way (Greenspan, 2003). If the student's defiant behavior is frequent and/or severe, the teacher should consult with a professional who

This is an agreement between ________________ and ________________

Student's name Teacher's name.

The contract begins on ________________ and ends on ________________. At this time, we will assess our progress.

The terms of the contract are as follows:

* Student will demonstrate the following behaviour(s) at the following time(s):

* Teacher will help the student demonstrate the expected behavior(s) by:

* When the student demonstrates the behavior, the teacher will:

________________ ________________

Student signature Teacher signature

Figure 2 Behavior Contract.

specializes in defiance. Colleagues, too, can assist in problem solving and the development and assessment of interventions.

Although the thought of managing students who exhibit defiance can be intimidating, a variety of strategies can help. Building a strong classroom community and avoiding common management traps are important for preventing defiance. When defiance occurs, one must consider the function the defiance serves in order to determine appropriate ways to intervene. The goal of intervention is to enable the student to meet his or her needs in more appropriate ways and to preserve a productive learning environment. With a repertoire of strategies for preventing and responding to defiant behavior, teachers can strive to maintain a psychologically supportive environment in which all students believe they can succeed. Under these conditions, defiant behavior is likely to be minimized.

References

Abrams, L., Pedulla, J., & Madaus, G. (2003). Views from the classroom: Teachers' opinions of statewide testing programs. *Theory Into Practice, 42*(1), 18–29.

Alderman, G. L. (1999). Management traps: Recognizing and staying out of common behavior management traps. *Beyond Behavior, 8,* 23–28.

Barkley, R. (1997). *Defiant children: A clinician's manual for assessment and parent training* (2nd ed.). New York: The Guilford Press.

Barksdale-Ladd, M. A., & Thomas, K. (2000). What's at stake in high-stakes testing. *Journal of Teacher Education, 51*(5), 384–401.

Behavenet® clinical capsule™. (n.d.). DSM-IV & DSM-IV-TR: Oppositional Defiant Disorder. Retrieved Aug. 17, 2004, from BehaveNet Inc Web site: www.behavenet.com/capsules/disorders/odd.htm.

Benard, B. (2004). *Resiliency: What we have learned.* San Francisco: WestEd.

Blendinger, J., Devlin, S., & Elrod, G. (1995). *Controlling aggressive students.* Bloomington, IN: Phi Delta Kappa Educational Foundation.

Bloomquist, M. (1996). *Skills training for children with behavior disorders.* New York: The Guilford Press.

Bondy, E., & Ketts, S. (2001). "Like being at the breakfast table": The power of classroom morning meeting. *Childhood Education, 77,* 144–149.

Brady, K., Forton, M., & Porter, D. (2003). *Rules in school.* Greenfield, MA: Northeast Foundation for Children.

Charney, R. (2002). *Teaching children to care: Classroom management for ethical academic growth, K-8* (2nd ed.). Greenfield, MA: Northeast Foundation for Children.

Day, H. M., Horner, R. H., & O'Neill, R. E. (1994). Multiple functions of problem behaviors: Assessment and intervention. *Journal of Applied Behavior Analysis, 27,* 279–289.

Diamond, N. (2003). Defiance is not a disease. *Rethinking Schools Online, 17*(4). Retrieved from www.rethinkingschools.org/archive/17-04/defi174.shtml

Eaves, L., Rutter, M., Silberg, J. L., & Shillady, L. (2000). Genetic and environmental causes of covariation in interview assessments of disruptive behavior in child and adolescent twins. *Behavior Genetics, 30*(4), 321.

Evertson, C., Emmer, E., & Worsham, M. (2006). *Classroom management for elementary teachers* (7th ed.). Boston: Allyn and Bacon.

Greenspan, S. I. (2003). The oppositional child. *Early Childhood Today, 17*(4), 24.

Gregory, A. (2005, September). *A window on the discipline gap: Cooperation or defiance in high school classrooms.* Paper presented at the Curry School of Education Risk and Prevention Speaker Series, Charlottesville, VA.

Henderson, N., & Milstein, M. M. (1996). *Resiliency in schools.* Thousand Oaks, CA: Corwin Press.

Jensen, E. (2001). Fragile brains. *Educational Leadership, 59*(3), 32.

Kohl, H. (1994). *"I won't learn from you" and other thoughts on creative maladjustment.* New York: New Press.

Kohn, A. (1996). *Beyond discipline: From compliance to community.* Upper Saddle River, NJ: Prentice-Hall.

Kriete, R. (2002). *The morning meeting book.* Greenfield, MA: Northeast Foundation for Children.

Levy, R., O'Hanlon, B., & Goode, T. (2001). *Try and make me! Simple strategies that turn off the tantrums and create cooperation.* New York: Penguin Group.

Nelsen, J. (1999). *Positive time-out.* Rocklin, CA: Prima.

Nelsen, J., Lott, L., & Glenn, H. (2000). *Positive discipline in the classroom: Developing mutual respect, cooperation and responsibility in your classroom* (3rd ed.). Roseville, CA: Prima.

Patrick, H., Turner, J., Meyer, D. K., & Midgley, C. (2003). How teachers establish psychological environments during the first days of school: Associations with avoidance in mathematics. *Teachers College Record, 105,* 1521–1558.

Ruef, M. B., Higgins, C., Glaeser, B. J., & Patnode, M. (1998). Positive behavioral support: Strategies for teachers. *Intervention in School and Clinic, 34*(1), 21–32.

Scott, T. M., & Nelson, C. M. (1999). Using functional behavioral assessment to develop effective intervention plans: Practical classroom applications. *Journal of Positive Behavior Interventions, 1*(4), 242–251.

U.S. Office of Special Education Programs. (1999, Winter). Positive behavioral support: Helping students with challenging behaviors succeed. *Research Connections in Special Education,* (4), 1–5. Retrieved from http://ericec.org/osep/recon4/rc4cov.html

van Lier, P. A., Muthen, B. O., & van der Sar, R. M. (2004). Preventing disruptive behavior in elementary schoolchildren: Impact of a universal classroom-based intervention. *Journal of Consulting & Clinical Psychology, 72*(3), 467–478.

Walker, H., Colvin, G., & Ramsey, E. (1995). *Antisocial behavior in school: Strategies and best practices.* Pacific Grove, CA: Brooks/Cole.

Warner, L., & Lynch, S. (2002). Classroom problems that don't go away. *Childhood Education, 79,* 97–100.

Zirpoli, T. J., & Mellow, K.J. (2001). *Behavior management: Applications for teachers* (3rd ed.). Upper Saddle River, NJ: Merrill/Prentice Hall.

Andrea Smith is a 4th-grade teacher, Alachua County Public Schools, Gainesville, Florida. **Elizabeth Bondy** is Professor, College of Education, University of Florida, Gainesville.

Bullying: Effective Strategies for Its Prevention

Put a halt to the name-calling, teasing, poking, and shoving, and make way for learning.

RICHARD T. SCARPACI

Some people view bullying as a normal aspect of childhood; teachers who prevent bullying know that this is not true. Bullying is a deliberate act that hurts young victims, both emotionally and physically. Aside from the victims, bullying affects people around them by distracting, intimidating, and upsetting them. Basically, bullying in the classroom is disruptive and prevents students from learning and teachers from reaching their students. Moreover, research has indicated that adopting programs which target antisocial behavior are likely to boost overall student academic performance (University of Washington 2005; Glew et al. 2005).

Though bullying among school children is hardly a new phenomenon, highly publicized media accounts have brought the topic a great deal of attention recently. In approaching this problem, research has suggested that reduction of bullying is best accomplished through a comprehensive, school-wide effort that involves everyone—especially teachers (Limber 2003).

Specific teacher behaviors may limit or prevent bullying in schools. When teachers respect student autonomy, while maintaining young people's sense of belonging, and teach cause-and-effect thinking that promotes development of a sense of right and wrong, schools are likely to deter bullying (Davis 2005). To accomplish this goal, teachers must confront their own beliefs and misconceptions about bullying, learn skills for recognizing the indicators of bullying, and practice strategies for addressing and deterring bullying.

What Is Bullying?

Bullying can be defined as when a more powerful person hurts, frightens, or intimidates a weaker person on a continual and deliberate basis. This behavior manifests itself in three distinct forms (Ritter 2002): physical (hitting, shoving, poking, tripping, and slapping), verbal (name-calling, insults, derision, racist remarks, and teasing) and social (persuading others to exclude or reject someone). Bullying in schools can be described simply as when a student is exposed repeatedly and over time to negative actions on the part of one or more other students (Olweus 2003).

Regardless of definition, some basic concepts provide insight and characterize bullies and bullying.

- Bullying takes at least two people: bully and victim.
- Bullies like to feel strong and superior.
- Bullies enjoy having power over others.
- Bullies use their power to hurt other people.

Though violent incidents are relatively uncommon, harassment in various physical and verbal forms is widespread. The American Medical Association (AMA) claimed that half of all children in the United States are bullied at some point in their lives, and one in 10 is victimized on a regular basis (Ritter 2002). A National Institute of Child Health and Human Development (2001) study found that 13 percent of children in grades six through ten had taunted, threatened, or acted physically aggressive toward classmates, while 11 percent had been the targets of such behavior. Six percent admitted that they both bullied others and had been bullied themselves. Boys were more likely to be bullies or victims of bullying than girls, who more frequently were the targets of bullying in the form of malicious rumors, electronic bullying, and sexual harassment.

Myths about Bullying

The belief that bullying is some sort of childhood disease is false. Olweus (2003) disputed several common assumptions such as this one, finding that many so-called causes of bullying and profiles of typical victims do not stand up to empirical data. Students who wear glasses, are overweight, or speak differently are not more likely to become victims of bullies. Actually, those who are passive or submissive tend to become victims almost 85 percent of the time. Comprising the other 15 percent are aggressive victims who are targeted because of some provocative feature of their personalities.

Myths have been exposed online by the U.S. Department of Health and Human Services (2003), School Bully OnLine (Field 2005), and For KidSake (2006). Some typical myths about bullying are:

1. Bullying is just teasing. "I was just kidding around!" is a refrain educators often hear from bullies.
2. some people deserve to be bullied.
3. Only boys are bullies.
4. People who complain about bullies are babies.
5. Bullying is a normal part of growing up.
6. Bullies will go away if you ignore them.
7. All bullies have low self-esteem. That's why they pick on others.
8. It's tattling to tell an adult when you're being bullied.
9. The best way to deal with a bully is by fighting or trying to get even.
10. People who are bullied might hurt for a while, but they'll get over it.

"Teachers must learn to recognize the indicators of bullying, in both the victims and the bully."

Though a couple of these—such as numbers 6 and 10—may be true sometimes, all the other statements are false. The challenge, then, is to get past the myths and to identify the true indicators of bullying.

Indicators of Bullying

Awareness is the first step in preventing bullying. Teachers must learn to recognize the indicators of bullying, in both the victims and the bully.

Recognizing the Victims

Teachers should be alert to students who have poor social skills and few friends; they may be victims of bullying. Teachers also should keep an eye on students who are physically smaller and act or look unlike other students; they too are potential victims.

Frankel (1996) described the key indicators for a child at risk:

- A child's grades begin to fall.
- A child shows a decrease in interest for school in general.
- A child feigns illness, such as frequent headaches or stomachaches.
- A child who chooses ubiquitous routes home may be hiding the fact that he or she is a victim of a bully.
- A child claims to have lost books, money, or other belongings without a good explanation.
- A child is caught stealing or asking for extra money.
- A child has unexplained injuries, bruises, or torn clothing; bullying may be the cause for any or all of these indicators.

The AMA warned that bullying can damage a child as much as child abuse (Ritter 2002), and has asked doctors to be vigilant for signs that their young patients might be victims of bullying or be bullies themselves. The psychological trauma of recurring harassment puts victims at risk of suffering from depression or low self-esteem as an adult. The younger the child, the more he or she ultimately will suffer from bullying.

To identify whether a patient is being bullied, the AMA suggested that parents and doctors ask a series of questions (Ritter 2002). The questions also are quite appropriate for teachers who suspect that bullying is going on in their classrooms. Developing the skill of asking the right questions may help deter bullying.

1. Have you ever been teased at school? How long has this been going on?
2. Do you know of other children who have been teased?
3. Have you ever told your teacher about the teasing? What happens?
4. What kinds of things do children tease you about?
5. Do you have nicknames at school?
6. Have you ever been teased because of your illness, disability, or for looking different than other kids?
7. At recess, do you usually play with other children or by yourself?

Though one might not think of a student who attacks others as a victim, that is sometimes the case. Bullies are characterized by hypersensitivity toward criticism—being teased, harassed, or generally picked on by those to whom they were violent. Of the 37 school shootings since 1974, the National Threat Assessment Center found that attackers felt persecuted, bullied, threatened, or had been previously attacked. Bullying is a prime factor in two-thirds of school shooting incidents (Viadero 2003). In more than half of the rampages, revenge was the motivation (Vossekuil et al. 2002).

Charles Andrew Williams, the 15-year-old Santee, California, student accused of killing two classmates and wounding 13 others (Reaves 2001) was tormented and bullied. Witnesses said that kids burned him with cigarette lighters and accused him of being a faggot. When he announced that he planned to pull a Columbine, two students called him a wimp and dared him to do it. Early intervention might have been able to prevent this tragedy.

Recognizing the Bully

Bullies may be more difficult to identify than the victims of bullying. While the stereotype is that bullies have low self-esteem, actually they're often self-confident, popular, and make friends easily (Cohen-Posey 1995). If slighted, however, they may take it out on someone who can't fight back. The reasons for this are based somewhere in familiar coping mechanisms that bullies have learned.

Bullies often manifest more violent behavior with age and tend to suffer from depression, suicidal behavior, and alcoholism (Olweus 1998). Many bullies come from homes where they're harassed themselves; they also tend to perform poorly at school; and, by age 24, 60 percent of former bullies have been convicted of a crime (Olweus 1998).

What Teachers Can Do

Teachers have dual roles: teach potential bullies social skills, while developing capacity to avoid intimidation. The next steps are to develop and implement the practices and strategies needed to stop bullying at school while assisting its victims.

Eliminating Harassment

Sexual harassment, when viewed as conflict, can be described as intentional or inadvertent conduct offensive to a reasonable person. A female victim of this type of harassment may appear angry, distrustful of her classmates, or self-conscious about her physical maturation as a result of untoward comments. A male may become passive following incidents of sexual insults, threats, or innuendo.

Teachers should investigate all complaints or rumors of sexual harassment. The best tool for the elimination of harassment is prevention. Affirmatively raise the subject in class. Express strong disapproval for untoward actions, develop sanctions (such as referrals to a higher authority), and inform students of their rights to raise the issue of harassment.

Encouraging Openness

To deter bullying, teachers should encourage and practice openness in class. Bullies tend to work in secret; they depend on the silence of their victims. If open communication is practiced, bullies will find it difficult to operate. Hold them accountable for their actions. Use or develop school antiharassment policies and hold bullies responsible for inappropriate behavior.

Practicing Bullying Prevention

Four basic principles for the prevention of bullying should be practiced by teachers (Olweus 2003):

1. Provide warm, positive interest and involvement from adults.
2. Provide consistent application of nonpunitive, nonphysical sanctions for unacceptable behavior or violations of rules.
3. Establish firm limits on unacceptable behavior.
4. Act as authorities and role models.

A bullying prevention program created by Olweus, Limber, and Mihalic (1999) incorporates having regular class meetings with students while establishing and enforcing class rules against bullying.

Neutralizing a Bully

Teachers should know how to neutralize a bully—to use the skill of acquiring information about incidents and then enforcing consequences if the negative behavior continues (Frankel 1996). Victims also should be taught how to deal with teasing so that they can help neutralize the bully. Teachers should practice being role models and encourage victims to make light of teasing by using statements such as:

- *So what?*
- *Can't you think of anything else to say?*
- *Tell me when you get to the funny part.*
- *And your point is?*

Responses such as these, perhaps surprisingly, generally do not incite bullies to further action.

The National Education Association has developed Quit It and Bullyproof—programs that work to neutralize bullies. These programs consist of interactive materials, including discussions and role-playing aimed at educating children about hurtful behaviors, and advice on how to deal with bullying situations (Froschl, Sprung, and Mullin-Rindler 1998).

Resolving Conflict

Bullying creates conflicts for both the victim and the bully. Conflict should be viewed as normal, and an opportunity to develop constructive practices to prevent bullying. Most bullying prevention programs invite teachers to intervene when children's conflict is about power and control, not negotiation (Craig and Pepler 1997). That is, teacher intervention is appropriate and necessary to prevent or end a physical conflict between students; violence, once started, stops only when someone is hurt. Intervention by a teacher is less necessary when students are involved in a conflict whose outcome can be negotiated.

Briggs (1996) advocated extending social and emotional learning by viewing incidents of conflict as teachable moments for social learning, and practicing skill streaming (social skills training), peer mediation, or conflict resolution. Phillips (1997) described how her high school attempted to alleviate and resolve conflicts by establishing a "conflict wall" (see below) that provided step-by-step guidance. If students cannot resolve a conflict, have them agree to disagree; sometimes that is the best we can do.

Closing Thoughts

Specific teacher behaviors can limit or prevent bullying in school. Reject myths about bullying. Believe that effective teachers manage classrooms with care and understanding, while creating an open, warm, nurturing environment that allows less opportunity or incentive for bullying to occur (Scarpaci 2007). Demonstrate active positive interest in student well-being.

Develop the skill of questioning and respectful listening to assess indications of bullying. By learning and teaching conflict resolution skills, teachers create environments that are less conducive to bullying. Employ the skills necessary to address the psychological needs of students: belonging, power, freedom, and fun (Glasser 1998). Focus on remediating student social-skill deficits by addressing classroom survival skills, friendship-making skills, dealing with feelings, and alternatives to aggression.

Teach students how to deal with behaviors that can be hurtful. Role-play in class to illustrate how to deal with teasing and threats of physical aggression. Bullying, when understood, can be prevented by doing what we do best—teaching! By combining education about bullying and establishing consequences for continued bullying, schools not only will neutralize bullying; they also might prevent it.

Conflict Wall: Steps for Resolving Conflicts

1. Cool down. Don't try to resolve a conflict when you are angry. Take time out and attempt to resolve the conflict when cooler heads prevail.
2. Describe the conflict. Each person should be given the opportunity to explain what happened in his or her own words. (Make no judgments!)
3. Describe what caused the conflict. Be specific and insist on exact chronological order. (Don't place blame!)
4. Describe the feelings raised by the conflict.
5. Listen carefully and respectfully while the other person is talking.
6. Brainstorm solutions to the conflict.
7. Try your solutions.
8. If that doesn't work, try another solution.

References

Briggs, D. 1996. Turning conflicts into learning experiences. *Educational Leadership* 54(1): 60–63.

Cohen-Posey, K. 1995. *How to handle bullies, teasers and other meanlees.* Highland City, FL: Rainbow Books.

Craig, W., and D. J. Pepler. 1997. Observations of bullying and victimization in the schoolyard. *Canadian Journal of School Psychology* 13(2): 41–60.

Davis, S. 2005. Schools *where everyone belongs: Practical strategies for reducing bullying.* Champaign, IL: Research Press. Available at: *www.stopbullyingnow.com.*

Field, T. 2005. Myths and misconceptions about school bullying. *School Bully OnLine.* Available at: *www.bullyonline.org/schoolbully/myths.htm.*

For KidSake. 2006. Breaking through the myths. Available at: *www.forkidsake.net/bully_myths_answer_sheet.htm.*

Frankel, F. 1996. *Good friends are hard to find.* Glendale, CA: Perspective Publishing.

Froschl, M., B. Sprung, and N. Mullin-Rindler. 1998. *Quit it! A teacher's guide on teasing and bullying for use with students in grades K–3.* New York: Educational Equity Concepts.

Glasser, W. 1998. *Choice theory: A new psychology of personal freedom.* New York: HarperCollins.

Glew, G. M., M.-Y. Fan, W. Katon, F. P. Rivara, and M. A. Kernic. 2005. Bullying, psychosocial adjustment, and academic performance in elementary school. *Archives of Pediatrics & Adolescent Medicine* 159(11): 1026–31.

Limber, S. P. 2003. Efforts to address bullying in U.S. Schools. *Journal of Health Educalion* 34(5): S23–S29.

National Institute of Child Health and Human Development. 2001. Bullying widespread in U.S. schools, survey finds, Rockville, MD: NICHD. Available at: *www.nichd.nih.gov/new/releases/bullying.clm.*

Olweus. D. 1998. *Bullying at school.* Malden, *MA:* Blackwell Publishers.

Olweus, D. 2003. A profile of bullying at school. *Educational Leadership* 60(6): 12–17.

Olweus, D., S. Limber, and S. F. Mihalic. 1999. *Bullying prevention program,* Book nine of Blueprints for Violence Prevention. Boulder, CO: Center for the Study and Prevention of Violence.

Phillips, P. 1997. The conflict wall. *Educational Leadership* 54(8): 43–44.

Reaves, J. 2001. Charles 'Andy' Williams. *Time,* March 9. Available at: *www.time.com/time/pow/printout/0,8816,101847,00.html.*

Ritter, J. 2002. AMA puts doctors on lookout for bullying. *Chicago Sun Times,* June 20.

Scarpaci, R. T. 2007. *A case study approach to classroom management.* Boston: Allyn & Bacon.

University of Washington. 2005. School programs targeting antisocial behavior can boost test scores, grades. Seattle, WA: UW. Available at: *www.newswise.com/p/articles/view/516342.*

U.S. Department of Health and Human Services. 2003. *Bullying is not a fact of life.* Washington, DC: Substance Abuse and Mental Health Services Administration. Available at: *www.mentalhealth.samhsa.gov/publications/allpubs/SVP-0052.*

Viadero, D. 2003. Tormentors. *Education Week,* Jan. 15, 24.

Vossekuil, B., R. Fern, M. Reddy, R. Borum, and W. Modzeleski. 2002. *The final report and findings of the safe school initiative: Implications for the prevention of school attacks in the United States.* Washington, DC: U.S. Secret Service and U.S. Department of Education.

Richard T. Scarpaci, a former teacher and principal, currently is an Assistant Professor and Director of Field Experiences at St. John's University, Staten Island campus. He has taught courses in Management and Methods as well as conducted Child Abuse and Violence Prevention Seminars. He is a member of the Alpha Beta Gamma Chapter of Kappa Delta Pi.

UNIT 6

Assessment

Unit Selections

Key Points to Consider

- What fundamental concepts from contemporary learning and motivation theories have specific implications for how teachers assess their students? Are such practices consistent with what is promulgated with standardized tests?
- Many educators believe that schools should identify the brightest, most capable students. What are the assessment implications of this philosophy? How would low-achieving students be affected?
- What principles of assessment should teachers adopt for their own classroom testing? How do we know if the test scores teachers use are reliable and if valid inferences are drawn from the scores? How can teachers make time to involve students in self-assessment?

Student Web Site

www.mhcls.com/online

Internet References

Further information regarding these Websites may be found in this book's preface or online.

Awesome Library for Teachers
http://www.neat-schoolhouse.org/teacher.html

FairTest
http://fairtest.org

Kathy Schrocks's Guide for Educators: Assessment
http://school.discovery.com/schrockguide/assess.html

Phi Delta Kappa International
http://www.pdkintl.org

Washington (State) Center for the Improvement of Student Learning
http://www.k12.wa.us/

In which reading group does Jon belong? How do I construct tests? How do I know when my students have mastered the course objectives? How can I explain test results to Mary's parents? Teachers answer these questions, and many more, by applying principles of assessment. Assessment refers to procedures for measuring and recording student performance and constructing grades that communicate to others levels of proficiency or relative standing. Assessment principles constitute a set of concepts that are integral to the teaching-learning process. Indeed, a significant amount of teacher time is spent in assessment activities, and with more accountability there is a greater emphasis on assessment.

Assessment provides a foundation for making sound evaluative judgments about students' learning and achievement. Teachers need to use fair and unbiased criteria in order to assess student learning objectively and accurately and make appropriate decisions about student placement. For example, in assigning Jon to a reading group, the teacher will use his test scores as an indication of his skill level. Are the inferences from the test results valid for the school's reading program? Are his test scores consistent over several months or years? Are they consistent with his performance in class? The teacher should ask and then answer these questions so that he or she can make intelligent decisions about Jon. On the other hand, will knowledge of the test scores affect the teacher's perception of classroom performance and create a self-fulfilling prophesy? Teachers also evaluate students in order to assign grades, and the challenge is to balance "objective" test scores with more subjective, informally gathered information. Both kinds of evaluative information are necessary, but both can be inaccurate and are frequently misused.

The articles in this section focus on two contemporary issues in assessment—standards and the use of high-stakes standardized tests, and classroom assessment that is integrated with teaching.

The first article in this unit provides a review of standards from all 50 states, identifying those that had standards that provided sufficient information regarding what students should learn to allow teachers to develop a core curriculum and a test developer to create aligned assessments. In the second article, Naomi Dillon, suggests that the formats of most standardized tests disadvantage students with different learning needs, particularly English Language Learners. In the third article, Rick Stiggins, an expert in testing, argues that classroom assessment and grading practices should focus on enhancing learning, rather than sorting students. James Allen shows how classroom assessment and grading practices can be implemented to accurately reflect student learning. In "Seven Practices for Effective Learning," Jay McTighe and Ken O'Conner, highlight assessment practices that can improve student learning and enhance teaching. The final article examines the experiences of two urban teachers in terms of the challenges of meeting the demands of high stakes testing in their classrooms.

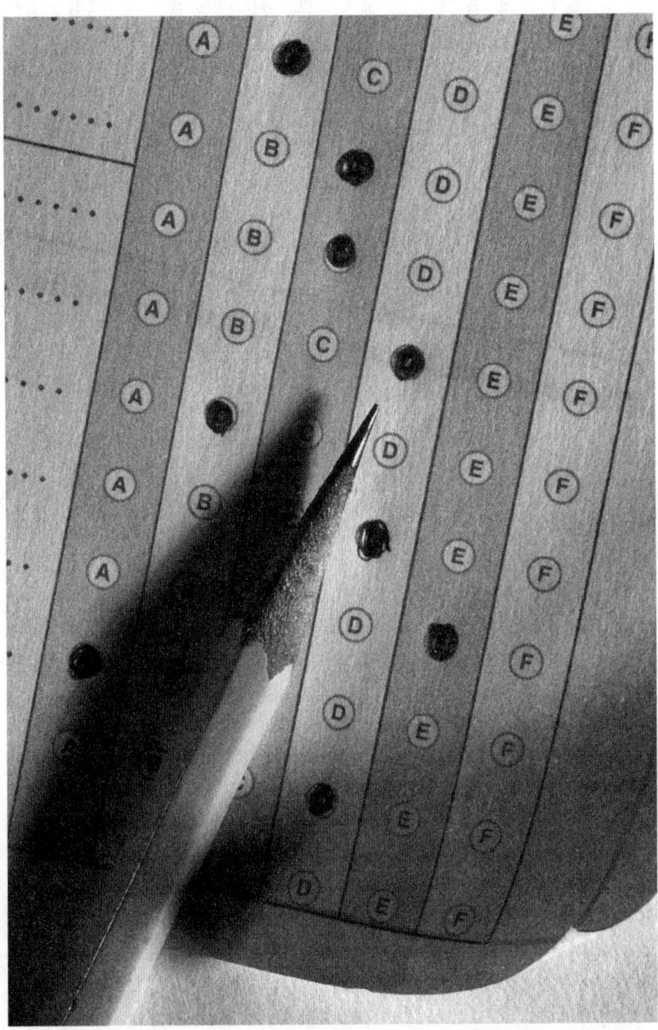

Comstock/Picture Quest

IOSIE: A Method for Analyzing Student Behavioral Problems

The author argues for a rational method to analyze behavior problems and proposes a method of identifying the problem, the objectives to be achieved, the solution, the implementation, and the evaluation (IOSIE) as a practical approach to assist teachers in resolving most classroom behavior management problems. The approach draws heavily on well-known classroom management strategies and encourages readers to put those into place by using the five-step IOSIE approach. The letters in the term IOSIE represent steps to follow when analyzing acts of classroom misbehavior.

RICHARD T. SCARPACI

A five-step process for looking at and reflecting on solutions for behavioral classroom problems is the method described here. The process requires one to identify causes of misconduct, determine objectives, and propose a solution. Implementation provides an opportunity to evaluate the executed solutions (IOSIE; Figure 1). The first letter of each italicized word indicates the steps to follow when analyzing misbehavior in classrooms. If this procedure is followed, disruption and discipline problems should be lessened in classrooms.

Identifying the Problem

Problem behavior analysis is something all teachers have to master. The procedure is unchanging; one cannot fix what is not recognized as broken. The process is not as simple as it might seem at first. Do not be deceived by appearances or biases when attempting to identify the cause of a problem (Danforth and Boyle 2000). A boy who is arguing with a girl in the classroom may not be the instigator of misbehavior. Children who are talking loudly are not automatically being disruptive; a student who is threatening another student is not necessarily the culprit. Do not jump to false conclusions.

In classrooms a problem only exists if it impinges negatively on learning. If this is the case, the teacher must assess seriousness and weigh the problem's impact on student learning. Acting out behaviors, such as threats, loud talking, arguing, and fighting, are problems that must be addressed immediately, but incomplete assignments, attendance, sloppy work, and lost books, although readily identifiable problems, can wait to be resolved. Another category that must be remedied without delay is incidents such as cheating, slander, theft, safety that involves moral codes, or physical well-being.

Problems concerning withdrawal behaviors such as not paying attention, depression, drugs, and alcohol indicate a desire to flee from reality and must be dealt with expeditiously (Curwin 1997). It should be understood that most misbehavior is caused by frustration, ignorance, conflict, displacement, or misunderstanding rules and procedures. In contrast, the reasons for misbehavior can be identified as a desire to achieve one of four immediate goals: attention, power, revenge, or to avoid failure. In the final analysis the choice as to what constitutes a problem is the teacher's decision (Glasser 1990, 1997; Mager and Piper 1997).

Objectives

Teachers are fortunate when it comes to objectives. In classroom behavioral situations two objectives always remain the same: to facilitate learning and encourage self-discipline (Scarpaci 2007). All other objectives relate directly to identifying problems. Objectives describe, in measurable terms, the behaviors needed to attain the desired results within a specific time frame: for example, Billy will complete all ten incomplete assignments satisfactorily by the end of the semester.

- The "I" represents the first step in the process, to identify and assess the problem.
- The "O" stands for the objectives that you wish to achieve through your intervention.
- The "S" stands for the solution, which should be the result of the plan you put into effect to achieve your objectives.
- The "I" indicates the implementation of your plan and the procedures to be followed by the people who should be involved.
- The acronym concludes with the letter "E" that stands for your evaluation and reflection on results.

Figure 1 IOSIE analysis model.

Objectives are specific statements of a learner's behavior. They are the outcomes one wishes to obtain within a specific time limit. They can also be described as statements that answer two questions: What do I want my students to know? How will I know if my students understand? Good objectives show learners what is expected, how the work will be done, and what the minimum standards are. They are explicit, quantifiable, and achievable; they create an end result that can be met within a specific time frame.

Solutions

One of the keys to the IOSIE process is selection of strategy. The steps are not rigid but should be followed in sequence. The method presumes that there are three generic approaches to solutions for classroom misbehavior: a consequence, group guidance, and a guidance approach. A consequence approach such as assertive discipline (Canter and Canter 1976) implies consequences for improper actions. A group guidance approach such as judicious discipline (Gathercoal 1993) encourages classes to establish rules to prevent inappropriate actions. Finally, in a guidance approach such as reality therapy (Glasser 1999), the teacher counsels the rule offender, encouraging students to take ownership of problems. The purpose of each strategy is to assist students to develop self-discipline and responsibility for their actions. A good strategy must be comprehensive and contain in its design components both preventive and intervention procedures. The ideal is to prevent problems before they occur.

Implementation

The most difficult step is the actual implementation. Putting solutions into action is not simply a "just do it" sequence. Basic questions must be addressed before implementation: Who is to implement the solution? How do you get the cooperation and support of everyone involved? How long do you expect it will take before a positive result is accomplished? What happens if the solution does not work?

The answers to the first two questions are easy when the teacher is the implementer. They only become difficult when support and cooperation of parents, staff, and professionals outside of the school need to be elicited. The answer to the third question depends on the severity of the problem, the objectives set, and the resistance met. The personalities of all involved parties should also be considered. The only way to resolve the final question is to go back to the drawing board and attempt a different approach to the problem. When these four questions are satisfactorily answered a guide to evaluation is created.

Evaluation

Assessment of results is often forgotten, ignored, or done incorrectly by teachers. The easiest way to evaluate is to look at your objectives. Are they specific, measurable, and attainable within a defined time frame? Outcomes are wishes achieved within an explicit period and should be easily recognizable and readily assessable. The basic premise of any evaluation is to determine if you achieved what you set out to achieve. If the success lasts for only a brief time, then the solution was not really appropriate. An example would be a child who no longer fights at lunchtime but fights after school. Obviously something is wrong with this picture. If the results are not positive, the whole process must be reviewed. Was the problem really identified? Were the objectives attainable in the time span anticipated? Was the proposed solution appropriate for the objectives you wished to achieve? Was the implementation done correctly? Are you sure you did not succeed, even partially?

Sample Case Studies

Below are three case studies, one for each of the basic approaches, beginning with a case study that lends itself to a consequence strategy, which might afford positive results if implemented properly.

Consequence Approach

Billy Williams, a seventeen-year-old in your twelfth-grade mathematics class, has been accused in an unsigned note of extorting lunch money from his classmates. Billy has a prior record of supposed misdeeds. One specifically, although never proven, was when he was blamed for the recent rash of drug activity outside the school grounds. Billy's misdeeds have never been proven because no one has stood up and charged Billy with any specific misbehavior. For all intents and purposes, he lives under a cloud of suspicion. There are those who believe that Billy is innocent of any major wrongdoing, but their numbers are few. You have spoken to Billy on numerous occasions with regard to his lack of class work, homework, and general deportment during your class with little or no results. He claims he does not know why everyone thinks he is a criminal, because he has not done anything wrong. When you ask about his homework, he again changes the subject by confiding to you that even the principal has threatened him for no reason. He believes people dislike him because he is African American and therefore make up false rumors.

His classmates as well as most of the student body are in deathly fear of Billy because of his physical size and menacing presence. There is a rumor that he has been in fights after school, yet no one has come forward to point him out for any wrongdoing. A colleague tells you that you also have reason to fear for your own safety. Recently, Ms. Kumar had her tires slashed. Ms. Kumar believes the slashing was retaliation for her failing Billy for the first quarter of the semester. You also had expected to fail Billy before this morning's incident when Billy came to you and explained that he had to pass your class to graduate. He pleaded for you to give him a break and pass him. He said if you did not pass him, his parents would kick him out of their house when he turned eighteen.

IOSIE Analysis Using a Consequence Approach

Identify the Problem

What exactly is the problem in this case? Is it the unsigned note claiming that Billy is extorting money? Is it Billy's prior record of misdeeds? Is it Billy's lack of class work, homework, and poor deportment? Is it Billy's charge of racial bias on the part of those who dislike him? Is it the fights after school or Billy's menacing demeanor? Could it be Ms. Kumar's belief that you are in danger because she thinks Billy slashed her tires for failing him during the first quarter? Or could it be the problem Billy presented to you this morning when he said his parents would throw him out of their house if he did not graduate?

You can see that it is not always easy to determine the problem in any given situation. There are usually a number of problems. Look at the potential problems we identified and place them in some type of priority order to better understand the case. A prior record of unproven misdeeds and unsigned accusations should go to the bottom of any list of potential problems. Rumors regarding one's behavior outside of school are usually just gossip and unconfirmed. Billy's size and someone's unfounded accusation regarding slashed tires are not your problems. Billy's belief that he is the butt of racial prejudice is certainly a concern. It is not necessarily a problem that you face with him, because he has confided in you. Billy's academic performance and poor deportment are the immediate problem that you face. His feelings regarding prejudice should also be addressed as a long-term problem.

Objectives

Once the problem has been identified you have to determine your objectives. What is it exactly that you want Billy to do? Based on your identification of the problem, it would appear that you would expect Billy to improve his academic performance and his general behavior in your class for the remainder of the school term. With regard to his personal feelings with "racial bias," you should refer Billy to the appropriate support personnel within your school. This would usually be the school guidance counselor or school psychologist. If these personnel are not available the principal should be notified and outside assistance could also be sought.

Solutions

The solution to this problem should go back to how you can most easily achieve your objective. It would appear that Billy himself handed the answer to this dilemma to you. He gave you a consequence he did not wish to face. He was fearful of being thrown out of his parents' house. This consequence must be corroborated to implement your solution.

Implementation

Once you have confirmed with his parents that they have spoken to Billy and learned exactly what they had told him, you are than ready to implement your solution for your immediate problem of getting Billy to improve academically and behaviorally. Although the consequence is outside of your control, you should offer to assist Billy in avoiding the consequence. Provide tutorial assistance and counsel him on exactly the way you expect him to behave in your class. You should also arrange with the guidance counselor for Billy to be counseled regarding his feelings of prejudice.

Evaluation

Your self-assessment of the results in this case study should be easy to recognize. Did you achieve what you set out to do in the time frame you set up? Did Billy's academic performance and behavior improve incrementally by the end of the term as a result of the consequence with which he was faced? It is important to remember that there should be interim evaluations prior to the final assessment. This affords you the opportunity to fine-tune your solution or change direction if it is not working. If the answer to the prior question of his academic success was yes, congratulations, your solution worked. If the answer was no, then you should go back to your solution and attempt a different approach.

Sample Case Study

Guidance Approach

Sara Ramirez, a thirteen-year-old girl in your eighth-grade social studies class, places her coat and books wherever she chooses, totally disregarding the comfort of her fellow classmates. Students have complained to you but seem to be fearful of addressing Sara directly. Sara comes from a privileged one-parent family in which she has always been the apple of her father's eye. Sara stays with her elderly grandmother when her father is away on business trips, which seems to be most of the time. Sara boasts that she can come and go as she pleases. Sara's mother is fighting for custody, but she is having a difficult time because of her prior drug and mental health issues.

Sara is an average student with definite adolescent tendencies. She is physically mature for her age, dressing way beyond her years, yet at times she acts like a child. She constantly discards her refuse by placing it on a neighbor's desk when she believes no one is looking or throwing it on the floor when they are looking. She is the first to push her way into the wardrobe at dismissal to retrieve her coat. She likes to push other students' chairs about the room thereby creating obstructions so that her classmates have difficulty finding their seats. Sara constantly laughs at the discomfort she creates for her classmates. She teases the boys, and then complains that they are bothering her. During class she is always calling out and gets angry when she is not called on. As a result her class work has deteriorated. You have spoken to her and warned her that her grade would suffer if she continues being disruptive in class. Sara, in true adolescent fashion, "yeses" you to death and continues to misbehave.

IOSIE Analysis Using a Guidance Approach

Identify the Problem

Is the problem Sara's apparent disregard for her classmates? Is it that she appears to be a physically mature child with less than adequate supervision? Is her grandmother too old and her father too distant? Is she reacting to her mother's attempt to gain custody? Could she just be a mean-spirited child, or are there deeper meanings for her antisocial behavior? Is the real problem the deterioration of her grades?

Again, this case study is overburdened with potential problems. Remember this child's specific actions—throwing papers, pushing, teasing the boys, laughing at others, and calling out—are really not the problem but indications that there is a problem. How do you identify the problems that you wish to address? The key is to prioritize. What is the first role of a teacher? Is it to see that her students are learning? In this case Sara's grades have fallen so her academic needs must be considered. Sara's family life seems to be unstable and uncontrollable. Emotional problems are rampant throughout this case description. Therefore, her immediate problem is to improve her grades. The question is how you attempt to do that while this child is facing so many emotional problems at home that are manifesting themselves in her actions at school.

Objectives

Your objectives are in two interrelated areas: improvement of academic standing and emotional well-being. Your objective should be to have Sara improve her grades before the end of the marking period. A second and concomitant objective should be to help guide Sara through the emotional upheaval in her young life.

Solutions

The objectives are easy to establish, but the resolution for Sara may be much more difficult. A guidance approach on your part requires a caring positive relationship with the child. You may want to have a private heart-to-heart in which you encourage Sara to confide in you. You should also explain to Sara that her grades are a major part of her life and must improve. The reason for this is that if Sara could get guidance she could learn to deal with her family environment, which would allow her to work at improving her grades. Her disruptive behavior and antisocial actions in class should stop of their own accord. Once Sara accepts responsibility for her actions and understands that she cannot necessarily change the actions of others, she will be on the path to understanding her problems. Once she understands that she is responsible for choosing her own behavior, she will be better able to deal with the problems she faces.

Implementation

In this case study the implementation is much more difficult than it was in the previous study. In this situation the teacher is expected to assume the role of guide and mentor. These are roles for whom not all are suited. Even if you were suited, the time needed would take away from your primary classroom duties. You would therefore have to seek the assistance of the guidance counselor and involve the family. Most likely the counselor would suggest family counseling as well as individual sessions with Sara. Your role would remain as guide and mentor, yet your actual functions are lessened.

Evaluation

When using a guidance approach, assessment of objectives should be ongoing. Emotional problems can be easily inflamed, especially when parents are fighting over custody. Your evaluation of success should be focused on her academic studies and classroom behavior. The counselor should keep you informed as to the steps she is taking with the child and family. The same cooperation and communication must be established with any outside counseling that might occur. In this case a positive report card would indicate movement in the proper direction.

Sample Case Study

Group-Guidance Approach

Third-grade student Abdul Hussein cries continually during your class. He complains that everyone is picking on him because of his religious beliefs and because he is Arabic. Abdul's behavior has gone from being cooperative, practically docile, to sulking and at times raging at his classmates. Recently Abdul's class work has gone from exceptional to abysmal. You have never seen any of the incidents even though they have been graphically described by Abdul and just as vocally denied by his classmates. The incidents described consist of stolen or spoiled lunches, torn textbook pages, missing homework, and obscene drawings in Abdul's notebooks. Abdul further claims that the other children claim he is responsible for 9/11. Abdul cries when he tells you that his uncle was killed in the World Trade Center while working. He implies that the children call him a liar and they blaspheme his faith. Abdul's parents have complained to you and request that you do something to stop the harassment of their son.

The president of the parents' association, whose son is also in your class, claims that her child thinks Abdul is a compulsive liar and is just acting the way he does to get your attention. She also claims that someone has been destroying other children's property in the class. She believes it is Abdul. Other parents of children in the class concur with the parents' association president. The situation comes to a head when you see the children fighting in the schoolyard at lunchtime. The children claim that Abdul attacked them when they said they would not play with him. He spit at them and called them dirty names.

IOSIE Analysis Using a Group-Guidance Approach

Identify the Problem

Is the problem Abdul's constant crying and whining during class time? Is it the charges of bias toward Abdul's religion and ethnicity? Is it the multitude of incidents in which Abdul's property has been despoiled? Or is it Abdul's academic performance? In this case study there seems to be a clear link between Abdul's academic performance and the incidents, real or imaginary, that have occurred recently. These incidents appear to have been motivated by group racial bias. In this case there are three distinct and interrelated problems that must be addressed: academic performance, racial and religious issues, and physical incidents of misbehavior.

Objectives

Your first objective is to have Abdul return to doing his superior academic work, while simultaneously educating the class with regard to racial and religious bias as well as eliminating incidents of violence and vandalism. If the first two objectives are achieved, the incidents will also end. The physical episodes are a direct result of the apparent racial intolerance that seems to have infected the class.

Solutions

The solution is based on dealing with the question of group tolerance. Guide the class to solve the problem by using a group guidance exercise. Prepare the class by having them read a children's version of *The Diary of Anne Frank* at home with their parents. Read it aloud to the class during a block of instructional time set aside specifically for this purpose. The project requires dividing the class into two subgroups by drawing straws out of a hat. The groups consist of those with red circles and those with green circles, which the children must prominently display on their clothing. The children with the red circles are to make all of the class rules, which must be obeyed by all green circle children. Focus the class by establishing the first three rules:

1. Green-circle children must never line up before a red-circle child at entrance, dismissal, or lunchtime; they must always walk at the back of the line.
2. Green-circle children must keep their heads lower than red-circle children at all times and never look them in the eyes.
3. In any discussion between circle children, the red-circle children will always be considered correct.

The class at the end of the experiment (no more than two days) will evaluate the impact and the result of creating an intolerant society in which there are rulers and second-class citizens. They will be asked to describe their feelings with regard to injustice and intolerance.

Implementation

To implement a scenario as described above takes the cooperation and support of parents, administration, and various mental health providers. The purpose of the exercise should be explained to parents, and be supported by the school administration. Mental health providers such as the school guidance counselor, school psychologist, and outside defamation organizations should be involved.

Evaluation

Assessments when dealing with mental health problems can only be made by evaluating the end product. What did the children describe as their feelings? Did the class want to continue the project? Have the incidents stopped and has Abdul stopped crying, and been allowed to rejoin the class? If the exercise achieves all of its objectives, it is a success.

It should be noted that a group-guidance approach is froth with potential for manipulation (Landau 2000). It is not necessary to be objective when dealing with a situation as described in this case. One should realize, however, that as human beings we do not see resolutions through the same perspective. Children must be given the opportunity to develop their critical-thinking abilities if we are to truly function as a democratic society. A democratic classroom is the single best precursor for a free and democratic nation.

Conclusion

The IOSIE management model is essentially a common sense way for analyzing student behavioral problems. It is a user-friendly approach that provides a framework for teachers to use in resolving the multitude of management problems faced every day. The mnemonic IOSIE applied properly acts as a rubric for guiding teacher actions needed to resolve student behavioral problems. The method provides teachers a strategy to analyze and resolve common, and some not so common, behavioral problems.

References

Canter, L., and M. Canter. 1976. *Assertive discipline: A take charge approach for today's educator.* Seal Beach, CA: Canter and Associates.

Curwin, R. 1997. Discipline with dignity: Beyond obedience. *Education Digest.* December 11–14.

Danforth, S., and J. R. Boyle. 2000. *Cases in behavior management.* Upper Saddle River, NJ: Merrill/Prentice Hall.

Gathercoal, P. 1993. *Judicious discipline.* 3rd ed. San Francisco: Caddo Gap.

Glasser, W. 1990. *The quality school.* New York: Harper and Row.

———. 1997. A new look at school failure and school success. *Phi Delta Kappan* 78:596-602.

——— 1999. *Choice theory: A new psychology of personnel freedom.* New York: Harper Collins.

Landau, B., and P. Gathercoal. 2000. Creating peaceful classrooms: Judicious discipline and class meetings. *Phi Delta Kappan* 81:450–54.

Mager, F. R., and P. Piper. 1997. *Analyzing performance problems: Or you really oughta wanna.* 3rd ed. Atlanta: Center for Effective Performance.

Scarpaci, R. 2007. *A case study approach to classroom management.* New York: Allyn and Bacon.

Richard T. Scarpaci is an assistant professor and director of Field Experiences at St. John's University Staten Island campus, New York. He has taught courses in management and methods as well as conducted Child Abuse and Violence Prevention Seminars.

Mismatch

When state standards and tests don't mesh, schools are left grinding their gears.

HEIDI GLIDDEN AND AMY M. HIGHTOWER

Imagine this: Sylvia and Steve are seventh-graders in different states. They're both eager, hard-working students, and do reasonably well in school. Come springtime, they join most students across the country in taking various state assessments in (at least) reading and mathematics. You know these tests: they're the ones that teachers give to students on behalf of their state to monitor how students are doing in school. They are also used for federal accountability purposes to determine if schools and school districts are doing a good job educating students.

Sylvia and Steve have had different experiences with these assessments. For Sylvia, they're just par for the course. Sure, she'd rather be playing softball, but taking a test of the things she's been taught that year in school has become routine. No huge surprises, no big deal.

But bluntly put, Steve is dreading assessment season this year, based on the state test he had to take last year in math. Last year, he'd worked hard to learn the material he was taught. He always submitted the homework his teacher assigned and listened hard as his teacher explained the concepts of mean, median, and mode. From fractions and ratios to probability and circumference, Steve felt like he was mastering some tough sixth-grade math concepts. His teacher thought so too, giving him *A*s and *B*s all year. When springtime testing came around, he'd been ready to strut his stuff. But when he sharpened his #2 pencil and sat down to take the state test, darned if they didn't ask him about the Pythagorean Theorem and three-dimensional objects!

These were things he hadn't studied and his teacher hadn't taught. Wait, wasn't his brother, an eighth-grader, studying some of this stuff? How was he supposed to know the answers now? Had someone given him the wrong test by mistake? No mistake: He just didn't have the knowledge he needed to answer the questions. So he did what anyone in this situation would do—he flipped through the exam and guessed. And he fidgeted. And he watched the clock, waiting for the uncomfortable moment to pass. He remembers the moment like it was yesterday.

What went wrong? Why did both Sylvia and Steve feel ready for the test, but only one of them was actually prepared? Here's a dirty little secret that educators know all too well: State tests and state content standards don't always match up. It's far too often assumed that what's expected, what's taught, and what's tested are cut from the same cloth. That's the way it should be. It's what advocates of standards-based education assumed. It's certainly rational, and it's something that's never even questioned by the general public once the test results come in—the results that judge students, schools, and sometimes teachers. But as it turns out, this assumption is too often untrue and a lot of things are at play behind the scenes.

As it happens, Steve's state isn't particularly clear about what it expects of students in each grade and in each subject. This puts his teachers in a guessing game about what to teach. It also has test developers guessing about what content to sample from as they design their assessments. Maybe they guess the same, and maybe they don't. But why leave it to chance?

Sylvia's state, in contrast, is more explicit about the grade-by-grade standards students are to meet. Her state doesn't direct teachers in *how* to teach or at what precise moment to introduce a particular concept, but it does set specific, helpful year-end goals for every grade and every subject. These standards are explicit enough for teachers like Sylvia's to build their curriculum around and for testing companies to know what content to draw upon for their tests.

While Steve and Sylvia are fictitious, the problem we've identified is real. Based on our research, just 11 states are like Sylvia's, with all of their reading and math tests clearly aligned to strong standards. The rest, to a greater or lesser extent, are like Steve's. In fact, nine states do not have any of their reading or math tests aligned to strong standards. The consequences are far-reaching since the results of these tests are used to make consequential, high-stakes judgments.

No Child Left Behind (NCLB) has led to the vast expansion of states' testing programs and heightened the stakes associated with testing results. Specifically in reading and math,[1] NCLB requires states to have grade-level standards in grades 3 to 8 and once in high school, and to annually test students in grades 3 to 8 and at least once in high school using assessments that are criterion-referenced/standards-based and aligned with the state's content area standards. The results of these assessments are used to determine if schools and districts are making adequate yearly progress. If not, NCLB imposes a series of escalating sanctions. (To learn more about NCLB, see www.aft.org/topics/nclb/index.htm.)

Given the fact that state standards are often deemed inadequate (see, for example, "The State of State Standards 2006" from the Thomas B. Fordham Institute; "Staying on Course" from Achieve Inc.; and "Making Standards Matter" from the American Federation of Teachers), we wondered how states are doing in developing assessment systems that meet NCLB's requirements and, therefore, can be legitimately used for accountability purposes. So we conducted a study to address two key questions. First, since (as we demonstrate in the next section) it is not possible to align a test to vague standards, are states' content standards in reading and math clear and specific? Second, for those standards that are clear and specific, is there evidence posted on states' Web sites for all to see that the state assessments are aligned with those standards?

For grades 3 to 8 and high school, we looked at all 50 states' and the District of Columbia's reading and math standards, as well as at the test specifications that the states and D.C. provide to their test developers.[2] Of course, we would have preferred to look directly at the actual tests, but they are confidential. Nevertheless, looking at the test specifications is the next best option; it seems highly unlikely that a test could be better aligned to the standards than the specifications upon which the test is based.

Just 11 states have all of their reading and math tests clearly aligned to strong standards. Nine states do not have any of their reading or math tests aligned to strong standards.

Our first step was to examine the strength, clarity, and specificity of the standards themselves. Content standards are at the heart of everything that goes on in a standards-based system, including testing. They define our expectations for what's important for children to learn, and serve as guideposts about what content to teach and assess. These state-developed public documents are the source that teachers, parents, and the general public consult to understand content-matter expectations. Content standards should exist for every single grade, kindergarten through high school, in every subject. Grade-by-grade content standards increase the likelihood that all students are exposed to a rigorous, sequenced curriculum that is consistent across schools and school districts. Grade-specific standards also make it possible to align not only assessments, but also curriculum, textbooks, professional development, and instruction. States that organize their standards grade-by-grade are best able to specify what students should learn and when they should learn it.

We examined each state's content-standards documents to determine whether there was enough information about what students should learn to provide the basis for teachers to develop a common core curriculum and for the test developer to create aligned assessments. There is no perfect formula for this; we made a series of judgments based on a set of criteria. **To be judged "strong," a state's content standards had to:**

- Be detailed, explicit, and firmly rooted in the content of the subject area so as to lead to a common core curriculum;
- Contain particular content:
  - Reading standards must cover reading basics (e.g., word attack skills, vocabulary) and reading comprehension (e.g., exposure to a variety of literary genres);
  - Math standards must cover number sense and operations, measurement, geometry, data analysis and probability, and algebra and functions;
- Provide attention to both content and skills; and,
- Be articulated without excessive repetition in both math and reading in grades 3, 4, 5, 6, 7, 8, and once in high school.

For any standard we found to be strong, we then examined the extent to which the state's test specifications were aligned with the standard. In our alignment review, each state received a yes/no judgment for each of the NCLB-related tests it administered. **To meet our criteria for alignment, a state must:**

- Have evidence of the alignment of its tests and content standards through documents such as item specifications, test specifications, test blueprints, test development reports, or assessment frameworks; and,
- Post the alignment evidence on its Web site in a transparent manner.

The need for alignment should be obvious, but the need for transparency may not be. Transparency "demystifies" how (or if) the pieces connect to function as a unified *system.* A transparent system is not necessarily an aligned system, but only with transparency can we determine if the tests and content standards are aligned. A transparent testing program provides information to parents, students, teachers, and the public about the development, purpose, and use of state tests. It also brings any problems within the testing program to light so that they can be addressed. This is why, in our review, states could not simply assert that their tests were aligned to their standards. And yet, our alignment criteria were still not as stringent as we believe they should be. A state could receive alignment credit for fairly minimal documentation. For example, if a state had grade-by-grade math standards organized by number sense, algebra, measurement, etc., we gave that state credit for evidence of alignment if it indicated the percentage of items devoted to each of these topics.

Grade-by-grade content standards increase the likelihood that all students are exposed to a rigorous, sequenced curriculum that is consistent across schools and school districts.

As our opening vignette indicates, what we found was not what the average person would assume. There were two basic problems: Standards that were too weak to guide teachers or test developers, and standards that were strong, yet mismatched with tests nonetheless. To explain the problems with the weak standards, in the following section, we provide examples of vague and repetitious standards—and examples that show why tests cannot be aligned with such weak standards. We wrap up that section with data on how widespread weak standards are. Then we turn to the mismatch between strong standards and test specifications. Once again we provide examples of the mismatch as well as data on how widespread this problem is.

Vague Standards Inevitably Lead to Mismatch

The quality of content standards matters greatly to teaching, learning, and testing, so it directly affects the fairness and validity of tests and the accountability systems they support. Despite this obvious and indisputable fact, we found that across the country, many states have failed to write clear and specific standards for every subject and grade. As you read the examples[3] of vague state standards in the table below, consider them from both the teachers' and the test developers' perspectives. None of these standards gives enough information to teachers about what to teach or to test developers about what to test.

Subject	Grade(s)	Examples of Vague Content Standards
Reading	4	Demonstrate the understanding that the purposes of experiencing literary works include personal satisfaction and development of lifelong literature appreciation.
	8	View a variety of visually presented materials for understanding of a specific topic.
Math	4	Students will describe, extend, and create a wide variety of patterns using a wide variety of materials (transfer from concrete to symbols).
	9-12	Model and analyze real-world situations by using patterns and functions.

In contrast, take a look at the following standards; they are clear and specific enough to eliminate the guesswork.

Subject	Grade	Examples of Strong Content Standards
Reading	4	Distinguish between cause and effect and between fact and opinion in informational text. Example: In reading an article about how snowshoe rabbits change color, distinguish facts (such as snowshoe rabbits change color from brown to white in the winter) from opinions (such as snowshoe rabbits are very pretty animals because they can change colors).
Math	4	Subtract units of length that may require renaming of feet to inches or meters to centimeters. Example: The shelf was 2 feet long. Jane shortened it by 8 inches. How long is the shelf now?

These latter examples are particularly strong—most states do not have standards this clear and specific. Instead, most states occupy a middle ground between these and the terribly vague standards shown previously. But even with middling standards, it's very hard for a teacher to know what to teach and a test developer to know what to test. Teachers may feel like they just have to make do—but test developers often do not. In states with weak standards, additional information is often given to testing companies that further clarifies or elaborates on the standard to be tested. In essence, these states are creating an additional layer or set of "shadow" standards, which are often more specific and detailed than the official standards from which they presumably came. However, it is the test developer who receives these "shadow" standards, not teachers.

Surprised? So were we. Let's look at an example to make this a little easier to understand. Here is a 4th-grade math standard and the corresponding test specification. Clearly, the test developer received much more specific information than teachers—information that would be just as helpful in preparing lessons as it is in preparing tests.

What 4th-grade teachers receive

Describe, model, and classify two- and three-dimensional shapes

What the test developer receives

Students demonstrate understanding of two- and three-dimensional geometric shapes and the relationships among them. In the grade 4 test, understanding is demonstrated with the following indicators as well as by solving problems, reasoning, communicating, representing, and making connections based on indicators—

- Using properties to describe, identify, and sort 2- and 3-dimensional figures [Vocabulary in addition to that for grade 3: polygon; kite; pentagon; hexagon; octagon; line; line segment; parallel, perpendicular, and intersecting lines]
- Recognizing two- and three-dimensional figures irrespective of their orientation
- Recognizing the results of subdividing and combining shapes, e.g., tangrams
- Recognizing congruent figures (having the same size and shape) including shapes that have been rotated

Clearly, it is possible for a teacher to believe she has covered a vague standard, and for a test developer to come up with an angle that she hasn't considered. In the example above, a teacher may do several lessons on describing, modeling, and classifying two- and three-dimensional shapes—but she may not think to teach students to recognize them "irrespective of their orientation," as the test specifications state. The only way to avoid such problems is for the teachers and the test developers to receive the same clear, detailed standards.

Some states are creating "shadow" standards, which are often more specific and detailed than the official standards. However, it is the test developer who receives these "shadow" standards, not teachers.

Repetition Makes Standards Vague

Even when states manage to write standards that sound reasonably specific, they sometimes poison the effort by repeating the standard over four or more grades. This problem is especially evident in states' reading standards. For example, one state's reading standards expect eighth-graders to, among other things, "develop a critical stance and cite evidence to support the stance;" "use phonetic, structural, syntactical, and contextual clues to read and understand words;" and "describe how the experiences of a reader influence the interpretation of a text." That may sound reasonable—but the exact same thing is expected of 2nd-graders, 10th-graders, and students in every other grade in between.

Repetition of standards makes it hard, if not impossible, for a teacher to know what content students have mastered in previous grades or to determine the specific differences in student expectations from grade to grade. It certainly isn't enough for a teacher to build his or her lesson plans.

Let's look a little more at that state that expects 2nd- through 10th-graders to develop a critical stance. The vast majority of its reading standards are exactly the same from grade 3 to grade 10 and, shockingly, *more than 40 percent of the 10th-grade standards come from grade 2 standards:*

- 71 percent of the 4th-grade standards are repeated (56 percent come from grade 2)
- 87 percent of the 6th-grade standards are repeated (44 percent come from grade 2)
- 92 percent of the 8th-grade standards are repeated (42 percent come from grade 2)
- 81 percent of the 10th-grade standards are repeated (42 percent come from grade 2)

What 3rd- and 4th-grade teachers receive

Determines meaning of words through knowledge of word structure (e.g., compound nouns, contractions, root words, prefixes, suffixes)

What the test developer receives

Determines meaning of words through knowledge of word structure (e.g., compound nouns, contractions, root words, prefixes, suffixes)

Grade 3 test

Assessment Indicators
Prefixes: *mis-, pre-, pro-, re-, un-*
Suffixes: *-ed, -er, -est, -ing, -ly, -y*
Only test prefixes and suffixes listed above

Grade 4 test

Assessment Indicators
Prefixes: *anti-, dis-, ex-, non-, under-*
Suffixes: *-en, -ful, -less, -ment, -ness*
Only test prefixes and suffixes listed above

One can easily imagine how 2nd- and 9th-grade teachers, for example, would develop different lesson plans based on these repetitive standards. But what would prevent 2nd- and 3rd-grade teachers from teaching almost identical lessons? And what happens to the unlucky student who is assigned in 4th, 5th, and 6th grades to use *Charlotte's Web* to "describe how the experiences of a reader influence the interpretation of a text." Or the unlucky student who is never assigned *Charlotte's Web* for any reason? A central purpose of state standards is to avoid such repetition and such gaps—but repetitive standards that do not specify what should be taught at each grade can't serve that purpose and, as a result, they can't be used to develop standards-based tests either.

Unfortunately, the example we've been using is a pretty typical one. Here's an example of reading standards from another state that are even more repetitious from grade to grade:

- 75 percent of the 3rd-grade standards are repeated from K-2
- 98 percent of the 5th-grade standards are repeated from grade 4
- 94 percent of the 7th-grade standards are repeated from grade 4

Repetitious standards are neither clear nor specific enough to guarantee that what's taught in each and every grade and subject is also what's tested. The result? Guesswork on the part of teachers and testing companies. Or, as we saw with the vague standards, sometimes the teachers are left to guess, but the test developers get the extra information they need.

In this example, 3rd- and 4th-grade teachers work from the exact same reading standard, with no indication of what is appropriate for a 3rd-grader versus a 4th-grader. The test developer, however, receives the standard *plus* specific indicators of what is appropriate for a 3rd-grader and what is appropriate for a 4th-grader:

Unlike teachers' information about the reading standard for grades 3 and 4, the test developers receive indicators that are unique to each grade. The indicators add information that would be useful to teachers, but teachers don't receive them—nor do they necessarily know that such an elaboration even exists. An excellent 3rd-grade teacher could, in good conscience and with good reason, deliver highly effective instruction on the prefixes *anti-, dis-,* and *non-,* but because she guessed wrong as to what would be on the 3rd-grade test versus the 4th-grade test, her test results would indicate that her students did not know anything about prefixes. Of course, the 4th-grade teacher is in an equally difficult position—how is she to know which prefixes the students have already learned and which will be tested?

Vague and repetitious standards are clearly a big problem, but just how widespread are they? It depends on the subject. States tend to have fairly good math standards, but weak reading standards. Here is what we found:

- **A majority of states have grade-by-grade reading and math standards in every grade that NCLB requires them to assess.** Six states still have not developed grade-by-grade standards in reading and math despite being required to do so by the guidance written for NCLB: Colorado, Illinois, Montana, Nebraska, Pennsylvania, and Wisconsin. At the high school level, 20 states clustered their reading standards and 22 clustered their math standards.

For example, while 3rd- and 4th-grade teachers work from the exact same standard, the test developer receives specific indicators of what is appropriate for a 3rd-grader and what is appropriate for a 4th-grader.

- **But, grade-by-grade standards do not guarantee clear, specific standards: Only a little more than one-third of states have strong reading and math standards in every grade that NCLB requires them to assess.** Just 18 states and the District of Columbia met our criteria for having strong standards in reading and math in all grades that NCLB requires states to assess: California, Georgia, Indiana, Louisiana, Massachusetts, Michigan, Nevada, New Jersey, New Mexico, New York, North Carolina, North Dakota, Ohio, South Dakota, Tennessee, Virginia, Washington, and West Virginia.
- **Across states and subjects, of all the 714 content standards reviewed, 70 percent met our criteria for being strong.** States had strong standards in mathematics: Eighty-seven percent of the math standards we reviewed met our criteria. In contrast, only about half of the states' reading content standards met our criteria (53 percent).
- **On average, the most vague and repetitious content standards are in reading.** Only 20 states had strong reading standards in grades 3 to 8 and high school; 12 states had weak reading standards in all of these grades. Twenty-one percent of all reading standards reviewed

Science Standards and Tests Suffer from Mismatch, Too

No Child Left Behind (NCLB) is somewhat more lenient with science than it is with reading and math. Science standards need not be grade by grade; academic expectations at each of the three grade-level ranges (such as grades 3 to 5, 6 to 9, and 10 to 12) are sufficient. Likewise, starting in the 2007–2008 school year, science must be assessed annually, but just once during elementary, middle/junior high, and high school—and the results are not incorporated into federally required accountability determinations.

Nonetheless, we still wanted to examine states' science standards and the extent to which their standards and test specifications are aligned. Unfortunately, as with reading and math, we found serious problems.

As we explained in the main article, grade-by-grade standards are essential for guiding instruction. And yet, 13 states cluster their science standards at the elementary level, 13 states at the middle-school level, and 21 states at the high-school level. While permitted under NCLB, clustering results in vague standards such as these:

- Grades 5 to 8—Describe the historical and cultural conditions at the time of an invention or discovery, and analyze the societal impacts of that invention;
- Grades 9 to 12—Analyze the impacts of various scientific and technological developments.

Besides getting frustrated, what is a teacher or a test developer to do with such a directive? The teacher can guess what will be tested, and the test developer can guess what will be taught. Or, they can demand more specifics from the state. For the test developers at least, such demands appear to be working.

Take a look at the following example of one 7th-grade science standard and the corresponding test specification—it reveals something we reported on in the main article with reading and math. The test designer gets the same standard that is given to teachers, as well as very specific examples that help clarify the focus of the standard.

What 7th-grade teachers receive:

The student will cite examples of individuals throughout history who made discoveries and contributions in science and technology.

What the test developer receives:

The student will cite examples of individuals throughout history who made discoveries and contributions in science and technology.

- Examples of individuals (and some of their discoveries or contributions) are limited to: Rachel Carson–*Silent Spring;* George Washington Carver–agricultural products, technology; Nicolas Copernicus–Copernican revolution; Charles Darwin–classification, ecology, and natural selection; Galileo Galilei–gravity and telescopes; Jane Goodall–primate research; James Hutton–geology; Anton van Leeuwenhoek and Robert Hooke–microscopy; Johann Gregor Mendel–genetics; Isaac Newton–gravity, mechanics, light, and telescopes; Louis Pasteur–pasteurization; and Alfred Wegener–plate tectonics.

As a teacher, wouldn't you feel like you covered the standard if you taught your students about Thomas Edison's light bulb, Eli Whitney's cotton gin, and Lord Kelvin's Kelvin scale? You might feel good, but you would not have prepared your students for a test that focused on Rachel Carson, George Washington Carver, and Johann Gregor Mendel. Teachers (and their students) would benefit significantly from the additional information provided to the test developers, but that information is not included as a part of the standards. Teachers wouldn't even know to look for this elaboration.

—H.G. and A.H.

were significantly repetitious across the grades (meaning word-by-word repetition across the grades at least 50 percent of the time). Fifteen states had reading standards that repeated the same reading standards in three or more grades.

In some states, the clarity and specificity of the standards are not the problem. The grade level and subject content to be taught are specific enough, but the tests simply cover other things.

Even with Strong Standards, Mismatch Can Happen

In some states, the clarity and specificity of the standards are not the problem; instead, it is the lack of follow-through. The grade level and subject content to be taught are specific enough, but the tests simply cover other things. For example, in one state, the 3rd-grade test pulls content from both the 3rd- and 4th-grade standards:

A 3rd-grade teacher in this state is unlikely to have her students prepared for questions relating to words with multiple meanings, antonyms, or synonyms because, according to the state's content standards, these concepts are not to be addressed until grade 4. As the example above demonstrates, the specific content standards that teachers receive from their state don't always match up with what the state gives test developers to create the tests.

Here's another example (taken from a different state) that reveals a similar problem. In this case, there are 8th-grade math standards and test specifications that *almost* match up. Both the standards and test specifications are about measurement, but they diverge in two important ways. First, although the standards say nothing explicitly about converting measurements, the test specification expects students to make several different types of conversions. Second, one of those conversions—moving from Fahrenheit to Celsius—involves content not even included in the 8th-grade standards.

The 8th-grade standards have content that would require students to have, as the assessment anchor requires, "an understanding of measurable attributes of objects and figures, and the units, systems, and processes of measurement." However, since teachers do not receive the specifics that the test developer receives, the 8th-grade teachers do not know to devote extra time to conversions, and the 8th-grade teachers—and their students—end up with the blame when the students perform poorly on the test.

What 3rd-grade teachers receive

Third-grade student uses a variety of strategies to determine meaning and increase vocabulary (for example, prefixes, suffixes, root words, less common vowel patterns, homophones, compound words, contractions)

What 4th-grade teachers receive

Fourth-grade student uses a variety of strategies to determine meaning and increase vocabulary (for example, multiple meaning words, antonyms, synonyms, word relationships, root words, homonyms)

What the 3rd-grade test developer receives

Third-grade test content limit—Vocabulary words for prefixes (e.g., *re-, un-, pre-, dis-, mis-, in-, non-*), suffixes (e.g., *-er, -est, -ful, -less, -able, -ly, -or, -ness*), root words, multiple meanings, antonyms, synonyms, homophones, compound words, and contractions should be on grade level

What 8th-grade teachers receive

Under the header "Measurement and Estimation" are the following seven standards:

- Develop formulas and procedures for determining measurements (e.g., area, volume, distance)
- Solve rate problems (e.g., rate × time = distance, principle × interest rate = interest)
- Measure angles in degrees and determine relations of angles
- Estimate, use and describe measures of distance, rate, perimeter, area, volume, weight, mass, and angles
- Describe how a change in linear dimension of an object affects its perimeter, area, and volume
- Use scale measurements to interpret maps or drawings
- Create and use scale models

What the 8th-grade test developer receives

Assessment Anchor: Demonstrate an understanding of measurable attributes of objects and figures, and the units, systems, and processes of measurement.

Convert measurements: Eligible Content

- Convert among all metric measurements (milli, centi, deci, deka, kilo using meter, liter, and gram)
- Convert customary measurements to 2 units above or below the given unit (e.g., inches to yards, pints to gallons)
- Convert time to 2 units above or below a given unit (e.g., seconds to hours)
- Convert from Fahrenheit to Celsius or Celsius to Fahrenheit

Because of NCLB's testing requirements, states have rushed to establish tests that comply with the law. However, there appears to be very little urgency to align those tests with the content standards or be transparent about which standards are assessed. Here is what we found:

Where and Why Does Mismatch Exist?

Only 11 states met our criteria for having tests transparently aligned to strong standards: Calif., Ind., La., Nev., N.M., N.Y., Ohio, Tenn., Va., Wash., and W.Va. This table shows why the others fell short.

State	Some test specifications not online	Some mismatch between standards and test specifications	Percentage of strong reading and math standards	Percentage of tests transparently aligned to strong reading and math standards
Alabama		✓	79	64
Alaska			79	79
Arizona			71	71
Arkansas	✓		79	0
Colorado		✓	14	14
Connecticut		✓	50	0
Delaware	✓		50	0
D.C.	✓		100	0
Florida			64	64
Georgia		✓	100	57
Hawaii	✓		50	0
Idaho		✓	57	50
Illinois		✓	0	0
Iowa	✓		0	0
Kansas			50	50
Kentucky			57	57
Maine	✓		50	7
Maryland	✓		57	57
Massachusetts	✓		100	43
Michigan	✓		100	43
Minnesota			50	50
Mississippi		✓	86	79
Missouri	✓	✓	50	0
Montana	✓	✓	0	0
Nebraska	✓	✓	29	29
New Hampshire			50	50
New Jersey	✓	✓	100	43
North Carolina	✓	✓	100	43
North Dakota	✓		100	0
Oklahoma			86	86
Oregon			71	71
Pennsylvania		✓	57	57
Rhode Island			50	50
South Carolina	✓	✓	64	14
South Dakota		✓	100	50
Texas			57	57
Utah		✓	71	50
Vermont	✓		57	57
Wisconsin		✓	21	0
Wyoming		✓	71	0

- **Eleven states met our criteria for having both strong reading and math standards and documenting in a transparent manner that their tests align to them in all NCLB-required grades.** They are: California, Indiana, Louisiana, Nevada, New Mexico, New York, Ohio, Tennessee, Virginia, Washington, and West Virginia. Eleven states is not a lot, but keep in mind that states could fall short for several reasons—having some content standards that are weak, not aligning their strong standards to their tests, and/or not providing evidence of alignment online. Of those who fell short (39 states plus the District of Columbia), 17 did so because at least some of their testing documents were not online, 32 did so because at least some of their standards were weak, and 18 did so because their standards and tests were not aligned.

- **An additional three states had at least 75 percent of their tests aligned to strong content standards.** With a few adjustments in particular grades or in just one subject, these additional three states would fully meet our criteria for alignment to strong content standards: Mississippi (meeting 86 percent of our criteria), Oklahoma (meeting 86 percent), and Alaska (meeting 78 percent).
- **Twice as many states met our criteria for having strong and transparently aligned standards and tests in math than they did in reading.** Twenty-six states have aligned math tests across all grades tested. But, just 13 states have aligned reading tests across all grades tested.

Overall, our results lead us to conclude that states are doing a better job in developing content standards than in using them to drive assessment. Simply put, in too many cases, tests that are not aligned to strong standards are driving many accountability systems. In order to comply with NCLB, states have been under enormous pressure to quickly develop new assessment systems. We hope this research provides some ideas on how they could improve those systems in the near future. For example, state departments of education need to post their content standards on their Web sites, along with information about how their state tests are aligned to these standards—they also need to keep this information current. When test developers or state officials clarify standards in order to write test items that align to them, the clarifications should be made public and should make their way back to the original standards document in the form of clearly marked revisions. This way, educators will be able to skip the guessing game and teach the content that the state believes is most important.

Detailed information about content standards and what will be tested should be readily available to anyone (teachers, students, parents, the general public) at any point, and should not have to be ferreted out. Educators, in particular, need to know that what will be tested draws from the content standards to which they are teaching. Where there's a mismatch, or a fuzzy match, or only an assumed match between the content that's expected and the content that's assessed—and when the results are used to judge students, schools, and teachers—it's no wonder that folks in schools toss up their hands in frustration.

Notes

1. NCLB also requires states to have science standards and, as of the 2007–2008 school year, administer science tests, but the law does not hold states accountable for their science results. Therefore, our main analysis focuses on reading and math, and we deal with science briefly in the box on page 195.
2. For brevity's sake, throughout this document when we refer to the states collectively, we are actually referring to the 50 states and the District of Columbia.
3. When providing examples, we chose not to name the states in the main article because it would unfairly place emphasis on them instead of on the broader problem. The examples are drawn from the following states: 1) vague standards—Arkansas, Connecticut, and Montana; 2) strong standards—Indiana; 3) repetitious standards—Connecticut and Texas; 4) mismatched standards and test specifications—Florida, Kansas, Minnesota, Montana, and Pennsylvania.

Heidi Glidden, assistant director, and Amy M. Hightower, associate director, are assessment and accountability specialists for the AFT teachers division. This article is based on a research brief they published in July 2006.

Assessment Through the Student's Eyes

Rather than sorting students into winners and losers, assessment for learning can put all students on a winning streak.

Rick Stiggins

Historically, a major role of assessment has been to detect and highlight differences in student learning in order to rank students according to their achievement. Such assessment experiences have produced winners and losers. Some students succeed early and build on winning streaks to learn more as they grow; others fail early and often, falling farther and farther behind.

As we all know, the mission of schools has changed. Today's schools are less focused on merely sorting students and more focused on helping *all* students succeed in meeting standards. This evolution in the mission of schools means that we can't let students who have not yet met standards fall into losing streaks, succumb to hopelessness, and stop trying.

Our evolving mission compels us to embrace a new vision of assessment that can tap the wellspring of confidence, motivation, and learning potential that resides within every student. First, we need to tune in to the emotional dynamics of the assessment experience from the point of view of students—both assessment winners and assessment losers. These two groups experience assessment practices in vastly different ways, as shown in "The Assessment Experience," p. 24. To enable all students to experience the productive emotional dynamics of winning, we need to move from exclusive reliance on assessments that verify learning to the use of assessments that support learning—that is, assessments *for* learning.

Assessment *for* Learning

Assessment for learning turns day-to-day assessment into a teaching and learning process that enhances (instead of merely monitoring) student learning. Extensive research conducted around the world shows that by consistently applying the principles of assessment for learning, we can produce impressive gains in student achievement, especially for struggling learners (Black & Wiliam, 1998).

Assessment for learning begins when teachers share achievement targets with students, presenting those expectations in student-friendly language accompanied by examples of exemplary student work. Then, frequent self-assessments provide students (and teachers) with continual access to descriptive feedback in amounts they can manage effectively without being overwhelmed. Thus, students can chart their trajectory toward the transparent achievement targets their teachers have established.

The students' role is to strive to understand what success looks like, to use feedback from each assessment to discover where they are now in relation to where they want to be, and to determine how to do better the next time. As students become increasingly proficient, they learn to generate their own descriptive feedback and set goals for what comes next on their journey.

Teachers and students are partners in the assessment for learning process. For example, teachers might have students study samples of work that vary in quality and collaborate in creating their own student-friendly version of a performance assessment scoring rubric. Or students might create practice versions of multiple-choice tests that parallel the content of an upcoming final exam, which they can then use to analyze their own strengths and weaknesses and to focus their final preparation for that exam. Students can accumulate evidence of their learning in growth portfolios. They can also become partners with teachers in communicating about their own learning successes by leading their parent/teacher conferences.

Assessment for learning provides both students and teachers with understandable information in a form they can use immediately to improve performance. In this context, students become both self-assessors and consumers of assessment information. As they experience and understand their own improvement over time, learners begin to sense that success is within reach if they keep trying. This process can put them on a winning streak and keep them there.

When we use assessment for learning, assessment becomes far more than merely a one-time event stuck onto the end of an instructional unit. It becomes a series of interlaced experiences that enhance the learning process by keeping students confident and focused on their progress, even in the face of occasional setbacks.

The goal of assessment for learning is not to eliminate failure, but rather to keep failure from becoming chronic and thus inevitable in the mind of the learner. Duke University basketball coach Mike Krzyzewski has pointed out that the key to winning is to avoid losing twice in a row (Kanter, 2004, p. 251). He meant that if you lose once and fix it, you can remain confident. Losing twice, though, can raise questions, crack that confidence, and make recovery more difficult. So when learners suffer a failure, we must get them back to success as quickly as possible to restore their confidence in their capabilities. This is the emotional dynamic of assessment for learning.

We can't let students who have not yet met standards fall into losing streaks, succumb to hopelessness, and stop trying.

Scenario 1: Set Students Up for Success

Here is an example of the use of assessment for learning that builds student confidence from the start. Notice who develops and uses the assessment.

A high school English teacher assigns students to read three novels by the same author and develop a thesis statement about a common theme, consistent character development, or social commentary in the novels. They must then defend that thesis in a term paper with references. To set students up for success, the teacher begins by providing them with a sample of an outstanding paper to read and analyze. The next day, the class discusses what made the sample outstanding.

As their next assignment, the teacher gives students a sample paper of poor quality. Again, they analyze and evaluate its features in some detail. Comparing the two papers, students list essential differences. The class then uses this analysis to collaboratively decide on the keys to a high-quality paper.

After identifying and defining those keys, the students share in the process of transforming them into a rubric—a set of rating scales depicting a continuum of quality for each key. The teacher provides examples of student work to illustrate each level on the quality continuum.

Only after these specific understandings are in place do students draft their papers. Then they exchange drafts, analyzing and evaluating one another's work and providing

The Assessment Experience

For Students on Winning Streaks	For Students on Losing Streaks
Assessment Results Provide	
Continual evidence of success	Continual evidence of failure
The Student Feels	
Hopeful and optimistic Empowered to take productive action	Hopeless Initially panicked, giving way to resignation
The Student Thinks	
It's all good. I'm doing fine. See the trend? I succeed as usual. I want more success. School focuses on what I do well. I know what to do next. Feedback helps me. Public success feels good.	This hurts. I'm not safe here. I just can't do this . . . again. I'm confused. I don't like this—help! Why is it always about what I can't do? Nothing I try seems to work. Feedback is criticism. It hurts. Public failure is embarrassing.
The Student Becomes More Likely to	
Seek challenges. Seek exciting new ideas. Practice with gusto. Take initiative. Persist in the face of setbacks. Take risks and stretch—go for it!	Seek what's easy. Avoid new concepts and approaches. Become confused about what to practice. Avoid initiative. Give up when things become challenging. Retreat and escape—trying is too dangerous!
These Actions Lead to	
Self-enhancement Positive self-fulfilling prophecy Acceptance of responsibility Manageable stress Feeling that success is its own reward Curiosity, enthusiasm Continuous adaptation Resilience Strong foundations for future success	Self-defeat, self-destruction Negative self-fulfilling prophecy Denial of responsibility High stress No feelings of success; no reward Boredom, frustration, fear Inability to adapt Yielding quickly to defeat Failure to master prerequisites for future success

descriptive feedback on how to improve it, always using the language of the rubric. If students want descriptive feedback from their teacher on any particular dimension of quality, they can request and will receive it. The paper is finished when the student says it is finished. In the end, not every paper is outstanding, but most are of high quality, and each student is confident of that fact before submitting his or her work for final evaluation and grading (Stiggins, in press; Scenario 1 adapted by permission).

Scenario 2: Help Students Turn Failure into Success

Here is an illustration of assessment for learning in mathematics used to help a struggling elementary student find the path to recovery from a chronic sense of failure. Notice how the teacher highlights the meaning of success and turns the responsibility over to the student. In addition, notice how the learner has already begun to internalize the keys to her own success.

Gail is a 5th grader who gets her math test back with "60 percent" marked at the top. She knows this means another *F.* So her losing streak continues, she thinks. She's ready to give up on ever connecting with math.

But then her teacher distributes another paper—a worksheet the students will use to learn from their performance on the math test. What's up with this? The worksheet has several columns. Column one lists the 20 test items by number. Column two lists what math proficiency each item tested. The teacher calls the class's attention to the next two columns: *Right* and *Wrong.* She asks the students to fill in those columns with checks for each item to indicate their performance on the test. Gail checks 12 right and 8 wrong.

The teacher then asks the students to evaluate as honestly as they can why they got each incorrect item wrong and to check column five if they made a simple mistake and column six if they really don't understand what went wrong. Gail discovers that four of her eight incorrect answers were caused by careless mistakes that she knows how to fix. But four were math problems she really doesn't understand how to solve.

Next, the teacher goes through the list of math concepts covered item by item, enabling Gail and her classmates to determine exactly what concepts they don't understand. Gail discovers that all four of her wrong answers that reflect a true lack of understanding arise from the same gap in her problem-solving ability: subtracting 3-digit numbers with regrouping. If she had just avoided those careless mistakes and had also overcome this one gap in understanding, she might have received 100 percent. Imagine that! If she could just do the test over . . .

She can. Because Gail's teacher has mapped out precisely what each item on the test measures, the teacher and students can work in partnership to group the students according to the math concepts they haven't yet mastered. The teacher then provides differentiated instruction to the groups focused on their conceptual misunderstandings. Together the class also plans strategies that everyone can use to avoid simple mistakes. When that work is complete, the teacher gives students a second form of the same math test. When Gail gets the test back with a grade of 100 percent, she jumps from her seat with arms held high. Her winning streak begins (Stiggins, Arter, Chappuis, & Chappuis, 2004; Scenario 2 adapted by permission).

Redefining Our Assessment Future

We know how to deliver professional development that will give practitioners the tools and technologies they need to use assessment effectively in the service of student success. (Stiggins et al., 2004; Stiggins & Chappuis, 2006). Thus far, however, the immense potential of assessment for learning has gone largely untapped because we have failed to deliver the proper tools into the hands of teachers and school leaders. If we are to fulfill our mission of leaving no child behind, we must adjust our vision of excellence in assessment in at least two important ways that will help us balance assessment *of* and assessment *for* learning.

First, we must expand the criteria by which we evaluate the quality of our assessments at all levels and in all contexts. Traditionally, we have judged quality in terms of the attributes of the resulting scores; these scores must lead to valid and reliable inferences about student achievement. As a result, schools have lavished attention on characteristics of the instruments that produce such scores. In the future, however, we must recognize that assessment is about far more than the test score's dependability—it also must be about the score's effect on the learner. Even the most valid and reliable assessment cannot be regarded as high quality if it causes a student to give up.

We must begin to evaluate our assessments in terms of both the quality of the evidence they yield and the effect they have on future learning. High-quality assessments encourage further learning; low-quality assessments hinder learning. Understanding the emotional dynamics of the assessment experience from the student's perspective is crucial to the effective use of assessments to improve schools.

Second, we must abandon the limiting belief that adults represent the most important assessment consumers or data-based decision makers in schools. Students' thoughts and actions regarding assessment results are at least as important as those of adults. The students' emotional reaction to results will determine what they do in response. Whether their score is high or low, students respond productively when they say, "I understand. I know what to do next. I can handle this. I choose to keep trying." From here on, the result will be more learning. The counterproductive response is, "I don't know what this means. I have no idea what to do next. I'm probably too dumb to learn this anyway. I give up." Here, the learning stops.

In standards-driven schools, only one of these responses works, especially for students who have yet to meet standards. Assessment *for* learning is about eliciting that productive response to assessment results from students every time. It can produce winning streaks for *all* students.

References

Black, P., & Wiliam, D. (1998). Assessment and classroom learning. *Educational Assessment: Principles, Policy, and Practice, 5*(1), 7–74.

Kanter, R. M. (2004). *Confidence: How winning streaks and losing streaks begin and end.* New York: Crown Business.

Stiggins, R. J. (in press). Conquering the formative assessment frontier. In J. McMillan (Ed.), *Formative assessment: Theory into practice.* New York: Teachers College Press.

Stiggins, R. J., Arter, J. A., Chappuis, J., & Chappuis, S. (2004). *Classroom assessment FOR student learning: Doing it right—using it well.* Portland, OR: ETS Assessment Training Institute.

Stiggins, R. J., & Chappuis, J. (2006). What a difference a word makes: Assessment FOR learning rather than assessment OF learning helps students succeed. *Journal of Staff Development, 27*(1), 10–14.

Rick Stiggins is Founder and Director of the ETS Assessment Training Institute, 317 SW Alder St., Suite 1200, Portland, OR, 97204; 800-480-3060. www.ets.org/ati.

Grades as Valid Measures of Academic Achievement of Classroom Learning

JAMES D. ALLEN

What is the purpose of grades? In this article I present one answer to this question from a perspective that many educators might see as somewhat radical or extreme. The perspective that I take is based on the fundamental educational psychology assessment principle of validity—the validity of what learning is being assessed and the validity of the communication of that assessment to others. I believe most teachers fail to give grades to students that are as valid as they should be. Because grading is something that has been done to each of us during our many years as students, it is hard to change the invalid "grading" schema that has become embedded in our minds. Now, as educators often required to grade students, and because of this embedded schema, we often grade students in invalid ways similar to how we were graded. Inadequate education in valid assessment and grading principles and practices is a reason many teachers continue to perpetuate invalid grading practices with students. Since educational testing and assessment is a major content knowledge area in educational psychology, the issues regarding assessment and grading that I address in this article could well be addressed in an educational psychology course. If our preservice and inservice teachers are going to learn appropriate assessment and grading practices then educational psychologists need to provide the relevant information in their classes.

The most fundamental measurement principle related to meaningful assessment and grading is the principle of validity (Gallagher 1998; Gredler 1999; Linn and Gronlund 2000; Stiggins 2001). Although there are many validity issues involved in classroom assessment that classroom teachers should consider, such as making sure the way they assess students corresponds to the type of academic learning behaviors being assessed (Ormrod 2000), the focus here is on the valid assessment and communication of final class grades as summaries of students' academic achievement of content knowledge of a subject. Validity addresses the accuracy of the assessment and grading procedures used by teachers (Gallagher 1998; Gredler 1999; Linn and Gronlund 2000). Do the assessment procedures and assignment of grades accurately reflect and communicate the academic achievement of the student? Validity is important because the sole purpose of grades is to accurately communicate to others the level of academic achievement that a student has obtained (Snowman and Biehler 2003). If the grades are not accurate measures of the student's achievement, then they do not communicate the truth about the level of the student's academic achievement. Unfortunately, as stated by Cizek, even as "grades continue to be relied upon to communicate important information about [academic] performance and progress . . . they probably don't" (1996, 104).

Assigning grades to students is such a complex (and sometimes controversial) issue that some educators have proposed their abolition (Kohn 1999; Marzano 2000). Although I find this an interesting proposal, especially if one is trying to establish a classroom learning environment that is student-centered and encourages self-regulation and self-evaluation, the current reality for most teachers is that they are required to assign grades indicating students' academic achievement in the subjects they teach. Therefore, grading should be as valid as possible. Not only is grading a major responsibility of classroom teachers, but it is also a practice with which they are often uncomfortable and that they find difficult (Barnes 1985; Lomax 1996; Thorndike 1997). The sources of the discomfort and difficulty for teachers regarding the grading of students seem to be threefold. First, the student activities that teachers think should constitute "academic achievement" and how to handle ancillary features of achievement such as students' efforts varies tremendously from teacher to teacher. Although ancillary information such as effort and attitude could be part of an overall student report, they should not be part of a grade that represents academic achievement (Tombari and Borich 1999). Second, teachers often seem to be unsettled regarding the communication function of grades, and they often try to communicate multiple pieces of information about students that can not possibly be contained within a single academic mark. This is an issue of making sure the grade is accurate as a valid communication to others. Third, because of the first two issues, many teachers assign grades that are invalid and not built on a solid principle of measurement (Cizek 1996; Marzano 2000). In addition, partially due to their long career as students experiencing invalid grading practices, as well as inadequate preservice and inservice education on assessment and grading, teachers continue to perpetuate invalid grading practices. Let us consider each of these points in greater depth.

Miscommunication and Confusing Purposes of Grades

Although students learn many things in the classroom, the primary objective is for students to learn academic content knowledge of a particular subject. In order for teachers to know if students are achieving this academic knowledge, they generally are required to not only assess students' knowledge in some way, but eventually summarize that assessment into a letter or numerical grade. This is known as "summative" evaluation. Hopefully, teachers are also gathering nongraded "formative" assessments of students to provide feedback to students as they learn, as well as considering how to motivate students to learn and encouraging them to be self-regulated learners. However, generally, teachers have to eventually place a grade on a grade sheet indicating what level of content knowledge a student has achieved in the subject listed. But why do we place a grade on a grade sheet, report card, or transcript? Why do we create a permanent written record of the grade? And why is the grade listed next to a name of an academic course such as English, U.S. History, Algebra, or Educational Psychology?

As illustrated by the title of the 1996 Yearbook of the Association for Supervision and Curriculum Development, Communicating Student Learning to interested parties is an important function of schools and teachers (Guskey 1996). Although there are various means to communicate student learning, currently a single report card grade for each academic subject is the most common and generally accepted system in middle and secondary schools (Bailey and McTighe 1996; Lake and Kafka 1996). Bailey and McTighe argue that as a communication system, "the primary purpose of secondary level grades and reports [is] to communicate student achievement" so that informed decisions can be made about the student's future (1996, 120). Similarly, authors of major texts devoted to classroom assessment suggest that the major reason for assigning grades is to create a public record of a student's academic achievement that can accurately and effectively communicate to others the level of mastery of a subject a student has demonstrated (Airasian 2000; Gallagher 1998; Gredler 1999; Linn and Gronlund 2000; Nitko 2001; Oosterhof 2001; Stiggins 2001). Nitko points out that: "Grades . . . are used by students, parents, other teachers, guidance counselors, school officials, postsecondary educational institutions, and employers. Therefore [teachers] must assign grades with utmost care and maintain their validity" (2001, 365). However, according to Marzano, in contrast to teachers', students', parents', and community members' assumption that grades are valid "measures of student achievement . . . grades are so imprecise that they are almost meaningless" (2000, 1). Due to the wide variability in the criteria used in grading practices from teacher to teacher, the validity of student grades is unknown and they have limited value as guides for planning the academic and career futures of students (Thorndike 1997). Thus, if a single grade on a report card or transcript is to effectively communicate information to all these varied parties, then that single grade has to have some shared and accurate meaning (O'Connor 1995).

This lack of shared meaning seems to be found throughout our education system. A study by Baron (2000) shows that there is lack of coherence in the beliefs about grades held by parents and students and those held by the education community. Even in the same school, teachers often hold very different views about the purpose of grades and fail to communicate with their colleagues about their grading practices (Kain 1996). Grading practices by teachers rarely follow the measurement principles and grading practices recommended in measurement textbooks (Cross and Frary 1996; Frary, Cross, and Weber 1993). New teachers often work independently and are left to figure out their own grading policies, gradually adhering to the school's norms. There is a similar lack of coherence and communication among college teachers (Barnes, Bull, Campbell, and Perry 1998). Friedman and Frisbie (1995, 2000) make a particularly strong argument for making sure that report card grades accurately report information to parents about a student's academic progress and that teachers and administrators share a common understanding of what information a grade should communicate. They suggest that since grades become part of a students' permanent record, the purpose of these grades must be to communicate a valid summary of a student's academic achievement in the subject that is listed next to the grade on the record.

Grading systems used by teachers vary widely and unpredictably and often have low levels of validity due to the inclusion of nonacademic criteria used in the calculation of grades (Allen and Lambating 2001; Brookhart 1994; 2004; Frary, Cross, and Weber 1993; Olson 1989). Teachers have been found to make decisions about grades related to student effort in attempts to be "fair" in their grading practices (Barnes 1985). Studies have found that two out of three teachers believe that effort, student conduct, and attitude should influence final grades of students (Cross and Frary 1996; Frary, Cross, and Weber 1993). It has also been shown that grades are used as a motivational tool as well as to develop good study habits (Oosterhof 2001) and desirable classroom management behaviors (Allen 1983). Grades should not be a hodgepodge of factors such as student's level of effort, innate aptitude, compliance to rules, attendance, social behaviors, attitudes, or other nonachievement measures (Friedman and Frisbie 2000; Ornstein 1994). Although these factors may indirectly influence students' achievement of content knowledge, subjective—and often unknown to the teacher—factors such as these complicate the ability to interpret a grade since these factors may directly conflict with each other and distort the meaning of a grade measuring academic achievement (Cross and Frary 1996; Guskey 1994; Linn and Gronlund 2000; Nitko 2001; Stiggins 2001; Stumpo 1997). Nonacademic factors are often used as criteria for assigning grades because some teachers consider the consequences of grades more important than the value of clear communication of information and the interpretability of the grades (Brookhart 1993). It follows then that instead of the grade being a function of what a student has learned it has become a function of many variables. Simply put, it would appear that grades are often measures of how well a student lives up to the teacher's expectation of what a good student is rather than measuring the student's academic achievement in the subject matter objectives.

A grade can not be a teacher's "merged judgment"[1] of these factors, since as a single letter or numeric mark, the reported grade must communicate a single fact about the student if it is to be a valid or accurate source of information coherently shared between the reporter of the grade and the grade report's audience. How is the reader of a student's single grade on a transcript to know which factors are included and how much each unknown factor was weighed by the grade-giver to determine the grade? Also, since many of these factors such as effort, motivation, and student attitude are subjective measures made by a teacher, their inclusion in a grade related to academic achievement increases the chance for the grade to be biased or unreliable, and thus invalid. The purpose of an academic report is to communicate the level of academic achievement that a student has developed over a course of study. Therefore, the sole purpose of a grade on an academic report, if it is to be a valid source of information, is to communicate the academic achievement of the student. If other factors about the student are deemed important, such as a student's attitude, level of effort, or social behavior, then other appropriate forms of reporting these factors must be made available and used. If a multidimensional view of the student is desired, then a multidimensional system of reporting is required. Using a single grade as a summary of a teacher's "merged judgment" of a student leads to miscommunication, confusion, and a continuation of the lack of coherence among stakeholders about what a grade represents.

Since important decisions are often based on a student's grade, invalid grades may result in dire consequences for the student. Grades can open up or close down important learning opportunities for students (Jasmine 1999). With high grades, students get admitted to colleges and universities of their choice and receive scholarships and tuition assistance, since grades are a major selection criterion in the college admission process. The reverse is also true. It is very difficult for students to get admitted to some schools if their grades are not sufficiently high. Invalid grades that understate the student's knowledge may prevent a student with ability to pursue certain educational or career opportunities. Also, based on principles of attribution and social cognitive theories, if students receive grades lower than ones that accurately depict their true level of academic knowledge, it may lead students to believe they lack the ability to succeed academically and lower their sense of self-efficacy as well as their motivation to learn (Pintrich and Schunk 2002).

Grading and Lack of Professional Training

Cizek argues that the "lack of knowledge and interest in grading translates into a serious information breakdown in education" and that "reforming classroom assessment and grading practices will require educators' commitment to professional development, [and] classroom-relevant training programs" (1996, 103). Cizek's statement implies that an important area that needs to be addressed is the training of teachers in grading practices based on sound measurement principles relevant to their classroom lives.

This lack of knowledge about measurement theory and application to grading practices is a pervasive problem with preservice teacher training at the college level (Goodwin 2001; Schafer 1991; Stiggins 1991, 1999). One of the goals of a teacher education program should be to prepare preservice and in-service teachers to develop effective methods to assess students and to communicate clearly and accurately through their grading practices that assessment to others. However, very few teacher education programs include measurement or assessment courses. Allen and Lambating (2001) found in a random sample of teacher education programs that less than one-third required an assessment course, and many of those that did were courses focused on "informal" assessments, or standardized assessment of students with special needs and not focused on classroom assessment and grading. Fewer than half of the fifty states require specific coursework on assessment for their initial certification of teachers (Lomax 1996; O'Sullivan and Chalnick 1991; Stiggins 1999).

Although assigning grades is probably the most important measurement decision that classroom teachers make, the coverage of grading in assessment textbooks is often not as fully developed as other measurement topics that are less relevant to teachers' day-to-day assessment practices (Airasian 1991; Lomax 1996). According to Stiggins (1999), how the concepts of "reliability" and "validity" are related to classroom grading practices is not addressed in the courses which introduce these terms to our preservice teachers. It is important to look at this issue because validity and reliability are considered the most fundamental principles related to measurement and therefore important to classroom assessment and grading (Gallagher 1998; Gredler 1999; Linn and Gronlund 2000).

Some argue that even when teachers are provided with some measurement instruction, they still use subjective value judgements when assigning grades (Brookhart 1993). Undergraduate teacher education majors, when asked about the criteria that should be used for their own grades, believe that "effort" is more important than amount of academic content learned (Placier 1995). One contributing factor may be that after sixteen years of obtaining grades based on factors other than academic achievement, teachers-in-training have a difficult time accepting theoretical principles that do not match with their personal experience. Many beliefs about school practices are well established before students enter college and often are resistant to change (Britzman 1986, 1991; Ginsberg and Clift 1990; Holt-Reynolds 1992; Pajares 1992; Richardson 1996). They form many of their perspectives about teaching from their years of observing teachers and their teaching practices (Lortie 1975). They have been recipients of hundreds of grades from their K–12 teachers and college professors before taking on the responsibility of assigning grades to their own students. Their perception regarding grades comes from their own long experience as students.

Brookhart (1998) suggests that classroom assessment and grading practices are at the center of effective management of classroom instruction and learning. Through the use of real classroom scenarios, preservice teachers need to be taught assessment strategies in relationship to instruction and not as decontextualized measurement principles. As the past president of the American Educational Research Association, Lorrie Shepard has stated: "The transformation of assessment practices cannot be accomplished in separate tests and measurement courses, but rather should be a central concern in teaching methods courses" (2000, 4). In addition to instruction on how to assess and grade using sound principles of measurement, research suggests that preservice teachers need hands-on experience in grading students and how to work with cooperating teachers who assess and grade in ways different than those learned by the preservice teachers (Barnes 1985; Lomax 1996).

What the literature suggests is that educators at all levels make decisions when assigning grades that are not based on sound principles of validity that ensure the grade is a meaningful communication of a student's level of academic achievement. The literature also suggests that students in teacher education programs may be more influenced by the grading practices they have experienced as students in the past, as well as in their current courses taught by their education professors, than by what they learn about assessment and grading in their courses. Additionally, teachers in the field, as products of teacher education programs, seem to exhibit grading practices that confirm that they have not been influenced by measurement courses (Lambating and Allen 2002). This may be because they did not take any assessment courses, or because their long-held beliefs about grading were left unchallenged and the courses did not focus on assessment and grading issues related to measuring classroom learning.

Educational Implications and Conclusion

Concerns about the validity and reliability of grades for communicating meaningful information about students' academic progress have been raised for a long time (see Starch and Elliot 1912, 1913a, 1913b; Adams 1932). In addition, trying to help teachers to understand the purpose and effective functions of grades in the overall evaluation system has been addressed repeatedly in the literature (Airasian 2000; Brookhart 1993; Cross and Frary 1996; Gredler 1999; Guskey 1996; Linn and Gronlund 2000; Marzano 2000; O'Connor 1995; Stiggins 2001). However, there seems to be little progress being made in this area in actual classroom practice.

Two major thrusts need to occur in reforming grading practices. First, if factors such as effort, attitude, compliance, and behavior are to be noted about a student on a report card, then they should be reported with a separate mark and not figured in as part of a grade for academic achievement of content knowledge. However, as in most situations, if a teacher must summarize and communicate a student's classroom progress in an academic subject through a single report card grade, then there must be a consensus that the grade represents the most accurate statement of the student's academic achievement, and only academic achievement. This is the essence of valid assessment. To include nonacademic criteria, such as the student's effort, compliance, attitude, or behavior, makes the grade impossible to interpret in any meaningful way. Perhaps, a simple way to reach this consensus is to teach ourselves and those we prepare to be teachers to reflect on the following question: "If I was given a student's transcript with a single letter grade listed next to the subject I teach, what would be the most logical interpretation I could make about what the grade represents about the student's knowledge of that academic subject?" Therefore, that is what I should try to have my grades communicate to whomever will read and interpret them in the future.

In order for teachers to act consistently in assigning valid grades based only on appropriate achievement criteria, a second major initiative needs to be undertaken to help teachers understand how to make good grading decisions. This initiative is best addressed through teacher education programs taking on the challenge to improve the assessment training of their students and improve their own grading practices. This entails several dimensions.

First, students' long-held beliefs about the purpose and use of grades need to be challenged by teacher educators. Students' beliefs and value systems related to grades need to be exposed and examined to help them understand the unscientific basis of their grading beliefs. Second, once these beliefs are exposed, instructors must provide students with the theoretical base for good assessment and grading practices as explicated by measurement experts that would replace students' naive notions of assessment and grading. This could be either through self-contained measurement courses taught in a relevant manner by educational psychologists, or integrated into methods courses through collaboration between educational psychology and teacher-education specialists. It would help if more teacher-education programs required adequate instruction on classroom assessment and grading practices. There also needs to be more effective and meaningful grading practices addressed in-depth in measurement textbooks. Third, teacher education students need to be provided with opportunities to encounter grading activities before they are placed into student teaching, in order to practice applying assessment principles and theory to classroom grading issues. Finally, during student teaching experiences, education majors must be given the opportunity, in conjunction with their cooperating teachers and the support of their college supervisors, to actually develop and implement a valid evaluation and grading plan. Schools of education need to work with school district teachers to help improve the communication system for which grades function. Providing in-service "assessment and grading" workshops for practicing teachers, especially those operating as cooperating teachers, might help to establish a consensus of what is appropriate criteria to use for determining and assigning valid grades to indicate academic achievement.

One way to accomplish many of the above steps is through the use of case studies that focus on assessment and grading dilemmas often faced by real teachers. Discussion of case studies can help students to reflect on and expose their belief systems about grades and grading, and analyze them in relationship to educational psychology assessment principles such as validity. One example is the Sarah Hanover case which focuses on a grading dilemma a teacher must deal with when the question of the validity of a student's grade is raised by the student's parent (Silverman, Welty, and Lyon 1996).

However, the area that may be the most difficult to address is the change in the grading practices that teacher educators use in evaluating students. As long as preservice and in-service teachers take classes from education professors who base grading decisions on more than academic achievement, they will have little reason to either believe what we say or practice what we preach about assessment and grading. As teacher educators, we need to model sound grading practices in our own courses in which grades accurately communicate students' achievement of content knowledge learned in our courses, and not how hard they work or how often they attend our classes.

My intention in this article has been to suggest that by giving serious reflection to the meaning of the educational psychology measurement principle of validity, grading practices can improve and the grades we assign to students as teachers can be more accurate and educationally meaningful. We need to begin to break the cycle of invalid grading practices that prevail throughout the education system, and the only behaviors we as teachers can truly control are our own.

Key words: grading, education system, assessment

Note

1. The author has borrowed this phrase from an anonymous reviewer.

References

Adams, W. L. 1932. Why teachers say they fail pupils. *Educational Administration and Supervision* 18:594–600.

Airasian, P. W. 1991. Perspectives on measurement instruction. *Educational Measurement: Issues and Practice* 10 (1): 13–16, 26.

———. 2000. *Assessment in the classroom: A concise approach.* 2nd ed. Boston: McGraw-Hill.

Allen, J. D. 1983. Classroom management: Students' perspectives, goals and strategies. Paper presented at the annual meeting of the American Educational Research Association, Montreal, Canada, April.

Allen, J. D., and J. Lambating. 2001. Validity and reliability in assessment and grading: Perspectives of preservice and inservice teachers and teacher education professors. Paper presented at the annual meeting of the American Educational Research Association, Seattle, April.

Bailey, J., and J. McTighe. 1996. Reporting achievement at the secondary level: What and how. In Guskey 1996, 119–40.

Barnes, L. B., K. S. Bull, N. J. Campbell, and K. M. Perry. 1998. Discipline-related differences in teaching and grading philosophies among undergraduate teaching faculty. Paper presented at the annual meeting of the American Educational Research Association, San Diego, April.

Barnes, S. 1985. A study of classroom pupil evaluation: The missing link in teacher education. *Journal of Teacher Education* 36 (4): 46–49.

Baron, P. A. B. 2000. Consequential validity for high school grades: What is the meaning of grades for senders and receivers? Paper presented at the annual meeting of the American Educational Research Association, New Orleans, April.

Britzman, D. P. 1986. Cultural myths in the making of a teacher: Biography and social structure in teacher education. *Harvard Educational Review* 56 (4): 442–56.

———. 1991. *Practice makes practice: A critical study of learning to teach.* New York: State University of New York Press.

Brookhart, S. M. 1993. Teachers' grading practices: Meaning and values. *Journal of Educational Measurement* 30 (2): 123–42.

———. 1994. Teachers' grading: Practice and theory. *Applied Measurement in Education* 7 (4): 279–301.

———. 1998. Teaching about grading and communicating assessment results. Paper presented at the annual meeting of the National Council on Measurement in Education, San Diego, April, 1998.

———. 2004. *Grading.* Upper Saddle River, NJ: Pearson/Merrill/Prentice Hall.

Cizek, G. J. 1996. Grades: The final frontier in assessment reform. *NASSP Bulletin* 80 (584): 103–10.

Cross, L. H., and R. B. Frary. 1996. Hodgepodge grading: Endorsed by students and teachers alike. Paper presented at the annual meeting of the National Council on Measurement in Education, New York, April.

Frary, R. B., L. H. Cross, and L. J. Weber. 1993. Testing and grading practices and opinions of secondary teachers of academic subjects: Implications for instruction in measurement. *Educational Measurement: Issues and Practice* 12 (3): 2330.

Friedman, S. J., and D. A. Frisbie. 1995. The influence of report cards on the validity of grades reported to parents. *Educational and Psychological Measurement* 55 (1): 5–26.

———. 2000. Making report cards measure up. *Education Digest* 65 (5): 45–50.

Gallagher, J. D. 1998. *Classroom assessment for teachers.* Upper Saddle River, NJ: Merrill/Prentice Hall.

Ginsburg, M. B., and R. T. Clift. 1990. The hidden curriculum of preservice teacher education. In *Handbook of research on teacher education*, ed. W. R. Houston, 450–65. New York: Macmillan.

Goodwin, A. L. 2001. The case of one child: Making the shift from personal knowledge to informed practice. Paper presented at the annual meeting of the American Educational Research Association, Seattle, April.

Gredler, M. E. 1999. *Classroom assessment and learning.* New York: Longman.

Guskey, T. R. 1994. Making the grade: What benefits students? *Educational Leadership* 52 (2): 14–20.

———. 1996. *ASCD Yearbook, 1996: Communicating student learning.* Alexandria, VA: Association for Supervision and Curriculum Development.

Holt-Reynolds, D. 1992. Personal history-based beliefs as relevant prior knowledge in coursework: Can we practice what we preach? *American Educational Research Journal* 29 (2): 325–49.

Jasmine, T. 1999. Grade distributions, grading procedures, and students' evaluations of instructors: A justice perspective. *Journal of Psychology* 133 (3): 263–71.

Kain, D. L. 1996. Looking beneath the surface: Teacher collaboration through the lens of grading practices. *Teachers College Record* 97 (4): 569–87.

Kohn, A. 1999. Grading is degrading. *Education Digest* 65 (1): 59–64.

Lake, K., and K. Kafka. 1996. Reporting methods in grades K–8. In Guskey 1996, 90–118.

Lambating, J., and J. D. Allen. 2002. How the multiple functions of grades influence their validity and value as measures of academic achievement. Paper presented at the annual meeting of the American Educational Research Association, New Orleans, April.

Linn, R. L., and N. E. Gronlund. 2000. *Measurement and assessment in teaching*. 8th ed. Englewood Cliffs, NJ: Merrill/Prentice Hall.

Lomax, R. G. 1996. On becoming assessment literate: An initial look at preservice teachers' beliefs and practices. *Teacher Educator* 31 (4): 292–303.

Lortie, D. 1975. *Schoolteacher: A sociological study*. Chicago: University of Chicago Press.

Marzano, R. J. 2000. *Transforming classroom grading*. Alexandria, VA: Association for Supervision and Curriculum Development.

Nitko, A. J. 2001. *Educational assessment of students*. 3rd ed. Upper Saddle River, NJ: Merrill/Prentice Hall.

O'Conner, K. 1995. Guidelines for grading that support learning and student success. *NASSP Bulletin* 79 (571): 91–101.

Olson, G. H. 1989. On the validity of performance grades: The relationship between teacher-assigned grades and standard measures of subject matter acquisition. Paper presented at the annual meeting of the National Council on Measurement in Education, San Francisco, March.

Oosterhof, A. 2001. *Classroom application of educational measurement*. Upper Saddle River, NJ: Prentice Hall.

Ormrod, J. E. 2000. *Educational psychology: Developing learners*. 3rd ed. Upper Saddle River, NJ: Merrill/Prentice Hall.

Ornstein, A. C. 1994. Grading practices and policies: An overview and some suggestions. *NASSP Bulletin* 78 (561): 55–64.

O'Sullivan, R. G., and M. K. Chalnick. 1991. Measurement-related course work requirements for teacher certification and recertification. *Educational Measurement: Issues and Practice* 10 (1): 17–19, 23.

Pajares, M. F. 1992. Teachers' beliefs and educational research: Cleaning up a messy construct. *Review of Educational Research* 62 (3): 307–32.

Pintrich, P. R., and D. H. Schunk. 2002. *Motivation in education*. 2nd ed. Upper Saddle River, NJ: Merrill/Prentice Hall.

Placier, M. 1995. "But I have to have an A": Probing the cultural meanings and ethical dilemmas of grades in teacher education. *Teacher Education Quarterly* 22 (1): 45–63.

Richardson, V. 1996. The role of attitudes and beliefs in learning to teach. In *Handbook of research on teacher education*, 2nd ed., ed. J. Sikula, T. Buttery, and E. Guyton, 102–19. New York: Macmillan.

Schafer, W. D. 1991. Essential assessment skills in professional education of teachers. *Educational Measurement: Issues and Practice* 10 (1): 3–6, 12.

Shepard, L. A. 2000. The role of assessment in a learning culture. *Educational Researcher* 29 (7): 4–14.

Silverman, R., W. M. Welty, and S. Lyon. 1996. *Case studies for teacher problem solving*. 2nd ed. New York: McGraw-Hill.

Snowman, J., and R. F. Biehler. 2003. *Psychology applied to teaching*. 10th ed. Boston: Houghton Mifflin.

Starch, D., and E. C. Elliot. 1912. Reliability of grading of high-school work in English. *School Review* 20:442–57.

———. 1913a. Reliability of grading work in mathematics. *School Review* 21:254–59.

———. 1913b. Reliability of grading work in history. *School Review* 20:676–81.

Stiggins, R. J. 1991. Relevant classroom assessment training for teachers. *Educational Measurement: Issues and Practice* 10 (1): 7–12.

———. 1999. Evaluating classroom assessment training in teacher education programs. *Educational Measurement: Issues and Practice* 18 (1): 23–27.

———. 2001. *Student-involved classroom assessment*. 3rd ed. Upper Saddle River, NJ: Merrill/Prentice Hall.

Stumpo, V. M. 1997. 3-tier grading sharpens student assessment. *Education Digest* 63 (4): 51–54.

Thorndike, R. M. 1997. *Measurement and Evaluation*. 6th ed. Upper Saddle River, NJ: Merrill/Prentice Hall.

Tombari, M., and G. Borich. 1999. *Authentic assessment in the classroom*. Upper Saddle River, NJ: Merrill/Prentice Hall.

James D. Allen is a professor of educational psychology in the Department of Educational and School Psychology at the College of Saint Rose in Albany, New York.

From *The Clearing House*, May/June 2005, pp. 218–223. Reprinted by permission of the Helen Dwight Reid Educational Foundation. Published by Heldref Publications, 1319 Eighteenth St., NW, Washington, DC 20036-1802.

Seven Practices for Effective Learning

Teachers in all content areas can use these seven assessment and grading practices to enhance learning and teaching.

JAY MCTIGHE AND KEN O'CONNOR

Classroom assessment and grading practices have the potential not only to measure and report learning but also to promote it. Indeed, recent research has documented the benefits of regular use of diagnostic and formative assessments as feedback for learning (Black, Harrison, Lee, Marshall, & Wiliam, 2004). Like successful athletic coaches, the best teachers recognize the importance of ongoing assessments and continual adjustments on the part of both teacher and student as the means to achieve maximum performance. Unlike the external standardized tests that feature so prominently on the school landscape these days, well-designed classroom assessment and grading practices can provide the kind of specific, personalized, and timely information needed to guide both learning and teaching.

Classroom assessments fall into three categories, each serving a different purpose, *Summative* assessments summarize what students have learned at the conclusion of an instructional segment. These assessments tend to be evaluative, and teachers typically encapsulate and report assessment results as a score or a grade. Familiar examples of summative assessments include tests, performance tasks, final exams, culminating projects, and work portfolios. Evaluative assessments command the attention of students and parents because their results typically "count" and appear on report cards and transcripts. But by themselves, summative assessments are insufficient tools for maximizing learning. Waiting until the end of a teaching period to find out how well students have learned is simply too late.

Teachers should set up authentic contexts for assessment.

Two other classroom assessment categories—diagnostic and formative—provide fuel for the teaching and learning engine by offering descriptive feedback along the way. *Diagnostic* assessments—sometimes known as *pre-assessments*—typically precede instruction. Teachers use them to check students' prior knowledge and skill levels, identify student misconceptions, profile learners' interests, and reveal learning-style preferences. Diagnostic assessments provide information to assist teacher planning and guide differentiated instruction. Examples of diagnostic assessments include prior knowledge and skill checks and interest or learning preference surveys. Because pre-assessments serve diagnostic purposes, teachers normally don't grade the results.

Formative assessments occur concurrently with instruction. These ongoing assessments provide specific feedback to teachers and students for the purpose of guiding teaching to improve learning. Formative assessments include both formal and informal methods, such as ungraded quizzes, oral questioning, teacher observations, draft work, think-alouds, student-constructed concept maps, learning logs, and portfolio reviews. Although teachers may record the results of formative assessments, we shouldn't factor these results into summative evaluation and grading.

Keeping these three categories of classroom assessment in mind, let us consider seven specific assessment and grading practices that can enhance teaching and learning.

Practice 1: Use Summative Assessments to Frame Meaningful Performance Goals

On the first day of a three-week unit on nutrition, a middle school teacher describes to students the two summative assessments that she will use. One assessment is a multiple-choice test examining student knowledge of various nutrition facts and such basic skills as analyzing nutrition labels. The second assessment is an authentic performance task in which each student designs a menu plan for an upcoming two-day trip to an outdoor education facility. The menu plan must provide well-balanced and nutritious meals and snacks.

The current emphasis on established content standards has focused teaching on designated knowledge and skills. To avoid the danger of viewing the standards and benchmarks as inert content to "cover," educators should frame the standards and benchmarks in terms of desired performances and ensure that the performances are as authentic as possible. Teachers should then present the summative performance assessment tasks to students at the beginning of a new unit or course.

This practice has three virtues. First, the summative assessments clarify the targeted standards and benchmarks for teachers and learners. In standards-based education, the rubber meets the road with assessments because they define the evidence that will determine whether or not students have learned the content standards and benchmarks. The nutrition vignette is illustrative: By knowing what the culminating assessments will be, students are better able to focus on what the teachers expect them to learn (information about healthy eating) and on what they will be expected to do with that knowledge (develop a nutritious meal plan).

Second, the performance assessment tasks yield evidence that reveals understanding, When we call for authentic application, we do not mean recall of basic facts or mechanical plug-ins of a memorized formula. Rather, we want students to transfer knowledge—to use what they know in a new situation, Teachers should set up realistic, authentic contexts for assessment that enable students to apply their learning thoughtfully and flexibly, thereby demonstrating their understanding of the content standards.

Third, presenting the authentic performance tasks at the beginning of a new unit or course provides a meaningful learning goal for students. Consider a sports analogy. Coaches routinely conduct practice drills that both develop basic skills and purposefully point toward performance in the game. Too often, classroom instruction and assessment overemphasize decontextualized drills and provide too few opportunities for students to actually "play the game." How many soccer players would practice comer kicks or run exhausting wind sprints if they weren't preparing for the upcoming game? How many competitive swimmers would log endless laps if there were no future swim meets? Authentic performance tasks provide a worthy goal and help learners see a reason for their learning.

Practice 2: Show Criteria and Models in Advance

A high school language arts teacher distributes a summary of the summative performance task that students will complete during the unit on research, including the rubric for judging the performance's quality. In addition, she shows examples of student work products collected from previous years (with student names removed) to illustrate criteria and performance levels. Throughout the unit, the teacher uses the student examples and the criteria in the rubric to help students better understand the nature of high-quality work and to support her teaching of research skills and report writing.

A second assessment practice that supports learning involves presenting evaluative criteria and models of work that illustrate different levels of quality. Unlike selected-response or short-answer tests, authentic performance assessments are typically open-ended and do not yield a single, correct answer or solution process. Consequently, teachers cannot score student responses using an answer key or a Scantron machine. They need to evaluate products and performances on the basis of explicitly defined performance criteria.

The best teachers recognize the importance on ongoing assessments as the means to achieve maximum performance.

A rubric is a widely used evaluation tool consisting of criteria, a measurement scale (a 4-point scale, for example), and descriptions of the characteristics for each score point. Well-developed rubrics communicate the important dimensions, or elements of quality, in a product or performance and guide educators in evaluating student work. When a department or

	Title	Labels	Accuracy	Neatness
3	The graph contains a title that clearly tells what the data show. ☐ ☐	All parts of the graph (units of measurement, rows, etc.) are correctly labeled. ☑ ☐	All data are accurately represented on the graph. ☑ ☑	The graph is very neat and easy to read. ☐
2	The graph contains a title that suggests what the data show. ☐ ☐	Some parts of the graph are inaccurately labeled. ☐ ☑	Data representation contains minor errors. ☑ ☐	The graph is generally neat and readable. ☐ ☑
1	The title does not reflect what the data show OR the title is missing. ☑ ☑	The graph is incorrectly labeled OR labels are missing. ☐ ☐	The data are inaccurately represented, contain major errors, OR are missing. ☐ ☐	The graph is sloppy and difficult to read. ☐ ☐

Comments: ________

Goals/Actions: ________

Source: From *The Understanding by Design Professional Development Workbook* (p. 183), by J. McTighe and G. Wiggins, 2004, Alexandria, VA: ASCD.

Figure 1 Analytic rubric for graphic display of data.

grade-level team—or better yet, an entire school or district—uses common rubrics, evaluation results are more consistent because the performance criteria don't vary from teacher to teacher or from school to school.

Rubrics also benefit students. When students know the criteria in advance of their performance, they have clear goals for their work. Because well-defined criteria provide a clear description of quality performance, students don't need to guess what is most important or how teachers will judge their work.

Providing a rubric to students in advance of the assessment is a necessary, but often insufficient, condition to support their learning. Although experienced teachers have a clear conception of what they mean by "quality work," students don't necessarily have the same understanding. Learners are more likely to understand feedback and evaluations when teachers show several examples that display both excellent and weak work. These models help translate the rubric's abstract language into more specific, concrete, and understandable terms.

Some teachers express concern that students will simply copy or imitate the example. A related worry is that showing an excellent model (sometimes known as an exemplar) will stultify student creativity. We have found that providing multiple models helps avoid these potential problems. When students see several exemplars showing how different students achieved high-level performance in unique ways, they are less likely to follow a cookie-cutter approach. In addition, when students study and compare examples ranging in quality—from very strong to very weak—they are better able to internalize the differences. The models enable students to more accurately self-assess and improve their work before turning it in to the teacher.

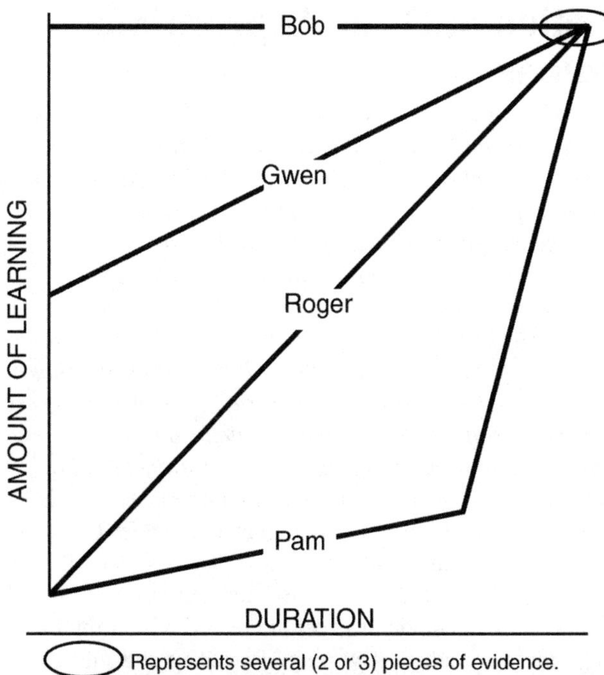

Figure 2 Student Learning Curves: Four students master a given learning goal by the end of an instructional segment but have vastly different learning curves.

Practice 3: Assess Before Teaching

Before beginning instruction on the five senses, a kindergarten teacher asks each student to draw a picture of the body parts related to the various senses and show what each part does. She models the process by drawing an eye on the chalkboard. "The eye helps us see things around us," she points out. As students draw, the teacher circulates around the room, stopping to ask clarifying questions ("I see you've drawn a nose. What does the nose help us do?"). On the basis of what she learns about her students from this diagnostic pre-test, she divides the class into two groups for differentiated instruction. At the conclusion of the unit, the teacher asks students to do another drawing, which she collects and compares with their original pre-test as evidence of their learning.

Diagnostic assessment is as important to teaching as a physical exam is to prescribing an appropriate medical regimen. At the outset of any unit of study, certain students are likely to have already mastered some of the skills that the teacher is about to introduce, and others may already understand key concepts. Some students are likely to be deficient in prerequisite skills or harbor misconceptions. Armed with this diagnostic information, a teacher gains greater insight into *what to teach*, by knowing what skill gaps to address or by skipping material previously mastered; into *how to teach*, by using grouping options and initiating activities based on preferred learning styles and interests; and into *how to connect* the content to students' interests and talents.

"With performance assessments, the juice must be worth the squeeze."

Teachers can use a variety of practical pre-assessment strategies, including pre-tests of content knowledge, skills checks, concept maps, drawings, and K-W-L (*K*now-*W*ant to learn-*L*earn) charts. Powerful pre-assessment has the potential to address a worrisome phenomenon reported in a growing body of literature (Bransford, Brown, & Cocking, 1999; Gardner, 1991): A sizeable number of students come into school with misconceptions about subject matter (thinking that a heavier object will drop faster than a lighter one, for example) and about themselves as learners (assuming that they can't and never will be able to draw, for example). If teachers don't identify and confront these misconceptions, they will persist even in the face of good teaching. To uncover existing misconceptions, teachers can use a short, nongraded true-false diagnostic quiz that includes several potential misconceptions related to the targeted learning. Student responses will signal any prevailing misconceptions, which the teacher can then address through instruction. In the future, the growing availability of portable, electronic student-response systems will enable educators to obtain this information instantaneously.

Practice 4: Offer Appropriate Choices

As part of a culminating assessment for a major unit on their state's history and geography, a class of 4th graders must contribute to a classroom museum display. The displays are designed to provide answers to the unit's essential question: How do geography, climate, and natural resources influence lifestyle, economy, and culture? Parents and students from other classrooms will view the display. Students have some choice about the specific products they will develop, which enables them to work to their strengths. Regardless of students' chosen products, the teacher uses a common rubric to evaluate every project. The resulting class museum contains a wide variety of unique and informative products that demonstrate learning.

Responsiveness in assessment is as important as it is in teaching. Students differ not only in how they prefer to take in and process information but also in how they best demonstrate their learning. Some students need to "do"; others thrive on oral explanations. Some students excel at creating visual representations; others are adept at writing. To make valid inferences about learning, teachers need to allow students to work to their strengths. A standardized approach to classroom assessment may be efficient, but it is not fair because any chosen format will favor some students and penalize others.

Assessment becomes responsive when students are given appropriate options for demonstrating knowledge, skills, and understanding. Allow choices—but always with the intent of collecting needed and appropriate evidence based on goals. In the example of the 4th grade museum display project, the teacher wants students to demonstrate their understanding of the relationship between geography and economy. This could be accomplished through a newspaper article, a concept web, a PowerPoint presentation, a comparison chart, or a simulated radio interview with an expert. Learners often put forth greater effort and produce higher-quality work when given such a variety of choices. The teacher will judge these products using a three-trait rubric that focuses on accuracy of content, clarity and thoroughness of explanation, and overall product quality.

Teachers need to allow students to work to their strengths.

We offer three cautions. First, teachers need to collect appropriate evidence of learning on the basis of goals rather than simply offer a "cool" menu of assessment choices. If a content standard calls for proficiency in written or oral presentations, it would be inappropriate to provide performance options other than those involving writing or speaking, except in the case of students for whom such goals are clearly inappropriate (a newly arrived English language learner, for example). Second, the options must be worth the time and energy required. It would be inefficient to have students develop an elaborate three-dimensional display or an animated PowerPoint presentation for content that a multiple-choice quiz could easily assess. In the folksy words of a teacher friend, "With performance assessments, the juice must be worth the squeeze." Third, teachers have only so much time and energy, so they must be judicious in determining when it is important to offer product and performance options. They need to strike a healthy balance between a single assessment path and a plethora of choices.

Practice 5: Provide Feedback Early and Often

Middle school students are learning watercolor painting techniques. The art teacher models proper technique for mixing and applying the colors, and the students begin working. As they paint, the teacher provides feedback both to individual students and to the class as a whole. She targets common mistakes, such as using too much paint and not enough water, a practice that reduces the desired transparency effect. Benefiting from continual feedback from the teacher, students experiment with the medium on small sheets of paper. The next class provides additional opportunities to apply various watercolor techniques to achieve such effects as color blending and soft edges. The class culminates in an informal peer feedback session. Skill development and refinement result from the combined effects of direct instruction, modeling, and opportunities to practice guided by ongoing feedback.

It is often said that feedback is the breakfast of champions. All kinds of learning, whether on the practice field or in the classroom, require feedback based on formative assessments. Ironically, the quality feedback necessary to enhance learning is limited or nonexistent in many classrooms.

To serve learning, feedback must meet four criteria: It must be timely, specific, understandable to the receiver, and formed to allow for self-adjustment on the student's part (Wiggins, 1998). First, feedback on strengths and weaknesses needs to be prompt for the learner to improve. Waiting three weeks to find out how you did on a test will not help your learning.

In addition, specificity is key to helping students understand both their strengths and the areas in which they can improve. Too many educators consider grades and scores as feedback when, in fact, they fail the specificity test. Pinning a letter (*B-*) or a number (82%) on a student's work is no more helpful than such comments as "Nice job" or "You can do better." Although good grades and positive remarks may feel good, they do not advance learning.

Specific feedback sounds different, as in this example:

> Your research paper is generally well organized and contains a great deal of information on your topic. You used multiple sources and documented them correctly. However, your paper lacks a clear conclusion, and you never really answered your basic research question.

Sometimes the language in a rubric is lost on a student. Exactly what does "well organized" or "sophisticated reasoning" mean? "Kid language" rubrics can make feedback clearer and more comprehensible. For instance, instead of saying, "Document your reasoning process," a teacher might say,

"Show your work in a step-by-step manner so the reader can see what you were thinking."

Here's a simple, straightforward test for a feedback system: Can learners tell *specifically* from the given feedback what they have done well and what they could do next time to improve? If not, then the feedback is not specific or understandable enough for the learner.

Finally, the learner needs opportunities to act on the feedback—to refine, revise, practice, and retry. Writers rarely compose a perfect manuscript on the first try, which is why the writing process stresses cycles of drafting, feedback, and revision as the route to excellence. Not surprisingly, the best feedback often surfaces in the performance-based subjects—such as art, music, and physical education—and in extracurricular activities, such as band and athletics. Indeed, the essence of coaching involves ongoing assessment and feedback.

Practice 6: Encourage Self-Assessment and Goal Setting

Before turning in their science lab reports, students review their work against a list of explicit criteria. On the basis of their self-assessments, a number of students make revisions to improve their reports before handing them in. Their teacher observes that the overall quality of the lab reports has improved.

The most effective learners set personal learning goals, employ proven strategies, and self-assess their work. Teachers help cultivate such habits of mind by modeling self-assessment and goal setting and by expecting students to apply these habits regularly.

Rubrics can help students become more effective at honest self-appraisal and productive self-improvement. In the rubric in Figure 1 (p. 210), students verify that they have met a specific criterion—for a title, for example—by placing a check in the lower left-hand square of the applicable box. The teacher then uses the square on the right side for his or her evaluation. Ideally, the two judgments should match. If not, the discrepancy raises an opportunity to discuss the criteria, expectations, and performance standards. Over time, teacher and student judgments tend to align. In fact, it is not unusual for students to be harder on themselves than the teacher is.

The rubric also includes space for feedback comments and student goals and action steps. Consequently the rubric moves from being simply an evaluation tool for "pinning a number" on students to a practical and robust vehicle for feedback, self-assessment, and goal setting.

Initially, the teacher models how to self-assess, set goals, and plan improvements by asking such prompting questions as,

- What aspect of your work was most effective?
- What aspect of your work was least effective?
- What specific action or actions will improve your performance?
- What will you do differently next time?

Questions like these help focus student reflection and planning. Over time, students assume greater responsibility for enacting these processes independently.

Educators who provide regular opportunities for learners to self-assess and set goals often report a change in the classroom culture. As one teacher put it,

> My students have shifted from asking, "What did I get?" or "What are you going to give me?" to becoming increasingly capable of knowing how they are doing and what they need to do to improve.

Authentic performance tasks help learners see a reason for their learning.

Practice 7: Allow New Evidence of Achievement to Replace Old Evidence

A driver education student fails his driving test the first time, but he immediately books an appointment to retake the test one week later. He passes on his second attempt because he successfully demonstrates the requisite knowledge and skills. The driving examiner does not average the first performance with the second, nor does the new license indicate that the driver "passed on the second attempt."

This vignette reveals an important principle in classroom assessment, grading, and reporting: New evidence of achievement should replace old evidence. Classroom assessments and grading should focus on *how well*—not on *when*—the student mastered the designated knowledge and skill.

Consider the learning curves of four students in terms of a specified learning goal (see fig. 2, p. 211). Bob already possesses the targeted knowledge and skill and doesn't need instruction for this particular goal. Gwen arrives with substantial knowledge and skill but has room to improve. Roger and Pam are true novices who demonstrate a high level of achievement by the *end* of the instructional segment as a result of effective teaching and diligent learning. If their school's grading system truly documented learning, all these students would receive the same grade because they all achieved the desired results over time. Roger and Pam would receive lower grades than Bob and Gwen, however, if the teacher factored their earlier performances into the final evaluation. This practice, which is typical of the grading approach used in many classrooms, would misrepresent Roger and Pam's ultimate success because it does not give appropriate recognition to the real—or most current—level of achievement.

Two concerns may arise when teachers provide students with multiple opportunities to demonstrate their learning. Students may not take the first attempt seriously once they realize they'll have a second chance. In addition, teachers often become overwhelmed by the logistical challenges of providing multiple opportunities. To make this approach effective, teachers need to require their students to provide some evidence of the corrective action they will take—such as engaging in peer coaching, revising their report, or practicing the needed skill in a given way—before embarking on their "second chance."

As students work to achieve clearly defined learning goals and produce evidence of their achievement, they need to know that teachers will not penalize them for either their lack of knowledge at the beginning of a course of study or their initial attempts at skill mastery. Allowing new evidence to replace old conveys an important message to students—that teachers care about their successful learning, not merely their grades.

Motivated to Learn

The assessment strategies that we have described address three factors that influence student motivation to learn (Marzano, 1992). Students are more likely to put forth the required effort when there is

- *Task clarity*—when they clearly understand the learning goal and know how teachers will evaluate their learning (Practices 1 and 2).
- *Relevance*—when they think the learning goals and assessments are meaningful and worth learning (Practice 1).
- *Potential for success*—when they believe they can successfully learn and meet the evaluative expectations (Practices 3–7).

By using these seven assessment and grading practices, all teachers can enhance learning in their classrooms.

References

Black, P., Harrison, C., Lee, C., Marshall, B., & Wiliam, D. (2004). Working inside the black box: Assessment for learning in the classroom. *Phi Delta Kappan, 86*(1), 8–21.

Bransford, J. D., Brown, A. L., & Cocking, R. R. (Eds.). (1999). *How people learn: Brain, mind, experience, and school.* Washington, DC: National Research Council.

Gardner, H. (1991). *The unschooled mind.* New York: BasicBooks.

Marzano, R. (1992). *A different kind of classroom: Teaching with dimensions of learning.* Alexandria, VA: ASCD.

Wiggins, G. (1998). *Educative assessment: Designing assessments to inform and improve student performance.* San Francisco: Jossey-Bass.

Jay McTighe (jmctigh@aol.com) is coauthor of *The Understanding by Design* series (ASCD, 1998, 1999, 2000, 2004, 2005). **Ken O'Connor** is author of *How to Grade for Learning: Linking Grades to Standards* (Corwin, 2002).

From *Educational Leadership,* November 2005, pp. 11–17. Reprinted by permission of the Association for Supervision and Curriculum Development. The Association for Supervision and Curriculum Development is a worldwide community of educators advocating sound policies and sharing best practices to achieve the success of each learner. To learn more, visit ASCD at www.ascd.org

Meeting the Challenge of High-Stakes Testing While Remaining Child-Centered

The Representations of Two Urban Teachers

PAMELA WILLIAMSON ET AL.

Current education policies aimed at accountability create pressing dilemmas for many educators. Much research points to the potentially harmful effects of high-stakes testing on students, such as narrowing school curriculum to only that which is covered on exams (Abrams, Pedulla, & Madaus, 2003; Barksdale-Ladd & Thomas, 2000; Cimbricz, 2002; Darling-Hammond & Wise, 1985). In addition, as Blackwell (2004) pointed out, accountability has many potential hidden costs, including a weakening of teachers' personal connections with students and the loss of shared learning journeys. Although these important concerns and others have been raised about the effect of high-stakes tests on students and about the relationship between students' test scores and learning, the fact remains that students' performance on high-stakes tests is of increasing significance for their futures. For example, some states retain students or withhold high school diplomas from students who do not pass the tests. Such potential consequences undeniably create tension for educators as they attempt to balance concern for the whole child's development with concern for his or her performance on a single test. Nowhere is this reality more painfully felt than in the lives of low-income students of color and their teachers.

Much evidence suggests that the achievement gap between white students and students of color has widened (Hedges & Nowell, 1998; Madaus & Clarke, 2001). Teachers everywhere are grappling with how to close this gap. Thus, it is incumbent upon the education research community to shed light on ways that some teachers have facilitated the success of low-income students of color on high-stakes state assessments, while remaining child-centered.

It is incumbent upon the education research community to shed light on ways that some teachers have facilitated the success of low-income students of color on high-stakes state assessments, while remining child-centered.

The Center for Research on Education, Diversity, and Excellence (CREDE), having synthesized research across multiple at-risk groups, developed five generic principles to guide the instruction of diverse learners: 1) facilitating learning through joint productive activity among teachers and students, 2) developing students' competence in the language and literacy of instruction throughout all instructional activities, 3) contextualizing teaching and curriculum in the experiences and skills of home and community, 4) challenging students toward cognitive complexity, and 5) engaging students through dialogue, especially instructional conversations (CREDE, 1997). With these principles in mind, we began a year-long study of exemplary teaching in an urban elementary school.

The previous year, the school had received a grade of "F" from the state's department of education, based on the students' poor performance on the high-stakes exam in reading, mathematics, and writing. Most of the students were living in poverty; 95 percent of the student body qualified for free or fee-reduced lunch. We selected two teachers to study, one from 3rd grade and one from 5th (hereafter referred to as Ms. Third and Ms. Fifth), whose students, in spite of the school's failing grade, did well on the exam. Both were nominated as exemplary teachers by their principal and other teachers and had been selected as teacher of the year. Despite their shared exemplary status, they differed in obvious ways. Ms. Third, a white female in her fifth year of teaching, never had a desk or a piece of paper out of place in her classroom. Ms. Fifth, an African American woman in her 26th year of teaching, taught in a class that was crowded, with piles of papers and student projects cluttering every corner.

Months of classroom observations and interviews with the teachers, their students, and others revealed that, despite their obvious differences, the two teachers believed in several common principles of practice. This article elaborates on just one of those principles—the use of a variety of strategies to help students make sense of and understand new skills and concepts. Referred to in the research literature as "representing," this principle was a cornerstone of both these teachers' efforts. By providing and seeking representations, the teachers collaborated with their students to promote mastery of new ideas.

Representing

Often used in the context of math and science instruction, "representing" refers to the ways teachers transform content so that students can understand it. Representations may include metaphors, analogies, explanations, illustrations, and examples (Wilson, Shulman, & Richert, 1987). In order for representations to work well for students, students must be able to relate to them (Resnick, 1989). Thus, teachers must have an understanding of the students' background knowledge in order to create powerful representations. A representation that works for one group of students may not work as well for another group. Therefore, simply providing a list of representations used by these teachers likely would be of little relevance for other teachers. Our analysis did reveal, however, the following salient features of the representations we found in the two classrooms that may be useful for all teachers to consider: 1) being explicit, 2) using the familiar to explain the unfamiliar, 3) breaking down larger concepts into smaller parts, and 4) providing multiple exposures to new concepts (see Table 1). Also, representing was not reserved only for the teachers. They sought representations from their students as a way to encourage them to think deeply about their learning. Although not a new instructional practice, representing takes on increased importance in a testing context that can promote content coverage over content appreciation and mastery.

Table 1 Representation Taxonomy

Explicit			Use of familiar to explain unfamiliar			Breaking down concepts into smaller parts		Providing multiple exposures			Demanding representations			
Naming and defining	Conspicuous strategies	Demonstrating how to solve academic problems	Use of the everyday language of students	Activation of background knowledge	Known concept to explain unknown concept/analogy	Use of constituent parts	Start with concrete and move toward abstract	Repeated exposures in multiple contexts	Thematic units of study	One problem ten times	Oral	Written	Artistic	Kinesthetic

Vignettes from the teachers' classrooms illustrate how the teachers provided representations. Each vignette also demonstrates how the teachers drew on multiple modes of representing within a single lesson or activity. (A fourth kind of representing, providing multiple exposures, is harder to capture in a brief vignette.)

In the first vignette, Ms. Third conducts a writing lesson that she crafted with the state's writing assessment in mind. For the assessment, students are given either a narrative or an expository prompt and are asked to plan and write an essay in 45 minutes. Although the lesson that follows does not characterize all of Ms. Third's writing instruction, it is a structure she uses frequently in order to prepare her students for the state test.

Vignette #1: Adventures With a Leprechaun

Seventeen students are seated on the floor surrounding Ms. Third as they discuss a story they will be writing. It is St. Patrick's Day, and students have been reading books about this holiday. They have started a chart listing what they have learned so far. Ms. Third begins, "When I was a little girl, my brother told me a story about a leprechaun named Sammy who lived in our backyard. I was wondering—If you met a leprechaun, what are some of the problems that might happen?" Students eagerly offer suggestions. "He might trick you and leave," offers Cody. "Or, he might be scared of you or something," suggests Monet. "I love those ideas," says Ms. Third. "Who has some other ideas?" "He might sneak food from your garden," offers Hedrika. "You could cut down his home on accident," says Jamal. "Or, he could get pushed out of his house with water from the hose," suggests Judy.

"These are all terrific suggestions for problems in a story. Let's look at the writing prompt. I want you to be thinking about what your story will be about." Ms. Third turns on the overhead projector, displaying the following writing prompt:

> "Wouldn't it be neat to meet a leprechaun? Imagine what might happen if you met a real live leprechaun. When you get your outline for your story plan, write your name on it."

"Okay, first we need to think about what kind of writing we need to do," says Ms. Third. "Oooo, there's a clue word in the prompt that tells me what kind of writing. It's the word 'story.' 'Story' means that it will be a narrative. Let's look at our plan to see how many parts a narrative story usually has in it."

Each student has a story outline that includes space for writing down brief information about the characters, setting, problem, events leading to the solution, and solution. The story outline is organized into three parts. Students readily notice this detail and tell Ms. Third that a narrative story has three parts. Ms. Third completes her story outline by using think-alouds. "Hmmm, characters. That is who will be in the story." She then writes down, "Me, the leprechaun, and the class."

"The next thing that I need to decide is where the story will take place," Ms. Third tells the class. "We call the place the 'setting.' I think my setting will be on a class field trip in the woods. Problem? That's something that makes readers want to read my story. It's also something I have to have fixed up by the end. I think I will keep my problem a secret!

"Now, I want you to begin planning your story by filling in this planning sheet. Remember, there should be three events in the middle of the story that lead us to a solution to the story's problem. Begin completing your planning sheet." With this, Ms. Third begins to circulate, answering individual questions. Students work hard to complete their planning sheets. Some students share what they have written with classmates; others work independently. After some time passes, she asks for students to tell the class what they have written on their planning sheets.

Next, Ms. Third begins to write her story on a large sheet of white paper. As she writes, students offer ideas for the story, which Ms. Third incorporates enthusiastically. When students seem stuck on how to write about the setting, Ms. Third reminds them they can always use real events from their own lives to help them. They decide to use events from a recent field trip.

"Let's see. We've introduced our characters and setting. We've introduced the problem in our story. That means that the beginning of the story is drafted. Now we have to decide what happens next. Remember, we need three events that will eventually lead us to a solution."

Being Explicit

Ms. Third named and defined new concepts for students, provided conspicuous strategies (Kame'enui, Carnine, Dixon, Simmons, & Coyne, 2002) to help them accomplish writing tasks, and demonstrated processes by which the students could solve academic problems. For example, Ms. Third named and defined the concepts of "character," "setting," and "problem" with clear, direct language. She also explained, and provided access to, two strategies often used by writers. First, she gave students a story planning sheet as a temporary scaffold for writing narrative stories. This helped the students think about the necessary elements of narratives. In rereading the story aloud, Ms. Third summarized for students what belongs in the beginning of a narrative. Thus, she made explicit for her students what often may be implicit—that stories have certain elements and that the beginning of a story generally contains a subset of those elements. She also explicitly stated that the middle of the story should contain three events that lead to a solution. Second, she told students that drawing on life experiences (e.g., using their own experiences from a recent field trip) is a useful strategy when they had trouble deciding how to continue their stories. By being explicit, Ms. Third provided these novice writers access to the kind of writing that they would be expected to produce on the state's assessment test.

Finally, Ms. Third also demonstrated an explicit process for solving an academic problem. The first task students encounter on the state's writing assessment is to determine what kind of an essay to write. By pointing out the clue word "story," Ms. Third showed students one way to determine what kind of essay to write. Furthermore, her think-alouds modeled for students a logical process for creating a narrative essay.

Using the Familiar to Explain the Unfamiliar

Ms. Third drew on her students' fascination with the leprechaun myth to engage them in a challenging writing lesson. She read to them about leprechauns, discussed leprechauns in the Morning Meeting, and created a chart of their knowledge and questions about leprechauns. Therefore, she paved the way for learning new writing skills by building and using familiar and interesting content. Ms. Third used this representing in another manner when she used words students knew (i.e., "who" and "where") to help them understand the two lesser known words, "character" and "setting." She helped them recognize their understanding of the concept of "problem" by having them generate examples of problems they might encounter with a leprechaun. Later, she used language that was familiar to them to define problem as "something that makes readers want to read my story," and "something I have to have fixed up by the end."

Breaking Down Larger Concepts Into Smaller Parts

Ms. Third used this form of representing masterfully in the writing lesson. Planning and writing an essay is a demanding task. The added challenge of completing the task within a 45-minute period can make the writing test a daunting experience. Ms. Third created the story outline form to help students grasp ideas about essay substance and structure. By breaking down the complex tasks into component parts, and relying on explaining, modeling, guided practice, and independent practice, Ms. Third gradually led students through the processes required for success on the writing test.

Vignette #2: We're Going to the Mall

Ms. Fifth walks to a table holding several items that one might find for sale at the mall. Approaching the table, she calls out, "We're going to the mall!" Jerome whispers excitedly, "Yes! I love this game!" Lifting a sweater from the table, Ms. Fifth says, "When you go to the mall, and you see an item that is $70, like this sweater, and then you see a percentage sign that says 30 percent off, you've got to know if you've got enough money to pay for it." She asks several students if they have enough money to buy the sweater at the sale price. They are unsure. "In order to figure this out, you've got to do some math. Here's how it works." She explains that three numbers are needed to figure out whether or not you have enough money—the original price, the discount, and the sale price. She writes on the board the information they have about the sweater. "Which is the original price?" she asks. "The discount? The sale price?" Ms. Fifth explains, "As I teach you how to calculate the price of a discounted item, I want you to carefully label each number. Once you really understand how to do these kinds of problems, you won't have to label the numbers. For now, labeling them helps you think about what you're doing and why. You know what I always tell you—you've got to make mind movies so you can really see what you're doing and why."

Being Explicit

Although explicit instruction is less evident in this vignette than it was in Ms. Third's writing lesson, Ms. Fifth hints at it as she names the three components of this kind of math problem. She leaves nothing to chance as she clearly states the elements and requires students to label each of them. Ms. Fifth's instruction was full of explicit representing as she named and defined concepts and skills and repeatedly demonstrated the logical thinking required to solve math problems.

Using the Familiar to Explain the Unfamiliar

In the vignette, Ms. Fifth draws on the students' familiarity with the mall to help them understand discounts. By referring to specific items and to the money in their pockets ("Do you have enough to buy it?"), she engages them in what might have been, on a textbook page, an abstract and incomprehensible problem.

Breaking Down Large Concepts Into Smaller Parts

By focusing on each component of the discount problem, Ms. Fifth breaks the problem into its constituent parts (i.e., the price, the discount, and the sale price) so that students understand precisely what numbers are needed for them to solve these kinds of word problems. Furthermore, they are able to make sense of the problem-solving process, because they spend time discussing the key parts, what they mean, and their relationship to one another.

Providing Representations: Multiple Exposures

Ms. Third and Ms. Fifth provided their students with multiple opportunities to learn new skills or concepts, although those opportunities may not have been immediately apparent in the two vignettes. Multiple exposures, which is different from practicing, helps students make sense of new concepts or skills, and ensures that practicing becomes more than rote repetition. The teachers deliberately planned for multiple exposures—sometimes within the context of a single lesson, sometimes distributed over time—to the same new idea. As Ms. Third explained, "The lesson is ongoing. For instance, Morning Meeting will have something dealing with the lesson. Then I try to bring it in as much as possible—weave it in through the day, and I try to relate it to other things." When asked whether or not she was concerned that some of her students did not seem to understand the concept of fractions during a lesson we observed, Ms. Third said she was not worried. She was confident that with multiple, varied presentations, "eventually, most will catch on." Similarly, Ms. Fifth used an approach to math instruction that she called "one problem 10 times." She often asked students to do one problem repeatedly—with a partner or alone, using a variety of solution strategies, in their heads or on paper, as a drawing or using numerals, or teaching it to someone.

Another way that Ms. Third provided multiple exposures was through her use of thematic units of study, which provided opportunities for students to experience concepts multiple times and in multiple ways. For example, in a unit on economics, students formed companies that manufactured and sold products. In the process, students examined the cost of production, including the cost of labor. Students created advertisements for their products, and they also learned how to make change. This thematic unit provided students with multiple opportunities to use math and language skills in authentic tasks, allowing for a deeper understanding of economics and math concepts than textbook lessons would have allowed.

Demanding Student Representations

Perhaps one of the most striking features in these classrooms was the demands these teachers placed on students to provide representations of their learning—orally, artistically, kinesthetically, and in writing. In Ms. Fifth's classroom, students often worked math problems on transparencies to orally defend their solutions. It was not an uncommon experience in Ms. Fifth's room to see students debate the veracity of their answers. Just getting the answer "right" was never good enough; students had to explain how they arrived at their answers.

The teachers also demanded student representations in writing. Until students could demonstrate what they knew in writing, these teachers did not assume students knew it. Scaffolds helped the students do their best. In Ms. Third's classroom, for example, students graded essays collectively. Carefully laid ground rules, as well as a climate of care, enabled even the weakest writers to achieve success. Peer criticism and support motivated struggling writers to be enthusiastic about trying to improve.

Students also were expected to offer artistic representations of their knowledge. Ms. Fifth's students often included drawings next to definitions in their math journals. For example, next to the definition of "perimeter," students might have a picture of a fence as a representation that perimeter measures the distance around something. As part of a thematic unit on medieval times, Ms. Third had students create stained-glass windows to represent various fractions.

Finally, both teachers often required kinesthetic representations from students. During a lesson on syllables, Ms. Fifth's students used drums to tap out the number of syllables in words. During a vocabulary lesson, Ms. Third and her students generated hand gestures for new vocabulary words. For the word "harvest," students decided to hold pretend baskets in which to place imaginary vegetables.

Discussion

At the end of the year in which the study was conducted, the school received a grade of "A" from the state's department of education—a remarkable jump from the previous year's grade of "F." Both Ms. Third's and Ms. Fifth's students excelled on the required tests. In Ms. Third's class, 100 percent of students earned at least a passing grade (a score of 3 on a scale of 1 to 5) on the reading test; 88 percent of her students passed the math test. In Ms. Fifth's classroom, 100 percent of the students passed both exams.

What can we learn from the instructional methods of these two elementary teachers in a small urban school? One lesson is clear to us: Teachers do not have to sacrifice high-quality, child-centered pedagogy that focuses on sense-making and understanding in order to get their students through high-stakes tests. In fact, the teachers' attention to representing new ideas for students and demanding representations of students fits well with the recommendations of researchers (CREDE, 1997), as is evident in the following examples from Ms. Third and Ms. Fifth's classrooms that demonstrate adherence to CREDE's recommendations (in italics):

- *Facilitate learning through joint productive activity among teachers and students.* Through the joint productive activity of learning and writing about St. Patrick's Day and leprechauns, Ms. Third created a "common context of experience within [the] school itself," thus enabling the kind of collaboration that can only happen when all parties share knowledge about the same topic. Notably, these kinds of activities are of utmost importance "when the teacher and the students are not of the same background" (CREDE, 1997, p. 1).
- *Developing students' competence in language and literacy throughout all instructional activities.* Students were presented with multiple opportunities to develop oral and written language skills. We watched as 5th-grade students, students some would define as at risk, passionately argued the merits of how best to solve a permutation problem. We watched as the teachers explicitly taught students how to recognize clue words and how to create outlines for essays that would exceed state standards. The teachers gave students access to the academic discourse of testing—specifically, how questions are asked and answered, and how knowledge claims are made and refuted.
- *Contextualize teaching and learning in the experiences of home and community.* Ms. Third stressed communication with her students' families, not just to inform them of what was happening at school, but also to learn about what was happening at home. When Ms. Fifth talked to students about going to the mall, she brought to life a lesson that could have been just words on the page. In another lesson, she used the concept of running out of gas to help students understand the importance of estimating.
- *Challenging students with cognitively complex tasks.* By refusing to water down assignments and minimize expectations, the teachers created an environment in which all students had to work to represent their knowledge in ways that would be expected on high-stakes tests. They offered the kind of "instruction that requires thinking and analysis, not only rote, repetitive, detail-level drill" (CREDE, 1997, p. 2).
- *Engage students in instructional conversations.* These teachers, "like parents in natural teaching, assume the student has something to say beyond the known answers in the head of the adult" (CREDE, 1997, p. 2). Evidence can be found in the nature of the kinds of questions Ms. Third asked of her students (e.g., "I was wondering—If you met a leprechaun, what are some of the problems that might happen?," or "Who has some other ideas?"), and in the fact that, each year, she asked students to tell her which activities they favored and those they did not. In addition, Ms. Fifth routinely encouraged students to find multiple ways to solve the "same problem 10 times" and share those solutions. Student knowledge was highly valued.

Ms. Third and Ms. Fifth have provided their students with the cultural capital necessary to avoid school failure and its increasingly damaging consequences. In the process, they avoided many of the hidden costs of high-stakes testing, including the loss of personal connections with students, and were able to share journeys of learning and exploration with their students (Blackwell, 2004).

References

Abrams, L., Pedulla, J., & Madaus, G. (2003). Views from the classroom: Teachers' opinions of statewide testing programs. *Theory Into Practice, 42*(1), 18–29.

Barksdale-Ladd, M. A., & Thomas, K. (2000). What's at stake in high-stakes testing. *Journal of Teacher Education, 51*(5), 384–401.

Blackwell, J. (2004). New accountability: Hidden costs for teachers and students. *ACEI Exchange, 80*, 146–A, 146–C.

Center for Research on Education, Diversity & Excellence. (1997). *From at-risk to excellence: Principles of practice.* ERIC Clearinghouse on languages and linguistics. EDP-FL-98-01.

Cimbricz, S. (2002). *State-mandated testing and teachers' beliefs and practice.* Retrieved October 11, 2002, from http://epaa.asu.edu

Darling-Hammond, L., & Wise, A. (1985). Beyond standardization: State standards and school improvement. *The Elementary School Journal, 85*(5), 315–336.

Hedges, L., & Nowell, A. (1998). Black-white test score convergence since 1965. In C. Jencks & M. Phillips (Eds.), *The black-white test score gap* (pp. 149–181). Washington, DC: Brookings Institution Press.

Kame'enui, E. J., Carnine, D. W., Dixon, R. C., Simmons, D. C., & Coyne, M. D. (2002). *Effective teaching strategies that accommodate diverse learners* (2nd ed.). Upper Saddle River, NJ: Merrill Prentice Hall.

Madaus, G., & Clarke, M. (2001). The impact of high-stakes testing on minority students. In M. Kornhaber & G. Orfield (Eds.), *Raising standards or raising barriers: Inequality and high stakes testing in public education* (pp. 85–106). New York: Century Foundation.

Resnick, L. B. (1989). Introduction. In L. B. Resnick (Ed.), *Knowing, learning, and instruction: Essays in honor of Robert Glaser* (pp. 1–24). Hillsdale, NJ: Lawrence Erlbaum.

Wilson, S. M., Shulman, L. S., & Richert, A. E. (1987). "150 different ways" of knowing: Representations of knowledge in teaching. In J. Calderhead (Ed.), *Exploring teachers' thinking* (pp. 104–124). London: Casell.

Pamela Williamson is a doctoral candidate, Department of Special Education, **Elizabeth Bondy** is Professor, **Lisa Langley** is a doctoral student, and **Dina Mayne** is a doctoral student, School of Teaching and Learning, College of Education, University of Florida, Gainesville.

Test-Your-Knowledge Form

We encourage you to photocopy and use this page as a tool to assess how the articles in *Annual Editions* expand on the information in your textbook. By reflecting on the articles you will gain enhanced text information. You can also access this useful form on a product's book support Web site at *http://www.mhcls.com/online/*.

NAME: DATE:

TITLE AND NUMBER OF ARTICLE:

BRIEFLY STATE THE MAIN IDEA OF THIS ARTICLE:

LIST THREE IMPORTANT FACTS THAT THE AUTHOR USES TO SUPPORT THE MAIN IDEA:

WHAT INFORMATION OR IDEAS DISCUSSED IN THIS ARTICLE ARE ALSO DISCUSSED IN YOUR TEXTBOOK OR OTHER READINGS THAT YOU HAVE DONE? LIST THE TEXTBOOK CHAPTERS AND PAGE NUMBERS:

LIST ANY EXAMPLES OF BIAS OR FAULTY REASONING THAT YOU FOUND IN THE ARTICLE:

LIST ANY NEW TERMS/CONCEPTS THAT WERE DISCUSSED IN THE ARTICLE, AND WRITE A SHORT DEFINITION:

We Want Your Advice

ANNUAL EDITIONS revisions depend on two major opinion sources: one is our Advisory Board, listed in the front of this volume, which works with us in scanning the thousands of articles published in the public press each year; the other is you—the person actually using the book. Please help us and the users of the next edition by completing the prepaid article rating form on this page and returning it to us. Thank you for your help!

ANNUAL EDITIONS: Educational Psychology 08/09

ARTICLE RATING FORM

Here is an opportunity for you to have direct input into the next revision of this volume.
We would like you to rate each of the articles listed below, using the following scale:

1. **Excellent: should definitely be retained**
2. **Above average: should probably be retained**
3. **Below average: should probably be deleted**
4. **Poor: should definitely be deleted**

Your ratings will play a vital part in the next revision.
Please mail this prepaid form to us as soon as possible.
Thanks for your help!

RATING	ARTICLE
______	1. A Learner's Bill of Rights
______	2. Letters to a Young Teacher
______	3. Memories from the 'Other'
______	4. The Skill Set
______	5. A National Tragedy: Helping Children Cope
______	6. Mind and Body
______	7. Understanding Families
______	8. The Curriculum Superhighway
______	9. The Role of the Generations in Identity Formation
______	10. Risk Taking in Adolescence
______	11. Extending Inclusive Opportunities
______	12. Thinking Positively
______	13. Technology to Help Struggling Students
______	14. Recognizing Gifted Students
______	15. Raising Expectations for the Gifted
______	16. Challenging Deficit Thinking
______	17. The Culturally Responsive Teacher
______	18. Boys and Girls Together
______	19. Learning and Gender
______	20. Differentiating for Tweens
______	21. Critical Thinking
______	22. Constructing Learning: Using Technology to Support Teaching for Understanding
______	23. Creating a Culture for Learning
______	24. Teaching for Deep Learning
______	25. The Changing Classroom: Challenges for Teachers
______	26. Improve Your Verbal Questioning
______	27. Designing Learning Through Learning to Design
______	28. Using Engagement Strategies to Facilitate Children's Learning and Success
______	29. Convincing Students They Can Learn to Read
______	30. Why We Can't Always Get What We Want
______	31. How to Produce a High-Achieving Child
______	32. "If Only They Would Do Their Homework"
______	33. The Perils and Promises of Praise
______	34. When Children Make Rules
______	35. Strategies for Effective Classroom Management in the Secondary Setting
______	36. "No! I Won't"
______	37. Bullying: Effective Strategies for Its Prevention
______	38. IOSIE: A Method for Analyzing Student Behavioral Problems
______	40. Assessment Through the Student's Eyes
______	41. Grades as Valid Measures of Academic Achievement of Classroom Learning
______	42. Seven Practices for Effective Learning
______	43. Meeting the Challenge of High-Stakes Testing While Remaining Child-Centered

ANNUAL EDITIONS: EDUCATIONAL PSYCHOLOGY 08/09

NO POSTAGE NECESSARY IF MAILED IN THE UNITED STATES

BUSINESS REPLY MAIL
FIRST CLASS MAIL PERMIT NO. 551 DUBUQUE IA

POSTAGE WILL BE PAID BY ADDRESSEE

McGraw-Hill Contemporary Learning Series
501 BELL STREET
DUBUQUE, IA 52001

ABOUT YOU

Name ____________________ Date ____________

Are you a teacher? ❐ A student? ❐
Your school's name ____________________

Department ____________________

Address ____________ City ____________ State ____________ Zip ____________

School telephone # ____________________

YOUR COMMENTS ARE IMPORTANT TO US!

Please fill in the following information:
For which course did you use this book? ____________________

Did you use a text with this ANNUAL EDITION? ❐ yes ❐ no
What was the title of the text? ____________________

What are your general reactions to the Annual Editions concept? ____________________

Have you read any pertinent articles recently that you think should be included in the next edition? Explain. ____________________

Are there any articles that you feel should be replaced in the next edition? Why? ____________________

Are there any World Wide Web sites that you feel should be included in the next edition? Please annotate. ____________________

May we contact you for editorial input? ❐ yes ❐ no
May we quote your comments? ❐ yes ❐ no